Georgia Backroads Traveler

by
Olin Jackson

Legacy Communications, Inc.
Roswell, Georgia

Georgia Backroads Traveler is published by Legacy Communications, Inc.
P.O. Box 127, Roswell, GA 30077, publishers of *Georgia Backroads*
magazine, the *North Georgia Journal of History* hardback series, *Moonshine,
Murder & Mayhem in Georgia, Tales of the Rails,* and other non-fiction
publications associated with the history and historic travel
destinations of Georgia.

ISBN# 1-880816-10-5

Contents

3 NORTH - CENTRAL GEORGIA

4 NORTHWEST GEORGIA

5 SOUTHEAST GEORGIA

6 SOUTHWEST GEORGIA

7 STATEWIDE

Georgia Backroads Traveler is designed as a handy and informative travel guide to the historic sites, interesting shopping opportunities, historic overnight accommodations, historic restaurants and scenic travel destinations in the state of Georgia.

The *Traveler* was born out of a direct need for a comprehensive guide to sites – both well-known and little-known – in Georgia for use by the state's many travelers. Legacy Communications, publishers of *Georgia Backroads* magazine, has published travel guides and volumes on the state's history since 1985.

As you read through the pages which follow, you will see we have included a broad cross-section of options for scenic and historic travel and entertainment in our great state, all of which we heartily recommend. This information was painstakingly compiled over a period of several years.

As a native of north Georgia, I have been exploring the backroads and scenic byways of our state for decades, searching for interesting travel destinations to report to the readers of *Georgia Backroads*. The pages in this guide reflect many of my own preferences, as well as those of a number of the supporting writers of *Backroads*, all of whom have made *Georgia Backroads Traveler* so popular with our readership.

Grateful appreciation is hereby extended to the numerous writers and photographers who have helped to make this publication possible, including Anne Amerson, Dr. Kristine F. Anderson, Mary Ann Anderson, Roy Anderson, Susan Brender Bagwell, Judy Woodward Bates, Ray Chandler, Robert and Liz Coleman, Robert S. Davis, Jr., Virginia Davis, Dr. Caroline M. Dillman, Gary Elam, Rutherford "Ruddy" Ellis, Doris English, D.J. Fenlon, Joe Griffith, Debbie Humphrey, Jackie Kennedy, Alline Kent, Deborah Malone, Sarah Hines Martin, Wayne McDaniel, Bill Merrick, Dr. Lloyd Newberry, Wm. Ellis Oglesby, Dr. Robin Pennock, Fran M. Putney, Susan S. Rogers, Daniel M. Roper, Jeff Samsel, Gordon D. Sargent, Carol Thompson, Kathleen Walls, Jeff Warren, Mitchell Yockelson, and Joe Zentner.

The state of Georgia has an abundance of recreational, scenic and historic destination opportunities. The trick is to know where they are and what to expect when you get there. We have tried our best to provide that information in this publication. It contains most of the best scenic and historic travel opportunities Georgia has to offer.

In the months ahead – and indeed even in the years ahead – I hope you will continue to find this guidebook a rewarding companion as you also seek out the interesting and intriguing travel destinations that make Georgia such a special place.

Olin Jackson,
Managing Editor

For additional copies of this publication, send your check or money order for $18.50 plus $3.00 per copy for shipping to Legacy Communications, P.O. Box 127, Roswell, GA 30077, or order by credit card by calling toll free 1-800-547-1625.

The Margaret Mitchell House

This cozy little apartment in midtown Atlanta witnessed the creation of the most popular novel of all time. Over the years, the historic structure weathered time, the elements and several fires before a preservation group was able to preserve it for posterity.

Today, a small Remington typewriter sits on a simple table in the living room alcove. A white towel, ready to hide the manuscript when company arrived, hangs over the chair. Stacks of manila envelopes covered with notes and dates fill the window seat. And one manila envelope filled with manuscript pages supports a leg of the nearby green velvet love seat.

Seated in this cramped, cluttered apartment she dubbed "**The Dump**," **Margaret Mitchell** pounded out *Gone With The Wind*, an epic that has become the most popular novel of all time. After two fires and an ongoing struggle to raise funds that is almost as dramatic as the story from Mitchell's novel, "The Dump" and the Margaret Mitchell House were finally opened to the public.

In 1925, newlyweds "**Peggy**" **Mitchell** and **John Marsh** had set up housekeeping in the three-room apartment at the corner of Tenth and Peachtree streets. The next year, Peggy, had been laid up with an injured ankle, and she took advantage of the opportunity to begin writing her **War Between The States** saga.

She created the story around her characters, beginning with the last chapters and sometimes rewriting a chapter as many as 60 times. But only her husband and closest friends knew the former newspaper reporter was working on a book that continues to sell more than a half million copies worldwide each year.

After she and Marsh moved into a larger, more fashionable home in 1932, the Tudor Revival house that had been converted into apartments in 1913 fell into disrepair. The once-stately home continued to deteriorate and was eventually slated for demolition.

Fortunately for Georgians and "**Windies**" around the globe, the nonprofit Margaret Mitchell House, Inc., worked to save the seven-year residence of the Pulitzer Prize-winning writer.

Mary Rose Taylor, executive director of Margaret Mitchell House, says "The apartment and museum tell the untold story of Atlanta's most famous author and explore the impact of her book and life."

With the phenomenal success of her novel, Mitchell began guarding her privacy even more. She had always shielded the manuscript she often called her "baby." At her request, her husband destroyed most of her personal letters as well as the famous manuscript, saving only a few pages as proof of authorship after her death.

Today, her first-floor residence at the Margaret Mitchell House has been recreated from furnishing inventories and notes from her family and friends. Along with the tiny apartment, visitors can tour the Margaret Mitchell House and see a short film on Mitchell's life, her Pulitzer Prize, and a considerable amount of memorabilia. Movie and history buffs can even see the doors used in Tara filmed in the famous motion picture in 1939, as well as the painting of "Scarlett" in the blue dress.

Visitors can also learn about Margaret Mitchell's volunteer activities during World War II and little-known philanthropic gestures, including scholarships she provided for African-American students attending the Morehouse College School of Medicine in Atlanta.

One-hour guided tours at the house begin at regular intervals. The two-acre site, located at 990 Peachtree Street NE, is open from 9:30 a.m. to 5:00 p.m. daily. Admission is $12 for adults, $9 for seniors and $5 for children ages 6-17. Free parking is also available. For more information, call (404) 249-7012.

The restaurant empire known as "The Varsity" has provided for the fast food needs of millions of youngsters since it was first opened in the late 1920s. It has also produced its share of celebrities, including actor **Nipsey Russell**. The founder of this drive-in mecca, however, never wanted anything but the best fast food restaurant in Georgia. Most of his customers insist he succeeded long before he realized it.

Atlanta

The Varsity

Famous for its chili dogs, onion rings, and chaotically entertaining service, this restaurant at 61 North Avenue has fed kings and street sweepers, paupers and presidents, and everything in between. Like Coca-Cola, Stone Mountain, or the FOX Theater, The Varsity is an icon of Atlanta, yet it is the creation of one man. His name is **Frank Gordy**.

Walter Frank Gordy was born in 1904. His parents, Robert and Kate Ingram Gordy, raised him and three other children in a simple, clapboard farmhouse in Thomaston, Georgia.

Even as a child, Frank reportedly had no intention of carrying on the family tradition of farming. It was the commercial businesses in Thomaston that held his interest, not agriculture.

Gordy attended high school at **Reinhardt Academy** in Waleska, Georgia, where he met his future wife. As of this writing, **Mrs. Evelyn Jackson Gordy-Rankin** is still the "Queen Mother" of The Varsity. With keen eyes and a gentle smile, she is both stately and approachable.

Sitting in one of The Varsity's booths overlooking downtown Atlanta, Mrs. Gordy-Rankin remembers her former husband in his youth. "He had tremendous zest and energy," she says smiling. "It was there in high school and it stayed with him all his life.

"We didn't date at Reinhardt Academy because I was too young," she continued demurely. "I was only thirteen at the time. In the summer he earned money packing peaches in **Fort Valley**, **Georgia**, where his relatives owned a packing plant. There wasn't much

chance for us to be together."

At his parents urging, Frank Gordy moved to Atlanta and enrolled at **Georgia Tech** in the fall of 1923. Legend has it that his vision for The Varsity began there. He reportedly was more interested in fast food than the core curriculum, and as a result, he dropped out of the historic educational institute after only one semester.

Gordy's friends remember he wasn't discouraged in the least. When he moved out of the dormitory, he reportedly told his roommates that he'd be worth $20,000 by the time they graduated. That proved to be a conservative estimate.

After finishing the academic year at **Oglethorpe University**, Frank and his brother, Herbert, moved to Florida to try their luck in the real estate boom occurring there. However, their dreams of overnight riches didn't materialize, and they returned to Atlanta in 1926.

At that time, the boys' uncle was operating a service station at the corner of Luckie Street and North Avenue. Behind the main building stood a shed. It was only twelve feet across, but that was all the space Gordy needed for a hamburger grill and a pot for boiling hot dogs. His first restaurant, **"The Yellow Jacket,"** was born.

The Yellow Jacket was so popular with the Tech crowd, that by 1928, Frank had decided to expand. His vision included a chain of restaurants feeding college students all over the South.

When he moved his restaurant to the present location at North Avenue and Spring Street, he renamed it "The Varsity," in order to appeal to a broader clientele. With that name, he promised his patrons the best of everything: atmosphere, food, and service. Nothing would be "second-string."

The original 20 by 40-foot Varsity building sat on a cinder parking lot. On its first day of business, it grossed almost fifty dollars - quite a sum considering a hot dog only cost a nickel.

The popularity of The Varsity with students is easy to understand. For a country kid who grew up on collards and ice tea, a chili dog and a Coke were exotic fare. In the twenties and thirties, there wasn't a fast food joint on every corner. The Varsity was one of the first.

The Varsity clientele soon grew beyond the Tech set. In a 1977 interview with *Buckhead Atlanta*, Mr. Gordy remembered, "When the FOX Theater first opened in about 1930, and the last show was over, 20,000 people just rolled down the hill to The Varsity. They didn't even have to crank up their cars. In those days, there were a lot of high school and college dances, and the young people always ended up at The Varsity."

By 1930, Frank Gordy had achieved enough financial security that he felt he could ask for Evelyn Jackson's hand in marriage. They were wed on July 7th, and they drove away from the church in a brand-new Buick coupe with running boards and a rumple seat. Mrs. Gordy-Rankin remembered her wedding day so fondly that she commissioned an artist to create a mural of their honeymoon car for one of the walls of The Varsity.

A restaurant at the University of Georgia became Gordy's step toward his goal of feeding all the college kids in the South. In 1932, he opened The Varsity in Athens, directly across the street from the famous University Arch. Soon, the students began to think of The Varsity as an extension of their campus, and they claimed it as their own.

Despite the Athens, Georgia restaurant's popularity, Gordy became discouraged with the problems of absentee ownership. He hated spending his time on the highway instead of behind the counter. He often said, "My footprints on the floor are the key to The Varsity's success," but he couldn't be in three or four places at once. Instead of enlarging the chain, Gordy decided instead to concentrate on expanding the capacities of his existing restaurants.

To accommodate his legions of customers as quickly as possible, Gordy struck upon a unique idea. He mobilized an army of car-hop waiters. A parking lot manager deployed these workers from a wooden tower. On his command, the waiters swarmed over the cars and placed a cardboard number on the windshield. After taking an order, the car-hop would then dash to the kitchen and return shortly thereafter with the meal.

Some car-hops with names like "**Snake-Eye**," "**Rochester**," and "**Pork Chop**" became local celebrities, and one in particular went on to international stardom as a professional comedian/actor. Nipsey Russell, who starred in the movie version of *The Wiz*, perfected his routine while catching cars and wearing a cardboard "46" on his chest at The Varsity. Like an esteemed athlete, Russell's number has been retired, and now rests in a glass case in The Varsity's Hall of Fame.

Nipsey Russell may be the most well-known of The Varsity waiters, but it was John Raiford, alias "**Flossie Mae**," who turned the skill of car-hopping into an art. He figured out that customers would tip him more if he gave them a good show, so he started singing the menu and wearing funny hats. Before his retirement, Flossie had done his meta-rap on the radio, at the **FOX Theater**, and on *MTV*.

At the height of the drive-in popularity in the 1950s, eighty percent of The Varsity's business was curb service, and the restaurant deployed over one hundred car-hops. While few earned national fame or even a storied spot in local lore, untold numbers of Varsity waiters sent themselves through high school and college by waiting on cars.

This hoard of curb-side eaters presented Gordy with yet another problem: parking. In the era between the Second World War and the Oil Crisis of the 1970s, automobiles grew in number and size. Accommodating these legions of land-yachts required plenty of space. Eventually, Gordy bought out a bowling alley and a barber shop, taking over the entire North Avenue block. To make the outdoor atmosphere more comfortable, he erected rows of red and white awnings to cover the parking spaces and to give the feeling of picnicking beneath shady trees.

At its peak, the parking area was so large that the car-hops coined names like "lower deck," "football," "Up front," and "Snellville" (after a manager named Mr. Snell) to denote the various sections. Traffic flow was also a logistical dilemma, and to keep the cars moving, Gordy hired more off-duty policemen than anyone else in Atlanta.

"Progress" also brought along special problems for Gordy. In the 1960s, the city of Atlanta condemned some of The Varsity's parking area for the construction of Interstate 75-85. To make up for this lost parking space, Gordy constructed a ramp-fed, double-decker parking area. When the WSB-TV helicopter flew in and landed for the opening ceremony, a regular customer pointed at it and yelled, "We've got a lunching pad!" Mr. Gordy, appreciative of the quick wit, gave the gentleman a thirty-day meal pass. The next day, a sign bearing the identity "**Lunching Pad**" was hung prominently above the ramp.

The car-hops could only deliver food to parked cars as fast as the kitchen could cook it up, and preparing up to 25,000 hot dogs a day is not a trivial task. Using his background in industrial management, Gordy set up The Varsity not as a kitchen, but as a factory. The entire process was automated. Conveyor belts carry the hot dogs through the assembly process, which keeps the cooks from running around and bumping into each other. Several of the machines - like the one that cuts potatoes into French fries and the fried pie press - were Gordy's own inventions.

Gordy's innovations included food as well. He didn't enjoy the orange sodas produced by the major soft-drink manufacturers, so he concocted his own "**Varsity Orange**." It's made in stainless steel tanks in the kitchen and piped to a faucet up front. A frozen variety - the "FO" or "Frosted Orange," is also available.

In 1967, Frank Gordy issued his only Varsity franchise. It went to his son, **Frank Gordy, Jr.**, who had worked as a securities analyst in New York. Gordy Jr. returned to Atlanta and purchased one of **John Portman's** first creations - The Raja Drive-In - at the corner of Lindbergh and Cheshire Bridge. He remodeled it and renamed it "**The Varsity, Jr.**," and served the same menu as the parent restaurant. When Frank Gordy, Jr. died in 1980, he willed the restaurant to his wife, Susan Gordy, who continues to operate the business in the family tradition today.

As Mr. Gordy aged, he delegated many day to day responsibilities to his managers. He spent his time checking the quality of the food and mingling with his customers. He loved to tell stories. His favorite was about the freshman student from south Georgia who came to The Varsity for the first time. He walked up to the counter and within seconds, found himself holding a tray of chili dogs and onion rings. The astonished fellow looked up and said, "But I just wanted directions to Underground Atlanta."

To his employees, Mr. Gordy was a stern boss who demanded perfection, but to his customers, he was the friendliest millionaire fry-cook in the city. It is said that he couldn't face his customers after a price increase. On those days, he was always "out of town." He could usually be found hunting deer, rabbit, quail or dove on his 1,500-acre ranch near Cartersville or fishing in his lake in Cherokee County.

The only other times he was away from The Varsity were when he took vacations. He and his wife traveled throughout the world in the fifties and sixties.

Frank Gordy was also known as a kind man, who seldom if ever spoke of his good deeds - even though they were many. His daughter, **Nancy Simms**, says, "To this day, folks I've never seen come up to me and say, 'I can't tell you how much your father meant to me. He helped me buy school books when I was running low,' or 'he once paid my father's hospital bill' or whatever."

When Frank Gordy fell ill himself in 1983, his daughter took over operation of the family business. Frank died on June 18th of that year.

Mrs. Gordy-Rankin says she remembers the funeral distinctly. "The parlor was so packed that they had to put loud speakers on the lawn to accommodate the overflow. More flowers were sent than I've ever seen. On the way to the interment, Nancy asked the procession to drive her father past The Varsity one last time. The doors were locked and a wreath hung over the doors. For the first time in over 20,000 consecutive days of operation, The Varsity was closed."

Great things can't be kept down, however. The following Wednesday, The Varsity reopened its doors. The personnel behind the counter once again greeted customers with the familiar "What'll ya' have?"

A few things have changed since Mr. Gordy passed on. Cash registers have replaced the huge jars into which the cashiers once tossed the customers' money, and there's finally a ladies restroom inside.

The menu now includes a chef salad, and the French fries and onion rings are now cooked in vegetable oil instead of lard. For the most part, however, The Varsity is the same gargantuan hot-dog stand it always was - a living monument to a gutsy kid with a good chili recipe.

The Varsity is located at 61 North Avenue in Atlanta. For more information, call (404) 881-1706.

Horseradish Grill

Reminiscent of a day and time when the pace was much slower, and nearby Powers Ferry Road was little more than a dusty horse trail, **Horseradish Grill** - Atlanta's oldest continuously-operating restaurant - is a dining experience into yesteryear.

Many Atlanta-area travelers are simply unaware of the existence of this popular eatery. . . and that's just fine with area patrons who have become accustomed to this little secret.

The restaurant actually began as a country store which once existed alongside Powers Ferry Road in the days when the byway was little more than a dusty dirt trail. Today, swank neighborhoods exist on what once was fertile farmland.

An early entrepreneur named **John Adam Langford** purchased 200 acres in this vicinity to grow corn, cotton and sorghum cane. He also planted an orchard of apple, plum, pear, and fig trees, and he built a small store where he sold canned goods, flour and other staples.

Unfortunately, Mr. Langford was too lenient with credit and when too many customers failed to pay, his store folded. The structure eventually was demolished when Powers Ferry was widened in the late 1930s.

Some years later, another Langford caught the family itch for retailing, and re-erected the store near its original site. In this tiny country grocery – which serves today as the bar area of Horseradish Grill – this later Langford sold hot dogs and hamburgers and other groceries.

Other tenants later operated the store, one of which expanded the site to include a two-pump gasoline service station. By the early 1940s, **Bill Daly** – who had owned **Daly's Health Club** downtown – had leased the little grocery/eatery. Following a round of golf, hungry players invariably stopped in to buy a sandwich, some home-made barbecue, or perhaps even a steak at Daly's little diner.

In 1946, with his business flourishing from post-war recreationers, Daly enlarged the store with a dining annex, and the place became a full-fledged restaurant.

A passion for horses prompted Daly to furnish his new restaurant – by then called **Red Barn Inn** – in a style reminiscent of a stable. Individual dining areas were partitioned to resemble horse stalls, and a variety of horse tack and equestrian gear and Kentucky Derby photos added to the atmosphere.

After Daly's death in the early 1960s, the Langford family sold the restaurant to Stefan and Kirsten Popescu. The Popescus changed little of Daly's decor. After all, why reinvent the wheel?

They kept the dark, beamed, carefully cluttered ambience; the eight-point moose head in the foyer; the red and white tablecloths; the cozy fieldstone fireplace hung with coach lamps and copper kitchen pots, and the complimentary relish tray of olives, onions, radishes and celery sticks.

Another new set of owners purchased the historic eatery in 1994, naming it Horseradish Grill. Today, the Grill continues to offer fine dining in a rustic, yet sophisticated atmosphere, with cozy tables and the sounds of Billie Holiday on a sound system.

The new owners kept the original framing of the old building, the hardwood floors, and of course, the warm fireplace, but they removed the old horse stall-type booths which had previously dominated the interior of the structure. They also rebuilt the bar area (comprising the original little store built by Mr. Langford back in the late 1930s) to include a raised ceiling to give more space and light there.

Despite the absence of the cozy old horse stalls, a stable atmosphere still pervades the structure. Horse tack and other equine paraphernalia still adorn some of the walls.

New owners Steve and Renee Alterman say they're firm believers in the adage that "*Good business doesn't just happen - it must be nurtured.*"

"We recognize that people go out to eat because they expect to have a good time, not just a good meal," says Steve. "It's our duty to see to it that our operation consistently exceeds their expectations."

Heirloom varieties of seeds have been planted in an organic garden out back of the Grill to provide fresh herbs and garnishes for the creations of the chef. Many of the entrees are Southern in preparation, but the management maintains they try to dispel the notion that Southern cooking is only fried chicken and green beans.

Horseradish Grill is located at 4320 Powers Ferry Road, NW opposite popular Chastain Park in Buckhead. It is open Monday thru Friday 11:30 a.m. to 2:30 p.m. for lunch and Monday thru Saturday 5:00 p.m. to 10:00 p.m. for dinner. Sunday brunch is served from 11:30 to 2:30 p.m. and dinner from 5:00 to 9:00 p.m. For more information and reservations, telephone: (404) 255-7277.

The interesting and exciting lore of the railroad has been preserved in song and story for over a hundred years now. The faded relics from this glory, however – the railroad locomotives, cars, and memorabilia – have been steadily disappearing. An organization in Duluth, Georgia, is attempting to change that, restoring the old cars, and preserving the memorabilia for future generations of Americans.

As a result of the efforts of these dyed-in-the-wool railroad preservationists, Georgians and area travelers now have an excellent way to spend a Saturday morning or afternoon in Duluth, where the Southeastern Railway Museum is picking up steam.

The Atlanta Chapter of the National Railway Historical Society (NRHS) was organized in 1959 with the goal of collecting, preserving and displaying items and data historically significant to our nation's railroads. As a result, the Southeastern Railway Museum, a project of the Society, has evolved into a bonafide entertainment complex and repository for railroad memorabilia and historic equipment.

Accomplished mostly from the donated time and labor of former and current railroad employees and enthusiasts, virtually all the displays at the museum (some of the locomotives and railcars are not yet refurbished) are well-worth a visit. They're all authentic equipment from a day long departed.

Much of the memorabilia has been donated, but a significant portion has also been purchased. Six of the most valuable locomotives and cars are exhibited in Building #1 at the museum. The remainder are maintained elsewhere around the museum complex.

Duluth

Southeastern Railway Museum

According to Atlanta resident Ruddy Ellis, many times, the easy part is obtaining old equipment. The hard part is finding volunteers willing to endure the heat, long hours and hard labor necessary to reclaim the old engines and railcars from the rust and rot of years of neglect.

The cost involved in new or refurbished parts is no small matter either. Still, the museum is making steady progress with its coterie of volunteers.

Today, visitors are treated to everything from an authentic train register with Casey Jones' signature, to tours of retired passenger coaches, aged steam and coal-fired locomotives (over 40 units of railroad rolling stock), and even rides in a caboose around the grounds of the museum complex.

One example of the items of interest here is a special Pullman car named "Superb," which was operated during the golden era of railroad travel. This special conveyance transported President Warren Harding on his journey to San Francisco in 1923, and following his death, returned his body to Washington, D.C.

The museum's library currently occupies an old Rail Post Office car and contains over 7,000 catalogued items of railroad memorabilia. Rail fans can, by appointment, leaf through train and railroad magazines dating from the early 1930s, old railroad posters, actual railroad company time-tables, and much more

The Southeastern Railway Museum is located on Buford Highway (U.S. 23) at South Old Peachtree Road in Duluth, 0.3 of a mile north of Pleasant Hill Road. It is open to the public every Saturday from 9:00 a.m. to 5:00 p.m. For admission rates and more information, contact the museum at (770) 476-2013.

Fayetteville

The John "Doc" Holliday House

He has been dead since 1887, but his legend is more profound and widely-known today than ever before. **John Henry "Doc" Holliday**, was born in Griffin, Georgia, but he spent a great deal of time in the Atlanta area visiting with family members and attending family gatherings. One of the homes at which he spent this time still stands in Fayetteville, Georgia.

The **Holliday-Dorsey-Fife House** Museum in Fayetteville, Georgia, is associated with additional figures of Georgia history beyond Doc Holliday too, including **Hugh Manson Dorsey**, a two-term governor of Georgia; **Margaret Mitchell**, author of the legendary *Gone With The Wind*; and many figures from the U.S. Civil War.

Built at least as early as 1855 by its first owner, **Dr. John Stiles Holliday**, the imposing home is located just off the town square in downtown Fayetteville. The Hollidays – originally from Ireland – settled in Fayette County via South Carolina in the 1830s. In 1846, Dr. Holliday acquired the property on which the antebellum home still sits today.

Dr. John Stiles Holliday was the uncle of gunslinger **John Henry "Doc" Holliday**. He was a medical practitioner (just as was his famous nephew) as well as a surgeon. He did not move into the home with his family until 1857, opting instead to allow students and faculty of the newly established "**Fayetteville Academy**" to board in the home. Dr. Holliday was a trustee of the new school, and was instrumental in its founding and early operation.

The connection between Dr. John Stiles Holliday and John Henry "Doc" Holliday is extensive. In fact, Uncle John even delivered his famous nephew in 1851 at the Griffin, Georgia home of Doc's parents – **Henry and Alice Jane McKey Holliday**. The newborn was given the name "John" in honor of his uncle who delivered him, and the middle name "Henry" after his own father.

Dr. John Stiles was the first of the Holliday family to obtain a college degree. John Henry was the second, and he spent considerable time visiting his favorite uncle and aunt in Fayetteville where he was very close to his first cousin, **Robert Alexander**, who grew up in the Holliday-Dorsey-Fife House.

During the U.S. Civil War, the Hollidays were staunch Confederates. Dr. John Stiles Holliday became a member of the 2nd Georgia Cavalry, State Guards, while his brother, Henry (Doc's father), became a major in the 27th Georgia Regiment. Another brother, Robert Kennedy Holliday, served as a captain (quartermaster) in the 7th Georgia Regiment.

Dr. Holliday's eldest son, **George Henry**, was a cadet at **Georgia Military Institute** in Marietta during the war, and saw action during Sherman's siege of Atlanta.

Mrs. John Stiles Holliday herself was not a stranger to the Confederate cause, having been one of the primary seamstresses to piece and sew together a Confederate banner for the first company (**Fayette Rifle Grays**) to leave for the war from the county. That particular flag reportedly was crafted in the Holliday-Dorsey-Fife House, and an exact replica of the historic relic is on display in the museum in the home today.

If young John Henry "Doc" Holliday had been old enough (he was 13 in 1864), he undoubtedly would have joined the Confederate cause as well. During his brief career in the Old West, his courage – despite his illness from tuberculosis – became well known.

Following the war, Dr. Holliday sold the Holliday-Dorsey-Fife House to his in-laws – the Wares – and moved to Atlanta, hoping to reestablish his medical and mercantile businesses in the rebounding city. The Wares, another prominent Fayette County family, sold the home in 1867 to a neighbor, Solomon Dawson Dorsey, a businessman, farmer, and leading citizen of Fayetteville.

As was his friend and neighbor John Stiles Holliday, Dorsey was a trustee of the

1 ATLANTA METRO

Fayetteville "Seminary" and also served in the Confederacy as a colonel in the State Militia. Two of Dorsey's sons served in the Confederate forces as well. The oldest – John Manson Dorsey – was a private in the "Fayette Rifle Grays," and was the flag-bearer for the flag that had its beginnings in the Holliday-Dorsey-Fife House.

Another son – Rufus Thomas Dorsey – joined the Confederate cavalry in April of 1865, one month before the end of the war, at the tender age of 16. Rufus Thomas's son – **Hugh Manson Dorsey** – was Georgia's World War I governor from 1917 to 1921.

Governor Dorsey was very fond of the old homeplace, even writing an article on the history of the house in 1937. The article eventually found its way into the *History of Fayette County*, published in 1977.

After the Dorsey occupation of the home, **Robert E. Lee Fife**, originally from Henry County, purchased the property. With his wife, Emily Hindsman of Coweta County, the couple moved into their "new" spacious residence.

Like his predecessors, Mr. Fife was a leading citizen of the town, councilman, merchant and very active in the Methodist Church. **Fife's Mercantile & Hardware**, located on the town square north of the courthouse, was more than likely the largest store of its type in the county. Mr. Fife's son, Cecil, a mayor of Fayetteville in the 1950s, was the last person to use the Holliday-Dorsey-Fife House as a residence. He moved out in 1968. The Fife family lived in the structure the longest – over 50 years – and were responsible for it being known solely as "the Fife house" for many years.

So what is Margaret Mitchell's connection to the house? When the then-unknown author penned her famous book, she placed her 16-year-old heroine – **Scarlett O'Hara** – as a student in the "Fayetteville Female Academy" in 1861. In real life, Margaret Mitchell's own grandmother – **Annie Fitzgerald Stephens** – did in fact attend the Fayetteville Academy, and boarded at one time in the Holliday house in the early 1860s.

Mitchell's family connections to the Holliday-Dorsey-Fife House did not stop with the fictional Scarlett. The writer's cousin from the Fitzgerald clan, Martha Anne **"Mattie" Holliday**, was the prototype for Mitchell's *Gone With The Wind* character of Melanie.

Mattie spent her childhood in Fayetteville and nearby Jonesboro. A close-knit Irish clan, family gatherings at the Holliday home were common. It was during these and other times that the strong bonds between Mattie and John Henry (Doc) Holliday were established. Only twenty months older than Doc, Mattie was his constant playmate and companion during these assemblies.

The secrets these two shared as children formed the basis of an intimacy that lasted throughout their lives. The depth and breadth of this relationship and its exact details are not known today. It however, has been fodder for considerable myth-making over the years. In the Hollywood motion picture *Tombstone*, the character portraying Doc confesses to **Wyatt Earp** that an affair with a cousin caused her to enter a convent and him to leave his home in disgrace.

Cousin Mattie, born December 14, 1849, was raised a Catholic, and became a nun at the age of 34. Interestingly, she took the name "Melanie," in honor of **Saint Melaine,** who, after marrying a kinsman, sought to live a life of complete devotion to God. Did Mattie take the name Melanie because she was in love with her cousin Doc?

Another link between Margaret Mitchell and the Holliday-Dorsey-Fife House existed in the fact that Robert Kennedy Holliday married Mary Ann Fitzgerald – a relative of Mrs. Mitchell's. The Fitzgeralds were the great-grandparents of Margaret Mitchell.

Today, the Holliday-Dorsey-Fife House enjoys the honor of being one of Fayette County's first historical museums. Inside is a room dedicated to the families that once occupied the home, a War Between The States room, a Fayette County History room, and a *Gone With The Wind* room. Each contains is own unique artifacts and treasures pertinent to its theme.

A gift shop in the rear of the museum offers one-of-a-kind gifts and souvenirs. Plans are underway to create other rooms as further attractions.

Today, the Holliday-Dorsey-Fife House lives on as a museum to the past.

The Holliday-Dorsey-Fife House is managed by the Fayetteville Downtown Development Authorty and the Main Street Program. It is located at 140 Lanier Avenue West, just off the town square in Fayetteville. It is open from 10:00 a.m. to 5:00 p.m. on Thursdays, Fridays and Saturdays. For more information, call 770-716-5332.

Doc Holliday and Griffin, GA

Recent investigations and research on the famous Old West gunman have revealed some captivating details, particularly as concerns his former homes in Griffin, Georgia.

Bill Dunn, a distant cousin to the Griffin native, wants to get the truth out about his famous forebear, to see the "real" Doc Holliday – the Southern gentleman as opposed to the reckless outlaw – presented, once and for all.

As simple as that might seem, it, in fact, is considerably difficult to achieve, especially when dealing with a Western legend whose fascinating life has inspired multiple interpretations.

Dunn, however, must have fate on his side. Since he began researching his famous relative 20 years ago, he has managed to uncover quite a bit of previously unknown information pertaining to the dentist-gambler and his Griffin roots.

For instance, Dunn has discovered evidence that Doc actually practiced dentistry in Griffin – a detail heretofore unsubstantiated. He also has researched two "Holliday" graves in the local cemetery believed to be those of Doc's father's slaves, and he vows two other graves in the same cemetery are "more than likely" those of Doc and his equally-elusive father.

Most recently, Dunn and fellow Doc enthusiasts have discovered the actual site upon which Holliday's plantation home in Griffin once stood. This find, says Dunn, is the most satisfying of all.

"While the other discoveries happened along the way, this is the one I've been pursuing for two decades," Dunn relates.

Hitting The Jackpot

John Henry "Doc" Holliday was born Aug. 14, 1851, in Griffin, a west-central Georgia town with a current population of 22,000. He was the only living child of **Henry Burroughs** and **Alice Jane McKey Holliday**. Prior to his birth, a sister, Martha Eleanora, died at the age of six months.

John Henry was born in a house at the corner of what today is Tinsley and North 9th Street, according to Dunn. A modest brick residence – the nicest house in this lower income neighborhood – now occupies this corner lot.

John Henry's father had served in both the Indian and Mexican wars by the time his only son was born. Ten years later, the elder Holliday joined the Confederate Army and fought in his third war. During the decade in-between, he had worked as a druggist in Griffin and served as the first elected clerk of court there. His family – though not wealthy – was stable and socially prominent. They attended Griffin's **First Presbyterian Church** where records today indicate the infant John Henry Holliday was baptized at the age of seven months in 1852.

When John Henry was two years old, the family moved to a 148-acre plantation in rural Griffin. It is the location of this homestead that had eluded historians and that Dunn had long hoped to find.

"I'd been looking for twenty years," he said. "I'd get close but just couldn't pinpoint the location." Destiny, however, walked through his door in 2003 and Dunn said he still gets goose bumps talking about it. An employee of Spring Industries – which owns the former Holliday property – had been researching water locations at the site when he reportedly came across a copy of a 140-year-old map. "Bill, I think you'll be interested in this," the worker said.

To his amazement, Dunn discovered the map describes in detail the lay of the land of **Camp Stephens** – a Griffin-based Confederate Army camp – in 1862. **Major Henry Burroughs Holliday** had sold 137 of his original 148 acres to the Confederate Army for construction of the camp, leaving 11 acres for his family's residence. There, on the map, was clearly listed "**H.B. Holliday's second home.**"

Confederate Private **Asbury H. Jackson** had given the original map to Doc's mother in March of 1862.

"You search for something for years, then somebody just walks in and hands it to you," Dunn smiled, still incredulous.

Walking Hallowed Ground

The map had barely exchanged hands when Dunn solicited help from two friends – fellow members of the **Doc Holliday Society** (of which he serves as president) who were in town that August weekend for Doc's annual birthday bash.

With Gene Carlisle, a Holliday researcher who has penned a manuscript on the Western legend, Dunn set out hiking. Using the map as their guide, the men followed the old **Macon and Western Railroad** line toward the house site, battling tree branches, vines and undergrowth as they searched for the site of the old homeplace. Veering off the railroad tracks, they cut their way through one particularly dense area of undergrowth for a short distance before stumbling upon a scattered pile of ancient fieldstones which the men now believe were used in the foundation of the Holliday house.

"Gene," Dunn uttered, barely able to breathe. "I think we've found it."

The next day, Keith Reed – Holliday Society member and the third explorer – entered the wooded area at a different angle, hoping to prove Dunn's assumption correct.

"He said he was practically eaten alive by redbugs," Dunn smiled, "but he stepped off the map's directives and landed on the exact same spot, confirming it as the former Holliday homesite."

The site is about two miles from Griffin's town square. Interestingly, Dunn says some earthworks from **Camp Stephens** – just as they appeared during the Civil War – remain in the vicinity adjacent to the homesite.

As the war worsened for the South in 1864 – and with the Confederate camp barely a hop, skip and a jump from the Holliday home – it does not take a rocket scientist to understand why Major Holliday moved his family to Bemiss (a south Georgia town near Valdosta) that same year, almost simultaneously as **William T. Sherman's** Army was marching toward middle Georgia.

"Surely," said Dunn, "the major (medically discharged in 1862 due to 'watery dysentery') reckoned Sherman would march right by his home with destruction in mind. Seeking safety, he undoubtedly moved his family farther southward, eventually settling in Valdosta where he acquired more than 2,000 acres and ultimately served four terms as the city's mayor."

John Henry's Georgia

Tangible reminders of Doc's days in Griffin are abundant even today, if one knows where to look. There is John Henry's birthplace on Tinsley Street and the Holliday plantation. There's the former site of First Presbyterian Church where he was baptized. (The Griffin Fire Station stands on this site today.) There's the old **Griffin Courthouse** where Major Holliday served as clerk of court. And at **Oak Hill Cemetery**, there's the final resting place of Doc's sister.

A bit beyond John Henry's sister's grave are the graves of Mariah and Harry Holliday, a black couple who, according to Dunn, probably were slaves on the Holliday plantation.

"By all indications," said Dunn, "the Hollidays were good and decent people who cared for their workers." Despite a common tendency to believe that hatred and violence sparked all relationships between whites and blacks of the pre-Civil War era, Dunn asserts that nothing could be further from the truth. He said this was particularly true in regard to the Holliday family.

According to family tradition, it was a slave girl – Sophie Walton – who taught a young John Henry the skills he later used to support himself as a gambler after tuberculosis robbed him of the ability to practice dentistry. She showed him a number of the tricks of the trade, such as 'skinning' cards and 'the put-and-take' technique of dealing cards.

Doc, the Dentist

One of the most intriguing "Doc sites" in Griffin is the building where he may have actually practiced dentistry. In a 1940 *Griffin Daily News* article, Judge L.P. Goodrich noted that his father had known the Hollidays. The article goes on to state, "Doc Holliday returned to Griffin after the war and practiced dentistry here in an office in the old **Merritt building**."

It is a matter of public record that John

Henry, in fact, was partial owner of what then was called the Iron Front Building. He had inherited half of the property from his mother's estate, and her family – the McKeys – had claimed the other half.

"They actually drew a line down the middle of the building, separating the two halves," Dunn added. "Doc later sold his half for $1,800, which was a good price for that property back then."

Dunn said he feels certain Doc practiced dentistry in an upstairs office at the Iron Front. After graduating from **Valdosta Institute** in 1870, Doc had entered the **Pennsylvania College of Dental Surgery** from which he was graduated in 1872. He subsequently returned south and worked for **Dr. Arthur C. Ford** in his dental practice in Atlanta, while living with his **Uncle John Stiles Holliday** a short distance away (*Readers see "Fayetteville's Doc Holliday House" in the metro-Atlanta section of this guide*). While Ford attended the Southern Dental Association Conference in Richmond, Virginia in the summer of 1872, Dr. John Henry Holliday was left in charge of Ford's practice. When the elder dentist returned, the younger was left with time on his hands – time to commute to Griffin to operate his own dental practice, said Dunn.

"If he practiced here, this is where he did it," Dunn said, pointing to four holes in the original wooden floor situated in strategic spots to accommodate a dental chair of that time period. Equally interesting is a tin cylinder discovered under a loose floor plank at *Holliday's Portions & Elixirs*, a restaurant that now occupies the building.

"He probably used this for dental supplies or to hide money in," says Dunn who researched the cylinder, stamped "Great Northern Manufacturing Company, Chicago," and found it to be of Civil War era vintage. Great Northern did, indeed, carry dental supplies.

"It sure does lend credence to the possibility that Doc practiced dentistry here for two or three months before heading out West," Dunn concluded.

Resting In Peace, But Where?

While history claims that Doc Holliday is buried in **Glenwood Springs, Colorado**, persistent rumors through the years have alluded that Major Henry B. Holliday brought his son's body back to Georgia for burial. It's one rumor in which Dunn places some credence.

"Yes, I sincerely believe that," he says. "Knowing Southern history as I do – and knowing the major had the motive, the money, the mode of transportation, and nothing to stop him – I believe he brought Doc back and buried him under that oak tree. Until someone proves otherwise to me, I'll believe Doc's buried right here beside the major."

The unmarked twin graves at Griffin's Oak Hill Cemetery are compelling. Set off to themselves, they are covered by unassuming concrete slabs with no etchings. Dunn theorizes that Major Holliday either went to Colorado himself or sent a relative to retrieve his son's remains, then buried his boy under the now-massive oak.

Interestingly, an ancient heavy-duty nail is driven, rock-solid, into a sprawling root of the oak, centered above what Dunn believes to be Doc's grave. Dunn conjectures the major quite possibly could have hammered in the nail and used it to work a pulley to lower his son's casket into its final resting place.

"The nail-pulley mechanism would have enabled him to accomplish the two-man job on his own," said Dunn. It's a plausible theory if you believe the major wanted his boy's gravesite to be kept a secret, but then, digging a proper grave is a substantial job, and the Major was getting on up in years by that time. It is, possible, however, that he obtained the services of a former slave or family member who could have been sworn to secrecy to accomplish the task.

Supporting Dunn's belief that father and son are buried in Griffin are these notes of interest:

1) While Doc is said to be buried at Glenwood Springs, the marker in the cemetery there reads, "This memorial dedicated to Doc Holliday who is buried someplace in this cemetery." It is a fact that no one today knows the actual gravesite in Glenwood Springs containing Holliday's last remains.

2) While some Valdostans believe the major is buried in that town, no one knows the exact location of his gravesite there either. Dunn finds it difficult to believe that the grave of a man of his prominence (veteran of three wars and a four-term mayor) would be completely unknown and unmarked today if indeed

it did exist in Valdosta.

3) The twin graves in Griffin are in the Thomas family plot. Dunn said the Thomas and Holliday families were socially connected and the Thomases may very well have acceded to Major Holliday's request and agreed to the anonymous burial of Doc Holliday in their plot.

"Why can't the folks in Glenwood Springs point to Doc's grave?" questioned Dunn. "It's because it's not there. Major Holliday had the motive and the means to bring his boy back to Griffin. A man of Southern heritage would want his son buried near him, and removing him to an anonymous location would prevent the vandalism that surely would have followed had Doc's gravesite been revealed."

They say you can take the boy out of Georgia but can't take Georgia out of the boy. John Henry Holliday left the South and lived as Doc Holliday his last 15 years out West, but did he long for home?

An 1882 *Atlanta Constitution* interview with Holliday family friend Lee Smith indicates he did. When asked if Doc ever spoke of returning to Georgia, Smith responded, "He would be back here today but for fear of being handed over to the Arizona authorities." (By that time, Doc was a "Wanted" man for his involvement with Wyatt Earp in what came to be known as the "Vendetta Ride," in which a number of noted murderers who had been protected by a corrupt legal system in Arizona Territory were systematically hunted down and executed.)

By the 1880s, the West had claimed Doc Holliday as its own. He ultimately died in the Glenwood Springs Hotel on Nov. 8, 1887, tuberculosis finally defeating him.

It's a matter of public record that John Henry died out West, but, if Bill Dunn's theory about the two graves at Oak Hill Cemetery in Griffin, Georgia is correct, the noted gunman did, indeed, come home to Georgia a final time.

Southern Gentleman, Western Legend

Bill Dunn said he likes **Tombstone (Arizona) Historian Ben Traywick's** description of Doc Holliday best: "He was an orchid in a cactus patch."

Several years ago, Dunn received a call from Traywick when the Tombstone historian was working on his book, *John Henry: The Doc*

Holliday Story.

"He asked me to help and I asked him how he intended to portray Doc," Dunn recalls. Traywick replied, "As the true Southern, educated gentleman that he was.'

"What can I do to help?" said Dunn. Published in 1996, the book, to Dunn's delight, "does nothing to discredit Doc."

Known best for teaming with the **Earp** brothers to defeat the **Clantons** and **McLaurys** in the 1881 gunfight at the **O.K. Corral**, Doc Holliday became a larger-than-life legend. Over the next century, stories of him would range from fact to fabrication with his reputation as a ruthless gunman dominating. Numerous publications and Hollywood movies would paint the picture of a merciless killer with murder in his heart.

The facts, said Dunn, paint a different picture – that of an educated gentleman who never abandoned his Southern roots. Either way, the intrigue of Doc Holliday continues, even as it did a century ago.

"This guy from Buckhead called to get information for a report his 11-year-old daughter was doing on Doc," said Dunn. "He said she was infatuated with him and that after seeing the movie **Tombstone**, she could recite all of actor **Val Kilmer's** dialogue in the movie."

While some insist on portraying John Henry as a killer without a conscience, Dunn vows the dentist from Griffin fired a weapon only when he had to, and he never became comfortable with killing. The handsome ash-blond, blue-eyed Georgian who departed his home for the drier climate out West to slow the stranglehold of tuberculosis was most likely "a very typical young guy, mischievous with an out-going personality," says Dunn.

Regardless of the circumstances, Doc Holliday has become a legend that will never die as long as there are Old West aficionados in existence. It's like they say in Tombstone, Arizona these days: "There are three names that will forever be magic in this town: **Wyatt Earp, Doc Holliday** and the **O.K. Corral.**"

For more information on Doc Holliday's roots in Griffin, Georgia, contact the Griffin, Georgia Chamber of Commerce.

Yellow River Game Ranch

It began as a type of petting zoo at Georgia's scenic **Stone Mountain** Park. Today, Art Rilling's wildlife ranch in Lilburn is one of the more interesting attractions in the metro-Atlanta area.

Mr. Rilling relocated his wildlife to the picturesque Lilburn location in the early 1980s in order to create a preserve which would appeal to young and old alike and which would allow children (or "citified" adults) the opportunity to observe first-hand a variety of creatures native to Georgia. This captivating preserve is located on twenty-four wooded acres near the Yellow River.

The complex is filled with wildlife. Deer and fawns cavorted effortlessly along the paths, leaping the fences at will. Some of the deer will even approach visitors because they (the deer) have become accustomed to accepting treats from humans. As one strolls through this park, he or she will notice other wildlife along the way, many of which lay among the base of trees or shrubs where they often are easily overlooked in their silent stillness.

In one of the enclosures in the park, the palatial home of "General Lee," the nationally-known weather prognosticating woodchuck is located. The counsel of **General Lee** is sought each year on Groundhog Day in an attempt to learn the probability of a long winter or early spring.

Shortly after General Lee's enclosure, visitors see the first of two cages of bear. The bears have also learned that visitors have treats for them and respond accordingly.

Further along, there is a goat enclosure where these energetic and inquisitive animals often put on an amusing show. At one end of the pen is a ramp leading to a house. The house leads to a suspension bridge over the trail and to an automatic feeder at the other end. When a visitor places money into a food dispenser, corn drops out of the feeder at the far end of the bridge and the "billy goats gruff" trot over the bridge to collect their prize.

Another interesting aspect of Yellow River Game Ranch is the wide range of fowl encountered throughout it – including peacocks which may or may not wish to impress the visitor with their finery.

Some wildlife have populated the ranch of their own volition. Squirrels and chipmunks quickly learned of the ample foods available on the ranch grounds, and have taken up residence to take advantage of the situation.

One of the most imposing animals at the ranch is the buffalo. Many children – as well as adults – do not realize how massive a buffalo actually is, and thus are awestruck upon meeting the huge beasts up close. Mr. Rilling's collection of the bison (the correct name for this animal) reportedly is the largest herd east of the Mississippi. A coin dispenser at this point on the walk releases feed into a nearby trough which lures the buffalo over for an even closer look by patrons.

As visitors stroll further along the river, other animals come into view. There are coyotes (some of which are as tame and playful as dogs), foxes and bobcats, all in humane comfortable enclosures.

Just beyond the raccoons, foxes and bobcats, there is a picnic area overlooking a small waterfall on the river. Many visitors like to pause at this spot to enjoy the soothing babel of the stream.

Further down the path, visitors encounter some ingeniously-designed bunny burrows. At this spot, patrons may even walk up and over a wall so they can mingle with all varieties of the rabbits. The furry creatures seem to enjoy the attention, but signs at this enclosure urge visitors not to pick up the rabbits, since this causes stress in the animals.

"They feel secure as long as they have their feet on the ground," Mr. Rilling explains. "When you lift them up, they become frightened and agitated."

One of the final animals on the path is **General Sherman** – a skunk. Many visitors to the park apparently agree that he is appropriately named.

When you come to the Game Ranch, bring a picnic lunch and spend the day. You'll find more than enough here to amuse and delight the entire family.

The Yellow River Wildlife Game Ranch is open from 9:30 a.m. to 5:00 p.m. seven days a week year-round. For more information see the Ranch's website at www.yellowrivergameranch.com or call (770) 972-6643.

For well over a century, this historic structure stood as a community landmark. It weathered the years as a beacon for travelers, and even as an observation post from which law enforcement officials once spotted moonshiners. In the early 1990s, its days had seemed numbered until a community rallied to its support.

Like armaments awaiting a battle, large earthmoving machines had lined up behind the old store perched on the last remaining hill at the red clay construction site. Beneath the structure's foundation, timbers and jacks had been positioned in anticipation of the men charged with removal of the historic structure. It was the last remaining obstacle to the construction of a new supermarket and strip shopping center at the busy intersection of Mars Hill Road and Dallas Highway in this burgeoning west Cobb County suburb.

Old Lost Mountain Store with its sturdy brick walls stuccoed in spots to keep the rain from pelting through the lime and sand mortar, offered no particular architectural beauty to warrant its preservation. Outside, its aged gas pumps stood in stark contrast to the changing times, while inside, only a single light bulb suspended from the tall ceiling gave credence to modern conveniences. The shotgun-style, one-room building with its rusted tin roof covering a broad front porch resembles many other structures which once existed in 18th and 19th century Georgia, some of which still dot the Georgia landscape today.

Over the years, an uncanny emotional bond had formed between this building and long-time residents in its vicinity. For well over a century, it had stood as a stalwart sentinel beside busy State Road 120 connecting Cobb County to Dallas and other points westward.

Situated at the foot of Lost Mountain, an area rife with Indian lore and Civil War history, old Lost Mountain Store represented a nostalgic link to the past, while all around it, muddy roads were being paved with asphalt, and the many-terraced cotton fields were being replaced by subdivisions.

Marietta

Old Lost Mountain Store

When **Judge A. Lafayette Bartlett** – a man of diminutive stature and snapping dark eyes – built the old building back in 1881, he hardly had a lasting monument in mind. The structure's purpose was solely utilitarian. It was simply one more rung in the ladder to financial security for this fascinating man.

Born February 15, 1851 on his father's farm near **Lost Mountain** in Cobb County, "Fate" was the youngest of nine children. In 1863, when he was 12 years of age, his mother passed away. Later that same year, federal troops burned the Bartlett family home, along with all of the family's personal belongings. This could easily have been "the straw which broke the camel's back," but Lafayette Bartlett was made of stronger stuff.

Trapped inside **General William T. Sherman**'s lines and separated from his family, Lafayette realized painfully that he was on his own, with only his sharp wit and initiative to help him survive. Managing to escape enemy sentries, he reached the Confederate lines where he reportedly offered his services to the men in gray.

General Joseph E. Johnston's scouts hired young Lafayette to observe enemy actions. His knowledge of the area allowed him to slip in and out of the federal lines continuously with vital information until the fateful day he paused to watch Marietta burn after Sherman had put it to the torch. Contingents of Sherman's army caught and arrested him as a spy.

Knowing his fate, the young man watched earnestly for an opportunity to escape. When night fell one evening, his chance suddenly arrived. The Confederate scouts who had hired him had learned of his predicament. Under cover of darkness, they stealthily rescued him and took him safely back home.

The war had left fourteen-year-old Lafayette alone and penniless – but it had also motivated him. According to accounts, he was possessed of a driving ambition to be successful; to make something of himself. No task was too menial; no project too difficult for him to tackle.

Following the war, he earned twenty-five cents a day by plowing. By 1868, he had managed to save $137.85, which was a lot of money for a young lad in those days. Just prior to his eighteenth birthday, he invested in his first business venture – a small general store in the Brownsville area between Douglasville and Dallas.

In 1870, Lafayette married Permelia Isabel Watson, daughter of one of the prominent families of the area. The young couple began their lives together in a modest log home with a dirt floor, but that was not to be their fate for long. "Melia" and "Fate" worked hard for the success of their store, and their business ultimately flourished.

In 1871, the door of opportunity opened once again to the diligent young man and he again stepped through it with the vigor of youth. When Cobb County auctioned off 200 acres at the intersection of Dallas and Lost Mountain roads at a sheriff's sale, Lafayette did not let the opportunity slip through his fingers. The farmland – formerly owned by Joshua Jackson – sold for the grand sum of $2.95!

Lacking the capital, however, to rebuild a large two-story wooden store on the site which had burned (or been burned by Sherman's troops), Mr. Bartlett had to put his plans for the site "on hold" for ten years. During this time, he studied law, worked hard and saved his money, waiting for the right opportunity to profit from his meager purchase.

In 1877, Lafayette was admitted to the Georgia Bar. He set up a law practice and later served two years as a deputy sheriff of Paulding County. With the money he earned, he built his bride an impressive two-story brick home in the Brownsville community.

After he had accumulated the necessary funds for his Lost Mountain property, he began reconstruction of the store there. Talented and priding himself in his self-sufficiency, he hand-made the bricks for his new store himself. He used the rich Georgia red clay he found on the property.

Lafayette enlisted the assistance of his wife's brother, **John Coleman Watson**, to help him set up the store, and in 1881, the same year as the famed shoot-out at O.K. Corral in Tombstone, Arizona, "**Watson & Bartlett General Store**" opened its doors for business at Lost Mountain, Georgia. They sold goods covering everything from the cradle to the grave. From food and yard goods to farm implements and seed, Watson & Bartlett's Store endeavored to meet all the needs of the lively community in their vicinity.

In 1882, the store became even more vital when it was named as the site of the **U.S. Post Office** for the community. Riders on horseback brought the mail to the store.

A tall walnut bookkeeper's desk (with pigeon holes bearing each family's name) held the mail until someone came to claim it. Watson remained at the store for a happy eleven year stint as manager. Prosperity smiled upon the young manager and in 1892, he moved his family to Dallas where he opened a store and livery stable with his brother.

When Mr. Watson moved to Dallas, Lafayette enlisted the services of **Joe Arnold** as manager of the store at Lost Mountain. He remained a fixture there for 30 years.

Young Joe was a man of modest means who lived nearby with his wife, the former Mintora Meadors. His connection with the Bartlett family must have come from an unlikely friendship between Bartlett and Joe's father, **Silas Pinkney Arnold**, a former Confederate soldier who could neither read nor write.

While the circumstances of the friendship are clouded, the affection and respect between the two families remain evident, even today. Dr. Judson Ward, grandson of Joe Arnold, relates that several successive Arnold generations have named their sons "Bartlett" and his aunts were close friends with Bartlett's daughter, Ruth.

Dr. Ward, who was ten years old when his grandfather left the business, enjoys fond recollections of times spent in the old store, and of the fields and streams surrounding it. He remembers running barefooted through the freshly-plowed earth and picking wild plums in the summertime. Memories of an occasional clandestine swim in the cool spring-fed waters of the Lost Mountain Baptist Church's outdoor baptismal pool are also recalled.

When the influenza epidemic of 1920 claimed the life of Joe Arnold's wife, Mintie Arnold, her husband was able to remain at the old store for only two more years. He then left to live with his sons who had moved to Florida.

At the time of Arnold's departure, the store had been in operation for an amazing forty-one years. This period witnessed the growth of young Bartlett who had built the store so many years earlier with high hopes and anticipation. He had become a moving force in the political life of Paulding County, serving in the state legislature and as a judge of the Superior Court of Tallapoosa Circuit.

In 1922, Judge Bartlett was semi-retired and in his seventies – the twilight of his life. He

needed the right replacement for Arnold at the old store at Lost Mountain, and he found that person in an individual by the name of **Newt Sandford**. In only three more years, Judge Bartlett would face life's ultimate challenge – death.

The large **Levi Sanford** family moved 12 miles east from their home on Cole Lake Road in Dallas, settling into the comfortable white clapboard home beside the old store. Levi's son, Newt, eighteen years of age, ran the store and helped his brothers and father eke out a living from the dense soils and rocky fields surrounding them. Seventy years later in 1992, when progress and the destiny of the old store collided head-on, Newt would close the doors for the last time. In its 115-year history, the business had only three managers.

In 1935, Effie, Newt's older sister who had been tragically widowed, returned home with her five children. She stayed on almost seventy years to help Newt in the store and to cook for her large extended family. Their father, Levi, had died in 1942, leaving Newt the head of the family.

Effie's children all have fond memories of those years at the old store. On Saturday evenings, after a long day's work, young people often met at the store which was a type of social gathering spot. Some carved their names on the backs of the old porch benches.

On special summer nights, those gathered at the site might have a watermelon for refreshment. They'd sit on the front porch and swap news. Many outsiders knew of the store too. Even Gene Talmadge once stopped for a spell to have "a chaw" with Newt.

In the winter, older folk would drop by to spin a yarn or two around the old potbellied stove that was in the rear of the store. The site was a peaceful respite from the howling wind and even harsher circumstances of life in the community during the oppressive 1930s.

Because money was tight and jobs were scarce, illegal activities flourished in the hills to the west. The store's porch, perched high above the road, offered a bird's-eye view inside passing automobiles. Before the advent of modern surveillance equipment, the local sheriff would often come to Lost Mountain Store to watch for whiskey runners from Paulding County. Many were apprehended as Newt often helped the sheriff by passing on what he had observed.

The depression years left Newt so cautious about the banking system that, according to him, he never wrote a check or borrowed any money, dealing strictly in cash. Consequently, he kept his money – all of it – on the premises, a fact which ultimately targeted him for a number of armed robberies.

Newt's beloved dog – "Smoky Joe" – was shot in one hold-up. Another time, when Newt was away, three men armed with shotguns tied up his brother, Ansel, and his sister, Effie. They pistol-whipped the two of them, seriously injuring "Miss Effie." This was more than Newt could tolerate. He armed himself thereafter, and word eventually got around that Newt Sandford was not a man to be trifled with anymore.

Travelers along State Route 120 no longer see Newt propped back in his chair on the shady front porch of the old store. Age finally forced him – just as all his predecessors – into retirement. He, along with the others whose lives have created the heritage of the old store, has retreated into history.

As a result of community support, however, old Lost Mountain Store has managed to survive. Although Environmental Protection Agency (E.P.A.) regulations required the store to be moved slightly, to facilitate the removal of old buried gasoline tanks which were contaminating the soil, the historic structure has found a permanent home a few yards to the west.

Independent Bank and Trust of Powder Springs purchased the property as their west Cobb branch office. The site plan, however, called for the complete restoration and preservation of the old building for use as part of the banking building.

With a commitment toward maintaining the original appearance of the building, the contractor – who was experienced in historical restoration – stripped, patched and refinished the old heart pine floors of the building. Today, their rich orange and gold patina is a thing of beauty, long-hidden beneath the dust and debris of a bygone era.

Old Lost Mountain Store stands today as proof positive that progress and history need not collide. Rather, with cooperation and vision, the history of yesteryear can be incorporated into the progress of today.

Old Lost Mountain Store is located at the intersection of Mars Hill Road and Dallas Highway in northwest Cobb County on State Road 120.

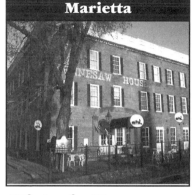

As soon as the big brick building is seen, it conjures up images of historic events in the mind of the beholder. Known originally as the Kennesaw House, a hotel of the U.S. Civil War era, this structure has witnessed the comings and goings of its share of the famous as well as infamous. Today, the second and third floors of the historic building house the **Marietta Historical Museum**, a very interesting attraction in historic Marietta.

Historic Kennesaw House / Marietta Museum of History

"Few buildings anywhere in Georgia have a history as interesting as that of the Kennesaw House in Marietta. It predates the Civil War (and provided accommodations) for the famous 'Andrews Raiders' on a night in 1862 before they hijacked a Confederate train pulled by the locomotive 'General.'" So wrote Joe Kirby in an article published in the *Marietta Daily Journal.*

Prior to the war, the Kennesaw House was a summer resort for the wealthy. Many of these visitors came to partake of the waters of a unique spring in the vicinity. Historical Museum founder **Dan Cox** rediscovered that spring behind present-day **Kennestone Hospital**. He maintains there is a lot of interesting history involving his community that is not well-known. That includes a "ghost" in the Kennesaw House.

Mr. Cox emphasizes that he doesn't believe in ghosts, "But I think I've seen one as I've worked here," he adds with a smile. The image Cox says he 'saw' stood about 5'6" tall and wore a flat hat with a brim, a cream-colored coat that hung three-fourths of the way down the thigh, and boots that came to mid-calf.

Cobb County Police Lieutenant Henry Higgins, a volunteer at the museum, supported Mr. Cox's contention. 'I've seen the

'ghost' three times,' he said. "We've attributed it to a lot of things up here – headlights reflecting on the windows, passing trains, and so forth. Just about the time you see him, he's gone."

Cox acknowledges that in this historic building, imaginations tend to run wild. "Doors swing for no reason (probably due to the air from a heating system vent), and boards creak."

History is not clear as to whether **Dix Fletcher** or **John Heyward Glover** (Marietta's first mayor) built the old hotel in the 1850s. However, it is a matter of public record that it was known as **Fletcher House**, and ultimately was later renamed the **Kennesaw House**.

Mr. Cox may be the first individual to have put a name to the specter thought to roam the Kennesaw House. He thinks it is **Dr. Daniel Wilder**, a Union Army physician and the nephew of Dix and Louisa Fletcher, Union sympathizers who once owned the property.

"When Union troops looted and pillaged Marietta during General William Sherman's occupation, Wilder prevented them from absconding with the Fletcher family's belongings, including a blind horse, flour and pots," says Connie (Mrs. Dan) Cox, who, with Henry E. Higgins, edited Mrs. Fletcher's diary for publication, renaming it *Journal Of A Landlady.* It covered the years 1857 to 1883 in Marietta.

Aside from its other early uses, the Kennesaw House also was used as a Confederate hospital where wounded soldiers were fed and treated following a number of area battles.

As enthusiastic as he is, Mr. Cox says he didn't always espouse his current love for history that has led him to develop the museum on the second floor of the Kennesaw House. "I didn't like it until my son, Carey, had an elementary school project on researching our family history."

The research revealed that their Cox ancestors could be traced back some 158 years in the Marietta area. In 1840, Dr. Carey Cox built the first hospital in the city, and specialized in homeopathic cures, particularly one using the waters from the spring behind present-day Kennestone Hospital.

According to accounts, patients would drink the water in small quantities and many reportedly experienced more healthful conditions thereafter. Mr. Cox says an analysis of the water revealed a high iron content. "My theory is that anemic people benefitted from drinking the water," he explains.

As a result of the research into his family genealogy, Mr. Cox says his work eventually fueled an almost overwhelming interest in the history of the area, ultimately expanding to include the preservation of historic real estate. Several years ago, while "just driving by the Kennesaw House," Cox's wife asked "Why doesn't the city buy the building and develop a museum?"

Dan almost immediately seized upon the idea. He got a city council member to set up an appointment with Joe Mack Wilson (then mayor and now deceased) in November of 1992. "I thought the process would take perhaps a year," he mused, but three weeks later, Wilson had gotten the Downtown Marietta Development Authority to buy the building for $525,000 to ensure its preservation.

"And because it was my idea," Cox laughed, "I got the job of Executive Director of the project. Most of the work, however, has been done by volunteers.'

The museum was founded by the Downtown Marietta Development Authority in 1992, and was officially opened to the public in 1995. "We've been lucky in the participation of people who have been members of the community for generations. That's meant a lot of donated items and volunteer help," Cox said.

The corner front room that overlooks the railroad tracks was the room in which several of **Andrews' Raiders** spend the night prior to hijacking the "**General**" locomotive from nearby Kennesaw (at a site called "**Big Shanty**") and speeding northward in the fabled chase. Today, this room is the Marietta Museum's Civil War Gallery and contains information about the Raiders. It also houses many Civil War artifacts.

Interestingly, following his arrest, **Marion Ross**, one of the spies, wrote **Eliza Fletcher** (a dyed-in-the-wool rebel in contrast to her parents) for help. She refused him. Ross ultimately was hanged.

Many items have been donated to the museum. Other items in the museum include historic memorabilia of old Marietta, period photographs, old furnishings, and one of "Sherman's hairpins" (a twisted piece of rail from the railroad). Union soldiers had a habit of heating the rails until they were red-hot, so they could then be twisted around a tree or some other object, rendering them useless to the Confederates.

The Marietta Museum currently is composed of a Homelife Gallery, a Civil War Gallery, and a General History Gallery on the second floor of the Kennesaw House. Visitors will also find the museum's conference room and a variety of displays on the third floor. The building also once had a fourth floor, but it burned during Sherman's occupation of the city.

The Marietta Museum of History is located just off the historic Marietta Square, facing the railroad. It is open Monday thru Saturday from 10 a.m. to 4 p.m., and Sundays from 1 to 4 p.m. Admission is $3 for adults and $2 for seniors and students. Members and children under 6 admitted free. For more information, call 770-528-0431, or see the Museum's web site at www.mariettahistory.org.

Rex

Historic Rex Mill

This aged mill has stood in downtown Rex since the early 1800s. It earned a well-deserved reputation for the excellence of the products it once produced. For decades, untold bushels of corn were ground into warm meal here. The years, however, eventually took a toll. Times changed and gristmills were no longer needed. To date, this historic structure has managed to avoid the wrecking ball, and is still privately-owned as of this writing. Rex Mill is one of the oldest water-powered gristmills in this part of the country, and the only gristmill left in Clayton County. In fact, it is quite historic since it is one of the few intact early gristmills remaining in north Georgia.

The mill pond, stream and nearby banks at the old mill have long been a favorite place for local residents for generations. Many a photograph – with the mill in the background – and many a picnic have been enjoyed at the site, not to mention the pleasures of swimming and fishing in the pond and wading in the stream.

Old photographs from about the time of the town's incorporation – 1916 – show ladies and gentlemen in their Sunday finery strolling near the mill sluice.

According to records, **Isaiah Hollingsworth** received this land that was once a swamp as part of a land grant in the 1820s. Hollingsworth built the mill at least as early as 1820, and an over-and-under turbine originally powered it. The mill was later converted to an overshot waterwheel.

The original dam in the millpond was a wooden dam. The roof of the two-and-a-half story structure was first covered with handmade metal. Side additions were added after the Civil War in the late 1860s.

"Touch" (Isaiah, Jr.) **Hollingsworth** operated the mill with a partner after his father's death in 1878. In 1881, the two men donated – for $1.00 – a right-of-way through a strip of land 150 feet wide. In 1882, rails for the railroad were laid into Rex. Family tradition maintains that Hollingsworth and his partner gave the right-of-way in return for an agreement that the railroad would construct its depot near the mill.

Different individuals owned or leased the mill in the ensuing years. It went by the name of **Hollingsworth's Flour Mill** during the U.S. Civil War. Its name later was changed to **Estes Mill**, and it is known today simply as **Rex Mill**. It was closed in 1959 after the bearings burned out from decades of use.

The town of Rex grew up around the mill – and the railroad. There used to be another mill on a dam slightly downstream. The lower dam supplied power for a cotton gin across the road from the mill.

Dr. William Callaway Estes, a physician and astute businessman, and his brother, Jimmy, bought the mill and surrounding 10 acres in 1887. The brothers had started a blacksmith and wagon repair shop in 1884 in **Yorktown**, a community about two miles west of Rex.

Josh Berry had designed a 14-fingered cradle scythe – a farm tool that farmers used to harvest wheat, oats and other grains – and had begun manufacturing it in a barn. The Estes brothers bought the business – along with the cradle's patent – in 1885.

The business soon outgrew the barn space, and the men also needed rail facilities. That year, they bought the village property which included the aged gristmill and cotton gin (on the lower dam), and converted the water-powered gin to a grain cradle factory. It turned out between 100 and 1,000 dozen cradles per year from 1887 to 1921.

The factory was so successful that both mills (lower and upper) ultimately were used to make the cradles. The cradle business, however, died out in the early 1920s, and the fact that the lower mill burned didn't help matters.

In 1918, Walter Estes, Dr. Estes' son, paid $3,000 for a big steel overshot water-wheel which he used to replace the old turbine in the upper mill. He had just gotten this new waterwheel installed when heavy rains flooded the creek and washed out the old wooden dam, letting the millpond go downstream with a loud "whoosh." Since the bridge had to be replaced, Walter decided to build a dam of fieldstones and cement. "If I hadn't just bought the wheel, I probably wouldn't have bothered to fix the dam," he said.

After the lower mill burned in the 1920s, the family converted the upper mill back into a gristmill. The aged enterprise once again was grinding the corn local farmers brought in. The Estes family then packaged the meal for sale in 10-pound bags. Water-ground corn meal from Rex eventually became a well-known commodity.

Walter Estes, former state senator, ran the mill after his father died in 1926. He also took over the chair company. He lived to be 102 years of age.

In an interview with the **Clayton Sun** newspaper published on July 30, 1981, Estes said a sidetrack from the railroad ran beside the mill, making the loading and unloading of products much easier.

"In those days, everything was shipped by rail," Estes explained. *"There were no trucks."* He added that he shipped most of the meal to the L.W. Rogers stores in Atlanta which later became the well-known **Colonial Store** chain of groceries.

In an article in the May 23, 1965 issue of

The Atlanta Journal and Constitution Sunday Magazine, Estes said, *"Early in the century practically all of our mill's work was custom grinding. Farmers brought their own corn and the miller kept one-eighth of the meal as a 'toll.' During World War I, with cotton up to 40 cents a pound, folks just about quit raising corn and I had to ship it in from the Midwest."*

Estes explained that the mill started losing money when the minimum wage laws came into effect.

"We couldn't pay the miller minimum wage and expect our profit to pay the expenses, so we sold the mill," he said.

The sale took place in the late 1940s. An individual named O.R. Longino bought the mill, then sold it to Elmer Partin in 1956.

In the May 23, 1965 article in *The Atlanta Journal and Constitution Sunday Magazine*, Partin said, *"I did hardly any custom grinding, since very little corn is grown in Clayton County. I bought corn, and sold a lot of fresh-ground meal at the mill and the rest to Atlanta stores. . ."*

The mill made some money for Partin for about four years. However, due to changes in the food business and customs in home kitchens, he eventually was forced to close. He sold the mill to a group of lawyers who planned to open a restaurant there. This venture, however, failed also.

Ironically, the law firm owed money to Walter Estes, so he took back the mill as a form of payment.

Subsequent owners installed new plumbing in the building, cedar and pine boards on the walls, and laid pine flooring on top of the original floor. They reportedly planned to open the mill as some type of public facility. The current circumstances of this historic site are unknown.

As of this writing, this historic site is not open to the public, but it is still worth a Sunday afternoon drive to the little town of Rex to view the old mill from the outside.

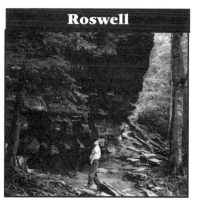

A ncient cliffside over-hangs provided shelter for prehistoric man, and if you're out hiking in the **Chattahoochee River National Recreation Area** (CRNRA) and get caught in a sudden summer rain, you might just find yourself taking shelter in one too!

Unless you don't get out much, you don't have to be told these days that Atlanta's **Chattahoochee River** corridor is a veritable magnet to modern development. It's becoming more and more difficult to find a stretch of the river in the Atlanta metro-area that doesn't boast (a term used loosely) just about all the modern riverside civilization it can stand.

Modern man, however, was not the first to "develop" this section of the Chattahoochee River. If one considers the situation from a historic perspective, various Native American inhabitants have called the river corridor "home" at least as far back as 8,000 years ago, and down thru the ages, they too "developed" the riverside to suit their lifestyle needs. Over those thousands of years of habitation, the ancients left millennia-worth of signs of their passing in the cool dim shadows of the **cliffside overhangs** that we call "**rock shelters**" today.

These shelters, however, have been very visible to modern man over recent years. That has made them prime targets for all manner of abuse, ranging from inadvertent damage by hikers and explorers to random and calculated acts of vandalism to excavation and pillaging by artifact collectors. In fact, according to one archaeological report, every one of CRNRA's dozen-plus rock shelters (as well as numerous other CRNRA sites of archaeological significance) has been disturbed to the point of diminishing or destroying its historic value. Alas, by the time archaeologists got around to investigating and cataloguing them, much of the value

Chattahoochee River Prehistoric Shelters

of the historic CRNRA rock shelters had already been lost.

Even so, these rock overhangs have yielded a number of intriguing artifacts. For example, a large rock shelter located above the floodplain in the Palisades East Unit of the CRNRA has at various times yielded small fragments of prehistoric pottery shards and "lithic (stone) material" despite being heavily pillaged in years past by artifact hunters.

So, where exactly are these rock shelters?

Well, if you ask a local archaeologist, he or she will probably (and understandably) only say, "Oh, here and there." Unless you're "In The Know" (and know the secret handshake), the line of thinking is that the relatively few undisturbed shelters will (and should) remain obscure and hidden away, protected from vandalism and pilferage.

There are, however, some you can visit – if you know where to look. . . .

Lovers' Leap Rock Shelter

One well-known CRNRA rock shelter is the so-called "**Lovers' Leap**" shelter group located in CRNRA's **Vickery Creek** Unit, behind historic **Allenbrook** just off Roswell Road.

Allenbrook – a worthy destination in itself – was built around 1845 as the office and residence for the manager of the nearby **Ivy Woolen Mill** (of which there are still Civil War-era ruins along Vickery Creek). Its solid brick walls are 18 inches thick, and its heart-of-pine flooring is crafted from 12-inch-wide planks – something one doesn't find too often anymore.

During the U.S. Civil War, Allenbrook was occupied by a French weaver named **Roche**, to whom James King (of the family owning **Roswell Mills**) had transferred ownership of the mills in a last ditch effort to preserve them. It was thought that Roche, who was French, could claim the mill(s) were French-owned (and therefore neutral as far as the war was concerned). Roche had hoisted a French flag in the vicinity of the mills in order to proclaim their nationality. However, when **Union Army General Kenner Jarrard** inspected the products produced by the mills and discovered the **"C.S.A."** insignia on them, he ordered the mills burned to the ground. The house, Allenbrook, however, was spared.

Even with all its aged history, however, Allenbrook is a "new kid on the block" compared to the nearby prehistoric rock shelters. Archaeological evidence suggests that this particular shelter grouping was used by Native Americans perhaps as far back as 1,000 B.C.

The Lovers' Leap shelter is easily (and legally) accessible today. From historic Roswell, go south on Roswell Road to the **National Park Service** parking area at Allenbrook, just north of the Chattahoochee. After paying the $2 parking fee, walk behind Allenbrook and look for a trailhead along the edge of the woods behind the house.

This area, however, is steep, with treacherous overhangs, so hikers proceed at their own risk. The trail carries you downhill, through lush stands of poison ivy – so beware – for about 80 paces. At that point, the trail ends at an intersection with a cross-trail.

At the intersection, you're almost on top of the Lover's Leap shelter. To best experience this shelter, you must make your way down to the level of **Big (or Vickery) Creek**. To do so, turn right at that trail intersection and hike south. You'll soon see a trail forking off to the left; it takes you down the hill, over some steps, and finally to the creekside trail which carries you to the shelter. Be careful if it's been raining; the steps are very slippery when wet.

At the bottom of the steps, go left and follow the trail upstream. This trail may be overgrown with briars of epic proportion, but the pathway itself is fairly distinct. You should have no trouble picking (and sticking) your way along.

When the Lovers' Leap shelter area was excavated by archaeologists during the 1980s, it yielded "faunal material" (Read: bones and such) that proved "useful in the reconstruction of dietary habits of prehistoric peoples in the corri-

dor." In other words, the stuff found here helped researchers figure out what the long-ago inhabitants liked to eat.

Favorite menu items apparently included deer, opossum, turtle, catfish and various mollusks. Alas, not a single Big Mac wrapper was found. Our own observations, however, confirm that such goodies (along with cylindrical aluminum or glass drink containers) are being actively deposited by careless hikers in parts of the area today. One has to wonder what the archaeologists of the future will make of such relics when they're excavated in another few thousand years.

Island Ford Rock Shelters

The Lovers' Leap rock shelters are some of the most spectacular awaiting explorers along the Chattahoochee. However, they are by no means the only ones. In fact, for casual explorers, it's impossible to beat the fascinating and highly accessible rock shelters at CRNRA's **Island Ford Unit**. You'll find no fewer than five of these shelters along this unit's wooded footpaths, and all but one are within just a few yards of the main riverside trail.

To visit these shelters, start at the **CRNRA headquarters building** located off Roberts Drive which turns east off Roswell Road just south of the Roswell Road Bridge over the Chattahoochee. Follow Roberts Road to the entrance of the Island Ford Unit, then continue on Island Ford Parkway as it winds hither and thither to the park's headquarters complex at the end of the road. There, pay the $2 per day parking fee, then put on your hiking shoes and get ready to step back in time.

The first thing you'll see is the log building that houses many of the park's administrative offices. Built over a six-year period in the 1930s, this structure originally was the summer home of the family of **Sam Hewlett**, a former judge in the Georgia Supreme Court. The building is said to be constructed of timber from the Okeefenokee Swamp and of stone from Stone Mountain.

To the left of the building, a graveled road bed leads down a hill. Follow the road to a level area, where a small covered picnic pavilion will be on your left. Just past the pavilion, the pathway – now an honest-to-goodness trail – continues over a little drop and takes you toward the woods and the river.

Making its way about 40 yards down a moderate slope, the trail quickly dead-ends in a cross-trail which parallels a little brook. Turning left takes you back up the hill to the parking area. But you want to turn right, toward the river, because that's the way to the rock shelters.

Continue right for 25 yards or so; you'll come to another cross-trail intersection. The right-hand trail will take you upriver toward a river overlook area; the left-hand trail immediately crosses a wooden footbridge and begins making its way downstream.

Just past the far end of the bridge, a trail takes off uphill along the creek toward another parking area. But you want to continue down-river. About 220 yards from the bridge, you'll see yet another path angling steeply up the hill on your left (It connects with the upland portion of the Island Ford trail system), but stay on the main riverside trail for an additional 200 paces or so. Then start looking to your left for the first of the Island Ford Rock Shelters.

How do you describe a rock shelter? It's an overhanging rock with a protected space beneath it, and this first one that you'll see at this spot is fairly typical. These large rock overhangs provide shelter from the sun, rain and the elements in general, particularly if a wall of tree limbs or stone is erected across the front of these shelters as quite probably was done by prehistoric man.

After you've explored this shelter, continue down-river for perhaps a dozen paces or so to a fork in the trail. The right fork (nearest the river) crosses a footbridge, then continues to eventually rejoin the left prong about 130 paces down the trail. The left fork, however, soon carries us to a spur trail which begins a gentle climb along a small creek.

By all means, follow this spur trail. It will take you to the second Island Ford Rock Shelter which is a spectacular site about 100 paces ahead.

This shelter, which is bordered along its front side by a tiny flowing brooklet, is arguably the most scenic of them all. Its large overhang shelters an equally large space, and there are several rocks that offer comfortable – if somewhat unyielding – seating. It's not hard to understand how prehistoric man could find this shelter to be an inviting refuge.

After exploring this shelter, rejoin the main trail and continue down-river. You'll quickly come to the third shelter and, about 60 yards farther, the fourth one.

The last of Island Ford's riverside rock shelters is located some distance down the trail. From that fourth shelter, hike on for perhaps 500 yards. Along the way, you'll pass a number of side trails entering the main riverside trail from the left. Near the end of this stretch, you'll cross a small rise, then – just a bit farther – you'll come to a final rock shelter not far from the point where the trail swings away from the river and turns uphill.

This last shelter is a small one, but it also includes rocks just right for "a rest," which you may well need at this point.

Seeking out these rock shelters, exploring them and listening to their whispered tales of ages past, is a great way to enjoy the Chattahoochee River National Recreation Area. One word of warning, however. . . Should you decide to become a shelter seeker, watch your head when you stand up. These shelters weren't designed with regulation eight-foot ceilings!

For more information on the Chattahoochee River National Recreation Area, contact the Chattahoochee River National Recreation Area offices.

Blue Willow Inn Country Restaurant

It began life as a portion of the estate of a wealthy Southern businessman, and came close to falling into disrepair in later years. Today, however, the elegant mansion known as Blue Willow Inn is known far and wide for its sumptuous meals and Southern charm.

The lovely Greek Revival mansion in **Social Circle**, Georgia offers a great weekend getaway opportunity for an excellent meal – or even series of meals, but the Blue Willow Inn is much more than that. Built in 1917, the captivating structure is approximately 100 years old today, has had some pretty interesting guests over the years, and has become the top attraction in Walton County.

When **Margaret Mitchell**, famed author of *Gone With The Wind* was courting first husband **Berrien Kinnard Upshaw** (on whom many believe she based her lead character, **Rhett Butler**), she would take the train from Atlanta to Social Circle to visit her beau. Known as "Red" because of his auburn-colored hair, Upshaw would travel the 10 or so miles from his home in Between, Georgia, gather Mitchell from the train station, and the two of them would lodge at his aunt and uncle's house in Social Circle.

During her visits, Mitchell respectably resided in a lovely Victorian cottage on the grounds, while her "intended" stayed next door in his family's Greek Revival mansion. Just as the private residence offered accommodations to Mitchell and Upshaw in the 1920s, today this distinctly Southern edifice and its gracious Southern charm continue to host guests under the auspices of the Blue Willow Inn.

Located in the historic district of Social Circle, the captivating mansion was built by Bertha and John Upshaw. The eldest of four boys, John was sure to inherit the wealth his parents had accumulated through the cotton industry, and his lavish home reflected that wealth. According to the Historic Preservation Society of Social Circle, the Upshaw mansion sits directly across the street from the residence of John's brother, Sanders, built in 1916. Ever the competitor, John built his home as a larger brick replica of his brother's home.

In the early 1950s, Bertha Upshaw gave the house and property to the clubs of Social Circle for use as a clubhouse and community center. The local clubs added a swimming pool, and the property was the center of social activity in Social Circle until the later 1960s.

In 1968, when integration arrived in the small Southern town and the clubs were court-ordered to integrate their swimming pool, they decided instead to abandon the Upshaw property, according to Louis Van Dyke, proprietor of the Blue Willow Inn. As a result, the historic home and property reverted back to the Upshaw estate until Homer Harvey purchased it in 1984 to establish the **Social Circle Church of God**.

Upon completion of the new church on the rear of the property, Louis and Billie Van Dyke purchased the by-then run-down main house and front two acres in 1991 to expand their restaurant and catering business.

'To open a restaurant in the mansion was my wife's idea," Van Dyke admits candidly today. "It was her dream and I joined her as it became a reality. At first, the banks laughed at the idea of financing the property and said such a business couldn't succeed in Social Circle."

But succeed it has. After the completion of major renovations to the property and despite the opinion of area naysayers, the Blue Willow Inn Restaurant opened for business on Thanksgiving Day in 1991. It quickly became the hit of Walton County, and indeed, one of the top attractions of east Georgia.

Inside the elegantly appointed mansion, where dining rooms such as the **Savannah Room** and the **Garden Room** are decorated in deep green and rich burgundy hues, the Van Dykes proudly display fine art, antique furnishings and accessories, along with part of their Blue Willow dish collection.

Since the early 1970s, the Van Dykes have been collectors of a historic pattern of china known as "Blue Willow." Their fondness for the pattern was extended to their new restaurant business.

Blue Willow china reportedly originated in the United Kingdom in 1790 and was made by Thomas Turner at **Caughley Pottery Works** in Shropshire, England. The pattern on the china includes a magnificent Chinese pagoda beneath the branches of an apple tree, a bridge extending across the sea to an island cottage, the drooping branches of the famous willow tree, and a pair of turtle doves.

The story behind the design dates back to a Chinese dynasty of long ago. According to the Blue Willow Inn website, a Chinese mandarin by the name of Tso Ling arranged the marriage of his beautiful daughter, Kwang-se, to an old but wealthy merchant. Kwang-se, however, had fallen in love with Chang, her father's clerk.

The two lovers eloped across the sea to the cottage on the island, quickly pursued by Kwang-se's father. Once the mandarin caught Kwang-se and Chang and was about to have them killed for their disobedience, the gods transformed them into a pair of turtle doves.

Each table in the Blue Willow Restaurant is set with Blue Willow china and adorned with fresh-cut flowers. However, though the restaurant's furnishings are beautiful and its décor elegant, it is the cuisine that attracts over 200,000 people each year to the facility.

Internationally acclaimed for its Southern-style cooking, this captivating mansion-turned-restaurant offers a sumptuous food line. Diners feast upon fried green tomatoes, sweet potatoes, chicken n'dumplings, black-eyed peas, collard greens, biscuits, "to die for Southern fried chicken," and much more.

"We wanted to do Southern cooking like the cooks of the Old South," Van Dyke explains. "We're not kind to diets, but you don't eat this way every day. We're a theme restaurant, not a buffet. . . kind of like Sunday dinners at grandmother's."

Honoring grandmothers all over the South, an average meal at the Blue Willow Inn features five meats, 12 vegetables, 10 desserts, two soups, salad fixings, biscuits, cornbread and muffins – all made from scratch – served with water, milk, coffee, lemonade and sweetened tea – "the champagne of the South." And just like at grandmother's, seconds and thirds are encouraged.

Treating each guest as if visitors in their own home, the Van Dykes are famous for their hospitality. They once hosted the late renowned humorist and writer **Lewis Grizzard**, and encouraged him to sample the buffet-style spread in the Walton Room. In 1992, the famed writer penned an article about the restaurant which appeared in over 280 newspapers nationwide. That one event took the Blue Willow Inn from obscurity to success in one weekend.

Today, there is a room dedicated to Grizzard who, through his nationally-syndicated column, proclaimed every dish to be "authentic and delicious," awarding the restaurant his "absolute highest mark, five bowls of turnip greens!"

Mirroring Grizzard's accolades, subscribers to **Southern Living** have bestowed the magazine's **"Readers' Choice Award"** to the inn since 1996, and diners, often arriving by the busload, back up their rave reviews with repeat visits to the popular eatery.

"I had heard of the Blue Willow Inn before," said Brenda Vaught of Woodstock, Georgia, "but when I finally decided to make a trip with a few of my friends and check it out, I had no idea that we would return time and time again afterwards. The mansion is beautiful, the hospitality is most gracious and the food is delicious. It reminds me of so many family reunions from my childhood."

And just like families pass down tried-and-true recipes from one generation to another, the

Blue Willow Inn Restaurant shares its favorites as well through the **Blue Willow Inn Cookbook**. Offered for sale at the restaurant's gift shop and also through the restaurant's web site, the hardcover cookbook includes not only delicious Southern recipes, but vintage photos of Social Circle and interesting anecdotes about the restaurant as well.

Lest one be deceived, however, this famous restaurant may not please every palate. "The Blue Willow Inn is not a place to grab a quick bite to eat," Van Dyke cautions. "It is a place to relax and dine. And, once the meal is over, guests are invited to browse the gift shop or rock in the oversized rockers on the front porch."

The Blue Willow Inn Gift Shop is located beside the pool, in the renovated Victorian cottage once occupied by author Margaret Mitchell on her weekend trips to see her beau. The shop is chock full of gifts, collectibles, home décor, cookbooks, jewelry and much more.

Beyond the inn itself, one may also wish to stroll the lovely streets in the historic district of Social Circle, partaking of the many antique shops and specialty stores in town. Social Circle offers a variety of treats, including a nostalgic turn-of-the-century soda fountain and a walking tour of the area's antebellum homes.

Visitors interested in a peek into the historic homes in the town may be interested in the annual tour of homes offered through the **Social Circle Historic Preservation Society**. This tour features six historic properties, including the home of internationally-acclaimed chef, **Nathalie Dupree**, where her PBS television show, *Nathalie Dupree's Comfortable Entertaining*, is filmed. Many historic residences in Social Circle serve as bed-

and-breakfast inns today.

Other extracurricular activities in the area include golfing at championship courses nearby, the hiking trails of **Hard Labor Creek State Park**, and wine tastings at area wineries.

It is the Blue Willow Inn, however, which continues to be one of the area's largest tourist attractions. Special events at the restaurant coincide with holidays or special days of recognition, such as Mother's Day.

"Mother's Day at the Blue Willow is our biggest event," Van Dyke continues. "It's the only day we don't take reservations and usually the wait is two to three hours long. However, we provide clowns to entertain the children, magicians to entertain everyone else, and horse-and-carriage rides to help pass the time."

Other special occasions at Blue Willow include daylong Easter Egg hunts for the children on Easter, and a Father's Day cookout where the restaurant provides chargrilled ribs in addition to its other buffet items.

During the warmer months, it is commonplace for guests at the inn to encounter antebellum greeters on the grounds of the inn. Ladies in hoop skirts, parasols in hand, and gentlemen in top hats often stop to have their photograph taken with diners. Their presence is yet another special touch the Van Dykes have added to recreate the grandeur and charm of the Old South.

Located 40 minutes east of Atlanta and 90 minutes west of Augusta, the Blue Willow Inn Restaurant is open Tuesday through Sunday for lunch and dinner. Reservations are recommended. For more information, call 800-552-8813.

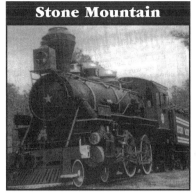

Stone Mountain

Stone Mountain Railroad

It is overshadowed by the world's largest granite outcropping – and most visitors and riders do not recognize it as a railroad museum. However, the five miles of standard-gauge track which encircle the monolithic landmark **Stone Mountain** – include a significant collection of antique and classic railroad equipment – not to mention three steam locomotives, four diesels, and a variety of passenger and freight cars.

The **Stone Mountain Scenic Railroad** has been part of **Stone Mountain Park** in DeKalb County since 1962. The railroad was initially operated with old steam locomotives until they gradually became too weary to pull the trains anymore.

All three steam locomotives at Stone Mountain Park are named for the locomotives involved in the Civil War's famed "**Great Locomotive Chase**" of 1862.

Number 104, named the "**General II,**" came to the park in 1962. It was built by the Baldwin Locomotive Works in August of 1919.

Number 60, the "**Texas II,**" was built in May of 1922.

Stone Mountain Railroad Number 110 – the "**Yonah II**" – is an entirely different type of steam locomotive. It is a 2-6-2 Prairie type, built in July of 1927. It is a much more squat-looking locomotive than Numbers 60 and 104.

The task of augmenting (and ultimately replacing) the steam locomotives at Stone Mountain Park has been accomplished with a collection of diesel locomotives.

The most historically-significant diesel on the Stone Mountain Railroad is a recent addition – Number 3499 – from the now defunct **New Georgia Railroad** which once provided excursions to Stone Mountain and elsewhere from downtown Atlanta. Another locomotive – Number 3498 – has also been obtained from the old New Georgia Railroad.

The next time you visit Stone Mountain Park, take an hour to ride around the mountain – starting from the recreation of the old pre-Civil War Atlanta train depot. The train will slow down to a crawl as it rolls through a recreation of Big Shanty, Georgia, the historic origin of the **Great Locomotive Chase**.

Most of the venerable rail equipment will be on the right side. Make note of it, because you'll be looking at a rare assemblage which has now virtually disappeared from the Southeast.

While you're visiting Stone Mountain Park, don't forget to stop by the unique collection of shops at **Stone Mountain Village** just outside the park. A refurbished caboose serves as the **Welcome Station** today for the village, and can provide much information concerning the shops and sites to see in the village.

For more information on Stone Mountain Park, call 770-498-5690.

Hight atop Amicalola Mountain in the northern portion of Dawson County, five springs bubble up and run together to become a tributary of Little Amicalola Creek. As the creek flows southward, it courses to the abrupt edge of a steep precipice and cascades majestically 729 feet to the foot of the mountain. The Cherokees called the falls "Um Ma Calo La," which reportedly translates to "tumbling waters."

Amicalola Falls

Today, thousands of people come to **Amicalola Falls State Park** not only to admire the waterfall, but also to picnic, camp, hike and fish. Until 1940, however, Amicalola Falls was "one of Georgia's most inaccessible beauty spots," as described in an article published in the October 6, 1940 issue of *The Atlanta Journal.*

In this article entitled *"New Road To Hidden Beauty,"* Georgia Highway Department Supervisor H.H. Johnson wrote, *"The scene could be reached only by a rough footpath until this fall, but the Highway Department is now completing a hard-surfaced road from Dawsonville which ends in two forks, one at the top of the falls, and the other at the bottom. The State Parks Department plans to begin work soon on a lake and recreational facilities at the head of the falls."*

As remote as the area was, white settlers began moving in even before gold was discovered in north Georgia in 1828-29. Family legend maintains that in 1820, **Abraham Cochran** settled near the foot of another nearby waterfall which came to be known as "**Cochran Falls.**" He reportedly stuck his walking cane into the ground to mark the spot where he wanted to build a home. When he returned (after going back to North Carolina to get his family), the cane had sprouted and subsequently grew into a huge sycamore tree.

Several of Abraham Cochran's sons and some of their kin later established a community further up in the mountains above Amicalola

Falls. It was called Buncombe, because the Cochrans originally came from Buncombe County, Ireland. Before coming to Georgia, they had settled Buncombe County in North Carolina.

"The Cochrans must have really loved the mountains because they always wanted to get as far back in the hills as they could," Abraham's great-grandson **Clarence Cochran** (now deceased) once mused of his ancestors. "They may have been isolated in Buncombe, but they built a schoolhouse for their children and a place of worship. I have a copy of the document the founding members wrote when they organized **High Shoals Baptist Church** on June 7, 1879."

In the spring of 1832, **William W. Williamson** was the adjutant general and subcommander of the Georgia Guards assigned to survey the area for the upcoming land lottery. The following is a portion of the five-page letter he wrote to **Governor Wilson Lumpkin**:

"I spared no exertions to obtain all the information on the subject of Survey Of The Country that my limited means would afford. . . . I passed through the mountains with only nine of the guards believing from report the almost impossibility of success. However, I had determined to make the trail. I had no pilot and was fortunate to pass without ever being lost.

"I passed the mountain town of Ellijay and several other smaller towns that I did not learn their names. In the course of my route in the mountains, I discovered a water fall, perhaps the greatest in the world, the most majestic scene I have ever witnessed or heard of – the creek passes over the fall I think can't be less than six hundred yards. The mountain is at least three fourths of a mile high. I made great exertion to get to the summit, but the ascent was so great that I was completely exhausted by the time I reached halfway. My position is such that I had a perfect view of the entire

fall. The stream is called Um-ma-calo-la from the fall (sliding water)."

(Author's Note: The letter from Adj. Gen. Williamson is maintained in the Telamon Cuyler Collection of Gov. Wilson Lumpkin's papers, University of Georgia Library, Athens, GA, and was quoted in a January 2, 1992 article in the Pickens County Progress by J.B. Hill.)

A post office called "**High Shoals**" was established in 1837 at the falls, with **Elias Turner** serving as the first postmaster. **Henry H. Ware** was postmaster in 1846, when the name was changed to **Amicalola Post Office**.

A Methodist campground was established near the bottom of Amicalola Falls not long after the area was settled. It was called **Amicalola Campground** and was originally a "brush arbor" where families from miles around gathered for a week of revival services after their crops had been "laid by" in August.

During the War Between The States, **Amicalola Campground** was used as a mustering ground not only for Confederate troops but also for a Union Army contingent composed of north Georgia mountaineers. There was a great deal of anti-Confederate sentiment in the north Georgia mountains at this time, especially against the quasi-military units known as "Home Guards" who frequently confiscated supplies from already lean larders of the mountaineers. The Home Guards also meted out harsh vigilante punishment, hanging men who refused to wear the gray uniform.

Company B of the 1st Georgia State Troops was composed largely of men from Dawson County who had deserted from Confederate units. They mustered at Amicalola before marching to Dalton, Georgia, to be formed into a Union battalion.

In November of 1864, **Col. James J. Findley** and his **1st Georgia State Cavalry Home Guards** (C.S.A.) camped near Amicalola Falls while in pursuit of some of these pro-Union north Georgia troops who had been raiding the area for horses and supplies. Findley and his men followed the raiders over the top of Amicalola Mountain to an isolated community in Gilmer County called **Bucktown** where a skirmish broke out. Several Union soldiers were killed in the engagement. Others were captured along with papers which provided the names of local Union sympathizers who were later captured and executed.

When a pioneer named **Bartley Crane** found his way to the foot of Amicalola Falls in the early 1850s, he reportedly became acquainted with a Cherokee woman named **Elizabeth Brock** who was living nearby. Some accounts maintain Elizabeth was a full-blood Indian. Stories about her described her as a very tall, slim woman who carried a double-barreled shotgun.

"She was a dear woman but different," is the way Mary Bridges remembered that her mother, Etta Crane, described her grandmother, Elizabeth Brock Crane. "Great-grandmother would take her children to church but never set foot inside the door herself," Mrs. Bridges explained. "I've always heard that she had coal-black hair and was part Cherokee.

"Even after marrying Bartley Crane in 1853, Elizabeth would periodically take her gun and two jugs of whiskey and ride her mule off into the mountains to stay for weeks at a time," Mrs. Bridges continued. "It's always been my belief that she took the whiskey to her people who had hidden out in the mountains to escape the Indian Removal in 1838. Back then, whiskey was used a great deal for medicinal purposes.

"My mother Etta was the daughter of Bartley and Elizabeth's son, Jim," Ms. Bridges continued. "Etta was born in 1890 and raised at the foot of Amicalola Falls. Although she was fair and blond, she had high cheekbones. She remembered Indians coming to her grandfather's store and bartering with gold and silver when she was a girl."

Etta had a brother who was named James Olin, but he was always called "Brock" because that was his grandmother's maiden name. Etta also had a sister named Ida, whose son Will, when recently interviewed, was able to remember his great-grandmother, Elizabeth Brock Crane well. He described her as "a tall, slim lady with black hair that she wore parted in the middle and pulled back in a single braid." Will clearly recalled how Elizabeth "cooked in big iron skillets in her fireplace and was always trying to give me something to eat. She was always very loving to me."

Bartley and Elizabeth's son, Jim, married

Martha Waters, and his brother, Miles, married Martha's sister Mary. Both girls were daughters of Moses Waters, who settled near Little Amicalola Creek in the early 1830s.

Mary Bridges and others remember hearing that Moses didn't want his daughter to marry Jim Crane. They speculated that it may have been because of Jim's Indian blood. Although people now take pride in having Indian ancestry, it was a source of shame in the 19th century when Native Americans were not officially allowed to own land, vote, hold public office, or attend public schools.

Other Crane descendants, including **Johnny Burt**, owner of the popular **Burt's Pumpkin Farm** located near Amicalola Falls, doubt that Bartley's wife was Indian. "I remember hearing Grandpa say that his daddy traded with the Indians when he first came to this area," Johnny recalls, "but I never heard anything about any Indian blood in our family, and our features don't show it."

Johnny's mother, Bonnelle, was the daughter of Bartley's and Elizabeth's son, John Hunter "Hunt" Crane and Carrie Fausett. Bartley ran a corn and flour mill on the creek below the falls, and Johnny Burt recalls that the old mill rocks were still in place when he was a kid. Bartley also ran a government-licensed liquor distillery in the vicinity and reportedly once got into trouble for making additional spirits on the side.

At one time, Bartley owned several hundred acres including the falls, but lost some of the property after using the land for collateral on a loan. The falls reportedly were sold for the grand total of $2.65 in a tax sale to pay the sheriff's cost of advertising.

The remaining property passed to John Hunter Crane, who repurchased some of the land his father had lost, but he apparently never regained possession of the falls. "Hunt" Crane operated a store and barber shop near the bottom of the falls. He also rented out several small cabins to people who wanted to spend a few days enjoying the natural beauty of the falls and the surrounding area.

Hunt Crane's daughter, Laverne, married

Clarence Kincaid, and they also operated a store near the falls (known as **Kincaid's Store**) from 1942 to 1998. Hunt was killed in a tractor accident in 1958, and his homeplace burned in 1947, unfortunately destroying all the family pictures.

Today, Bartley and Elizabeth Brock Crane sleep peacefully in the cemetery at **Nimblewill Church** a short distance east of Amicalola Falls. Many of their descendants still live within a few miles of the site of the Cranes' old log homeplace which once existed near the foot of the falls. Other great-grandchildren were raised elsewhere, like Mary Bridges and her sister, Helen Talton and brother Frank Roberts, all of whom eventually returned to the home of their ancestors to live out their retirement years.

Amicalola Falls State Park consists of 1,020 acres and boasts an impressive 57-room lodge with restaurant and meeting room facilities at the top of the falls. Accommodations also include 14 rental cottages and 17 tent and trailer sites for campers.

The park is especially popular with hikers, since it provides three and one-half miles of trails as well as an 8-mile approach trail to the southern end of the Appalachian Trail which runs from Springer Mountain in north Georgia, all the way to Maine.

Other popular attractions include spring wildflowers, colorful autumn leaf displays and overnight backpacking trips in the fall, and a Christmas Open House with Santa and carolers at the lodge. The Visitors Center has a number of interesting exhibits of native animals indigenous to the area, including deer, bear, bobcat, and pileated woodpeckers. Year-round naturalist programs feature "Owl Prowls," "Ssssnake Shows," Cherokee stories and crafts, scavenger hunts in the woods, and fireside fun with stories, games, and marshmallows.

Amicalola Falls State Park and Lodge is located between Dahlonega and Ellijay on Highway 52 East. For reservations and more information, call 706-265-8888.

Amicalola Falls

Burt's Pumpkin Farm

You want pumpkins? They've GOT pumpkins!

"We sell about 3,000 every day on weekends from September 1 through November 15," Kathy Burt says, as she shows visitors around Burt's Pumpkin Farm near **Amicalola Falls** in Dawson County. Kathy and her husband have operated the farm there since 1972.

You want choices in pumpkins? They've got myriad sizes: big pumpkins, little ones, tiny ones, and enormous ones that range in price from $2 to $60. The choice is yours.

The largest pumpkins at the farm can weigh up to 340 pounds, and they've got seven different varieties too.

"Some are better for cooking, while some do better for decoration," Kathy explains.

Despite their prominence at this scenic attraction, pumpkins are only the beginning at Burt's Pumpkin Farm. "Chow chow and apple butter are the best sellers among our canned items," Kathy says. Her sister offers homemade crabapple jelly, apple relish, candied tomatoes, pickled carrots, and pickled pumpkin. And if gourds are what you're looking for, the Burts offer them too – especially dried painted apple gourds.

The Burts grow most of the fruits and vegetables used in the goodies they offer. "We have a limited supply of wild fox grape jelly because those grapes grow wild and are hard to find," Kathy adds.

The store at Burt's Farm also has pies, rolls, muffins, and bread – all made from what? . . . .Why, the delicious pumpkins of course. You'll find apple bread, too. And if you follow your nose, you could even take a peek into the kitchen where cooks are baking the products on the premises – guaranteeing that whatever you buy is fresh from the oven.

And then there's the popcorn. . . The Burts grow 40 acres of popcorn and "cutie pops" (a variety that grows three to four inches in length) every year.

"We actually grow nine different varieties, including colors," Kathy smiles. "We recently added blue and white corn. Seed companies do research and we keep in touch with their new varieties."

Another unusual item – popcorn meal – is also good for the creation of bread. And before you leave, don't miss the beautifully-colored Indian corn (which does not pop). It, of course, is only good for use in decorations.

You'll also find baskets, dolls, Christmas decorations, and tee-shirts in the shop. There's more to do at Burt's Pumpkin Farm than just buy gifts and foods too – especially if you take your children.

Kids can take a two-mile ride on the hay wagon (adults have been known to enjoy this ride too). Participants will cross a stream and then go up through the mountains where you'll pass fields filled with popcorn and pumpkins. Along the way, you'll see a road in the forest "paved" with hundreds of pumpkins. You just can't get away from those things at Burt's Pumpkin Farm!

You might ask, "Are the Burts a 'Johnny come lately?'" and the answer would be a resounding "No." The property has been in the Burt family for many generations according to Johnny Burt, Kathy's husband.

"My great-grandfather, Bartley A. Crane (on my mother's side) once owned so much land around here that he owned Amicalola Falls," Johnny begins. "But somewhere along the way, he wasn't able to pay his taxes, and the government took the land away and sold it."

Sometime later, Burt's grandfather – Hunter Crane – bought back 400 acres of the lost property. His other grandfather – Alonzo Burt – whom Johnny remembers as "a tough old bird," brought still more of the property back into the family by working hard during the Great Depression. His toughness has paid off for his descendants.

At age 12, a young Johnny Burt was a farm-loving boy who had grown up helping his mama grow things. Suddenly, one day, however, young Johnny found himself living in Chicago. Later, as a young man, he trained to work in the Wrigley's chewing gum factory. "I didn't like it," he recalled. After having lived in the open countryside as a child, he says he found life in an apartment to be too confining.

In 1972, Johnny says he returned to north Georgia, where he found employment at Lockheed in Marietta, at General Motors in Doraville, and at a factory in Flowery Branch. He says he gradually worked himself back to his first love – farming in the north Georgia mountains.

When he first returned from Chicago, Johnny says he planted some pumpkins in Granny Crane's yard. He later built a house and sold pumpkins out of his dad's yard until 1990. "After I built a barn on Grandpa Crane's land, I began to see the possibilities of opening a business," he says. It wasn't long before he rented 240 acres where he began growing pumpkins and gourds.

"I always felt I could make a living out of growing and selling pumpkins and other farm products," Burt says. He and his wife now have the largest pumpkin farm in the state, owning 189 acres of which 162 are planted in the crop.

Johnny makes no bones about it. . . He says he loves the farm despite the hard work it takes to keep it going. "We couldn't live through it if we didn't love it," he smiles. "Nobody actually knows how to farm," he adds. "The weather is different every year, and a farmer has to know how to deal with it . . . and adapt.

"For example, in the year 2,000, we ran a

pump (for water from the creek) 12 to 14 hours a day due to the drought," he continued. "Our products would have turned out better with the rainwater than with the creekwater, because the rain has certain chemical elements that the creek water doesn't, but it was better than doing without water completely."

Pumpkins just naturally require a lot of attention anyway if one wants a really good product. The crop's natural pest – the mosaic virus – is a disease which comes from Kansas wheat that is transported here by aphids. Some summer nights, the men stay out till midnight spraying the pumpkins.

Despite all the hours of hard work, Johnny sighs with satisfaction as he surveys his realm. "Our family works together in this business. We couldn't do it without my sons, Russell and Cameron." Grandson Johnny Tyler Goodwin is the youngest family employee.

The practice of growing pumpkins is a tradition as old as the days when prehistoric Native Americans grew this same crop in these hills prior to the white settlers. It also is a tradition which the Johnny Burt and his family intend to continue for many years to come.

Burt's Pumpkin Farm is located at 4801 Highway 52 East in Dawsonville, one-half mile from the entrance to Amicalola Falls State Park. From Atlanta, take Georgia 400 north to Highway 136 west. Highway 136 will intersect with Highway 183. Follow Highway 183 until it dead-ends into Highway 52. Turn right and continue to the farm. From Marietta, take Interstate 75 north to Interstate 575 north. Take Highway 108 east to Highway 53 east. Take Hwy 183 north to Hwy 52 east. For further information, call 706-265-3701 or 800-600-BURT (2878).

The Double Barreled Cannon in Athens

Ever heard of a double-barreled cannon? One is on display for public viewing on the grounds of the Athens, Georgia City Hall. You can walk around it. You can touch and take pictures of it. For many years, it was believed that it was the only one of its kind in the world, but recent revelations now indicate a second version of this killing machine may still exist.

There is anecdotal evidence that two castings of the double-barreled cannon were made for testing in this community in 1862 during the early years of the **War Between The States**. So if one is now displayed on the city hall grounds, what happened to the other one? Where is it today?

The story of the **Athens double-barreled cannon** actually began in August of 1861. **John A. Gilleland** watched as two of his sons, William and John Wesley, marched off to war in Virginia as members of Cobb's **Legion, Georgia Volunteers**. William was wounded in battle and returned home to Athens, minus a hand, in 1862.

The senior Gilleland learned from his sons that the army leaders lined up their troops, shoulder to shoulder, and when the soldiers were in range of their muskets, they would stand or slowly walk in ranks, blazing away until one side or the other was decimated and forced to withdraw in defeat from the battlefield. To Gilleland's mind, such rigid parade-ground type tactics presented an ideal opportunity for an area type weapon that could mow down advancing troops *"as a scythe cuts wheat."*

Thus, John Gilleland, an Athens, Georgia house builder, had an inspiration for just such an efficient killing machine of war. His idea was to fire two chain-linked cannonballs simultaneously from two slightly divergent barrels of a single cannon. When the chain was tautly extended in flight by the weight and trajectory of the two cannonballs attached to each end, it would ideally act as if a 100-feet-long razor-sharp steel blade was slashing from waist to head high into the enemy ranks, mowing down everything in its path. In his mind, Gilleland was convinced that the two balls and chain fired from the double-barreled cannon had the potential to become the ultimate "grim reaper" of the battlefield.

The First Cannon

John Gilleland lived on Jackson Street in Athens. Although he was a carpenter and contractor by trade, he not only built houses, he made cabinets, doors, windows and even coffins at his shop behind his home.

At the beginning of the war, a number of individuals realized there were substantial income opportunities in munitions manufacture. Gilleland was one of the first of these to try to seize the moment.

With the intent of manufacturing his double-barreled cannon in Athens, he gathered contributions from 36 interested investors for a total of $350 to finance the cost of making a double-barreled cannon for testing. In early 1862, using the facilities and mechanics of the **Athens Foundry and Machine Works**, Gilleland put his plan to work, casting an experimental version of his cannon.

His principal associates in the design, casting, and testing of the gun were his son William, Johnson Garwood, and William Bain, who along with Gilleland, were members of the local home guard unit called the **Mitchell Thunderbolts**. Other members of the unit assisted in the project by acting as crew members for the test firing of the weapon.

The barrels of the double six-pounder were cast in one piece, and diverged by three degrees from parallel. It weighed 1,290 pounds. It had three-inch smooth bores with overall barrel lengths of 32 inches which were the usual dimensions of the typical three-inch cannon of that day.

The breech was designed so that the powder from both barrel vents met at a central point. When fired, both barrels were designed to discharge simultaneously.

Loading the cannon involved ramming a powder charge and then a ball down each of the two muzzles with the balls connected by a 50-foot chain which dangled to the ground between the two muzzles prior to firing. The 50-foot chain was only half the length envisioned by Gilleland for his weapon, but as the design progressed it became obvious that the weight of the 100 feet of chain was far to much drag on the projected balls to extend the chain in flight.

After the cannon and its ammunition were assembled at the foundry, the gun was mounted on a two-wheeled shop truck and taken to the outskirts of Athens on Newton Bridge Road near Dr. Linton's woods for test-firing. A wide tract of land had been cleared of trees, and poles had been erected to represent the ranks of an advancing enemy as a target. The cannon was positioned in front of the target and a group of invited spectators were positioned at a safe distance to the rear of the cannon to observe the much-anticipated test-firing.

Then, with a bit of ceremony, the cannon designers, foundry workers, and assisting members of the Mitchell Thunderbolts loaded the cannon by ramming the powder charges and two five-pound iron balls into position down the muzzles with the connecting chain dangling to the ground between the two barrels.

The signal to "Fire!" was given and the lanyard pulled. The cannon roared horrendously and the smoke bellowed. One ball went out ahead of the other, snapping the chain that whipped wildly around, diverting the course of the left-side ball into the standing pines to the left of the firing range. The right-side ball went wide to the opposite side of the range plowing up the ground as it skipped along. When the smoke had cleared, it was also clear that the target poles representing the enemy troops were untouched by the fury of the blast.

As a result of the wild explosive violence around them, the invited spectators quickly scattered. By any measure, the first public demonstration of the double-barreled cannon had been a dismal failure.

A Second Cannon

John Gilleland was greatly embarrassed and publicly humiliated by the failure of his much-heralded ultimate weapon invention. For most of the citizens of Athens, the test-firing was the end of John Gilleland's dream of a secret weapon whose use would bring an end to the war. As far as they knew, Gilleland never fired the cannon again and the device was turned over to the local home guard to be used as an alarm signal (firing powder charges only) should the Yankees ever appear on the approaches to town.

However, in reality, Gilleland and his associates were undaunted in their continuing efforts to make the cannon function successfully, let alone to gain a contract to produce the weapon for the Confederacy. The major difference in their approach was that the public would no longer be looking over their shoulders. They would bear with good humor the ridicule and jokes about their initial efforts from the public, but from then on, they would keep their new work and testing on the cannon to themselves.

In assessing the results of the first firing test, it was decided by Gilleland and his men that the

barrels of the cannon were not cast at the same range (it is unknown today exactly what the word "range" meant in that context), thus causing the chain to break which began the disastrous events that followed.

So, during the summer of 1862, at the Athens Foundry and Machine Works, Gilleland and his associates continued to work on improving their cannon design. The pattern for the cannon was changed to correct the so-called "range" problem and a new improved second gun was cast in the foundry.

When completed, the second cannon was taken out and tested. A cluster of pines served as a target. Still chagrined from their first public test firing disaster, Gilleland and his assistants invited no spectators this time. However, Johnson Garwood, one of the three cannon-makers, wrote that *"Major Ferdinand Cook, Captain W.H. Dorsey, Joe Browning, Dr. Frank Hill, Dr. Billups, and Captain Reuben Nickerson observed the test."*

The result of the second test-firing was again far off the intended target. This time, however, the chain did not break and a group of pines were sliced off as if someone had cut them with a saw. For this test, the size of the chain was described as about the size of a horse halter chain with a five-pound iron ball at each end of the chain. Further, this time the length of the chain was only about eight feet which was little more than the distance needed to stretch the chain from ball to ball when loaded for firing. The eight-foot length of chain was a drastic reduction from Gilleland's originally planned killing zone of 100 feet wide.

In 1862, in response to Gilleland's insistence that his cannon had been perfected and "was a success in every way," the device was moved to the Augusta, Georgia Arsenal where it was to undergo War Department acceptance testing.

In March of 1863, the War Department tests at Augusta were concluded and the cannon was declared impractical due to its failure to fire both barrels simultaneously. On March 5, 1863, in a letter of protest to the Confederate Secretary of War, Gilleland complained that "the officer-in-charge of the tests had dismantled the gun, laid it on the ground with a piece of timber under the muzzle, and fired away."

Gilleland demanded to know what could be expected from such an inept procedure. He argued that he had fired the double-barreled cannon several times before intelligent people and they, as well as he, were convinced that it was a perfect success.

Eventually, John Gilleland's letter of complaint to the Secretary of War found its way to Colonel Josiah Gorgas, the Chief of Ordnance, who, in turn, requested a full report from Colonel George Washington Rains, commandant of the Augusta Arsenal. Colonel Rains basically explained it was impossible to fire off two charges by any means so that the quantities of powder would burn precisely the same at any given moment in time. And in addition, he pointed out that the difference between the amount of friction generated by the cannonballs passing through their respective barrels would in itself be sufficient to prevent the weapon from functioning as designed.

Gilleland's persistence with the Confederate authorities eventually proved fruitless. He would not get money from the government for further testing nor his much-desired contract to manufacture the cannons at Athens.

Gilleland also sought help from Georgia Governor Joseph E. Brown, but Brown also declined to provide any money for further development of the double-barreled cannon.

Finally, John Gilleland, having no further options to pursue, turned over his cannon to W.H. Dorsey to serve as a signaling device in the event of a Yankee attack. It supposedly was positioned in front of the Athens Town Hall.

Later, the double-barreled cannon actually saw action in one skirmish during the war. On Tuesday, August 2, 1864, it was placed about three miles from Athens on the outer defenses and fired conventional shot without chain at Stoneman's Raiders who were reported to be approaching to burn the town. The Union soldiers retreated, but the performance of the cannon was reported by James W. Camak, a Confederate veteran who was present that day, as "not accurate."

Perhaps no one had told Camak or the gun crew that the double-barreled cannon fired cockeyed by design and when the gun was aimed directly at a target, the cannonball would actually be directed to one side or the other, depending upon which barrel fired the round.

After the war, the double-barreled cannon was fired with black powder charges on special occasions. In more recent years, however, for safety reason, the weapon was spiked so that it would not fire. It was placed on display as a relic of war.

Which Cannon Is It?

The old gun presently on display at the City Hall may be either the first or the second experimental model cast by John Gilleland. No one knows for certain today, because the cannon which lay unmounted in the yard of the old Town Hall, which once stood in the middle of Washington Street between Lumpkin and Hull Streets in the years after the Civil War, was lost from public view about the time that the Town Hall was gutted by fire in 1893.

In either 1895 or 1898, depending upon your source of reference, a double-barreled cannon was literally unearthed near the old blacksmith shop on Jackson Street. It was reported by the individual who dug it up that Mr. Gilleland, who lived further down Jackson Street from the blacksmith shop, had put it there planning to do more work on it. This would seem to indicate that it was not the cannon turned over to the town after Gilleland had exhausted all hopes of gaining its acceptance by the Confederate government sometime after March, 1863.

Assuming there were two test cannons cast as previously described, then which one is now on display at the Athens City Hall and where is the other one?

After researching this article, it is this author's opinion that the first cannon cast by Gilleland and his associates is the one on display today at the Athens City Hall. Put simply, the decision to change the pattern of the first cannon to correct its range problem necessitated casting another gun and the first one was just forgotten and left laying abandoned in front of the old blacksmith shop, later to be dug up, refurbished, and placed on display at City Hall.

The location of the second casting of the double-barreled cannon is unknown today. Without a doubt, however, its recovery would be a wonderful find for a weapons enthusiast or collector!

Points Of Interest To Visit

Regardless of the version of the casting, an interesting weapons specimen rests on a relatively new carriage on an attractive plaza at the Athens City Hall today. A Georgia State Historical Marker nearby commemorates the history of the device.

The Athens Foundry and Machine Works, where the double-barreled cannons were cast, has been remodeled inside today, and is now the **John Gilleland Conference Center of the Days Inn** at **Athens History Village** located at the junction of Dougherty and Thomas streets, across Dougherty Street from the Athens Welcome Center.

John Gilleland's home no longer exists. However, it was located on Jackson Street, which is now within the University of Georgia campus, on the present site of the Visual Arts Building. The exact location of the old blacksmith shop on Jackson Street, where a cannon was dug up in 1895 or 1898, is not known today, other than being described as "*located up Jackson Street from Mr. Gilleland's house.*"

Although, today, the Athens' double-barreled cannon is a classic example of deficient technology and often the brunt of good-natured humor, it has remained for more than a century as a popular curiosity or oddity of war for the thousands of tourists that visit it each year. It seems appropriate to consider it simply as a failure of invention rather than to commemorate its intended role as the grim reaper of the battlefield.

Athens

The Iron Horse

A curious and once scorned sculpture in a Greene County cornfield is a familiar landmark to many north Georgia travelers, but few of them know the unusual story of its origin.

Alert travelers driving the 25-mile stretch of Georgia Highway 15 between Greensboro and Watkinsville, Georgia, are often surprised and puzzled to see a bizarre, twelve-foot-tall sculpture of a horse set atop a knoll in J.L. Curtis's cornfield. This unusual piece of art faces south towards the Oconee River and, consequently, its tail-end points north in the direction of nearby Athens. One suspects that the horse's orientation is not accidental – despite its owner's protests to the contrary – when the circumstances of its arrival in Greene County are explained.

In 1954, J.L. "Jack" Curtis, a geography student at the University of Georgia in Athens, paused in the Fine Arts building and watched Abit Pattison, a noted sculptor from Chicago, welding pieces of iron into the shape of a horse. Pattison had been commissioned by the University to create a piece of modern art that would, it was hoped, add a touch of class to the old-fashioned campus.

When it was completed, the iron horse was placed in a position of prominence across from Memorial Hall and the football players' dormitory. Few, if any, of the football players or students were impressed with Pattison's Picasso-like creation. They collectively felt it simply represented a grotesque caricature of a horse.

Soon, a sizeable gathering of students were not only unsupportive of the artwork, but were calling for its removal wholesale. "When their demands were not met," Curtis chuckles, "they took matters into their own hands."

In what Curtis describes as a near riot, the students stuffed old tires and other debris under the iron horse, doused it with gasoline, and set it afire. When the all-metal structure emerged from the conflagration unscathed, they tried again. (One has to wonder about the I.Q. of students who try to "burn" an all-iron work of art.)

Shaken by this unusual and unprecedented uprising at the formerly sleepy university, representatives of the administration removed Pattison's horse from the campus and placed it in a barn outside Athens for storage.

Three years later, after a tour in the Navy, Curtis returned to Athens and, curious about the horse's fate, made a few discreet inquiries about it. "My father," Curtis recalls, "was a faculty member and knew Lamar Dodd (former director of the art department). Through this connection, we eventually learned that the horse was available, and in 1959, we were given permission to 'take it off of the University's hands.'"

Unfortunately, when the time came to get the horse, Jack Curtis was in California. His father, however, and his friend Henry Compton who owned a John Deere dealership in Athens, agreed to transport the hulking structure to Curtis's farm.

"Compton," Curtis says, "did not want to be seen carrying the iron horse, which he thought was an embarrassment, and he therefore hauled it here in the middle of the night. We had previously discussed where to place it, but our field was wet and Compton, after nearly getting stuck in the mud, decided to unload the horse right where it sits today."

Along with the horse, Curtis garnered some trouble with University students and officials. "For several years after it was acquired," Curtis remembers, 'student pranksters would sneak out late in the night and topple the horse over." This was an inconvenience, since the structure weighs an estimated twenty-four thousand pounds and is very difficult to upright. Curtis, however, put a stop to this activity by embedding the horse's legs in a 12-inch thick base of concrete.

And so, for thirty-seven years now, this well-recognized landmark has stood watch over a Greene County cornfield with its nose pointed south, and its backside conspicuously aimed toward the spot from which it was so unceremoniously banished. But that, Curtis insists, is just a coincidence.

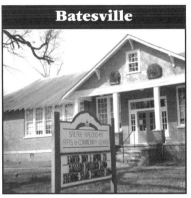

Batesville

A Beautiful Drive To Old Batesville

Ever wanted to just get away for a day or two on a beautiful country road with lots of historic sites and beautiful scenery? I think that's something we all can admit we've wanted to do from time to time. Northeast Georgia is a good place to start, and State Route 17 in the Sautee-Nacoochee Valley to State Route 197 up to Batesville, Georgia, has to be one of the prettiest and most interesting routes.

To begin this little weekend trip, you really ought to plan to spend the night at one of the Helen, Georgia bed & breakfast inns or motels, or perhaps one of the lovely historic bed & breakfast inns in the Sautee-Nacoochee Valley. That way, you can really enjoy the trip and take your time. However, for Atlanta-area residents, this trip can also be done in one day.

We've talked about scenic and historic attractions and sites in Helen and the Sautee Valley in previous articles. There are many many sites worth spending a day or two to visit along this route on the way to Batesville.

Historic Sites Along The Way

Look to your left as you head north on State Road 75 toward the intersection with State Road 17 (just outside Helen, Georgia), and you will notice a small building which is strangely reminiscent of a railroad depot. It looks this way for a reason. . . This is the historic old **Nacoochee Depot** at which the **Gainesville-Northwestern Railroad** from Gainesville, Georgia to Robertstown, Georgia, once stopped. This railroad once provided passenger and mail service for area residents, and was originally built to service the immense timber industry which once operated in this region. The rails were taken up in the 1930s.

Visit historic **Nora Gristmill** on the Chattahoochee River just north of the intersection of State Routes 17 and 75. This historic structure is well over a century old, and offers a unique glimpse at a working mill from yester-

year. In the summer of 1950, several scenes in the major motion picture *I'd Climb The Highest Mountain* were filmed around this gristmill. The movie, starring Susan Hayward, Rory Calhoun, Barbara Bates, William Lundigan and others, was filmed at various sites across White County.

Stop and admire the historic **Nichols home** at the intersection of State Roads 75 and 17. Confederate Captain James Hall Nichols built this beautiful Italianate summer residence after the U.S. Civil War, and lived here for many years.

Opposite the Nichols house out in the pasture you'll see the historic **Nacoochee Indian Mound**. Drive a little further up the road and you will encounter lovely **Crescent Hill Baptist Church** on the hillside on the left. It was also built by Captain Hall. Take time to walk inside this lovely little chapel – which is still used today – and admire it's interesting architecture. This structure was strongly considered as a filming site for several scenes in *I'd Climb The Highest Mountain* in 1950, but church elders at Crescent Hill felt it would be sacrilegious to allow Hollywood filmmakers to use their sanctuary for a movie, so **Chattahoochee United Methodist Church** in nearby Robertstown was used instead.

Farther down State Route 17 (heading east), turn left on State Route 197 and visit the Old Sautee Store. Located on the route of the pioneer **Unicoi Turnpike**, this store from yesteryear was built in 1873, and is still in operation today.

A short distance down Route 197, **Sautee-Nacoochee History Museum** is located in old Nacoochee school. It offers a great deal of information about the early history of this vicinity and is well-worth a visit.

Farther up State Route 197, one soon encounters one of the oldest (and shortest) original covered bridges still in existence in the United States. The aged **Sautee Covered Bridge** is well over a century old, and has been popularized by artists and photographers for many decades.

From here, proceed on up lovely 197 to our ultimate objective – Batesville. To find this little community, the easiest way is to look to South Carolina on a map. The western tip of the "Palmetto State" forms an arrow that points directly toward Batesville, Georgia. Originally a militia district, and now a voting district in Georgia's Habersham County, Batesville forms the northwestern portion of the county.

Prehistoric Travel Route

The **Soque** (pronounced so-kwee, with the accent on the second syllable) **River** flows through Batesville District. In pioneer days (and earlier), an Indian trail forded the Soque near a Cherokee village called "Suki" or "Sakwi-Yi" that once was located beside the river. Local folklore maintains the Cherokee word meant "squealing pig," but that probably is just a figment of some good ole boy's humorous imagination.

When the Unicoi Turnpike was chartered in 1813 to provide white settlers with a trade route between Tennessee and Georgia, it followed the Indian trail and ford across the Soque. Today, Georgia Highway 17 which runs through Clarkesville reportedly follows much of the original route of this trail.

As a result, numerous Native American artifacts – including arrowheads, stone hatchets, clay pottery shards, broken pieces of clay pipes, and more – have been discovered from time to time along the Soque in the vicinity of this ford. The artifacts provide a mute testament to the native people who once inhabited this region.

At one spot, a horseshoe-shaped stone ring has been examined by archaeologists from both the Smithsonian Institute and Cornell University. Both were impressed with the stone semi-circle's antiquity, believing it to pre-date even the Cherokees.

Historic Batesville

As more and more white settlers immigrated southward, the Cherokees were under constant pressure to sell or barter their land. In 1817, they were persuaded to cede a large tract which included land between the Chattahoochee and Oconee rivers. Habersham County was created in 1818.

The Batesville area must have been settled about this time, for Providence Church was established in 1825, and Providence School in 1826. Today, no one seems to know how Batesville actually acquired its name. According to one local historian, it was originally called "Captain Harris" for the military leader who once drilled soldiers in the area.

Archer Jarad Harris was a respected member of the community who was elected "captain" of the Batesville militia district several times. There were sixty families in his district according to the 1840 Census.

Despite the wilderness circumstances, it was important to the early settlers that their children get a good education. Land for both **Providence Church** and **Providence School** was donated by another early settler of Batesville – **Joshua Sutton** – who reportedly was a "pillar of the church," serving as deacon, clerk, and trustee. According to one of his descendants, the Suttons were in the Batesville area as early as 1818.

Talk to anyone in the Batesville area today, and it won't be long before the name of the late **Ellene Gowder** comes up in the conversation. Ellene was the great-granddaughter of Joshua Sutton, and was born in the house he built for his family perhaps as early as the 1820s. This house, which still stands (as of this writing), is on land owned today by Sutton descendants. It, however, is uninhabited and reportedly is full of honey bees. Its remarkable stone chimneys are works of art.

"It was the first sawed-plank house in the county and was built by slaves," Ellene is quoted as having said in an interview published in the book, *Foxfire 10*. "There's a slot in the door that people would drop their letters in." In addition to being an affluent farmer and merchant, Joshua Sutton also served as postmaster of the Soque Post Office.

One of Ellene's most prized possessions was the old desk once used by her great-grandfather Sutton when he enlisted the young men of Batesville to serve in the Confederacy during the U.S. Civil War.

Early College

In order to provide a quality education for his children, Sutton hired tutors until **Providence School** was built circa 1826. When he saw the need for a school of still-higher learning, Sutton established Providence College in the little town.

"The college was small, but it was very good for the time," Ellene recalled in her Foxfire interview. "It was particularly noted for producing good teachers, musicians, doctors, lawyers, and preachers. The reason I know about it is that my family was connected with it, and it was on our property. I know where it stood, but there are no documents or anything left, as everything burned."

Providence College unfortunately suffered the fate of many all-wood public structures of the 17th, 18th and 19th centuries. When it was destroyed by fire in 1896, some of the students moved to nearby Dahlonega to attend **North Georgia Agricultural College**. According to longtime Batesville native Edgar Stamey, his father, Emery S. Stamey, and his "Uncle Ferd" (Fernando) Stamey were among those who left Batesville to enroll at the Dahlonega school.

Ellene Gowder was also the descendant of another early pioneer family – the Hills – who arrived in the Batesville area in the 1820s. Amos Hill's son, Bryant, married Ruth Daniel in 1831, and they were the parents of thirteen children. When their first son was born in 1833, they named him Wilson Lumpkin Hill in honor of Wilson Lumpkin, then-governor of Georgia. The land grant Bryant Hill received in the Cherokee land lottery of that era was signed by Governor Lumpkin.

Batesville General Store

Today, the Wilson Lumpkin Hill House – reportedly built in 1867 – is a "Bed & Biscuit" place (as of this writing) and is located (appropriately) on a hill just prior to the intersection of Highways 255 and 197 in "Downtown Batesville." W.L. Hill owned and operated a store in front of his home, a site occupied today by the Old Batesville General Store and Restaurant. The present building was erected sometime in the early 20th century.

Old **Batesville General Store** was operated during the 1940s by Edgar Stamey. A photograph of Wilson Lumpkin and his wife, Sarah Cole Hill, hangs inside the restaurant portion of the store. One or more of the Hill descendants is likely to be eating lunch at one of the tables on any given day.

Wilson Lumpkin Hill and five of his brothers fought in the Civil War, and four were captured. However, all six returned home without serious injury. Although he was only a teenager at the time, Amos Jackson Hill (Bryant and Ruth's eighth child) served as a spy with the 11th Georgia Cavalry during the Georgia campaign. Unlike the other four, he and his older brother, Isaac Newton Hill, escaped capture throughout the war.

Early Gristmills

Wilson Lumpkin's father (Bryant Hill), grandfather (Amos Hill), and great-grandfather (Isaac Hill), were all millers. Bryant established a number of different types of mills, beginning with a gristmill on the Soque River in the 1830s. Other Hill mills included two planing mills and a furniture factory on the Soque River, as well as a number of mobile saw mills.

After a century of being run by the Hills, the last **Hill's Mill** on the Soque River ground to a halt sometime in the late 1920s. It was abandoned for a time until **Robert Watts** and his father, **Allen**, purchased the mill and set about repairing it. Allen (known as "**Grandpa Watts**") was a veteran miller who had previously operated several mills further north on Burton Road. Father and son reportedly restored the mill building, repaired the dam, built a new raceway and had the mill up and running within a month's time.

Despite the Watts' repairs, however, the old building was badly deteriorated with age and disintegrating rapidly. Thus the decision was made to tear down the old mill and replace it with a new structure built from timber cut and sawed on the property.

The foundation of the old Hill's Mill supported a generator house that produced twelve-volt electricity for the new Watts' Mill. The raceway was transferred from the old building to the new mill on the day it began operations, so that Watts' Mill did not miss a single day of grinding during the transition.

Robert gradually expanded his business by building a small mercantile store across the road from the mill. He and his wife **Letie** ran the store for many years back in the days when the gas pump in front sold gasoline for fifteen cents a gallon.

Some local people still remember the delicious butter that Letie churned and sold in the store along with milk from her cows. She reportedly was a strong woman who thought nothing of hefting 100-pound bags of cornmeal.

It, reportedly, was also Letie who noticed the big native brown trout swimming in the waters of the Soque near the mill. She began feeding them spilled cornmeal and the stale bread from her store. The trout reportedly proliferated.

After Allen and Robert Watts passed on, the mill continued to be operated by Eugene and Woodrow Free until 1966 when a flood washed out the raceway and part of the dam. The waters of the Soque reportedly were so high that they came up over the road and into the mill, silencing its machinery forever.

Even though no meal has been ground in over three decades, a *Grandpa Watts Water Ground Meal* sign still hangs on a pole beside the mill. Another sign hangs beside it announcing its contemporary name and modern-day use as a pottery shop.

Although the road leading to this site is full of curves, Ellene Gowder claimed it to be so beautifully banked that one could drive it with closed eyes.

"A cow was the original engineer," Ellene was fond of saying. "You know that a cow will always take the path of least resistance, so when they got ready to build the road, they turned a cow loose and followed her to determine the route the road should take!"

Batesville Historic Celebration

In 1999, when Ellene Franklin Gowder was ninety years of age, she presented a program on "Food Preservation Through The Ages" on the porch of the house her great-grandfather Wilson Lumpkin Hill had built in the 1860s. Her demonstrations of drying food, making "leather britches" beans, and canning in crocks and jars were a popular attraction at the first Batesville Historic Celebration. She was attired in an old-fashioned dress with hoops and crocheted collar topped off with a matching bonnet.

As Ellene attempted to maneuver the unaccustomed hoops through narrow doorways and into a sitting position, she commented that she had developed a great deal more respect for the ladies who had worn them as a matter of course in years past.

After she retired from teaching, Ellene frequently visited local schools wearing old-fashioned hoop dresses to do presentations on early schools and education in the area. She was working on a history of Batesville when she died on July 4, 2000, while picking berries in her yard.

The first **Batesville Historic Celebration** took place in 1999, but the event had been gestating for a number of years prior to that. It all began when Batesville folks rallied together in the mid-1980s to raise money for a much-needed local fire station. A group of women who called themselves "The Fire Belles" put on suppers and held quilt raffles. The men organized turkey shoots and sold barbecue.

The Batesville residents ultimately were successful in their fund-raising efforts too. The new fire station was built entirely with the raised funds.

"That first festival in 1999 was successful beyond our wildest expectations," smiled Dave Thomas, who helped organize the event. "We had volunteers from all over the county donating their time and talents. They demonstrated old-time skills like chair-caning, spinning, making hominy, splitting logs and much more. Musicians played bluegrass music all day long. Everything was free to the public except the food.

"Our goal was – and continues to be – to bring people together to have a good time and learn more about the history of this area," Thomas added. "I hope we can continue to do that for a long time."

The Batesville Historic Celebration is held annually on the third Saturday in October. For more information, call 706-947-1619.

Blairsville

Alexander's Store

A country store has stood on or near this site for much longer than anyone can remember. It is a unique area, once was called "**Choestoe**" by the Indians. The name meant "land of the dancing rabbits."

Travelers in north Georgia don't encounter many country stores like **Alexander's Store** anymore. They just don't make 'em that way today.

As visitors walk thru the store's front door, their eyes are immediately drawn to the store's sign. It reads, "*Everything Under The Sun*," and words are not far off the mark.

The late **Hoyt Alexander**, founder of this impressive enterprise preferred to put it this way: "If we don't have it, you don't need it."

Hoyt bought the store in 1957. It was housed in a turn-of-the-century 1,200-square-foot building, which is somewhat small by today's store standards, but more than enough for him and his community.

"I was one of the best customers the original owners had, and they were ready to retire," Hoyt once said. "One afternoon, I stopped by and made an offer to buy the place, and the next day, I had a deal."

Hoyt's son, Eddie, is the driving force in the business today. He says a store has existed on or very near the site of the current Alexander's Store building on-and-off since the late 1800s, when the Town Creek community was settled.

A Cherokee influence has existed in the area for centuries, and continued right up until the **Native Americans** were forcefully rounded up and relocated to Oklahoma in the 1830s. Interestingly, an Indian influence continues to this day according to the Alexanders, who maintain they are descended from Cherokee ancestors.

"Almost every old-timer in this community is part Cherokee," Eddie states, matter-of-factly. Eddie says his maternal great-great-grandmother was a full-blood Cherokee. Ruby Alexander, Eddie's mother, had jet-black hair, smooth skin and dark eyes, typical Indian features which have been inherited by Eddie.

As the youngest of Hoyt's three children, Eddie is the only child active in the mercantile business today.

Hoyt started out professionally as a farmer. He later bought the store and ran it in conjunction with his farm.

When son Eddie had to work on the farm as a child, he used to cry and have a fit to come to the store. "I started pumping gas for Dad as a teen," he smiles. "That's where I met Sandy (his wife) who was working in the clothing department of the store."

As Eddie looked toward the future, though, he thought, "There's bound to be an easier life." When he left Town Creek and the store for an education at nearby **North Georgia College** in Dahlonega, he kissed his mountain home goodbye.

"I began to see things a little differently though after I graduated from college and began living in Atlanta," he says. "I didn't even know my neighbors." He says he missed the style of his home where "people know everybody's business because they care."

Eddie subsequently called his mom, begging her to "let me come home. I'll pump gas, anything." She finally relented and he returned. "I wouldn't live anywhere else, now," Eddie smiles.

In 1961, Hoyt had torn down most of the original store building, but he kept the 4" tongue-in-groove pine flooring and the 6" pine wall boards. He added additional floor space that doubled the size of the little enterprise. And later, as a result of Eddie's work, there were more enlargements.

"Each addition has doubled the previous space," Eddie says. When he returned home to work, Eddie says the store's floor space was 2,760 square feet, with 1,500 of the footage in warehouse space. Today, the total square footage of

2 NORTHEAST GEORGIA

Alexander's Store is an impressive 50,000 square feet. Quite a thriving development.

But space doesn't make a successful store. It's the relationship with the community that really counts.

"If they have a dime or a thousand dollars, we treat them all the same," says Eddie's wife Sandy.

Eddie explains that he has shopped places where he's felt pressured to buy something. "We want people to feel free to just look if that's all they want to do," he says.

"Alexander's is a tourist site," laughs Sarah Williams, who has lived one mile from the store for the past 12 years. "The parking lot is always full of out-of-state license plates. If people visit Union County, they invariably go to Alexander's."

After having traveled around the world with her husband, Sarah says she knows something good when she sees it. "People can't believe all this is out here in the middle of nowhere," she laughs again.

During the **Blizzard of 1993**, Sarah and her granddaughter were able to walk to the store even though the area was snowed-in for days. Alexander's stayed open to provide things people needed, such as candles, kerosene lamps, peanut butter crackers and other snacks. "The very fact that they opened showed their sense of obligation to the community," Sarah says.

Until 1994, the store operated seven days a week, 364 days a year. On Sundays, the store closed during church hours and opened from 1:00 to 6:00 p.m. It even opened half a day on Christmas mornings, but that was mainly because "Some people always forgot to buy something for someone," Eddie smiles.

Today, the store employs several dozen people and offers some 50,000 different items. A cross-section of the commodities here include men's and ladies' clothing; cowboy boots; cowboy hats; groceries; candy; sporting goods; appliances, including window air-conditioners and huge freezers; pottery; guns; almost anything involving hunting; small appliances; grills; baking ingredients; and much more – even Beanie Babies!

If you want to visit a unique and sizeable country store, do yourself a favor and drive on up to Alexander's. Even if you have no need for any of the items mentioned above, you're bound to find something else that you just have to have. It's always been that way at Alexander's. And if you don't buy it, you can always just look at it. . . .

To reach Alexander's Store, take Highway 19/129 south out of Blairsville for three miles. Turn left onto Town Creek School Road. The store will come into view four miles up the road on the right. It's open six days a week, 9:00 a.m. to 7:00 p.m. It is closed on Sundays. For further information, call (706) 745- 6450.

Blairsville

The songbird sings melodiously; sparkling streams rush from clefts along the towering precipice, and a peaceful calm seems to indefinitely pervade Union County's Blood Mountain. For energetic outdoors enthusiasts, the breath-taking beauty of this area with its abundance of waterfalls, hiking trails, and exhilarating diversions, can help create a great weekend getaway in the north Georgia mountains – all only 85 miles away from Atlanta.

Located in the general vicinity of U.S. Highway 129 at the county line between Lumpkin and Union counties (at **Neel Gap**), Blood Mountain earned its name from a time in prehistory which was not always so peaceful.

According to tradition and Andrew W. Cain's, 1832 *History Of Lumpkin County-1832-1932* (The Reprint Company Publishers, Spartanburg, South Carolina), a portion of north Georgia was once contested by the native Creek and Cherokee Indians. In the dawns of pre-history, warring nations regularly met on the field of battle. Blood Mountain, it seems, marks the spot of one of these bloody confrontations.

Today, hikers on the Appalachian Trail which traverses Blood Mountain, still find arrowheads, undoubtedly from this ancient engagement. Winton Porter, owner of **Mountain Crossings At Walasi-Yi**, a shop catering to campers and hikers, says it's not unusual at all.

Winton, with wife Marge, operates one of the finest backpacking and outfitting centers in the area. His shop enjoys the luxury of being located in a historic structure (owned by the State of Georgia) right beside the Appalachian Trail where it crosses U.S. Highway 129 at Neel Gap.

Built by the **Civilian Conservation Corps** in the 1930s, and originally designed as a restaurant and stopover point, the large imposing building is hard to miss. Constructed of native stone and huge chestnut beams, it is as solid today, as when originally built by the CCC, and offers a panoramic view from its rear deck.

Blood Mountain Cabins, located approximately 100 yards south of Mountain Crossings At Walasi-Yi on U.S. 129, is an excellent and very scenic overnighting opportunity in this most scenic of spots in the north Georgia mountains.

Blood Mountain Cabin / Old Walasi-Yi Inn

George and Colley Case are the owners of these comfortable structures, and are about as accommodating as any owners could possibly be. George is well-versed on all the hiking trails and waterfalls in the area, as well as all the other scenic spots, and will patiently explain directions and all the "dos" and "don'ts" to even the most uninformed outdoors enthusiast.

All of the cabins have fireplaces for a crackling fire should you desire it. A word to the wise, however – bring you own firewood if you wish to use the fireplaces. Wood is available for a price, but you might be surprised at how fast your money goes up in smoke. If you don't want a fire, all the cabins have central heat and will stay toasty warm with heat generated in the modern manner.

All of the Blood Mountain Cabins also include most of the basic necessities of life (except food). This includes clean towels and soap, dish-washing detergent, a coffee-maker, a toaster, a wide range of cooking utensils, pots and pans, clean bed linens and extra blankets.

And lest you be uninformed, the extra blankets can come in handy, even in the summertime. At 3,000 feet above sea level, the temperature in the mountains here can easily catch the unassuming traveler off-guard.

The Cases also own and operate **Blood Mountain Cabins Country Store**, a comfy general store full of most anything you might need during a weekend in the mountains. With a warm wood-burning stove in one corner, and a snack bar in another, this establishment offers many food items as well as basic necessities. Aside from an array of snack items, ice, propane tanks, camping necessities, baskets, pottery, reading materials, games, novelties, and much more are all offered.

Rates at Blood Mountain Cabins range from $79 to $99 a day, and $389 to $469 a week. There is a two-night minimum stay on weekends, and a three-night minimum stay on national holiday weekends. VISA, Discover and MasterCard are accepted. For more information and reservations, contact the Cases toll-free at (800) 284-6866 or at (706) 745-9454.

Clermont

Old Clermont Hotel

Built in 1895, historic **Clermont Hotel** has seen good days and bad, weathering tornadoes and abandonment. The unique structure has recently been renovated and reopened as a mountain inn, convenient to many scenic and historic destinations in the north Georgia mountains.

The tiny town of **Clermont**, Georgia, thirteen miles north of Gainesville, was once a thriving community which boasted a 12-grade boarding school noted for its academic excellence, a two-story brick hotel, a bank, drug store, furniture store, three blacksmith shops, and a railroad depot on the **Gainesville & Northwestern Railroad**. Young people came from miles around to attend **Chattahoochee High School**, and travelers and businessmen overnighted regularly at the hotel where they enjoyed the fresh air and a clear view of nearby Wauka Mountain.

Originally called **Concord Church Community**, this town was known as "**Dip**" when a post office was opened in the vicinity in 1892. The more glamorous name of Clermont (meaning "clear mountain") was not adopted until 1905.

T.C. (Tom) Miller grew up in the little community. It was he who originally recognized the need for a hotel where guests and travelers could obtain overnight accommodations, especially with the Gainesville & Northwestern Railroad making plans to construct a rail line through town. Miller was a well-to-do merchant and landowner, and so had the capital necessary for the erection of a fine two-story brick hotel.

It was at about this time that several timber companies were milling lumber from the abundant forests in neighboring counties to the north, and the railroad was being constructed in large part to provide a means of transportation for these wood products. Railroad workers overnighted in the hotel during construction of the rail line, and double tracks were ultimately laid within a few feet of one end of the hotel. A depot was built almost directly across the street.

Sylvia Gailey Head, 94 at the time of this interview, remembered the heady early days of Clermont and business endeavors of Tom Miller.

"The hotel that Tom built had a lobby, dining room, and kitchen on the ground floor," Sylvia explained. "The rest of the downstairs was partitioned off to house a department store. An attractive young lady named Mae made hats which she sold in the store. It wasn't long before Tom's mechanic – Shug Matthews – fell in love with her and married her."

Louise Rogers Woodcock Murphy was born in one of the upstairs rooms of the hotel. "My mother was actually planning for me to be born in Gainesville, but she said I got in too big a hurry," Mrs. Murphy smiles in remembrance. "Mother's name was Ida, and she was Grandfather Miller's oldest daughter by his first wife. She married Frank Rogers, and they lived at the hotel and ran it for a number of years before moving to Gainesville when I was two years old."

"Ida was a lovely person and a good friend of ours," is how Ida Miller Rogers was remembered by the late Essie Hudgins Jordan. Mrs. Jordan, interviewed in 1997 at the age of 97, still had vivid memories of the early years in Clermont.

"I was born at **Sugar Hill**," Mrs. Jordan explained, "but my family moved to Clermont in 1912 when I was twelve years old so that I and my brothers and sisters could attend Chattahoochee High School. I had an older brother and sister who had boarded at the school, but with eleven more children to educate, I guess they thought it would be better to just relocate the whole family."

Mrs. Jordan's father, **James Zacheas "Jim-Zack" Hudgins**, moved his general merchandise business from Sugar Hill to Clermont and erected a store building across from the new Clermont Hotel. **"James Z. Hudgins, Mercantile"** sold a bit of everything, including books for students at Chattahoochee High School.

"Father had a soda fountain in the store

and made carbonated drinks for customers," Essie recalls. "My favorite was called 'peach phosphate.'"

Most of Mr. Hudgins' merchandise came by rail. The new railroad was just a few yards from his store which was near the depot, so there was a siding to unload goods. Mountain people traveling through Clermont on their way to Gainesville (where they marketed their produce) also brought him apples, sorghum, and chestnuts. Most of them camped out in their wagons. If their funds (and available rooms) allowed it, however, a few lucky ones spent the night in the Clermont Hotel.

"I loved to play tennis on the hard clay courts behind the Millers' hotel," Essie adds. "Eugenia Rogers and I used to play together in our middy blouses and box-pleated knee skirts. 'Jean,' as she preferred to be called, later married my older brother Carl, and the wedding was held in the hotel. They honeymooned at **Porter Springs**, a popular mineral spring spa north of Dahlonega."

Essie's younger sister, **Dorothy Hudgins Shaw**, was friends with Jean's younger sister, Frances Rogers. Dorothy has fond memories of the tennis court, a duck pond, and a seesaw behind the hotel where the girls played together. She also says she spent many nights in the hotel with her childhood friend and remembers crying her heart out when the Rogers moved to Gainesville in the early 1920s.

"Frank Rogers was a salesman, and a larger town offered him more opportunities," Dorothy explains, "but all I understood back then was that my best friend was moving away. I didn't think I would ever see her again, but actually, we stayed in touch by telephone, and I sometimes visited her in their new home near Brenau College."

The Hudgins family lived in a house Mr. Hudgins built for them on King Street in 1912. As of this writing, this fine old home still stands in Clermont. Dorothy says she had to cross the railroad tracks to get to her father's store and the hotel to play with Louise. She remembers being afraid of the trains when she was five or six years of age. Later, she says she learned to enjoy buying a ticket and riding the train to Gainesville to visit with Frances.

Trains weren't the only scary experience remembered by early residents of Clermont. The Hudgins family had only been living in their new home there for about a year when a tornado damaged the community, blowing off the front porch of the hotel, among other things. In her interview, Essie Hudgins Jordan said she remembered the day vividly.

"My father had gone to the store, and Mother had gone to visit my grandmother, who was ill," she explains. "My brothers and sisters and I were eating breakfast when we heard a strange noise. We ran to the window to look out, and we saw things flying up into the air. Our first thought was that we needed to get to our parents, but my older brother insisted that it was safer to stay where we were. I had no idea about the horrible circumstances that were taking place outside."

The terrible tornado Mrs. Jordan remembered possibly was the same one which destroyed part of nearby Gainesville on June 1, 1903. This violent storm destroyed approximately 70 homes, damaged another 120 homes, and killed 40 people in the **New Holland Mill** village in Gainesville. Luckily, however, Clermont suffered little damage.

A family named **Tumlin** lived in the Clermont Hotel during the early 1930s. They had a daughter named Nell who was the same age as Dorothy Hudgins, and Dorothy frequently visited her there. Dorothy says that the upper rooms of the hotel had deteriorated quite a bit by this time.

Unlike others who moved away from Clermont after the railroad was removed and business dried up, 90-year-old **Lorena Oxford** remained behind, living in the century-old white frame house on Main Street where she grew up. "T.C. Miller, who built the hotel, was my uncle. His first wife was my mother's sister," Lorena explained. "My father, **John Milton Haynes**, bought the hotel sometime in the 1930s and owned it a pretty good while. He rented it out to several different people over the years. He also owned a store and the **Clermont Banking Company**.

"I remember Jean Rogers very well because we started to school together," Lorena continued. "We lost touch when she married after high school and I went on to college."

Bill White of Dahlonega was graduated from Chattahoochee High School with **Ben Haynes** in 1933. The railroad tracks were still in place at that time, but the trains were no longer running. The wealth of timber on the heavily-forested slopes of the mountains in northeast Georgia had been depleted, and the lumbermen had all moved on to other places. As a result, the Gainesville & Northwestern

Railroad struggled to survive during its last years of existence.

The rails were finally taken up during the mid to late 1930s and probably sold as scrap metal which was bringing a premium price during the onset of World War II. With the demise of the railroad, the little town of Clermont also began to decline. The hotel, with its lifeblood choked off, closed its doors due to a lack of paying customers. For approximately 30 years, it stood empty and forlorn. Local residents watched it decay and worried about its fate.

One weekend in the early 1970s, **Sarah Herndon**, 82, was on her way back to Atlanta following a visit to her brother at **Unicoi State Park**, when she happened upon the aged and abandoned structure. Sarah had run a successful antique business in Atlanta for twenty years, and her first thought was, "That building is big enough to hold me and all the furniture I want to have!"

Her inquiries, however, revealed that the hotel had just been sold the previous week. She was further disappointed to learn the individual who had purchased it planned to demolish the structure to sell the bricks of which it was built. To Sarah's delight, however, the new owner changed his plans and agreed to sell the old building to her.

The hotel was in deplorable shape and literally falling down. Part of the roof, in fact, fell in almost on top of one of her workmen. Sarah had to replace the roof and do a great deal of repair work inside. She recalls that the hotel had been divided into apartments by that time.

Despite Clermont's distance from Atlanta, Sarah Herndon's "**Colony House**" was so popular that customers from the capital city and Gainesville patronized it faithfully. Unfortunately, Sarah had to sell the hotel herself in 1982 due to an illness.

When Cheryl and Glenn Plumlee discovered the hotel in 1993, it was once again abandoned and in dire need of repairs. "The roof was leaking; mold was growing in the carpet, and a cottonwood tree was trying to grow through one of the walls," Cheryl recalls with a smile. "Worse, bees had taken up residence above the first-floor ceiling, and honey was dripping through the boards!"

The old hotel required not only money for repairs, but also someone with artistic talent and creative imagination to revive its historic appearance while making it comfortable enough to attract paying guests. With her experience in interior decorating and interior construction around the Atlanta area, Cheryl was perfect for the job.

The original flooring in the dining room (located to the left of the lobby) had rotted out, so the Plumlees replaced it with century-old marble which was recovered from an old bank building in Chattanooga, Tennessee. The hotel restaurant is not open on a regular basis, but may be reserved by groups for luncheons, dinners, and receptions with a choice of catering services. The seating capacity is approximately 50, and meals are served buffet-style.

The Clermont Hotel originally boasted twenty upstairs rooms. Since the rooms did not contain plumbing (guests lined up in their bathrobes for the bathroom at the end of the hall), the Plumlees decided to combine every two rooms to make one suite with a sitting area and private bath. Cheryl selected bedspreads, wallpaper, and drapes that resemble early 20th century decor.

The rooms open onto an upstairs lobby, where guests are served a buffet breakfast each morning. In nice weather, they may also opt to take their coffee and sit in rocking chairs on the veranda, just as travelers and businessmen undoubtedly did in days of yesteryear.

The hotel has become a popular spot for weddings, rehearsal dinners and receptions. A huge framed antique mirror in front of the honeymoon suite provides an interesting setting in which to photograph the bride. Steps leading down to the lobby provide her with a dramatic "aisle" to walk down. The bridal suite features a four-poster canopied bed with a white satin coverlet.

Guests who discover the charming old Clermont Hotel frequently make comments like, "I can't believe what a great place this is. Why didn't we know about it before now?"

"It is a wonderful building," Cheryl Plumlee agrees. What I'm trying to do here is to create a place where people can get away from the hectic pace of city living and relax in a pleasant and peaceful setting. Sometimes I wish I could check in here myself!"

For more information on historic Clermont and the Clermont Hotel, call (770) 983-0704, or check the Website www.clermonthotel.com

Costley Mill

During the European settlement of America – prior even to the founding of Savannah, Georgia – fur traders, trappers, Indian agents, and pioneer settlers had often overnighted near a pleasant waterfall in what today is Rockdale County. Even today, it's still a very popular spot. . . Just ask Syl and Beverly Bowman, the current owners.

In the early days, it was a simple stop-over on a trade route to Augusta and points eastward. In later years, one of these travelers who was an entrepreneurial fellow, realized the value of the spot, and built a mill there, making "Costley Mill" the first settlement in Rockdale, and one of the oldest mills in the state. Today, it's a very popular recreation site.

Nestled in a thick woods amid rock outcroppings, Costley Mill was an outpost on the western frontier in the early 1800s. It endured several attacks from marauding Creek Indians who were not fond of their encroaching white neighbors, and somehow managed to survive into modern times. Sadly, after making it that far, the mill burned to the ground in the 20th century. Despite this fact, a lot of interesting history and scenic beauty still survive at this historic site.

James Luther Thomas Costley bought the property in 1875, giving the site the name it carries to this day. The Costleys once owned thousands of acres in this vicinity, eventually selling most of it.

The remaining acreage was subdivided between three brothers – Oscar, Bud, and Will. Oscar ultimately inherited the mill acreage, but he and his wife had no children, so his wife's side of the family inherited that portion of the property.

In 1982, Syl Bowman and his wife, Beverly, purchased 105 acres. The Bowmans had been searching specifically for a piece of property which included a historic mill site, so they were quite happy with their acquisition.

The new owners had a lot of cleaning up to do since the road into the site had been overtaken by undergrowth over the years, and trespassers had discarded many years'-worth of trash throughout the swimming area adjacent to the old mill site on Big Haynes Creek. The Bowmans named their new property **Costley Mill Park**, and eagerly went about the task of restoring the beauty of the site and preserving the historic aspects which still remained.

A recreated Old General Store at the site offers visitors a look at a variety of curios from days gone by. Photos of the original mill hang in the store. Visitors can sit and play a game of checkers laid out with old soft drink bottle caps beside a pot-bellied stove, and catch up on local news and gossip.

"If you're interested in history, come to the store," the Bowmans tell their guests. "If you want a yarn, take the train ride."

Now when the Bowmans say "train ride," they don't really mean "train" ride. . . Their "engine" is actually the frame of a four-wheel-drive vehicle which has been converted to the appearance of an old locomotive, with cars pulled along behind. The ride, of course, still thrills children as Syl takes the youngsters on a short trip along "Thrill Hill" beside the creek and to a "Gold Mine" Syl built under a hillside. All the time, he admonishes his young charges with "Watch out for buffalo crossing the tracks and for Injuns!"

Luckily, Syl and Beverly were able to restore many of the old buildings in the little township which once existed on their property. The Bowmans jacked up and repaired several ancient barns original to the site, restoring them to use.

Other structures have survived as well. An original dressing room/outhouse (a three-seater) provided accommodations for guests to a resort which once existed at the site in the early 1900s. It was Rockdale County's main recreation destination with cabins, picnic tables, concession stands, a barbecue shed, and much more. Some locals still tell stories of the dances which once were held in a large structure beside the water.

In the dressing room, women changed into bathing suits which, according to a sign, once could be rented for 25 cents each. Swimming cost 10 cents per person.

The Bowmans say they also appreciate and value the wildlife of the area, and accordingly, have left much of their acreage as nearly natural as possible.

"We've always been animal people," Beverly explains. Rockdale County officials and the U.S. Environmental Protection Agency have declared the far side of Big Haynes Creek a protected wetlands area. "We were concerned about the otter, raccoon and wild geese that either live here or come here," Beverly adds.

Beverly and Syl live in a completely remodeled 1900s-era home on the property. When they first moved to Costley Mill, they incorporated one of the original cabins into their home design.

A former tenant on the property – Mr. L.B. Baker – lived in one of the old homes for 70 years. Prior to his death, he explained to the Bowmans that most of the wood in the five houses and old barns on the property had been planed at Costley Mill. He also said that operations at the mill once included a gristmill and a cotton gin in addition to the planing or sawmill.

Nearby a family rents the home in which the miller at Costley Mill once lived. According to the Conyers, Georgia Historical Society, this structure is one of the oldest homes in the county.

The Bowmans had always entertained a lot, so Syl built a 72- by 36-foot pavilion just for family use down by the beach soon after they moved in. In 1986, a friend asked to host a company picnic under the pavilion. After first protesting, the Bowmans reluctantly agreed, and soon thereafter, they found themselves in the recreation sales business.

After people began patronizing the site for picnics, they began asking for a ball park. A former cow pasture was improved for that purpose – basebags replacing cow paddies.

Today, Costley Mill Park hosts about 50 private events (weddings, company parties, church groups, etc.) each year. Syl and Beverly both grew up in nearby Stone Mountain, and share a deep love of history.

By a stroke of coincidence, they have also both returned unintentionally to their roots. Syl learned that his great-grandparents are buried in the cemetery of Salem Baptist Church (Est. 1820) a short distance across the creek. Beverly used to come to that same church as a child, when an uncle preached there. She also swam in the creek which was a public swimming area in those days.

The Bowmans are continuously refining their growing enterprise. They have built a small chapel (which is used for weddings) and a large gazebo. One day, they hope to host camping clubs and other organized functions on the opposite side of the creek. A newly-constructed bridge now makes that area accessible to automobiles.

The park opens April 1st for guests and closes October 31st of each year. Reservations can be made beginning in January. A basic event package includes volleyball, horseshoes, softball and swimming, not to mention tours of the historic structures and just plain old peaceful country beauty. Pony rides, clowns, magicians, bingo and a dunk tank can also be arranged.

To reach Costley Mill Park, take Interstate 20 east to Exit 82. Turn north onto Georgia Highway 138. After approximately six miles, turn right onto Costley Mill Road. Take the park's second entrance. For reservations and further information, call 770-483-2455. The mailing address is Costley Mill Park, 2455 Costley Mill Rd., Conyers, GA, 30013.

Dahlonega

Chestatee Wildlife Preserve

Driving into Dahlonega, Georgia, one day on old GA Highway 115 (present-day Old Dahlonega Highway), a long-time resident caught a glimpse of an odd-looking animal in a pasture where she had often seen horses in the past. The animal resembled a small horse, but it appeared to have dark stripes almost like a zebra.

Zebras don't live in Lumpkin County, the lady thought to herself. *The stripes must have been shadows or else my imagination is working overtime.*

When she passed the pasture the next day, she found herself hoping to see the puzzling critter again, just to be sure what it was. Sure enough, there was not a zebra in the pasture. . . . There were two of them, grazing on the grassy hillside!

Shortly thereafter, a sign which reads "*Chestatee Wildlife Preserve*" appeared, and a new travel destination was born for the residents of Georgia. The preserve couldn't have a better patron than its owner, Mr. **C.W. Wathen**, who is a wildlife enthusiast extraordinaire, to say the least.

Visitors to CWP not only get to see wild zebras up close, they can hand-feed them! Zebras are known to be ill-tempered creatures, but these appear to be quite docile.

When they noticed the zebras being fed, a pair of llamas sometimes will also venture over to the fence for their share of the treats, all the while keeping a close watch on their precocious wooly three-week-old baby.

Since most of the animals usually encountered in zoos appear to be either very shy and retiring or else totally disinterested in their human visitors, it may come as a surprise to the visitors at Chestatee Wildlife Preserve to discover how friendly are the animals owned by Mr. Wathen.

"I handle (almost all of) them daily to keep them gentle and trusting," he explained. "That makes all the difference. However, it is important to remember that they are wild animals and you must respect that. We wouldn't want to take the wild out of them."

"**George**," a white-faced Capuchin monkey, had never been handled much when the Preserve acquired him, and C.W. was told it wasn't safe to enter his cage. However, he kept talking to the little monkey and giving him treats through the bars.

Eventually, the day arrived when C.W. had to enter the cage. To his surprise, George immediately climbed into his lap wanting attention.

"He soon became one of the most loveable animals in the Preserve," C.W. says. "He hugs my neck, and he's so polite that when I give him a treat, he offers me the first bite."

At the big cat cages, "**Baka**," the Bengal tiger, greets C.W. like a rambunctious overgrown kitten. "He only weighed ten pounds when he was donated to us, and we had to feed him with a bottle until he was old enough for solid food," C.W. said, petting him like an overgrown house cat. "Now, he's six months old (as of June, 2000), weighs 90 pounds and eats ten pounds of raw meat twice a day."

The first thing one notices about this "little" tiger is its enormous paws, an indicator of his impending adult size. "I still walk him on a leash to the mailbox every evening, but I probably won't be able to do that much longer," C.W. smiles knowingly.

Today, the Center includes a wide variety of wildlife, all of it extraordinarily interesting. And Mr. Wathen seems to be constantly enlarging the complex.

"I hope to get a baby elephant as soon as I can create a habitat for it," C.W. adds, explaining his plans. He says he would also like to add a giraffe to his menagerie in the near future too.

"We really need a nursery to house all our baby animals," he went on. "This past spring we had nine babies on bottles that had to be fed every three or four hours 24 hours a day. I am grateful to three 'godmothers' who took the babies home with them and bottle-fed them around the clock."

The success of the breeding program at the Preserve is a strong indication of how healthy and contented the animals are. As recently as early June of 2000, newborn wildlife at the Center included cougar, tiger and lion cubs, deer fawns, a one-day-old buffalo calf, and a Patagonian Cavy baby. Known as the world's largest rodents, Cavies have long ears which make them look somewhat like rabbits, but they also have long extremely slender legs which make them swift runners.)

When C.W. first opened the Chestatee Wildlife Preserve in 1995, he did all the work himself in the evenings after driving to Atlanta and putting in a full day's work as a contractor. Fortunately, the animals soon attracted a number of volunteers who made time in their busy schedules to clean out cages and help C.W. with the feeding, watering and upkeep during the Center's early years.

C.W. says that today, his daughter, Shawn, and her husband, Jack Ashworth, drive up from Marietta every weekend along with their children, Aaron and Jaclyn, to help with the animals. And his sister, Judy, her husband Russ, and their son Matthew, drive down from Kentucky to spend their vacations helping out also. Three other people – Donna Erwin and Warren and Toni Howe also help out. Donna has been commuting from Cumming, Georgia, ever since the Preserve was opened, and she takes care of all the paperwork in addition to helping out with the animals.

A former veterinary technician – Charlotte Johnson – donated her time for two years before being hired as the permanent full-time animal caretaker. "I love all the animals at the Preserve," Charlotte says. 'They're like my children.'

All one has to do is to visit the Preserve to be impressed not only with the gentle disposition of the animals, but also with the cleanliness of all the animals and their cages. There is never a trace of odor, and all the animals are obviously well cared for and healthy.

"Keeping the animals well-fed keeps them from being a threat to each other and to us," C.W. explained. "Of course, feeding them doesn't come cheap. In fact, it takes 90% of everything I make in construction."

With information like this, it quickly becomes obvious to even the most casual observer that C.W. is creating and maintaining his little kingdom because he loves the animals. . . and not because he's making money from the project. In fact, the Preserve is a non-profit organization, and the modest $5.00 admission fee isn't enough to even provide appetizers for his menagerie, much less pay the vet bills.

In order to generate additional funds to feed and house the animals, Chestatee Wildlife Preserve solicits outside aid. The Preserve has managed this in a variety of ways – sponsoring a golf tournament at Royal Lakes Country Club in Flowery Branch, visiting schools and getting the word out generally. Other benefits have also been conducted.

Corporate sponsorships are also available to organizations who are interested in helping Chestatee Wildlife Preserve in its mission of protecting and breeding endangered species as well as educating the public about why these now rare animals need to be protected. C.W. says individual donations of food and money are also gratefully accepted (and would probably be tax-deductible too).

"**Red**" is another of the endangered species that has found a home at Chestatee Wildlife Preserve. He is one of less than 25 Barbary lions left in the world. "Those magnificent beasts used to live in Africa, Europe, and India, but now there are so few left that they are no longer even generally recognized as a breed," C.W. says with a note of sadness in his voice. "They are different from other lions in that their manes grow almost back to their hind quarters." C.W. is hoping to find a mate for Red in some other animal preserve via the Internet so the species can be regenerated.

Another rare resident at CWP is a white Siberian tiger named "**Majestic**." He is one of less than 100 in the United States. The Siberian snow tiger is the largest tiger in the world and can weigh up to 1,200 pounds, as opposed to Bengal tigers like Baka, who only weigh half as much. Siberian tigers have not been seen in the wild since 1951. Chestatee Wildlife Preserve also has a young three-quarter white tiger named "Aurora" and a Siberian cub.

The Preserve is also providing safe habitats for a number of other animals that are on the brink of becoming endangered species, such as lemurs and a baboon named "**Handsome**" who is so rare that C.W. has been unable to find a mate for him. Many visitors to the Preserve wonder why Handsome is in such a small cage when all the other animals have more spacious accommodations.

"We originally put him in a larger cage, but he just stayed in one corner and moped," C.W. explained. "We finally put him in a smaller enclosure and he apparently is accustomed to less space, because he seems to feel more secure there."

There are strict government controls on owning wild animals, but Chestatee Wildlife Preserve is licensed for all animals and is allowed to purchase any non-endangered species. Endangered animals must be donated or swapped by agreement with another wildlife preserve or zoo.

C.W. says he recently donated a Scottish Highlander calf to a preserve in Alabama. "We had raised him on a bottle, and he followed us around like a puppy dog," he reminisced. "We hated to see him go, but we didn't have room to keep him, and the folks in Alabama were delighted to get him."

As visitors turn off Old Dahlonega Highway at the Chestatee Wildlife Preserve gate, they pass between pastures where zebras, llamas, bison, and unusual cattle graze nearby. In addition to the Scottish Highlanders is a Texas Longhorn and a pair of African Watusi cows. The latter are still juveniles, but will eventually have horns that are 54 inches in diameter with an eight-foot spread!

Across from the parking area, a great two-humped Bactrian camel stands waiting to greet guests at the gate of his enclosure. "**Sebastian**" loves attention and is especially fond of children according to C.W. His favorite treat is a two-liter bottle of orange soda or Koolaid, which he guzzles down by holding it between his lips and tilting his head back.

Sebastian had a close call early in the year 2000. He was stretching his head and neck through a gate trying to get to the ostrich food when he got stuck. When caretaker Charlotte Johnson found him, he was lying on his side with his feet tangled up and barely conscious.

Whom does one call to rescue a 2,500-pound camel? Charlotte just ran for the phone and dialed 911. Lumpkin County Fire Chief Ed Eggert and five firemen soon arrived and, in an unusual demonstration of the usefulness of the "Jaws Of Life," cut through the heavy metal of the gate. It took several cuts before Sebastian was freed and able to stagger to his feet. He has since made a full recovery from his misadventure. When asked if he had ever made such an unusual rescue before, Chief Eggert admitted that "camel extrication" was so rare that there was no place on the computer for it.

The primates are among the Preserve's most popular attractions, particularly the chimpanzees. "They are always up to something," C.W. says with a smile. "One of our chimps named "**Kima**" knows sign language, and she loves to dress up in clothing. She always picks the brightest colors, and if a garment is wrongside out, she will carefully turn it to the right side before putting it on."

I was amused to learn that the chimps have their own cable television to keep them entertained in the evenings until 10:30 p.m. when a timer shuts the set off. "They love cartoons, which really get them to whooping and hollering," C.W. laughed. "They also like to watch nature programs on the Discovery channel." Since the chimps are sensitive to temperature extremes, they have heat and air-conditioning in their inner living quarters.

Many exotic sounds are regularly heard in the vicinity of CWP, but C.W. reports that they have great neighbors who are very tolerant and supportive, despite the fact that the lions' roars can sometimes be heard two miles away. The noisiest time is during the full of the moon. "The roars and brays and howls can go on all night then," C.W. admits with a rueful smile. His house is only 150 feet from the lion and tiger cages, so he should know. Needless to say, he is a light sleeper.

Who is this remarkable man who loves animals so much that he works tirelessly caring for them and spends everything he makes providing for their well-being? C.W. Wathen grew up on a dairy farm in Kentucky, and says he has always been around animals. His earliest memories are of watching his dad milk the cows and seeing the calves being born.

C.W. says that as an adult, his interest switched from cows to horses, and he began raising and showing quarter horses.

When he moved to Cumming, Georgia, 15 years ago, C.W. scaled down to miniature horses. He got his first exotic animal when somebody wanted to trade a zebra for one of his colts. Then he says he became interested in llamas, and buffalo and lions and tigers and bears, etc. etc. He moved to Lumpkin County in 1995 to have more space to house his growing family of animals.

Today, Chestatee Wildlife Preserve has over 450 animals, including more than 100 different species, and more are being added all the time. Cages and pens are well-labeled with the names of the occupants and information about them. If you love animals, this can be a great weekend destination in the mountains.

If you want to visit the preserve, guided tours for groups of 25 people or more are available by advance request, and school field trips are welcomed. The Preserve is open to the public from 10:00 a.m. to 4:00 p.m. daily. General admission is $5.00 per person. To schedule a tour or request additional information, call 706-864-9411.

Dahlonega

Consolidated Gold Mine

For almost three-quarters of a century, the gold fields in north Georgia's Lumpkin County were worked by countless prospectors seeking their fortune from the rugged mountain terrain. Some were successful, but most searched in vain for the precious yellow metal. The **Consolidated Gold Mining Company**, organized in Dahlonega in 1898, was reputed to have been the largest gold mill ever constructed east of the Mississippi River, but even in this grand venture, failure became inevitable, that is, until the early 1980s, when entrepreneur **Bryan Whitfield IV** discovered where the real gold was buried.

For years, visitors had been coming to Dahlonega looking for old gold mines to explore. Inevitably, they were told that the mines were all on private property and unsafe as well. Bryan and his wife Donna thought the Consolidated could fill that need, and so they set out to see what they could do to make their idea bear fruit.

After several years of cleaning out and reinforcing the old **Knight Vein** at the Consolidated, the Whitfields opened the site for tours in October of 1991. To their amazement, their mine tour drew almost 20,000 people the first year it was open, and Bryan and Donna realized they may have discovered a hidden motherlode, just like in the gold rush of 1829.

When gold was first discovered in north Georgia in 1828, men from every walk of life were soon wading in every creek and branch in search of the yellow metal. For those who came early, a simple pan was the only tool needed to separate the shining flecks and nuggets from the sand in the stream beds. Eager to speed up the process, however, men soon began inventing new tools that would allow them to sort more ore in less time.

The huge Consolidated Mines site included a 300 x 100-foot 4-story 120-stamp mill; a 128 x 128-foot 4-story chlorination plant; an assay laboratory; and a blacksmith and machine shop. The *Engineering And Mining Journal* described it as "*the first systematic attempt at deep mining and intelligent milling in Georgia.*"

According to local resident and veteran miner **Marion Boatfield**, the company went broke because they just plain ran out of ore to process. "You can't run stamps without ore or it will bust the mortars," Boatfield explained.

Today, visitors to the Consolidated don yellow plastic hard hats to keep off occasional drips of water and follow a guide down a ramp into a gaping hole in the side of the mountain. Once inside, they find themselves with an awesome view of what is known as "the glory hole," a yawning 250-foot vertical shaft. The gold vein discovered there actually runs through a supporting pillar in the center of the shaft, but it had to be left untouched to provide support for the shaft.

Steep steps lead down into the main shaft, where visitors follow the old ore cart tracks deeper into the historic mine. Admission to the attraction includes not only a 45-minute tour of the mine, but also a pan of ore and a demonstration on panning techniques in a water trough behind the gift shop. The ore is taken from the nearby Chestatee River, and nearly everyone finds at least a few flecks of gold.

The Consolidated Gold Mines site is listed on the **National Register of Historic Places**, and the Whitfields were awarded the **Lumpkin County Historical Society's "Madeleine K. Anthony Award"** in 1992, for their protection of the property.

The Consolidated Gold Mine is open for tours from 10:00 a.m. to 4:00 p.m. seven days a week. The cost of admission is $11.00 for adults and $7.00 for children ages 4 to 14. Children age 3 and under are admitted free of charge. For more information, call (706) 864-8473.

NORTHEAST GEORGIA

Dahlonega

Crisson Gold Mine

Most of the gold mines in Lumpkin County have been bought and sold many times over the years. An exception to this practice however is the **Crisson Mine**, owned and operated by the same family for well over a century. This mining site is also a popular tourism destination in Dahlonega.

Originally opened as the **Rider Mine** circa 1846, this operation was purchased in 1883 by E.E. Crisson, who processed ore with a 10-stamp mill. E.E. also farmed and ran a general merchandise store on the property located two and one-half miles from Dahlonega on old Wimpy Mill Road (present-day U.S. 19 Connector in Dahlonega).

By 1920, maintenance on the Yahoola Ditch (which provided water from the Yahoola River to power the mill) had been so neglected that most of the water along the line was leaking out before it ever reached the mines. Without water, work at the Rider/Crisson Mine came to an end except for a small one-man operation maintained by E.E.'s son, Charlie Crisson. The abandoned mill deteriorated and finally collapsed.

E.E.'s other son, Reese, moved his family to Atlanta in search of work during the lean years of the Great Depression. Reese's son, John, was thirteen years of age at the time. He took with him many memories of the days when he would slip off to climb the abandoned stamp mill and watch his Uncle Charlie mine for gold.

All the years that John was in military service, he dreamed of moving back to Dahlonega and reactivating the Crisson Mine. "I never figured on going anywhere else," he says today. "I remembered Dahlonega not only for its gold, but also for having the finest people I had ever met anywhere in the world."

After returning from a tour of duty in Vietnam, John was assigned to a U.S. Army Recruiting post in Atlanta, and was finally near enough to Dahlonega to begin working the mine on weekends.

At the time, John says his plans involved nothing more than a limited commercial operation at the old mine site. However, local television programs featuring the mine attracted growing numbers of tourists wanting to try their hands at gold-panning. As a result, John was soon persuaded to put in panning boxes to take advantage of the tourist traffic.

The mine was initially open only on weekends, and there was no building at that time to serve as an office. John's wife – Dorothy – remembers sitting at a folding table under an umbrella (to escape the sun), taking in money in a cigar box. Hopeful prospectors could pan all day for $1.00.

John also continued his limited commercial operations at the mine during this period too. His brother, R.L., operated the stamp mill while John was working in Atlanta. In 1970, the price of gold was still fixed at $35 an ounce, but even at that low price, the mine proved profitable. On an average eight-hour day, the plant reportedly processed 500 tons of ore, requiring 650 gallons of water per minute to move the ore from stage to stage.

After retiring from the Army in 1972, John was able to move to Dahlonega permanently and operate the Crisson Mine on a full-time basis. He and Dorothy built a home next door, putting white quartz rocks from the mine to attractive use in their walls and fireplace.

These days, the Crisson Mine and gift shop are operated by Tony and Tammy Ray, since John had to retire from active mining after a heart attack in 1990. Visitors can buy the mine's rich ore by the pan or the bucket, and guides will instruct "gold grubbers' in the art of panning.

In the Crisson Mine Gift Shop, gold jewelry, nuggets, and mining supplies are available for sale.

The Crisson Gold Mine is open seven days a week year-round, with indoor winter panning facilities. The mine is located two and one-half miles northeast of Dahlonega on U.S. Highway 19 Connector. For more information, call (706) 864-6363.

Dahlonega

Dahlonega General Store

A ten-foot-high carved oak bear, mountains of jams and jellies, mounds of old-fashioned candies, aromatic coffees, tasty peanuts, antiques, collectibles, a large selection of pocket knives and oddities galore, are just a few of the array of retail items awaiting the lucky visitor to the **Dahlonega General Store** – one of north Georgia's best-kept secrets.

Located on the town square in this historic gold rush community in the mountains of north Georgia, the Dahlonega General Store is the product of entrepreneur **Jon Stone**.

A native of Atlanta, Stone disavows any special expertise in his business endeavors. He does, however, profess a certain amount of luck and intuition – and a lot of hard work. He also admits that he listens closely to the comments made by his customers and quite often reacts in relation to their desires as he stocks his products and wares.

In 1970, Stone had leased a portion of the old **Henry Moore Hardware Store**, a historic structure on the south side of the town square. He converted it into a restaurant which he named "The Lodestone," operating it for 14 years.

"I leased the building the first seven years, and then finally bought it in 1977," Stone explains. "When it reached the point that I was going to have to remodel it, I started thinking about the general store concept, as opposed to another restaurant"

Today, Stone's shop is one of the most popular in this tourism-dominated community which annually enjoys the visitations of tens of thousands of travelers, campers, and college students.

It undoubtedly is the atmosphere and the uniqueness of the products in the Dahlonega General Store which continue to attract tourists and travelers day-in and day-out. As one enters the building, the first thing that catches the roving eye is an immense carving (from a 100-year-old oak) of a huge grizzly bear which rears ten feet high in the center of the shop. "Kids are just amazed with it," Stone whispers.

And once the casual visitor has recovered from the bear carving, an almost overwhelmingly delicious smell of roasted peanuts is encountered. "We roast them and the smell drifts throughout the building," Stone says with a smile. "Most people can't resist them once they smell them. On some days, we'll sell six hundred dollars-worth of peanuts."

Then a fascination with the many novelties (all of which are for sale) in the store sets in. As did the old-timey general stores of yesteryear, Stone's shop offers everything from big cast- iron dinner bells like the one used in the movie *Gone With The Wind* (actually it's known as a #2 farm bell), cut-glass items, and octagon soap, to myriad candies, knives of all make and description (all the way from a Bowie knife to a pocket knife), and a player piano.

Most items in the Dahlonega General Store are inexpensive and perfect for vacation gifts and collectors of Southern memorabilia. One of the most popular is Stone's special blend of coffee.

And for shoppers with a sweet tooth, the store is "the cat's meow." Ever the businessman, Stone packages some 180 varieties of jellies, jams and preserves under the private Dahlonega General Store label. A wide selection of old-fashioned candies and other treats make this section of the store a must-see attraction.

Females seem to be unreservedly impressed with Stone's wide selection of cooking items too. Again, doing his homework, Stone has painstakingly stocked everything from moonshine jelly and Watkins Products ("Every good cook insists on using these," Stone smiles again), to sorghum syrup, sourwood honey and a plethora of country cookbooks.

Rounding out this country store are a variety of china cabinets, pottery, baker's racks, old-fashioned wooden toys, 'coonskin caps, oddities such as a "penny press" which converts a penny into a bit of memorabilia, huge washtubs of marbles which are sold by the cup, gold pans, traditional copper weather vanes, a selection of travel & history and cooking books, and much much more. One has to experience this shop to truly appreciate it.

The Dahlonega General Store is located on the south side of the town square in historic Dahlonega. It is open 10:00 a.m. to 6:00 p.m. seven days a week. For more information, call (706) 864-2005. Shop online at www.dahlonegageneralstore.com.

Dahlonega

Hall's Block Shops

Frank W. Hall built a monument to himself in downtown Dahlonega in the late 1800s. It has survived for well over 100 years, and today is one of the most captivating structures in this historic community where gold was once king.

The large, historic brick building – with "**Hall's Block**" emblazoned in the cornice stone across the top of the structure – is filled with interesting shops today, and is found on the northwestern corner of the town square of Dahlonega. The heavy iron bars across its windows imply it was built with protection in mind. In fact, it was designed as a general store in the days when rowdy gold miners still frequented the area.

Completed in 1883, the marvelous structure, now listed on the **National Register of Historic Places**, was only one of a number of prominent structures built by Hall, described as "the richest man in Lumpkin County" in his obituary when he died in 1901.

Hall was a Vermont native who had come to Dahlonega in 1868 as a millwright. Possessed with a keen sense of business savvy and a strong desire for success, he managed to advance from what was essentially a penniless prospector.

An astute entrepreneur, Hall realized early in his career that the real money was not made from mining gold from the ground, but from selling merchandise and equipment to the men who did the mining. About fifteen years after he first arrived in Dahlonega, Hall opened what then was a huge mercantile center on the square in the lusty gold mining town.

Hall built his showpiece to last, and the pine flooring and heart-pine main beams are even more solid today (having seasoned for over 100 years) than they were when Hall originally installed them. Present-day owner, C. Jon Stone, purchased the building on January 3, 1984.

Today, Stone leases space in the attractive Victorian-style building to 10 or more businesses, and on most days during the tourist season of May through October, a steady stream of visitors browse through the shops.

Hummingbird Lane, a nature-oriented shop and gallery, occupies the entire top level of Hall's Block. The Hummingbird Lane stock includes a unique array of handcrafted items ranging from pottery, birdhouses, clocks, and redwood tables to wood-carvings, metal sculptures, rocking chairs and much more. Other buyables include hammocks, wind-chimes, and many one-of-a-kind items associated with the shop's nature-oriented theme.

A large gallery of original paintings from regional artists emphasizes one end of the 4,000-square-foot space. A wide selection of nature, travel and history publications are positioned along another wall atop the old bookkeeper's table which once graced the upstairs business office when Hall's Block was renamed "**Moore's Store**," by a subsequent owner – **John H. Moore**.

It was during his renovations of Hall's Block that Jon Stone uncovered some interesting relics from previous owners. He found a faded and crumbling ledger book full of receipts dating back to Frank Hall's ownership in the 1890s. He also uncovered two dusty vintage appliances, at least one of which was a marvel in its day: a unit which doubled as both a dish and clothes washer with a sink. A six-burner kerosene stove was discovered near the washer.

"I think they were accidentally shoved together with a lot of other things that needed to be repaired, and were just forgotten," Stone explains. They are just a couple of the many novelties available for purchase in these unique shops.

(The Hall's Block shops are open most weekdays and weekends. For more information on these shops, contact the Dahlonega-Lumpkin County Chamber of Commerce.)

2
NORTHEAST GEORGIA

Dahlonega

The aged **John A. Parker Storehouse** standing proudly on the old town square in Dahlonega has survived approximately 150 years now, and is the oldest commercial structure on the square. It was built before much of the American West was even settled. Today, it houses the **Crimson Moon Gallery & Coffee Shop**, an after-hours gathering spot for musicians and other creative talent.

Crimson Moon Gallery & Coffee House

Dahlonega resident Dana LaChance owns the historic building today. Dana is a descendant of Rev. Joseph McKee, the gentleman who discovered an unusual mineral spring north of Dahlonega in 1868 which ultimately grew into a famous destination called **Porter Springs**.

The original owner and builder of Parker Storehouse, **John A. Parker**, was a prominent merchant and large property owner in Dahlonega in the mid-1800s. He purchased the property on the town square in 1857, and it is believed he constructed the building on the site the following year. He was a successful businessman until he encountered financial problems in the 1880s. A newspaper item reporting his departure from Dahlonega in 1890 to join relatives in Indian Territory suggests that Parker was part Cherokee Indian.

The Parker Storehouse was sold at a sheriff's sale to I.C. Head for $485.00 to satisfy a suit against Parker. In 1893, Head sold the property to E.E. Crisson, who in turn sold it two years later to partners named William H. Jones and John M. Brooksher. In 1919, Jones purchased his partner's half interest to become sole owner.

Local pharmacist George Lipscomb remembers when his family moved into the building next door to "**W.H. Jones Mercantile Co.**" about 1924.

"It wasn't just a grocery store," Lipscomb recalls, "but a general store that carried everything from horse collars to clothing to old-timey jewelry. I have to confess that I loved to snitch apples from the big wrought-iron baskets that Mr. Jones kept outside the front door - as did every other kid in town.

"There wasn't any way to drive around back at that time, so supplies were unloaded at the sidewalk onto what was called 'the Dahlonega railroad,'" Lipscomb continued. "There were iron rails that ran the length of the alley between Will Jones' store and our house (present-day Norman Adams Insurance Agency) and a loading cart rolled over them."

"I always looked forward to Saturday nights when people would gather at **Will Jones' Store** for some 'pickin' and grinnin,'" George says with a big grin of his own. "Folks sat around under the store's one faintly-glowing light bulb and listened to the fiddles and guitars playing hymns, folk songs, and hillbilly music. I was just a little fella then and probably wouldn't have been allowed out if we hadn't lived right next door."

In 1936, the property was leased and later sold to Nelson A. Nix, who would operate **N.A. Nix Grocery** for almost half a century and become a legend in his own lifetime. During that period, numerous articles about Nix were published in newspapers all over the country. He had the unenviable distinction of having been robbed at least seven times over the years - in a shop right in the middle of town.

"One robber hit Daddy over the head with a steel pipe," Nix's daughter, Lorene Higgins, remembers. "He was taken to the hospital but was back in the store the next day.

"Daddy wasn't bitter about his misfortunes and he never dwelled on them," Ms. Higgins continued. "He loved people, and he enjoyed having them come sit by the wood heater in the middle of the store and chat. He was always generous in extending credit to his customers."

Nelson Nix faithfully opened the doors in all kinds of weather until two days before his death in 1983 at the age of 99. At that time, local businesses closed and proprietors stood outside their doors in respect as the funeral procession passed by.

The next owners – a Roswell, Georgia, couple named Esther K. and Marcellus Anderson – discovered the old storehouse shortly after they purchased a

farm in Lumpkin County. They were intrigued by the building's character and history. The Andersons purchased the store from Mr. Nix's heirs and embarked upon an extensive restoration project, following stringent guidelines necessary to have the building listed on the **National Register of Historic Places**.

"The building was in such poor condition that trees were growing through the side walls in back," Esther recalled wryly. "The only lighting was from one naked light bulb hanging from the ceiling. We rewired the place with electric lamps that were reproductions of old lanterns. We also had to re-roof and replace a number of rotting floorboards. The old rounded counter in the back room - reportedly a saloon bar - was in real danger of falling through the floor."

The Esther K. Anderson Gallery offered quilts and various types of antiques until it closed its doors in 1996.

In 1997, Dana LaChance purchased the property and operated an old-time trading post called "Appalachian Outfitters" for a number of years. The original shelves, counters and display cases in the historic store were reused as displays for clothing, equipment and supplies for hikers and outdoor enthusiasts.

Since 2001, the building has been home to the **Crimson Moon Gallery & Coffee House**. Local north Georgia artists display their work on the coffee house's walls, and songwriters and musicians gather to share their acoustic music with patrons from 8:00 p.m. until 11:00 p.m. Wednesday thru Saturday evenings, much as is done in the famous **Bluebird Café** in Nashville, Tennessee. The coffee house offers beer and wine, baked goods, pita bread and other light fare.

(The historic Parker-Jones-Nix Building (Crimson Moon Gallery & Coffee House) is located on the town square in Dahlonega. For more information, telephone 706-864-3982.)

Dahlonega

WHOL LIVE RADIO
COUNTRY JUNCTION
JAN 15   8 PM

Holly Theatre

During major movies such as "**Gone With The Wind**" and so many others, the **Holly Theatre** was a bright jewel in the crown of north Georgia's small-town movie-houses in the 1940s. As its age and societal customs changed, however, its luster was dulled and the once popular weekend attraction was patronized less and less, until it ultimately was abandoned. Just when times seemed the darkest, a group of Dahlonega residents came together to save and revitalize it.

The historic gold-mining town of Dahlonega had enjoyed an early introduction to motion pictures when the **Fox Film Company** transported its cameras and actors to the tiny north Georgia town in 1915 to film a silent movie entitled, "*The Plunderer.*" Dahlonega's abandoned gold mines and mountainous scenery offered a setting very similar to that of the southwestern United States, and yet, Dahlonega was much more accessible, since the film companies – at that time – were based in New York.

"Although a number of long-time Dahlonega residents recalled incidents about the filming of *The Plunderer*, no one remembered actually seeing the motion picture at a Dahlonega theatre. This, no doubt, was because there was no theatre in Dahlonega at that time. It wasn't until the mid-1920s that **Robert D. Howser, Sr.,** converted the lower floor of the **Price Building** (built in 1897) on the Dahlonega Public Square into a movie theatre, and began showing movies for the paying public.

Interestingly, the projector was operated with electricity generated by a huge waterwheel which Robert Howser had installed at nearby **Cane Creek Falls** in 1921. It provided electricity not only for the theatre, but for the whole town!

Howser's movie theatre apparently was short-lived, however, for an individual named **Randall Holly Brannon** from Roswell, Georgia, began bringing a portable projector to Dahlonega in the early 1930s. He showed films in the old high school auditorium, and these

Saturday night productions were big events that were anticipated all week by many local citizens. Some walked from many miles out in the countryside just to be able to watch these early movies.

Brannon made arrangements through the president of the local Parents & Teachers Association – Mrs. Lula Ash – to show the movies. Mrs. Ash, herself, was soon pressed into service taking up tickets at these events.

The movies ultimately proved so popular that Brannon was encouraged to expand his services. In April of 1939, he took a two-year lease on the Price Building – where Howser had shown films a decade earlier – and announced the grand opening of the "**Holly Theatre.**"

On January 9, 1943, the Holly Theatre was temporarily closed due to a disastrous fire which completely destroyed the adjoining century-old frame building – "**Moore Hall**" – which had been originally built as the **Eagle Hotel**. The structure was being used in 1943 as a dormitory for **North Georgia College** cadets.

The aged Price Building was damaged by the flames, necessitating some repairs, including a re-roofing. Undaunted, the Holly Theatre was reopened for movies shortly thereafter.

Interestingly, the movie projectors of that day were operated by shining light – provided by an arc lamp – through the film. An arc lamp is a high intensity incandescent light created when electrical current leaps between two closely-spaced electrodes. Normally, the film would spin past the lamp too quickly to be affected by the intense heat, but sometimes, the film would jam, and would burn through before the projectionist could close the shutter between the film and the lamp.

This was only one of numerous problems with the equipment used to show films at the Holly during World War II. Mr. Brannon, however, was already hard at work attempting to correct the situation in order to improve his business. He applied to the War Production Board stating his need for new "*projector mechanisms, stands, magazines and reflector arc lamps,*" and citing the equipment breakdowns and the usefulness of the movies as morale boosters to back-up his requests.

When **World War II** came to an end, Randall Brannon began making plans to erect a new Holly Theatre. The old theatre was not only inadequate in size (containing only 224 seats) but was also in such poor condition as to be unsafe. The new theatre would be built at the foot of the hill below North Georgia College in Dahlonega, a site which was anticipated to guarantee the movie-house a steady clientele.

On July 12, 1948, the grand opening of the new Holly Theatre was celebrated by a capacity crowd of 600 amid festivities, including speeches of thanks to owner R.H. Brannon. The movie shown that night was **Metro-Goldwyn-Mayer's** production of "*The Bride Goes Wild*," with **Van Johnson** and **June Allyson**. It was billed as "*the funniest film in 10 years.*" Randall Brannon was probably laughing loudest of all in sheer relief.

The solidly-built brick building with its facade of Georgia marble and brightly-lit marquee was quite elegant for its day, particularly for a little town in north Georgia. The interior of the brick walls was covered with fabric, and the matching curtain was electrically-operated.

Mrs. Ash proudly occupied the ticket booth of the new Holly Theatre, and she loved seeing and greeting the people of all ages who lined up in front of her window to purchase their tickets. As patrons settled into the comfortable cushioned seats with their popcorn and drinks, there was a keen sense of anticipation as the lights went out, the great curtain was opened, and the production appeared on the large screen.

Saturday features at the movies usually were Westerns, starring cowboys like **Roy Rogers**, **Gene Autry** or **Hopalong Cassidy**.

Mrs. Ash was the unofficial chaperone of all that went on in the theatre and made regular rounds down one aisle and up the other with her flashlight to make certain that her patrons didn't have their feet on the seats in front of them and that everyone behaved themselves.

Mrs. Ash also checked to make sure the couples on the back row were not excessively ardent in expressing their affection. She didn't allow any "hanky-panky" in her theatre, but she did her chaperoning in a motherly way that didn't offend anyone. More often than not, when a couple became engaged, Mrs. Ash inevitably would be one of the first to hear the news and see the ring.

In retrospect, Lula Ash was as much a part of the Holly Theatre as were the movies. Since the Brannons lived in Roswell, they usually sent the films up by bus and depended upon Mrs. Ash to keep the Holly running smoothly.

A number of Dahlonega's young people got their first jobs at the Holly Theatre working as ticket collectors, popcorn vendors and projectionists. It was the projectionist's job to arrive early enough to splice the previews and other "shorts" onto the first reel of the movie and thread it into the #1 projector.

In the early days movie houses when there was only one projector, there was a short break in the middle of the movie when the reel of film had to be changed by the projectionist. Since the Holly had two projectors, there was no interruption between reels if the projectionist was alert enough to switch over to the #2 projector at just the right moment. A warning bell and inconspicuous numbers in the upper corner of the screen were his signals to make this switch-over.

After the second reel was running, the projectionist had to rewind the first one and thread the next reel into the #1 projector. He continued this process until the final reel was played and rewound. "Movies generally came in 6 to 8 reels," explained Charles Fitts, who started working as a Holly projectionist when he was fourteen years old, "but it took about 13 reels for '*Gone With The Wind*.'"

Many former "youngsters" who are middle-aged today, remember a television program called "*The Popeye Club*" which featured Atlanta television personality **Don Kennedy** as "*Officer Don.*" This program was widely popular in Georgia, and aired on **WSB-Television** from 1956 through 1970. It became so popular, in fact, that Kennedy took the show on the road, doing promotions in movie theatres throughout Georgia.

In 1959, the little theatre in Dahlonega was graced with his presence, much to the delight of many youngsters in the area. One Dahlonega native, who asked to remain anonymous, said she paid to see Officer Don when he visited the Holly Theatre, and she remembered the occasion clearly. "That was the time when there was a big measles epidemic in Dahlonega, and many of the people who went to the Holly that day came down with the measles that week," she smiled in remembrance.

The Holly apparently did well in its new location from the late 1940s through the 1950s. But as with many things, "*The Times They Were A'Changin'*" to paraphrase a popular song of the 1960s. Attendance began to drop for diverse reasons. According to Mrs. Ash's daughters, she was greatly annoyed with television because she saw it taking people away from her beloved Holly Theatre, and she wouldn't allow a set in her home for a long time.

After Randall Brannon's death, his widow, Mary, kept the theatre going as best she could through the 1960s. In general, however, as television and the divergent lifestyles of the 1960s caught on, theatre patronage dropped off.

In attempting to make ends meet in the face of rising expenses and decreasing income, Mary Brannon hiked the price of admission to 75 cents in 1967. She also apparently started renting less expensive films, for Geraldine Adams, who assisted Mrs. Brannon in operating the theatre, wrote to her to say that people had been complaining about the quality of the movies being shown and had even walked out of the theatre after the first thirty minutes. She also advised Mary that the sound system was not working well and was either too loud or too low.

Finally, the end became obvious for the faded little movie-house. On January 7, 1970, Mary Brannon wrote a letter to the City of Dahlonega, asking that the water at the Holly be turned off pending further notice. "*Due to the extreme cold weather and since the theatre is closed at the present, I am concerned about the water freezing,*" she explained.

Several people attempted to operate the Holly Theatre during the 1970s. One of these hopefuls was J.L. Proctor, who reopened the newly-renovated movie-house in the fall of 1976. The April 1, 1977 issue of *The Dahlonega Nugget* noted, "*J.L. Proctor has done an excellent job showing first-run movies at Dahlonega's Holly Theatre, but there is a danger he cannot keep Dahlonega's only moving picture theatre open unless patronage improves.*" A later tenant left town abruptly, owing Mary Brannon seven months of back rent, and even taking the keys to the Holly with him. By this time, the roof was beginning to leak badly enough to cause sections of the ceiling to sag. It was a sad time for the once-proud little theatre.

Mary Brannon tried whatever she could. She leased the theatre to a congregation who converted it into a church. During Dahlonega's annual **Gold Rush Festival**, the Holly was used as "**The Red Dog Saloon**," and is fondly remembered by many North Georgia College students in that context. But unfortunately, the building was steadily deteriorating with age and neglect. More time passed, and it was finally abandoned altogether. Pigeons moved in

through a broken window and left a regular layer of droppings in the interior. One could almost hear the clock of doom ticking ominously.

Although many people deplored the sad condition to which the Holly had descended, no one could afford to purchase and/or repair it. Finally, in 1991, a group of determined citizens decided that the Holly was a structure worth saving. They formed the **Holly Theatre Community Center, Inc.**, and began the laborious and expensive process of bringing it slowly back to life.

Funds donated by charter members and many local organizations were used to purchase the building from Mary Brannon and repair the ruined roof. The pigeons were evicted, and many volunteers over many months donned old clothes and gloves to help with the un-glamorous clean-up work. Electrical, heating and air-conditioning systems were updated, and theatre seats were taken apart and hauled to Toccoa to be cleaned and rebuilt.

A stage was added to allow for live performances, and concrete was poured into the dirt basement to create a rehearsal hall. The old projectors were sold as museum pieces – literally – and replaced with a modern projection system. Slowly – ever so slowly – life was being breathed back into the Holly.

Every effort was made to restore the Holly authentically and to utilize all the original furnishings whenever possible, including much of the original lighting and marquee letters.

After more than two years of dedicated work, with much still remaining to be done, the Holly Theatre was reopened on Saturday, November 6, 1993. Since that time, the renovated movie-house has hosted dozens of live performances as well as weekly family movies. The stage and fine acoustics in the building make it an ideal location for concerts, fashion shows, beauty pageants, puppet and magic shows, story telling events, and all types of drama. An active Little Theatre Group – **The Holly Theatre Company** – presents a number of plays and musicals every year, including "*The Sound Of Music,*" which drew full houses to no less than eleven performances in 1999.

Today, the Holly has gained a regional reputation as it attracts both patrons and performers alike from the surrounding areas as far away as Atlanta.

Dahlonega

This fortress-like building in which the **Bank of Dahlonega** was located for many years, has stood on the southeast corner of the Dahlonega Public Square for approximately 100 years. For much of that time, it was a beacon of reliability, serving the citizens of Lumpkin County reliably and fairly in their banking needs. Today, however, the banking business is no longer located in the old building, but a popular restaurant attracts patrons inside.

Jack's Cafe / Old Bank of Dahlonega

Part of the charm of Dahlonega's historic Public Square is its happy marriage to the many attractive buildings around it – both old and new. The old Bank of Dahlonega building was erected in 1910 and today houses **Jack's Cafe**.

At first glance inside, it is obvious the cafe's owners enjoy a keen awareness of the building's historic significance, for prominently displayed on one wall is a large old photograph of the bank in earlier days. Surrounding it are other early photos depicting Lumpkin County's history.

Jack Peck comes by his interest in local history naturally. He is a descendant of one of Dahlonega's earliest gold miners.

Adam Peck, a veteran of the War of 1812, arrived on the Lumpkin County scene *"very early in the third decade of the (19th) century,"* and was credited by one source as probably being *"the first man to attempt vein mining"* in the area. His arrival could not have been long after gold was first discovered in 1828, and he may well have been among the miners present at the first session of court held in the then-new county of Lumpkin on August 22, 1833. The small log courthouse used that day was located "a few yards north" of the brick Greek Revival courthouse erected in the center of the Public Square a few years later in 1838.

Jack Peck says his ancestor could well have stood on the very site where Jack's Cafe is located today. "That thought makes history very personal," he smiles.

Also hanging in the cafe is a painting by a local artist which depicts a well-known scene in local history. It shows **Matthew Stephenson** standing on the balcony of the courthouse shortly after gold was discovered in California in 1848, trying to dissuade Lumpkin County miners from leaving the area to seek new opportunities out West. In the painting, Stephenson points dramatically over the heads of the individuals in the crowd to **Findley Ridge** on nearby **Crown Mountain**, once described as the mother-lode of all the gold in the area.

Stephenson, assayer for the **Dahlonega Branch Mint** from 1850 to 1853, became famous for the words he spoke that day. "Boys, there's millions in it!" he exclaimed. His impassioned rhetoric, however, didn't deter most of the miners from pulling up stakes and heading West. His words, however, did become a popular expression which famed writer **Mark Twain** put in the mouth of one of his characters in his book *The Gilded Age*. The sentiment was also repeated over and over in the more colorful vernacular thereafter by Georgia gold miners as *"Thar's gold in them thar hills."*

Jack Peck selected the painting not only for its historic significance, but also because Jack's Cafe looks out on the old courthouse building from the same perspective as chosen by the artist. Some of Jack's customers were undoubtedly among the local people who donned clothing reminiscent of the early 1800s and posed for the painting in 1992.

Gold nuggets no longer wash up after a heavy rain as they once did before the Dahlonega Public Square was paved. The old gold miners have also disappeared, going to their just rewards many many years ago. The old courthouse, however, remains, and today is the home of the **Dahlonega Gold Museum**.

It is unknown today what buildings may have preceded the Bank of Dahlonega building on its site on the Square. However, the manner in which it was constructed is a story in itself.

At first glance, the old building appears to be made of hewn natural stone. Upon closer inspection, however, the viewer discovers that each "stone" is identical in size and appearance. The building is actually constructed of solid concrete blocks made from a mold designed to give the more elegant appearance of stone. The owner of the only other structure in Dahlonega built with the same concrete blocks provided some interesting information not only about the buildings, but the builder as well.

"A Lebanese man named **Galuscha** came to Dahlonega from North Dakota in the early 1900s to cut hardwood timber for flooring," **Elizabeth Moore** explained a few years prior to her death in 1996. "He brought with him a mold used to form the solid concrete blocks. Both my home 'Moorehill' (on West Main Street) and the Bank of Dahlonega building were erected using blocks made in that mold."

Elizabeth went on to explain that this was at a time when trees were becoming increasingly scarce in the Midwest and builders were looking for alternative materials. Concrete blocks resembling stone cost much less than natural stone, but their popularity was short-lived. Masons didn't like working with the blocks because they were very heavy – as much as 100 pounds each. The heavy blocks slowed construction time considerably, and many architects also did not consider the blocks to be aesthetically desirable.

Jack Peck likes to point out the cafe's historic mode of construction as well as its historic significance as the home of the Bank of Dahlonega for over half a century. He also likes to hear the chuckles when he shows his customers an article written by **Editor W.B. Townsend** in the June 5, 1914 issue of *The Dahlonega Nugget* shortly after the bank was reorganized and re-chartered.

According to the famed editor, *"the Bank of Dahlonega was organized when there was no such enterprise in Dahlonega. Business men had to send their money off to Gainesville to be deposited. If not, they kept it hid about their stores and residence, moving it from place to place. We had a little and changed it so much that the dollar bills got ragged and the nickels wore slick."*

In 1931, the **Bank of Lumpkin County** merged with the Bank of Dahlonega. The late Lillie Sanders, whose husband Fred was the Bank of Dahlonega's cashier at that time, described how all the equipment – including the heavy safe – had to be moved from the Meaders Building across the Square to the Bank of Dahlonega building. "It (the safe) was on wheels, but it was very heavy," she said when interviewed before her death in 1991. "Moving it was no easy matter."

Lillie's son, Howard, although only a youngster at the time, also has vivid memories of the event. "The Square wasn't paved at that time, so they laid 2 by 8-inch boards in front of the wheels and pushed the safe along on those boards, pulling the ones out from behind and bringing them back to the front," Howard explained. "The safe was made of iron and was as tall as a man. It was so heavy that a bunch of men were straining to push it."

As far as other unusual events at the bank were concerned, Mrs. Sanders said she remembered distinctly the day in 1932 that came to be known as **"Black Tuesday."** "We heard on the radio that the president of the United States had ordered all the banks in the country to be closed. That was during the **Great Depression** when so many banks were failing. The Bank of Dahlonega, however, was sound, and we saw no reason in the world why we should close down," she explained. "We opened the door at 9 a.m. as usual, but a few minutes later, here came the sheriff and his deputy. They said that if we didn't lock the door, they would have to lock it for us. There was nothing to do but put all the money back into the vault and go home," she continued with a sigh. "We didn't know how long we would have to stay closed, but as it turned out, the bank was allowed to reopen three days later for business as usual."

Another unusual event was a disastrous fire on the south side of the Public Square which caused considerable anxiety to the Bank of Dahlonega officials. The late Alma McGuire, a retired Lumpkin County schoolteacher who died in 1991, recalled (in an interview prior to her death) when **Moore Hall** (originally the historic **Riley Hotel** dating from the 1840s) burned to the ground on January 9, 1943.

"I remember watching them remove all the money and records from the bank in case the fire took the whole block," Alma related, describing how **North Georgia College cadets** bravely fought the fire in vain. Only the solid brick construction of the adjoining **Price Building** (originally built as the law offices of W.P. Price in 1897 and being used as a movie theater in 1943) prevented the fire from destroying the other buildings on the south side of the Public Square.

Bill Grindle grew up in Dahlonega and remembers the Moore Hall fire well. He was assistant cashier at the Bank of Dahlonega when it was remodeled in 1954 and remembers how it looked in earlier days. "The old wrought-iron cage that enclosed the bank employees was replaced by a long counter, and a large vault was built to improve security," he explained. "A thick concrete floor was poured to take the place of the old wooden boards. After the remodeling, we thought the Bank of Dahlonega was really 'uptown.'"

When J.R. Fields started working at the Bank of Dahlonega in 1955, his duties included doing everything from waiting on customers and keeping books using the old "hand-cranked posting machine," to sweeping the floor and locking the door.

By the time Claudine Jones became bookkeeper for the Bank of Dahlonega in 1958, Fred Sanders was the president and had an office at the rear of the bank. "Bank statements always went out the last day of the month so they could be delivered on the 1st," she recalls, "and that meant working until late at night, sometimes even midnight, preparing the statements. Most of the statements were taken to the post office to be delivered the next morning, but J.R. Fields personally hand-delivered them to businesses located on or near the square."

By 1963, the Bank of Dahlonega had outgrown its location on the Public Square and the bank directors decided to erect a new building on West Main Street. Bill and Effie Kate Fry, former owners of the well-known **Smith House Restaurant and Hotel**, bought the old bank building and operated **Dahlonega Loan Company** there until 1986. The building is still owned as of this writing by members of the Fry family.

When asked how he learned how to cook, Jack Peck admits with a laugh that it was a matter of self-preservation. "After my first marriage ended in divorce, I got hungry, so I got some cookbooks and started experimenting," he explains. I had some friends who ran small restaurants on St. Simon's Island where I was living at the time, and I started helping them out on weekends. Before long, I was hired as assistant manager of the Crab Trap nearby. Later, I went through the Shoney's restaurant training program which taught me how to cook everything served in their expansive breakfast."

A few weeks after the restaurant's grand opening, Jack expanded the hours and the menu to include a country breakfast offering grits, biscuits, bacon, tenderloin, sausage and pancakes made from Jack's own special recipe which he has perfected over the years.

"I like to prepare food the old-fashioned way, the way my grandparents did," Jack smiles, explaining his philosophy of cooking. "Here at Jack's Cafe, we make our own chicken, tuna and egg salads and 'old-timey' slaw. As an added touch, we butter our buns and toast them on the grill. Our aim is to serve food that tastes as good or better than anything our customers could fix at home. In the process, we save them the work of preparing the meal and cleaning up afterwards."

Although the cafe bears Jack's name, he is quick to point out that it is a family business which he and his wife, Erin, operate together as a team. There is also an obvious family atmosphere among the Pecks and their employees. "We treat everybody like family, whether they're local or from out-of-town," Jack adds.

{Jack's Cafe serves country breakfast starting at 8:30 a.m. on Saturdays and Sundays, and lunch from 11:00 a.m. until 5:00 p.m. seven days a week. The most popular luncheon items are hamburgers and cheeseburgers with all the trimmings, but the menu also includes sandwiches, subs, salads and pierogies. Veggie burgers are available for vegetarians. And as a tasty dessert, there are sixteen tempting flavors of Greenwood ice cream from which to choose. Take-out orders are also available (706-864-9169).}

Dahlonega

North Georgia College

Built in 1837, a massive building on this site turned out gold coins until operations ceased in 1861. It was donated to the state of Georgia in 1871, and became a branch of the **University of Georgia** shortly thereafter. It was destroyed by a horrific fire in 1878, but on the old mint foundation, a new structure was built which still impresses visitors today.

It was shortly after midnight on the morning of December 20, 1878, that residents at **North Georgia Agricultural College** in Dahlonega were awakened by the smell of smoke and the terrible cries of "Fire!" "Fire!" Flames were already lighting up the night sky as faculty members and students living in the 27-room brick building hurriedly grabbed what they could and groped their way to safety.

The college's president, **David W. Lewis**, and his family narrowly escaped being trapped by the flames, lingering as long as they dared trying to save books from his personal library by throwing them out the second-story windows. Although rescued from the fire, the volumes were badly damaged in the process.

By daylight the following morning, the building lay in ruins. There was no loss of life, but the college's only building – including its library, instruments, and other equipment – as well as the personal possessions of those who lived in the structure, had all been destroyed.

The headline of an article which appeared in the December 24, 1878 issue of Atlanta's newspaper, The Daily Constitution, called the Dahlonega fire *"North Georgia's Great Calamity."* The article went on to note, *"The recent burning of the North Georgia Agricultural College is justly considered a misfortune to the whole state. It affects northeast Georgia as a peculiar calamity. Full accounts of the burning which come from Dahlonega state that the destruction was almost total, and that the remains of the well-equipped institution are blackened walls and smouldering ruins."*

The cause of the fire could not be precisely determined, but it was generally believed that it originated from a beam of timber supporting the second floor located in the extreme end of the south wing of the T-shaped building. On one end, the beam rested in a groove in the brick chimney and may have been set so deep that it was ignited by flames in the fireplace. It probably smouldered for hours – perhaps even much longer – before actually igniting. Since the south wing was used for classrooms and was unoccupied at night, the fire was not discovered until a substantial portion of the building was ablaze.

Before the ashes were even cold, however, trustees, professors, and students of the college – supported by many local citizens – resolved that the college must not die. A mass meeting was held in the courthouse (present-day Gold Museum on the town square) three days later to plan for the reconstruction of the important building.

Immediate arrangements were made for classes to be held in the courthouse, the old Academy, and the Baptist Church (then located on what is now the college's front campus).

"We are glad to see that the faculty of the college have preserved their pluck in spite of disaster," the article in **The Daily Constitution** continued. *"The work of rebuilding will, we learn, be commenced at once."*

Among those taking an active part in the administration of the reconstruction was **Col. William Pierce Price**. This congressman from Dahlonega worked tirelessly to promote education in north Georgia when the area was still a remote backwoods region. He therefore was no stranger to adversity.

Back in 1871, Representative Price had been the individual responsible for the introduction of a resolution in Congress authorizing the Secretary of the Treasury to donate the old **United States Branch Mint** building in Dahlonega "for educational purposes."

The Dahlonega Mint had operated from 1838 until shortly after Georgia seceded from the Union in 1861 at the onset of the U.S. Civil War. Following Lee's surrender at Appomattox, federal troops were quartered

---

in the abandoned Mint building, and an inspector from the U.S. Mint in Philadelphia was sent to assess wartime damage to the structure and its equipment. The machinery was found to be rusty but salvageable and was shipped to the Philadelphia Mint.

The **U.S. Treasury Department** put the Dahlonega Mint building up for sale but declined selling it when the highest offer was only $1,525. Thus Col. Price's resolution authorizing the Secretary of the Treasury to donate the $70,000 building (which had become something of a "white elephant") for educational purposes fell upon receptive ears. The new facility was named North Georgia Agricultural College (NGAC).

Although the trustees of the newly-established college (present-day **North Georgia College & State University**) were custodians of a fine building, they had no funds for repairing or furnishing it or for the hiring of teachers to teach there. The trustees subsequently agreed for the college to become a part of the University of Georgia in order to receive the necessary financial support.

Soon, rooms which formerly had housed crucibles and dies for the conversion of bullion into gold coins were filled with blackboards and desks. Upstairs rooms which had served as quarters for the Mint officers and their families became the living quarters of President David Lewis and his family.

When NGAC. opened its doors on January 6, 1873, with the invitation of *"Whosoever will may come,"* it became the third public college in the state and the first to admit female students. *(Note: The University of Georgia didn't admit female students until nearly fifty years later.)* More than 200 students attended the college that first year, of which nearly half were coeds, including President Lewis's daughter, Willie, who would later be the only female in NGAC's first graduating class.

Notices in the local newspaper advertised *"Free Education!"* at NGAC, with only a $5.00 entrance fee per 5-month session. Ads also advised that *"the healthfulness of the climate and cheapness of board make N.G.A.C. a desirable school for young men and women from those sections of the state visited with chills and fever."* They also pointed out *"the entire absence of temptations to vice which its location affords."*

The fledgling college had only two faculty members initially, but two students were soon hired to teach the preparatory department. A "sub-freshman class" was a necessity, since there were no public high schools in Georgia at that time. Other students gained valuable teaching experience by providing summer school instruction to hundreds of children living in rural areas.

NGAC was unique in being both a coeducational and a military institution. The first commandant of cadets was Lieutenant Joseph Garrard. An item from the April 3, 1873 *Dahlonega Signal* newspaper noted, *"The Secretary of War, General Belnap, recently assured the President of the Board of Trustees that he would supply the college with all the necessary guns, accoutrements, and the like as soon as the number of male students reached one hundred and fifty."*

On December 15, 1876, the newspaper reported that 150 Springfield Cadet Rifles and other military equipment would soon be shipped to NGAC. Since there was space for only a small percentage of NGAC's students to reside in the old Mint building, the great majority boarded with families in town. When the building burned in 1878, some rifles and munitions were destroyed, but most of the military equipment was safe because it had been issued to cadets and was kept with them in their various boarding houses.

Less than two months after the fire, the editor of the *Signal* wrote, *"The flocking of such a large number of students to the North Georgia College presents a strange phenomenon. They come every day just like the grand old building had never been wrapped in flames. . . . It was feared that the students would go away and not return. But nothing of the sort has happened. . . . it really looks as if two new students had already taken the place of every one who had gone away."*

Four months after the fire, plans had been drawn for a new building and bids from contractors were coming in. On June 13, 1879, *Signal* reported: *"At this writing the old walls are being torn down to the foundation upon which will be erected according to the plans and specifications of Messrs. Parkins and Bruce, architects of Atlanta, the new building."*

The cornerstone of the new structure was laid with Masonic ceremonies on June 25, 1879. Col. Price, president of the college's board of trustees, donated generously to the institution from his own personal assets, and the new building that rose on the foundation of the old Mint was eventually named **Price Memorial Hall** in his honor.

Although erected on the Mint's original T-shaped, hand-hewn granite foundation, Price Memorial's appearance was considerably different from that of the Mint, due largely to the addition of a lofty steeple which towered above the building and the town. It was a magnificent addition, but its construction was not problem-free.

While carpenters were raising one of the tower trusses in the steeple in August of 1880, lightning struck the building. Three workmen who were operating a large hoist were reportedly *"knocked senseless."* Another workman who was on the roof of the building fell to the ground but miraculously survived both the shock of the lightning bolt as well as the long fall to the ground.

The brick walls of the new structure were not stuccoed over as had been done on the old Mint building, and the second story rose to twice the height of the 12-foot ceiling in the Mint. In the center portion of the building, the Mint's plain rectangular windows were replaced with five tall Gothic arched windows, the tallest one in the center pointing upward to the bell tower.

In time, as the college continued to grow, other buildings were erected on the campus, but Price Memorial continued to dominate the college and town over the years both with its tall spire and historic presence. The steeple became even more eye-catching and impressive approximately 100 years later in 1973, when it was covered with gold leaf in time for North Georgia College's centennial celebration.

Other exterior changes made to Price Memorial include a large front porch with tall columns thrusting up to support its second-story roof. Ralph Fitts, a former custodian, recalls when there were two porches – one for each floor. "At that time the steps were on either side of the lower porch (instead of in front of the building today)," Ralph recalls, "and the military cannons were rolled under the center of the porch and into the basement for storage."

Numerous changes have been made to the interior of Price Memorial over the years to adapt it to current needs. Fireplaces were closed off when steam heaters were installed, and the extraordinarily high ceilings were lowered twice to make the rooms more economical to heat. Unfortunately, the lowered ceilings concealed the tops of the great arched windows on the second floor. In time, other arched windows and doors were sealed up to create new office con-figurations, and walls were added to conceal plumbing pipes.

Over the years, Price Memorial has housed not only classrooms, but also administrative offices, a military armory, the college library, bookstore, planetarium, Y.M.C.A. room, campus post office and "canteen," and much more. The second story was originally an auditorium with a slanted floor where students and faculty gathered weekly for an assembly called "Chapel."

Erskine Rice, who followed in his father's footsteps to become a cadet at North Georgia College in 1937, relates a story his father, George Erskine Rice, Sr., told him about Chapel when he was a student there shortly after the turn of the century.

According to the tale, Erskine says the dignified old president of the college mounted the steps to the stage to speak to the assembled student body one morning, when suddenly, the curtains behind him opened to reveal his horse and buggy – all hitched up there on the stage – to the amazement and titillation of all in the audience. "How the pranksters managed to get the horse up those steep high steps to the second floor remains a mystery to this day," Rice smiles.

Price Memorial was vacated in 1994 in preparation for a complete restoration. Prior to the renovation work in the late autumn of 1997, college workmen removed all paneling and interior alterations which had been added over the years, exposing the original floors, walls, and ceilings for the first time in many decades. It proved to be a dazzling revelation.

Today, North Georgia College & State University in historic Dahlonega, Georgia has been recognized in most quarters as an excellent education facility. Many students have profited and many more hopefully will continue to profit from the grit and determination of a mountain congressman and his band of college and civic leaders following the terrible fire of 1878.

(North Georgia College and State University in downtown Dahlonega, is the only state-supported, coeducational, liberal arts, military college in the world. Coeds have participated in the military program since 1974. NGCSU has been recognized nationally and by the University System of Georgia for its academic excellence in admission standards, student retention and graduation rate. The campus has also been rated as one of the 20-safest in the United States.)

Dahlonega

Old Lydia School

Lumpkin County once had thirty-eight one-room schoolhouses scattered throughout its boundaries. Despite this fact, many students still had to walk several miles just to reach the nearest school. Today, most of those old schoolhouses have long since disappeared, but one – **Lydia School** – has been lovingly restored by local preservationists, and looks much as it did when students in seven different grade levels gathered there in years gone by to learn "readin', writin', and 'rithmetic."

Little is known of the first Lydia School except that it was a log structure built on land donated by J.P. Smith near **Macedonia Baptist Church** circa 1890. When it burned only a month after its completion, a second Lydia School was hastily erected about a mile away not far from the famed Porter Springs Hotel.

The second structure was unceiled, heated only by a fireplace, and remembered as "one cold place" by pupils who attended there. In time, this primitive building was replaced by a third Lydia School built a short distance away on the site of the abandoned old Cedar Mountain Campground.

The name "Lydia" (sometimes spelled "Liddia") may have been drawn from Biblical history. According to Andrew Cain's *History of Lumpkin County*, the school was named for the apostle Paul's first convert at Macedonia. However, another source maintains the school was named for the first teacher who taught at the school.

Loudean Jarrard Seabolt was eighth of the twelve Jarrard children who attended Lydia School. She still has a deed showing that her father, Josiah Jarrard, deeded an acre-and-a-half of land for the school. The deed was recorded in 1915, but some individuals maintain the school was already in session two or three years previously.

"I remember my brother Ernest telling me that he and my brothers Richard and Emory gathered rocks from the surrounding fields to build the foundation pillars of the school," Loudean recalls.

"I started at Lydia School when I was five years old and went through all seven grades there," she adds. "We were supposed to be at school at eight o'clock in the morning, but that wasn't a problem for us Jarrard children since we lived so close. We weren't dismissed until 4:00 p.m., so during the winter months, many students left for school in the dark and didn't arrive back home until the sun was setting. That seems like a long day compared to the hours students are in school today, but we had two 30-minute recesses and a full hour for lunch."

Loudean says she and her classmates began each day by chanting together, "Good morning, teacher." "Then we had a Bible reading and prayer, followed by the Pledge of Allegiance to the flag," she explains with a smile. "Some teachers had us sing patriotic songs like 'America,' while others preferred religious hymns."

Loudean says she and her classmates didn't have individual desks. "We sat on long benches with our feet dangling in the air. Boys were on one side of the room and girls were on the other. We wrote in our laps.

"There were no such things as free textbooks back then, either," she continued. "We children all had to work during the summer making money to buy our own books. Everybody had a job to do, and we frequently picked fruit and produce to sell to the Porter Springs Hotel. Students didn't get free textbooks until Governor Rivers made that a project in 1937.

Loudean also says the teacher left no illusions about who was in charge at the school. "She kept a hickory stick on her desk to use as needed, but she usually tried other kinds of discipline first." Smiling in remembrance, she explained, "One day I had been talking my head off despite all her warnings. Finally, in exasperation, she drew a circle on the board and told me to go and stand with my nose in it until I thought I could control my tongue. I was coming down with a cold, and the chalk dust kept irritating my nose and making it drip down the board. It seemed like hours before I got to go sit down again. . . Incidentally, the chalkboard we had then was just a big space painted black on the boards of the wall. An old rag served as an eraser.

"We all brought our lunches with us, carrying them in lard or syrup buckets. Mama would pack what was left from supper the night before. We might find a baked potato or corn-on-the-cob or even a dish of beans. Ham biscuits were popular too, although I remember some children being ashamed of having ordinary homemade biscuits instead of store-bought loaf bread."

Loudean says sweets were rare back then, but her parents grew a lot of syrup cane from which they extracted sorghum syrup. "Sometimes, Mama would put in a jar of syrup mixed with butter for us to spread on our biscuits. We carried milk with us in pint jars and put it in the spring nearby to keep it cool until lunchtime."

Back in those days, there wasn't any playground equipment, but the children had fun playing games like "Drop The Handkerchief." "We used homemade bats and balls made of twine to play 'Town Ball,' which is like baseball except that you got a player out by throwing the ball and hitting the person instead of tagging him," Loudean reminisces.

Indoor plumbing was also not a convenience enjoyed by the students of this early school "There weren't even any outhouses when I first started at Lydia School," she remembered. "At recess time, the girls headed in one direction to a wooded area, and the boys headed in another!

"After I graduated from 7th grade in 1932, I was excited about going to high school in Dahlonega," Loudean smiled again. "At the same time, though, I hated to leave Lydia School. I always wanted to go back as a teacher, but my teaching positions took me to other schools."

Though it seemed to be a rewarding profession to many teachers in those days, a professional teacher earned a paltry salary. . . But then, it didn't take a lot of money to live in those days either. "I still have a teacher's con-tract signed by my aunt, Cona Jarrard Hamilton, showing she was paid $20 a month in 1910. By the time my sister Christella was teaching there in 1929-1930, the salary was up to $40."

In the mid-1940s, Loudean's sister-in-law, Zora Duckett Jarrard, taught at Lydia School for four years. She drove an A-Model Ford, picking up children who lived along the way to ride in the "mother-in-law's seat" in the rear. Apparently, little had changed in the decade since Loudean was a pupil there. Students still sat on long benches and held their tablets in their laps to write.

Students were still fetching water from the spring, too, but most of them were delighted to be "chosen" for this chore. "That was their outing," Zora explains. "They liked getting out of the classroom and whatever work was going on. We also had to provide our own wood for the stove, and I frequently went with the class to pick up whatever we could find out in the woods."

On any given day, Zora says she usually taught thirty or thirty-five children of all ages and grade levels, but she doesn't recall having any problems. And there were actually advantages. "The younger pupils learned from the older ones," she beamed. "I learned fractions long before my age group got to them because I watched the higher grade work with them on the board."

Wyman Walden says he was a student at Lydia School in 1953 and 1954. He started school in January after his fifth birthday. By that time, the school had electricity, but still had no running water. Students were still fetching water from the spring, but one additional item of "progress" had been installed – outhouses.

"By that time, we had a school bus, too," Wyman recalled, "but Porter Springs Road had not yet been paved, and there were days when the bus couldn't make it to the school. Then we would have to walk the rest of the way in ankle-deep mud."

One of Wymans' most vivid memories is of the time some of the older pupils accidentally set the woods afire during a recess. "They sent us younger students back to tell the teacher and get some water," he recalls. "By the time Mrs. Smith got there, the fire had gotten pretty big, and we were all scared to death.

She knew what to do, though. She quickly had us form a circle and rake out a fire break."

Lydia School was one of the last of the little one-room schools to be phased out during consolidation with the county elementary school in town. The sad day arrived in 1957. After that, the property reverted back to Loudean's father, as was stipulated in the deed under which the land had been originally donated for educational use.

Loudean says her brother David ultimately purchased the property for $50 and used the little school building to store hay for a number of years. Over that span, the structure gradually deteriorated. Vandals removed the bell from the belltower and even took away part of the tower itself.

Unwilling to see the old school fall into total disrepair like most of the other historic one-room schoolhouses in the county, Loudean says she began to dream of restoring it. When she retired from teaching, she persuaded her husband, N.R. Seabolt, to assist her with the project.

After purchasing the land, Loudean says she and her husband began the formidable task of clearing out the hay and repairing the damage done by vandals and neglect. The bell tower and front porch had to be completely rebuilt, and the mud-chinked rock flue for the stove was replaced with a brick one. The floorboards and tongue-and-groove ceiling boards were still in good condition, but all new furnishings had to be collected, including a wood-burning stove. Many people, excited by the project, began donating their own personal memorabilia for display there. These items ranged from old school books and photos from days gone by at Lydia, to lunch pails, lanterns and much more.

When the restoration was complete, more than 300 people attended a special open house held on June 24, 1984 to commemorate the preservation project. Attendees included many former pupils, including nine of Loudean's brothers and sisters, and teachers.

Today, Loudean maintains Lydia School as a kind of museum where, on special occasions, visitors can see a typical one-room schoolhouse as it was used in early education in the mountains. Although the little structure is not open on a regular basis, it is occasionally used for special meetings, reunions and school field trips, though Loudean has cut back drastically on the time she is able to contribute to the school.

In the recent past, some individuals who visited the old school were fascinated by the boards nailed to the wall to create a ladder leading up into the attic. Loudean explained simply that the clapper frequently fell out of the bell and, and when that happened, one of the male students had to climb up the ladder into the belltower to replace the clapper. The cord used for ringing the bell still hangs down through the small hole in the ceiling.

A kerosene lantern gives Loudean an opportunity to explain that electricity did not come to Lydia until 1950. Before then, the room was lighted by kerosene lamps or lanterns placed on shelves on each side of the room. Lunch baskets and pails (minus the culinary contents) are lined up on a shelf at the back of the room, just as Loudean and countless other students had placed them in days of yesteryear. Pupils hung their coats on the pegs below the shelf. Old photographs of the school and people associated with it line the walls.

Today, historic Lydia School is a shining example of early education in the north Georgia mountains. Preserved for generations yet to come, it often encourages the youth of today to seek excellence through higher education, by demonstrating the considerable lengths to which students of yesteryear were willing to go to obtain their education.

(Visitors are welcome to drive by and view the old Lydia School from the outside. No tours of the structure, which is located on private property, are presently conducted.)

This impressive old home a couple of blocks from the public square in downtown Dahlonega, Georgia, has stood for well over 65 years. It is a structure fondly held even today in the memories of some citizens and former residents of the town who are now in their golden years. It was in this house that a renowned Lumpkin County figurehead from yesteryear – **Nina "Aunt Nine" Head** – spent her last years.

Dahlonega

The Royal Guard Inn

Nina Head contracted for construction of the home in 1937 following the death of her husband, Dr. Homer Head, a prominent physician in Dahlonega for many years. The new house was built next door to the couple's original home on one of the town's most attractive residential streets.

Though she originally had intended for the new smaller residence to serve as a rental property (for much-needed additional income), Mrs. Head ultimately decided to move into the new home herself, and rent out the larger house she had shared with her late husband for so many years.

The Heads were so well-known and respected in the community that they are remembered by a number of individuals today who never even met them personally. Their amusing experiences as a dedicated, highly-pragmatic country doctor and his faithful and intrepid spousal assistant, have become the subject of at least one book and numerous newspaper and magazine articles over the years.

When Farris and John Vanderhoff purchased the little home in 1989, they decided they would have to enlarge it in order for it to serve their needs. As they began the renovation project, they discovered that the years had not been kind to the old home. Rotted walls were discovered in some areas, but the Vanderhoffs were able to preserve much of the original structure.

All of the original hardwood floors remain, as well as a freestanding center chimney which had been partially hidden behind closets after Aunt Nine passed away. The tongue-in-groove mantel trim and paneling were created from lumber which had been salvaged from the old Dahlonega Baptist Church next door which was demolished in 1900. A big platter which still hangs on the kitchen wall as of this writing actually belonged to Aunt Nine.

Instead of making use of the history of the structure in their selection of an identity for their new inn, the Vanderhoffs decided to name it after Farris's Norwegian ancestry. Her grandfather reportedly was a captain in the Norwegian Royal Guard in the 1880s, and, having had a previous Scandinavian-themed bed-and-breakfast inn in California, the couple continued the tradition.

The four bedrooms in the inn are all uniquely named and decorated today, and each has its own modern bath and queen-size bed. Two rooms offer additional rollaway beds. The accommodations are upstairs with an outside entrance and ample windows for light and views of the historic town of Dahlonega.

Afternoon tea is served daily between 3:00 and 6:00 p.m. A full hot breakfast is served each morning at 8:30 a.m. on the wrap-around porch (weather permitting) or in the snug dining room. Following coffee or tea, juice and fruit, guests savor such delicacies as Suzanne's blueberry pancakes, Steve's apple-pecan waffles, Farris's Scandinavian egg & sausage casserole, and homemade muffins or scones.

(The Royal Guard Inn is located on South Park Street in Dahlonega. Prices range from $100 to $125 per night, depending upon the season. No pets please. Smoking is permitted on the porch. Major credit cards are welcome.)

It is situated in one of the most historic and picturesque locales in Georgia. That alone is enough to keep guests coming back time and again. Just like a fine wine that improves with each passing year, the Smith House just keeps getting better according to many folks.

The Smith House Restaurant and Inn

Ask people in other parts of the country if they've ever heard of Dahlonega, Georgia. If they're familiar with it, their response often will be, "Oh yes, that's where the Smith House is located, isn't it?" Since the 1920s, folks have been coming from all directions to enjoy this famous family-style restaurant located one block south of the town square in this historic gold-mining town in the north Georgia mountains.

Articles describing the vast array of mouth-watering dishes prepared for Smith House guests have been published over the years in numerous newspapers and magazines from California to Michigan to Florida. Even the Japan Times once weighed in on the subject, listing the price of a Smith House meal in both U.S. dollars and Japanese yen. Writing about the Smith House in the early 1970s, noted travel writer **Dick Enwright** described it as a six-star restaurant where *"one eats for a spell, then rests, and if able, begins the second course."*

Captain Frank W. Hall, an early entrepreneurial businessman was the first to own the property known today as the Smith House. One of the most popular stories told about the site is that it sits atop a rich vein of gold.

Captain Hall was probably unaware of gold on the property when he purchased it in 1895, because the November 3, 1899 issue of The Dahlonega Nugget contained a news item which reported *"Capt. Hall's workmen while excavating the cellar for his new warehouse on the corner of Chestatee and Water streets . . . . struck a rich gold bearing*

vein several feet wide, depth not known." Editor W.B. Townsend went on to note that Capt. Hall had informed him that he would not develop the vein since it ran under his building and was on a town lot.

The upstairs of Hall's new building on the property which later came to be known as the Smith House was designed as living quarters for he and his wife, Esther, but they never occupied the premises. Instead, they moved to Ingleside near Atlanta a few months later. Hall died the following year from typhoid fever at the age of 56.

The Smith House "restaurant" was actually born in 1922, when **Ben and Bessie Smith** purchased the old Frank Hall property and opened an inn on the premises. Dahlonega was still quite rural at this time – without even city water or sewage. The inn, however, had its own well, with a pump powered by electricity. The electricity was generated by a giant waterwheel at nearby Cane Creek Falls.

Ben and Bessie charged $1.50 a day for room and board. Word about Mrs. Smith's delicious home cooking soon spread, and it wasn't long before she had to hire kitchen help to assist her in cooking and serving meals (which cost a grand total of 35 cents for those not rooming at the Smith House).

The list of diners at the Smith House over the years reads like a "Who's Who" of prominent politicians and entertainers. These have included the late **Thomas P. "Tip" O'Neil**, former congressman and speaker of the U.S. House of Representatives; the late **Lester Maddox**, former governor of Georgia; U.S. President **Jimmy Carter**; General **William C. Westmoreland**; the late noted author and columnist **Celestine Sibley**; the late comedian **Bob Hope**; and well-known author and

Methodist minister **Dr. Charles Allen**, just to name a few.

In 1946, the Smiths sold the entire Smith House block to **William B. Fry**, the son of a gold miner who came to Dahlonega in the late 1800s to be superintendent of the **Crown Mountain Mining Company**. Bill Fry did some prospecting himself, and often took his Smith House guests on tours of the local mines.

By this time, the carriage house next to the main Smith House had been converted into living quarters and was home to Bill and Effie Kate Fry and their three children.

It was about this time that Bill Fry decided he needed someone to run the Smith House dining room and kitchen. He found just the person in local resident **Fred Welch**. "You might say that I was raised in a restaurant," Fred once said.

Fred's wife, Thelma, took over much of the cooking, and Effie Kate Fry taught her to make the famous snowflake rolls that had become such an important item on the Smith House menu.

"We were fortunate to have good cooks over the years," Fred said. "Fred Riley was especially good at seasoning vegetables to perfection."

The elder Welch and Thelma served three meals a day, seven days a week for nearly 25 years. Guests began eating breakfast at 7:00 a.m. and ate supper until 7:30 or 8:00 p.m. If people came in later, food was heated up for them – no matter the hour. Just try finding that kind of hospitality today.

Seeing how hard his parents worked, young **Freddy**, the Welch's only son, had no plans that included the Smith House when he was growing up. He remembers thinking that there was no way he would ever go into the restaurant business.

Things changed, however, after he was grown. He also discovered that he was very capably schooled in the profession, even if he hadn't consciously intended to learn

important elements of the hospitality industry. Today, he expresses pride in the fact that he, his wife and children – **Chris** and **Freda** – are carrying on the family business.

After Freddy entered into a partnership with his father in 1968, Mr. Fry began thinking about retirement and urged the Welch family to purchase the Smith House. It took Freddy a couple of years to persuade his father who was opposed to going into debt, having been raised with the philosophy that "if you can't pay cash, you don't need it."

In 1970, however, the family finally took the plunge. Mr. Fry sold the Smith House to his faithful long-time employee – Fred Welch – and his son Freddy. Eight years later, after 32 long years in the business, Fred and Thelma retired themselves, turning the operation over to Freddy and Shirley.

Chris and Freda both studied hotel management in college, and today, they assist their parents in much of the Smith House's overall operations.

The menu remains essentially the same as that established by Bessie Smith: several meats (which always include fried chicken), numerous vegetables, the famous snowflake rolls and/or Thelma Welch's angel biscuits, and a fruit cobbler for dessert.

The hotel rooms looking out on the town are still spacious, even after the addition of bathrooms and closets. Their windows are framed with small panels of the original stained glass believed to have been imported all the way from England by Capt. Frank Hall back in the 1890s.

Guests also still enjoy sitting in large rocking chairs on the front porch of the Smith House while their dinner digests, just as have countless other guests down through the years.

(The Smith House is located at 84 South Chestatee Street in Dahlonega. For room rates, meal times, and other information, call 706-867-7000.)

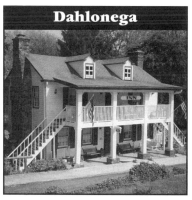

The Worley House B&B Inn

Driving into Dahlonega, Georgia, on the old Atlanta Highway (West Main Street), the traveler's eye is quickly drawn to a two-story brick building topped by a glittering gold steeple on the campus of North Georgia College & State University. Price Memorial Hall was built in 1879-'80 as the college's first building. Just across the road and down the hill on the left, a two-story frame building appears somewhat benign compared to the impressive structure across the street, but in actuality, it enjoys a distinguished history of its own, and its date of construction predates that of Price Memorial by at least 35 years.

Signage on the aged home identifies it today as the "Worley House Bed & Breakfast Inn," and indeed, travelers and tourists from across the United States enjoy the accommodations in this structure as they visit the historic goldrush community. Down through the years, this structure has been the home of many colorful personalities connected with either the United States Branch Mint (which burned in 1878 and on whose foundation Price Memorial was built in 1879) or the college.

Early Owners

Today, the inn fronts directly on a short segment of the original historic road to Atlanta. The first owner of the town lot fronting this road and on which this home was built was an early settler named Brice Howard, who purchased it in 1835, soon after Dahlonega was established. It is not known today when the house was actually built, but when the property was sold in 1846, it was described as "the lot on which the said Brice Howard has resided for several years past."

Howard may have been building his home at the same time the United States Branch Mint was being erected across the road. Whatever the circumstances, in May of 1846, the property was sold to David Hastings Mason, who came from Philadelphia to be the coiner at the Mint.

Mason and his family had lived in an apartment in the Mint building since their arrival in Dahlonega in 1837. When Mint Superintendent James Fairlie Cooper desired to occupy those quarters, Mason purchased the Brice Howard home across the road and moved into it in the summer of 1846.

David H. Mason died in 1848 while still in the employ of the Mint. His son-in-law, John D. Field (also a Mint employee, from 1845-1849 and 1853-1861), was the executor of the estate. The Mason family may have continued to live in the house for a time, but it later became a rental property.

The George A. Gordon family lived in the house during the U.S. Civil War. George was an engineer who came to Dahlonega in August of 1860 to be superintendent of gold mining property located two miles south of town on Cane Creek.

Living just across the road from the Dahlonega Branch Mint made it an easy matter for Gordon to convert gold from the mine into ingots and coins. When Mint operations were halted after the onset of the Civil War, George was appointed caretaker of the building.

Civil War Years

Sometime later, George received an appointment as a 2nd lieutenant and assistant quartermaster for a Georgia State Line unit popularly known as the "Blue Ridge Rangers." His descriptive letters offer more than a glimpse of the life of a Confederate soldier during this terrible war.

During his absence from Dahlonega, Lt. Gordon wrote regularly to his family, describing military movements and actions, life in camp, and the trials and tribulations of war. Ann Gordon's weekly letters to her husband related her struggles to locate food and fire-wood, the children's illnesses, and constant fears of raids.

The next family known to occupy the Howard/Mason/Worley house was that of Robert Hughes Moore. Moore succeeded David Mason and John D. Field as coiner at the Dahlonega Mint, a position he held from 1849 to 1853. When the winds of political change brought his employ as a coiner to an end in 1853, Moore sold the home he had built on nearby Church Street and moved back to Floyd County.

When the Civil War broke out in 1861, the 52-year-old Moore served as colonel of the 65th Georgia Volunteers, C.S.A., and was referred to for the rest of his life as "Col. Moore." A widower by this time, he returned to Dahlonega to resume his earlier gold-mining activities following the war.

In 1868, Moore married 26-year-old Clarissa Lucinda Morrison, and the couple moved into the house which the Gordons had rented during the war. The Moores' sons, Tom and John, were born there.

A few years later, Col. Moore built a new home for his growing second family, which eventually included eight children. Known as "Moore Cottage," it still stands today at the corner of Hawkins and North Chestatee Streets.

Later in his life, Col. Moore was appointed a member of the Board of Trustees for North Georgia Agricultural College which had been established in 1873 in the abandoned U.S. Mint building where he had served as coiner many years earlier. By this time, however, the Mint building had burned and been replaced with the present structure, Price Memorial Hall, built on the original T-shaped, hand-hewn granite foundation of the Mint.

Not long after Col. Robert Hughes Moore and his family moved to "Moore Cottage," the house which he had been renting was purchased by William Jasper Worley. The Worleys apparently had been in the area for some time, for the land upon which the Dahlonega Mint was built in 1837 was purchased from either William Worley (grandfather of William Jasper), or from his son, James H. Worley, for $1,050.00.

James H. Worley (1807-1869) was

Dahlonega's sheriff for two terms in the 1850s and clerk of court for fourteen years after that. His four oldest sons fought in the Civil War, two of them in the Battle of Atlanta.

William Jasper Worley (named for a Revolutionary War hero) was in the same State Line unit as George A. Gordon, and was appointed acting quartermaster sergeant on July 28, 1863. There are a number of references to Worley in George's letters. William Jasper was promoted to the rank of captain in January of 1864, and for the remainder of his life, was referred to as "Captain Bill."

After the war, William Jasper served as clerk of the Superior Court of Lumpkin County and later as Justice of the Peace. He also studied law and was admitted to the bar of the Superior Court.

Later Owners

From his front porch across the road, "Captain Bill" undoubtedly watched with interest as the abandoned Mint building reopened its doors as North Georgia Agricultural College in 1873. So keen was his interest in the new school that he became a charter member of the Board of Trustees and served as its secretary for seventeen years.

William Jasper was undoubtedly one of the first on the scene when flames appeared in the windows of the old Mint building on a fateful night in December (19), 1878. Although there was no loss of life, the building was completely destroyed.

Captain Bill was also among the loyal local citizens who played prominent roles in rebuilding the college. His daughter, Lee Anna Worley, graduated from NGAC in 1891, and was the college's librarian for several years.

The historic homestead remained in the Worley family until 1932, when it was sold to Lt. Charles Carlton, assistant professor of military science at the college from 1928 until 1933. Lt. Carlton remodeled portions of the house, including the conversion of the long upstairs porch to a stoop.

In 1945, Carlton sold the property to Bob Edwards. The Edwards removed the tall aged cedar trees in front of the home and lined the upstairs walls with the aromatic wood.

They slept in a huge "cannon ball bed" custom-made for them by Lewis Roberts, a local miller who operated Wimpy Mill on nearby Yahoola Creek. Each of the four tall bed posts was mounted with a wooden ball the size of a cannon shot.

At Christmastime, everybody in town was invited to the Edwards' "Open House" held each year. Since Bob was a big hunter, wild game was always plentiful on the menu to be served to guests.

Many people in Dahlonega still remember the café and pool room (popularly known as "Dirty Bob's") that Bob and "Chink" Edwards operated on West Main Street just off the Public Square. Chink reportedly earned her nickname from her dark eyes which reminded Bob of chinkapins, a type of chestnut once abundant in north Georgia.

The Edwards family kept the house until, in the early 1980s, Mitzi Francis noticed the old home was slowly dying during a trip she made through Dahlonega. Mitzi was the granddaughter of Capt. Bill and Georgia Victoria Worley's daughter, Maude Victoria, and therefore had a personal connection to the historic structure. She badly wanted to return it to its original state and preserve it for future generations to enjoy.

After purchasing the home, Mitzi began the task of rehabilitating it. The front sill was so rotted by run-off water from the road in front of the home that the whole structure was in imminent danger of collapsing into the stacked-stone-supported basement. After hiring workers to jack up the home with huge jacks, Mitzi contracted to have the sill and other supports replaced beneath the home, ultimately returning it to its original sound condition.

On May 4, 1984, Mitzi Francis opened the Worley Homestead Inn, an attractive bed-and-breakfast inn which took advantage of the home's history to capitalize on the multitude of visitors to the historic goldrush community of Dahlonega. Her mission completed, she leased the business to Bill and Mary Scott, so that she could return home to Florida.

Since 1996, the Worley Homestead Inn has been owned and operated by Bill and Frances Mauldin. The Mauldins are so enthusiastic about the history of the area and the Worley Inn that they offer "living history" events which reportedly draw guests from all over the world.

In April/May of 2002, a Civil War Encampment and Garden Party was held in the Inn's two courtyards. Men and women attired in authentic 1860s period dress performed reels and other dances to music of the era.

Young women in long 19th century dresses were again seen in both the Worley Homestead and the historic Vickery House next door in December of 2002 and January of 2003. They entertained guests with readings and enactments from Louisa May Alcott's classic, *Little Women*.

"We do lots of research and make our events as authentic as we possibly can," says Innkeeper Frances Mauldin, one of the organizers of "The Club," a group of local women who plan and carry out these living history events.

All of the Worley Inn's seven guest rooms are named for members of the Worley family and have plaques on the doors imprinted with the names of their former occupants – including young Claude, who died in a train accident when he was fourteen and whose benign presence reportedly has been felt by more than one guest in years past.

The Worley Homestead Inn serves a full Southern country breakfast and other meals by advance reservation. It is a popular location for such special events as wedding receptions, anniversary parties, family reunions, banquets and even luaus. "Give us a theme for an event and we'll create and organize it for you," Frances guarantees in her characteristic "Let's do it!" manner.

(The Worley Bed & Breakfast Inn is located at 168 Main Street West in Dahlonega. Telephone 706-864-7002 for more information and reservations. Also visit their web site at www.bbonline/ga/worley.)

Dahlonega

Turner's Corner Restaurant

For generations of early Georgia travelers to the Blue Ridge Mountains, **Charlie Turner**'s restaurant where he and his pet bear held court just north of Dahlonega was an eagerly-awaited stop. Though "tamer" today, this folksy site continues to attract steady customers.

Located at the intersection of Highways 19 and 129 in northern Lumpkin County, this landmark beckons warmly to tourists, hunters and campers, just as it has for generations. Not much has changed at **Turner's Corner**; it's just that in the days when Charlie Turner was still alive, things were just a little more exciting.

Travelers have been stopping at Turner's Corner for food and gasoline on their way up to the mountains almost since the day the road to Neel Gap was completed in 1925. That's because Charlie Turner knew how to get folks to stop.

When he first opened his store, Charlie would settle for a whistle and a wave to attract customers. Then he started using animals.

Charlie had a big bird-dog named "Jack" that he had trained to wear glasses and do tricks. When Charlie put a piece of candy on Jack's nose, the dog would flip the candy up into the air and then catch it. Naturally, everybody who stopped wanted to buy some candy, just to get Jack to do his trick. And of course both Charlie and Jack were more than glad to oblige.

Charlie's greatest claim to fame, however, was his pet bear "**Smoky**," a north Georgia black bear which Charlie had raised from a cub. Smoky was so unusually tame that, amazingly, Charlie sometimes allowed children to ride on the beast's back. It was a rare and heartless parent who could ignore a child's pleas to "stop and pet the bear at Turner's Corner." As a result, business boomed for Charlie Turner.

Interestingly, in much of his early life, Smoky – as gentle a wild bear as could possibly have existed – was allowed to freely roam the river banks in the vicinity of Charlie's little enterprise. Despite the fact that he was tame as a house cat, the big bear's fearsome countenance nevertheless struck abject terror in the hearts of most people. Ultimately, Charlie, much to his sadness, was finally forced to put Smoky into a cage to calm the fears of neighbors and passersby – and to protect the big bear from the guns of hunters.

Despite the cage, Charlie and Smoky continued to enjoy many happy years together, and Charlie still freed his pet from the enclosure on occasion during off-hours. Even though he was still a wild animal, Smoky had strongly bonded with Charlie. When the big bear finally died of old age, Charlie was almost inconsolable. He couldn't seem to imagine life without his wild companion.

Eventually, Charlie's loneliness forced him to search for a replacement for Smoky. He had a friend over the mountain in Suches – a ranger with the U.S. Game & Fish Department named **Arthur Woody** – who was renowned for his skills with wildlife. Ranger Woody occasionally came upon orphaned bear cubs in the mountains, and Charlie told him if he ever located another one, that he wanted it. It wasn't long before the restaurateur got a message that a new cub was waiting for him, and shortly thereafter, Charlie had his replacement.

Just as he had done with Smoky, Charlie solicitously raised his new cub on a bottle. He named the precocious animal "**Herman**," after **Governor Herman Talmadge** who occasionally stopped to visit with Charlie who was a strong political supporter.

The years passed by. Charlie lived a full and rewarding life in the wilds of northern Lumpkin County, entertaining and providing meals for travelers for years. Time, however, eventually caught up with him, and he passed away at the age of 75 in the late 1960s.

Without Charlie, the once-exciting restaurant at Turner's Corner languished for years. The business eventually was purchased and run by a series of seasonal operators. It had been closed for several years when **Joyce Gowder**, purchased it in 1991.

Joyce had grown up "just down the road," and some of her earliest memories were of Charlie Turner's bear on which she herself had ridden as a child. Her fondest memories of Charlie were of his "tall tales."

According to Joyce, Turner's Corner Restaurant hasn't changed much since Charlie ran it. It still has the same stove on which Charlie cooked – one of the first gas stoves in the area – and Joyce claims it still makes wonderful biscuits.

Turner's Corner was purchased by Kari L. and Jerry L. Morris in 1999. Despite the change in ownership, the traditions of mountain hospitality and delicious food remain indelibly stamped upon this site. Charlie Turner, undoubtedly, would be pleased with his legacy.

(Turner's Corner is open Thursday thru Sunday, 11:00 A.M. to 9:00 P.M. For more information, call 706-865-6150.)

Kangaroo Conservation Center

Take a drive thru the countryside of Dawson County, and you might be surprised by one site which contains wildlife that you know are not native to north Georgia . . . . That's right . . . Those large unusual-looking animals really are kangaroos, and you can visit them up close.

The development – the **Kangaroo Conservation Center** – is the only such facility in the United States, and has the largest collection of kangaroos outside of Australia.

The business is owned by **Roger** and **Debbie Nelson**, and it actually contains a collection of exotic animals. In addition to the "roos," the Nelsons have burros, dik-diks, East African crown cranes, kookaburra, fallow deer and ducks in their menagerie of wildlife.

Roger and Debbie have both been trained in animal husbandry, and have devoted their lives to the profession of captive wildlife management. For the past 20 years, they have conducted independent studies in zoological animal husbandry, ecology, and wildlife conservation. They both hold certification from the **American Zoo & Aquarium Association** (AZA) – the foremost such organization in the world – and they both have recently completed an extensive five-year re-certification process.

Within their wildlife sanctuary, the Nelsons have a total of 250 animals, of which 200 are kangaroos. "We have no children by choice, so the animals are our babies," Debbie says fondly. "It's a labor of love. We don't exploit the kangaroos and as such, we won't sell them for meat, hunting or for laboratory experiments."

The Nelsons do sell their kangaroos to zoos and zoological parks all over the world. However, before they'll let one of their "babies" go, they first conduct research on the interested facility to determine if it is actually qualified to properly care for the animal(s).

Debbie says they have sent animals to the **Cleveland Metroparks Zoo** – a walk-thru park in Cleveland, Ohio – as well as to zoos in **Sao Paulo, Brazil, Europe**, and other places. Working through an independent broker in England, they most recently have sent 20 kangaroos to two different zoos in **China**.

Roger says that he and Debbie have also allowed their kangaroos to be used in commercial advertising and television productions. "We've made appearances for the **Australian Tourist Commission**, ABC Television's 'Good Morning America,' 'Jack Hanna's Animal Adventures,' on **CNN** (and for programming) on local **ABC**, **CBS** and **NBC** television affiliates," Debbie adds. "It's always a big hit with audiences to see a kangaroo 'in person.'"

Both of the Nelsons were born in Connecticut. Debbie earned her degree from **Emory University** in Atlanta, where she majored in art history. Roger majored in mechanical engineering at the **University of Central Florida**. The Georgia climate seemed to be moderate enough to suit different species of animals, so the couple decided to begin working here with their animals.

Based on years of experience, the couple was able to design a very serviceable facility in Dawsonville. Roger did much of the mechanical construction.

The Nelsons live at the Center, and have six full-time staff personnel who rotate duty so that someone is always on the premises. All staff-members have degrees in animal science, zoology or biology.

The animals at the Nelsons' development can and do experience medical problems similar to any livestock. "We practice preventative medicine," Roger says. "We worm the animals and

2 NORTHEAST GEORGIA

screen them for internal parasites. Our kangaroos don't get external parasites such as ticks or fleas."

Despite the medical screenings and care they give their animals, the Nelsons say that injuries inevitably occur. As one example, kangaroos can become startled in a thunderstorm and run into a tree or fence, causing bones to be broken and concussions to occur. But all in all, the Nelsons' maintain that their wildlife domain offers a rewarding experience for their animals.

Down in the Center's food compound, a staff writes the food schedule on menu boards. The kangaroos consume a total of 150 pounds of Purina horse feed daily. They get hay in the morning, and in the afternoon, they get grain, bananas, and whole wheat bread.

The 'roos also graze and eat hay set out in racks. The Nelsons rotate the animals from pasture to pasture. When one pasture has been grazed completely, it is plowed and re-seeded for continued use.

In order to move from one field to another, the animals must pass through a 7,200-square-foot central arena. It is in this facility that the Nelsons train animals for public appearances. The pastures radiate like the spokes of a wheel from this central spot.

Yet another facility – the Center's nursery – is used to monitor and nurse newborns. It even contains an incubator where newborns can be closely monitored and nursed to good health.

Another animal at the complex is the **dikdik**. These African natives – one of the smallest of the antelope family – stand 10" at the shoulders. Intelligent, quiet and very graceful, they also are rarely seen in captivity. Their diets are similar to that of the kangaroos, and they enjoy apples and raisins as treats.

Kangaroos normally should not be approached by humans. Those that Debbie and Roger have raised, however, will allow strangers to actually pet them. The others, however, are shy and avoid human contact.

Kangaroos can live up to 20 years in captivity, but die younger in the wild as a result of predators and disease.

"They also enjoy a climate similar to humans," Debbie added. "When it's cloudy or rainy with temperatures in the 30s, they go into the inside stalls to keep warm. The Reds – the largest kangaroos – particular dislike wet weather since they rarely see it in the Outback."

To reach the Kangaroo Conservation Center, take Georgia Highway 400 north to the intersection with State Highway 136. Turn left onto #136 and follow it for approximately 12 miles, turning right onto Bailey-Waters Road.

Visitors are allowed to tour the center by reservation only. A 2-hour tour (maximum of 55 visitors at a time. No one under 8 years of age admitted) costs $24.95 for adults and $19.95 for ages 8 thru 18.

The tour includes a safari ride and an educational program in an arena where the animals may be observed up close. It also includes the main barn facility and a drive-thru of the 88-acre wildlife preserve over hilly terrain in a converted U.S. Army surplus military truck. Visitors receive explanations of animal biology, husbandry and general farm operations as applies to exotic animals. The Nelsons do stress that **the center is not a petting zoo**.

(For further information or to schedule a tour, call (706) 265-6100, or email a request to roofarm@aol.com. There is also a website at www.kangaroocenter.com.)

Old Lumpkin Campground

When Highway 9-E was built in the early 1960s providing Dahlonega with an easier access to Atlanta than old U.S. 19, many travelers were intrigued by a cluster of rustic buildings just south of Dawsonville. Some of these individuals soon learned that what they were seeing is one of the oldest religious campgrounds in the state.

White settlers had begun moving into the vicinity of old Lumpkin Campground in north Georgia while it was still part of the Cherokee Nation. Most of these pioneers were not fortune-seekers such as the gold miners feverishly panning the streams farther north. They were simple farmers who wanted nothing more than to till the fertile river bottomlands adjacent to the Etowah River as they cleared the virgin forests in the area.

"Camp meetings" as they are called, actually came into being in the early 1800s at a time when many groups of people left established communities along the eastern seaboard of the United States to move south or west in search of land on which they might homestead. The land lotteries held in Georgia between 1805 and 1832 attracted many of these hardy migrants. In the absence of already-established churches, these pioneers gathered in outdoor settings both for religious worship and to socialize.

In the north Georgia wilderness of the 1830s, the isolated pioneer families in this vicinity were hungry for social interaction spiritual refreshment as well. Annual camp meetings to fulfill these needs gradually were popularized.

Eventually, a central location for the meetings was selected, and a brush arbor was built with tree branches placed over a wooden post frame. It provided shade from the blistering sun or a modicum of shelter from the rain. The month of August became the traditional time to hold these camp meetings because crops were "laid by" at this time and needed no more attention until the time for harvesting had arrived.

Surprisingly, it took a lot of preparation for these early settlers to get away for a week at a time. Families loaded up a horse or mule-drawn wagon with quilts on which to sleep and food to last the week or more that they would be gone. They carried not only hams, eggs, cakes and pies, but also coops of chickens to kill and eat later in the week. They also had to take hay for their stock, which usually included the mules pulling the wagon and the family cow which had to be milked twice a day.

At first, the families slept in their wagons or in some make-shift shelter. Later, as the custom became a regular annual event, the families began building more permanent "tents" or lean-tos of sawed boards which were used and reused year after year. These annual camp meetings eventually were so well attended that the brush arbor ultimately was replaced by a large open-air pavilion constructed with substantial beams held together with wooden pegs and roofed with hand-split wooden shingles. Despite this sturdily-constructed shelter (a custom eventually adopted all across the eastern U.S.), these structures continued to be called "arbors."

It is not known today exactly when the campground near present-day Dawsonville became known as "**Lumpkin Campground**," but it was probably about the time that Lumpkin County was organized by an act of the Georgia State Legislature on December 3, 1832. The name may have been chosen to honor Governor Wilson Lumpkin or because the campground was actually located in Lumpkin County at that time. (Note: Dawson County was not created until 1856.)

In 1845, the site *("Lot 284, Lumpkin*

County, formerly Cherokee County") was deeded to the trustees of Lumpkin Campground by James M. Cooper. According to local folklore, 40 families donated a dollar each for the purchase of the lot. It has also been said that friendly Cherokees helped to build the large heart-pine arbor on the site (built circa 1837 and still standing today) prior to the Indian Removal on the "Trail of Tears" in 1838.

In 1846, the trustees agreed by resolution that *"if any tent falls down and is not rebuilt by the next camp meeting, the lot shall revert to the trustees. Sixteen feet only shall be allowed in front for a tent to stand on."*

Bonnelle Patterson, a former Dawson County school teacher born in 1910, attended camp meetings at Lumpkin Campground all her life.

"Services were held at 8:00 a.m., 11:00 a.m., 3:00 p.m., and 8:00 p.m.," Bonnelle recalled, "and there were always chores to do between services. After the three o'clock service, my grandmother would holler, 'We got to kill some chickens to eat.' After Grandma had wrung their necks, we children were responsible for picking the feathers off.

"We also had the job of hauling water up the long, steep hill from the spring," Bonnelle continued. "Water was all we had to drink besides milk which was kept cool by setting it in tubs of water we carried from the spring. Our buckets were made of cedar which gave the water a good smell and taste. The older boys and girls did most of their courting on their way to and from the spring.

"We cooked on wood-burning stoves in our 'tents.' We slept on beds built from wall to wall and piled high with straw and spread with quilts brought from home. We mostly ate what we had brought with us, but occasionally someone would bring a calf to the campground and we could buy portions of it for steaks or stews.

"It was 1940 before we got electric lights at the campground. Before that, we used kerosene lamps or lanterns. It was crude, but we loved it just as it was. Our lives were measured from camp meeting to camp meeting.

"In all my life, I've only missed three camp meetings," Bonnelle smiled in remembrance. "One year I had typhoid and was too sick to go. Another time I was still recuperating from surgery, and another year, I was away on a trip.

Bonnelle said her grandmother, Alpha Elliott, traditionally blew a conch shell ten minutes before the services were scheduled to begin to let the campers know it was time to head toward the arbor. The shell, which was found by Alpha's son Bunyan on the Gulf of Mexico, reportedly is still sometimes blown before services at the camp meetings which continue to be held annually at this historic site.

In his book, *A Feast Of Tabernacles: Georgia Campgrounds & Camp Meetings*, historian Harold Lawrence records the story about a gang of outlaws known as "the Taylor clan" who disrupted services during the 1869 camp meeting. The outlaws were so rowdy during the Saturday services that women and children were afraid to go to the spring to fetch water. According to reports however, the next night, the outlaws became curious and ventured nearer to the meeting to see what was actually going on. The Rev. J.D. Anthony preached such a powerful sermon that day that nine of the trouble-makers joined the church at the end of the service!

Author Lawrence and those who attend camp meetings today do not view them as merely a nostalgic way of preserving the past, but rather as a way of providing a time and atmosphere of spiritual retreat much needed in today's hectic and stressful world.

(For more information of Lumpkin Campground, contact the Dawson County Chamber of Commerce in Dawsonville, Georgia.)

Dillard

The community of **Dillard**, Georgia, was founded by a family of the same name sometime around 1820. A small close-knit community eventually grew up around the site, and as the road was widened and re-routed, the old part of town was forgotten by tourists. Today's travelers are rediscovering this unique spot.

Thousands of vacationers and tourists traveling up U.S. Highway 441 north pass through this quaint mountain community every year. Many of these wayfarers browse the shops along Main Street without ever noticing the treasures a block or two away. These "overlooked shops" are located along a portion of the old original road a block off the main highway in the old part of town. They're a real treat if you haven't seen them!

John Dillard's family runs the popular **Dillard House Restaurant** in the community. John's ancestors were among the first settlers in this community that ultimately came to be known as "Dillard," Georgia. When the first highway was built into this area, it included a short stretch of what is known as **Franklin Street** along which the first commercial buildings of Dillard were built. When the route of the old highway was slightly changed years later, new businesses sprang up along this new stretch, and the old portion – to a large degree – began to be overlooked by tourists.

A good place to stop first when visiting "Old" Dillard is **Valley Pharmacy** out on the main highway. Here, as of this writing, an honest-to-goodness old-time soda fountain is still in operation.

Next, stop in at the old shops on Franklin Street. These quaint old buildings from Dillard's early years have been refurbished and filled with all sorts of unique and interesting businesses.

In the **Old Feed Store Mall**, a shop called **Stikeleather's** offers an amazing assortment of antiques, collectibles, and even a section of rare and out-of-print books. One entire side of the

Old Dillard Restaurants & Shops

building is filled with hand-made items and incredible clothing created by Mrs. Stikeleather herself – also known as "the rag lady." The Stikeleathers own this roomy structure and Mr. Stikeleather has stocked the place with an array of impressive handcrafted furniture.

If you'd like to overnight at this locale, you won't find a much better opportunity than The Dillard House. However, **Whitehall Inn** is a circa-1846 home that has been renovated into an attractive bed-and-breakfast inn. Owners William and Charlene Johnson have styled the home's furnishings after its original use. It features feather beds and much more, and is located at 485 Carolina Street. (Tel.: 888-883-7708 or 706-746-5511).

Good food abounds in this mountain valley burg, and if you have a hankering for smokehouse cuisine, there is one really good place to get this – **The Blue Pig** – right in the heart of town. The tastebud-tingling fragrance of slow-cooked barbecue draws a person magnetically to this restaurant. Once inside, the mouth-watering aromas get even better.

"Old Dad" runs the show at The Blue Pig, and if you ask him to describe the restaurant's specialty, he'll probably just smile and say, "It ain't nothin' but good ol' country cookin'."

Dillard is a very good place to spend a day – or even a couple of days – shopping and browsing. Plan to be there in late summer and autumn too. Early August witnesses the **Dillard Bluegrass and Barbecue Festival**. Teams from all over the country compete in the preparation of barbecue culinary delights such as sauces, chicken, beef, and pork. A number of bluegrass bands will be performing; there will be a street dance, and mouth-watering barbecue everywhere.

(For more information about Dillard and the surrounding area, contact the Rabun County Chamber of Commerce at (706) 782-4812.)

2

NORTHEAST GEORGIA

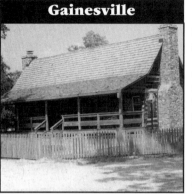

Gainesville

Chief White Path's Cabin

It stood for centuries not too far from downtown Ellijay, Georgia, and might have been a lynchpin for a dynamic tourism industry there. Today, however, the historic **Chief White Path** cabin attracts visitors to Gainesville, Georgia.

Hopefully, the old cabin is finally at rest. A new location and face lift have rescued it from the vandals and varmints which had threatened for years to destroy it forever. In the process, this preservation project has provided an opportunity to permanently recognize a heroic and often-forgotten Cherokee chieftain.

The ancient structure was built by the parents of a Native American named Nunna-tsunega or "White Path," a tribesman who was born circa 1761, and who quickly rose to prominence in the **Cherokee Nation** in the late 1700s. White Path's accomplishments and his stature among the Cherokees ranked among the highest in existence at that time, yet his name is not nearly as well-known as that of his counterparts such as **John Ross, The Ridge,** or **George Gist (Sequoyah).**

Until the early 1980s, White Path's old cabin – the last tangible reminder of his former residence in north Georgia – still stood on its original site some four miles north of Ellijay, Georgia, near present-day Georgia Highway 515. It, however, was a perilous existence at best.

Realizing the cabin was not likely to survive much longer, Gainesville, Georgia resident **Don Cooley** moved the old home from Ellijay to Gainesville in 1981. He had made a valiant effort to interest the leadership and preservationists of Gilmer County in restoration of the structure on its original site. Unfortunately, he found little support. As a result, Gilmer County lost a very valuable historic treasure (and tourist attraction) –

and Hall County gained yet another one.

Mr. Cooley, now deceased, reportedly traced his genealogy back to White Path (some say arguably), and therefore had a personal interest in the project. He spent a reported $75,000 transporting the old cabin to Gainesville and restoring it, but he still needed a protected permanent site for the years ahead.

Hall County businessman **James Mathis** luckily came to the rescue. He and his wife Frances took up the cause to find a permanent home for the historic cabin.

By virtue of an agreement between **Brenau University** in Gainesville and the **Georgia Mountains Museum** (also in Gainesville) on whose board Mr. Mathis served, a permanent site was provided near the University on land owned by Brenau. The situation was further facilitated by the fact that Mr. Cooley donated the cabin to the museum prior to his death.

Finding the permanent homesite at Brenau meant yet another move for the aged cabin. Mathis and the experts he consulted ultimately decided the best procedure would be to move it – more or less – in one piece. The roof was removed and loaded by crane onto a flatbed truck. Steel support beams beneath it held it firmly together. The same technique was used on the remainder of the large two-story log building.

"It's an amazingly sturdy and well-built cabin," Mathis stated following the relocation. "It came through the move with all of its logs and nearly all of the chinking still in place."

White Path lived in the cabin for most of his life. His parents were buried near the cabin's original site at Ellijay.

James Mooney, a well-known author and historian traveled among the Cherokees in the late 1700s. He knew White Path and described him in his writings as *"tall and light-skinned, with raven black hair and obsidian eyes that could glint with fire when he spoke out against ceding more Cherokee lands to the whites."*

For most of his life, White Path, according to historians, was an impressive leader and an eloquent speaker. He fought against the colonists during the American Revolution, but fought with General **Andrew Jackson** during the **Creek Indian Wars**. He was honored with a medal for bravery during the **Battle of Horseshoe Bend**.

In 1819, when Cherokee Chief **John Ross** became president of the **Cherokee National Committee**, one of his main allies was Chief White Path who often accompanied him to Washington, D.C. for talks with **President Adams** and **Congress**.

When the Cherokees were rounded up for their forced relocation to the West in the late 1830s, White Path was a calming and reassuring voice in their midst. Unfortunately, the trip proved to be his last. He died enroute, at a little spot near Hopkinsville, Kentucky, known at that time as **Gibson's Mill**.

Both he and another elderly chief named **Fly Smith** died the same night and were buried side by side nearby. As time passed, the site around the two graves alternated between pastureland and forest land, and eventually, the graves were virtually forgotten.

This historic site quite likely would have been lost to posterity forever had it not been for a gravestone placed upon White Path's plot at the time of his burial. According to folklore, the headstone was purchased with a silver watch White Path had owned.

In 1954, an individual named **Woodrow Hunter** was removing thick undergrowth from a plot of land he owned when he discovered the aged headstone. Today, the graves of White Path and Fly Smith are identified with monuments provided by the **Trail of Tears Commemorative Park** in Hopkinsville, Kentucky.

Back in Ellijay, Georgia, concerned citizens finally placed a commemorative marker at the former site of the White Path cabin, but by that time, the cabin was long gone. Another has been placed at the former site of **Fort Hetzel** (at the east corner of First Street and Georgia Highway 515) the compound within which the Cherokees (including Chief White Path) were imprisoned just prior to the **Trail of Tears** march.

Today, there is much speculation as to how much of the English language Chief White Path could speak and read. It is known, however, that he made a number of trips to Washington, speaking eloquently on behalf of his people.

There is also speculation regarding the lineage of White Path. According to some records, he had no children. According to others, he had ten children. Whatever the circumstances, no member of his family sought reimbursement from the U.S. government for reparations following the removal westward. As a result, no claim was ever submitted for White Path's lonely cabin back in Ellijay, Georgia.

And in downtown Gainesville, the original one-pen room in the old cabin is decorated as it would have been when White Path owned it. The later additions to the structure (those portions of the cabin added by the Aaron Pinson family) reflect an early settler lifestyle.

Aaron Pinson and his family (as a result of the last Georgia Land Lottery) became the new owners of the cabin following White Path's departure in the late 1830s. Descendants of the Pinson family continued to live in the structure for more than a hundred years, and added the second story to the cabin, as well as a room joined to the main structure by a dog-trot.

(To reach the Chief White Path cabin in Gainesville, take the E.E. Butler Parkway exit off U.S. 985 and proceed into Gainesville. After crossing the Jesse Jewell Parkway, look for Brenau Avenue on your right approximately four blocks down. White Path's cabin is on the left, just after the turn onto Brenau campus. For further information, call (770) 532-2698.)

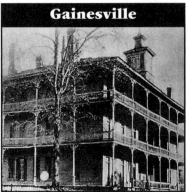

General Longstreet's Piedmont Hotel

Garland Reynolds, a local architect and historian for the Gainesville, Georgia-based **Longstreet Society**, was searching for the original site of the old **Piedmont Hotel** once owned and operated by **Confederate General James Longstreet** after the U.S. Civil War. The old structure had been demolished in 1918, and Reynolds was curious about its former site. Little did he know that he was about to make a startling discovery.

Walking up Maple Street which had many rundown clapboard buildings, Garland's eye fell upon one of the old structures. Long abandoned, the house somehow looked strange – as if it didn't belong with the neighboring homes.

Things that only an architect could detect began to bother Reynolds. The spacing and shape of the windows and doors, the porch and foundations, were all somehow vaguely familiar. Making a few quick measurements and sketches of the dilapidated looking structure, the curious architect returned to his office, then impulsively dug out old drawings and photographs of the Piedmont Hotel.

To his amazement, Reynolds realized the structure on Maple was one wing of the huge old hotel which had somehow survived the demolishment. Beneath the dirt and clapboard siding, a sturdy building was destined to be returned to its former splendor, renamed the **Longstreet Museum**. Today, this building houses the offices of what is known as the **Longstreet Society**.

Most everyone had previously believed the historic structure had been completely destroyed almost 80 years ago. The lumber had been salvaged – most of it used to build a few rental houses. The remaining lumber was donated to **Beulah Rucker** who built a vocational school for poor rural blacks. Nothing else had been saved – or so everyone thought.

Ironically, many Gainesville residents considered the loss of the old hotel to be good riddance. No need to leave any reminders behind of a man they considered a traitor to the Confederate cause and betrayer of the great **Robert E. Lee**. It was bad enough, they agreed, to have to endure that huge marble monument over in the city's main cemetery – Alta Vista – which marks Longstreet's final resting place.

Longstreet purchased the Piedmont Hotel in 1875, just before he settled in Gainesville. By that time, "Lee's good right arm," as he was called, had been in disgrace for some ten or eleven years. He had become what the South (and a few acrimonious Southern leaders) so badly needed at that time – a scapegoat to blame for the humiliating defeat at the hand of those "Godless Yankees." To put it bluntly, he was shunned by the general public.

Yet, through it all, Longstreet persevered. The Piedmont was just one of the many projects in which he immersed himself. It had three stories and was a substantial hostelry for that day and time. It offered forty spacious rooms and was surrounded by covered porches on all three floors.

Today, no one knows exactly what prompted the general to choose Gainesville as his final base of operations. He grew up in nearby White County, Georgia, so that undoubtedly had an impact. It is also believed the railroad lured him, along with the centralized location of the impressive structure he owned. The hotel was an easy walk from the train station and trains were a big part of post-Civil War life in the United States. This was especially true for Longstreet who admired trains and later became the nation's commissioner of railroads.

After settling his family in Gainesville, Longstreet didn't allow the grass to grow under his feet. He stayed on the move constantly. He served for many years as Gainesville's postmaster. He also was appointed to other positions in Washington in addition to his railroad job. He even served as the U.S. Ambassador to Turkey for a short time.

Through it all and into the early 1890s, Longstreet maintained his expansive hotel in Gainesville, using it as a home base for his many endeavors. The Piedmont became a popular aspect of the local hospitality industry and was patronized regularly by such notables as **President Woodrow Wilson** and his family, writer and *Atlanta Constitution* editor Joel Chandler Harris and many old soldiers of both the Blue and the Gray – ranking generals to lowly private soldiers.

President Wilson and his wife and the Longstreets were good friends. The Wilsons' second daughter, Jessie, was even born in the hotel, while the old cigar-smoking general and the President anxiously paced the long corridors.

In her old age, Mrs. Wilson was asked to identify from a photograph of the old hotel, the room in which she and the President had stayed. By a stroke of luck, the room she marked is included in the wing of the old structure which was recently discovered by architect Garland Reynolds.

Longstreet was famous for presiding over his hotel's sumptuous table laden with his homemade wines and home-grown meats and vegetables. He was especially noted for having the best Southern fried chicken in all of Dixie.

While the Yankees were busy praising the general's hotel and table, however, Southerners heartily wished he had settled somewhere else.

Today, Longstreet's postwar actions are seen as those of a visionary by most historians, but in the post-Civil War South, those actions were destined to alienate his neighbors and make him a pariah on the streets of Gainesville.

When Longstreet and his family entered old **Grace Episcopal Church** and took a seat in any pew, those individuals sitting nearby would immediately vacate their seats, even if there were no other seats available. They would rather stand in the rear than sit near "the Judas."

While serving as Gainesville's postmaster, Longstreet was fond of sitting in a favorite chair in front of the post office. Most residents made a point of ignoring him. War veterans, especially the common soldiers who had served under the general were noted exceptions. They invariably rendered a greeting and saluted their old commander.

What was Longstreet's crime that he should be so severely ostracized by the local citizens? Soon after war's end, Longstreet – contrary to many of his compatriots – returned to the Union fold. From his longtime friend and relative by marriage, **President Ulysses S. Grant**, he accepted a post as surveyor for customs of the Port of New Orleans. The position was prestigious and carried with it the job of leading the mostly black City Metropolitan Police force and militia.

The "**Radical Republicans**" in Congress had forced **Reconstruction** upon the South, a move which ultimately was as divisive as it was curative. Grant declared martial law in the South, requiring Southerners to take loyalty oaths to the Union and additional measures before being allowed to vote. And not coincidentally, the **Freedman's Bureau** assisted the many eager freed blacks to obtain voting rights and elective office at a time when most Southern whites were still refusing the terms required to rejoin the Union (and thus were unable to vote their representatives into political office).

It was in this incendiary atmosphere that an unfortunate Longstreet was forced to function. His acceptance that the South had lost the war and must take measures to reconcile with the North was far from popular with his Southern brethren, and he also seemed just a little too quick to take such odious Northerners as Grant into his family circle. His decision to become a Republican (at a time when the "Solid South" was totally composed of Democrats) flew squarely into the face of Southern tradition as well.

Longstreet, to his credit, simply felt that by accepting defeat graciously, and by becoming a Republican, Southerners would have more control over their destiny. He also felt that voting rights for blacks were inevitable and therefore should be instituted without delay. Here again, he was just a little too receptive too quickly to social circumstances which steadfastly "went against the grain" in the South.

Despite his unpopular status, Longstreet continued to hold his post in New Orleans until a fateful day in September, 1874. Federal Republican rule was so unpopular in Louisiana that on September 10, 1874, more than 8,000 members of a group calling themselves **The White League**, most of whom were former Confederate soldiers, threatened to storm the State House in New Orleans.

Standing between the White League forces and the State House were fewer than 3,000 defenders made up mostly of black Metropolitan Police and Louisiana National Guardsmen led by Longstreet. Undaunted by Longstreet's stature, the 8,000 soon overran the defenders and seized the city government. A slightly wounded Longstreet was pulled from his mount and taken prisoner. The incident only added fuel to the growing fires of distaste that many Southerners harbored for the once-popular general.

Longstreet was soon released, but the damage had been done. Disgraced and with his reputation in a shambles, he turned his back on New Orleans forever. He looked instead to an area he had known from his childhood – northeast Georgia. He subsequently moved his family there in the hope of beginning a new life.

Longstreet had been born in Edgefield District, South Carolina on January 8, 1821. His mother was visiting relatives when she delivered her soon-to-be-famous son. His roots actually ran deep into the red clay soil of north Georgia.

The Longstreet family cotton plantation was near Cleveland in White County. James grew up there and attended school in Augusta before going north to attend West Point. Though he was graduated there, some historians are quick to point out that he finished near the bottom of his **West Point** class. In his defense, members of the Longstreet Society will quickly point out that any number of former prominent U.S. military leaders also finished near the bottom of their class, not the least of which was Ulysses S. Grant.

Architect Garland Reynolds and other society members also point out that being near the bottom of a West Point graduating class is deceiving, because so many cadets never make it to graduation, falling victim to the tough discipline and academic standards required at "The Point."

Whether or not Longstreet was a great general is as much a controversy as is the man himself. Most Civil War leaders have been labeled as good, bad or mediocre, and have found their historical niches years ago.

"Longstreet was late at Gettysburg," cried Jubal Early and William Pendleton. They both were seeking to clear not only Lee of the shameful defeat, but themselves as well. They maintained that if "Old Pete" had been more punctual in his attack on the final fateful day of the battle of Gettysburg, the South would have carried the day in this battle which literally turned the tide of the war.

Lee, himself, had no such delusions. Sitting beside a fire with Colonel W.M. Owen and the retreating Washington Artillery on July 5th, he told the colonel "It's my fault, all my fault." Even more compelling were Lee's later comments to Colonel T.J. Goree which maintained, "If I had permitted Longstreet to carry

out his plan, instead of making the attack on Cemetery Hill, we would have been successful."

Longstreet's plan at Gettysburg reflected his strategy for most battles. Take the high ground, dig defensive trenches and then let the enemy come to you. He is considered by most military historians as a pioneer in trench warfare which was so widely used in World War I.

A reflection of this mentality ironically is also found at Longstreet's final resting place – Gainesville's **Alta Vista Cemetery**. Driving into the cemetery from its Jessee Jewell Parkway entrance, the land seems perfectly flat. It isn't until you reach the Longstreet family grave site that you discover it also sits on the most commanding spot in the area. Rolling hills drop rapidly away from the plot.

The grave has become something of a shrine to the general's memory. Local people and travelers from across the United States come to pause beside the huge marble gravestone. Mementos such as small flags and letters sprinkle the plot.

The Longstreet Society which honors the famed general today was formed in 1994 by a dozen or so Civil War buffs who shared a common interest in Longstreet. The group hoped to abate some of the controversy surrounding Longstreet and to help set the record straight on this most unique of the U.S. Civil War generals. What began with a handful of people has grown into an organization of nearly 300, with members from every state and several foreign countries, including Belgium, Denmark and England.

Restoring the remaining wing of Longstreet's Piedmont Hotel is another major undertaking of the Society. The hotel, as pointed out above, was believed to have been completely destroyed in 1918, until Garland Reynolds' discovery. Beneath the obscuring clapboards of what was believed to be an old rooming house stood one of the most historic structures remaining in Gainesville. The remnant was also the most historic portion of the old hotel – a wing in which a U.S. President's child was born.

Ten members of the Society, with the help of the Gainesville Bank and Trust, purchased the property for $80,000. Work on the renovation of the wing continues as of this writing, but additional funding in the amount of $50,000 is necessary to complete the project according to Reynolds.

Rudolph's on Green Street Fine Dining

Looking for a highly-rated restaurant in northeast Georgia that has historic atmosphere as well? Look no further than **Rudolph's on Green Street**.

Opened in 1980, Rudolph's is the only **three-star restaurant** (as rated by **Mobil Travel Guide**) north of Atlanta. The **American Automobile Association** (AAA) has awarded the restaurant its **three-diamond rating,** and national publications have described it as "classic cuisine," "food with a flair," and "creative continental."

As an added bonus, Rudolph's is listed on the **National Register of Historic Places**. The elegant former private residence was built in 1915-16 by **Mrs. Annie Perry Dixon** for herself and her daughter and son-in-law, **Dr. John Rudolph**. Dr. Rudolph was the oldest son of **Judge Amzi Rudolph**, one of Gainesville's most prominent and esteemed citizens who migrated from Ohio in 1826.

Prior to construction of the Rudolph home, the property was owned by the **Baptist Female Seminary,** a girl's boarding school and forerunner of **Brenau College**. The president of the college lived in a home on the premises until it was leveled by a tornado.

Diners have come to expect atmosphere, quality food and quality service – in that order – at Rudolph's. Accordingly, they are treated to white-clothed tables, highback chairs, pastel-colored rooms and delicious foods.

Apart from the main courses, delicious desserts are also offered to patrons with a sweet tooth. Most of these must be seen and enjoyed to be fully appreciated.

The wines at Rudolph's are well-selected, as well as nicely-priced. Several vintages are available by the glass. The restaurant also offers some very expensive wines and champagnes to satisfy all palates. A full bar is also available.

Many of the patrons at Rudolph's come from the Lake Lanier area. Some rent homes on the lake by the month in the summer and simply like to dine at Rudolph's. Other guests are long-time patrons and area residents.

Rudolph's can seat 100 people on the ground floor, and an upstairs banquet room seats 60. Private parties for 12 or more can be accommodated at lunch, and the restaurant caters for special occasions.

Rudolph's also features **The Attic**, a delightful piano bar upstairs.

{Rudolph's is located at 700 Green Street in Gainesville (Tel.: 770-534-2226). Dinner is served from 5:30 p.m. to 10:00 p.m. Monday through Saturday. Lunch is served Tuesday through Friday from 11:30 a.m. to 2:00 p.m. Sunday brunch is also served from 11:30 a.m. to 2:00 p.m. Reservations are recommended. A non-smoking area is available. Information on a historic walking and driving tour of the historic district in which Rudolph's exists is available at the Greater Hall County Welcome Center at 770-532-6206.}

Gainesville

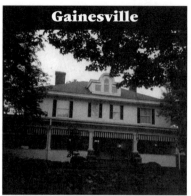

The Dunlap House

This expansive structure began life in 1910, as a grand family home on the outskirts of Gainesville. Today, **The Dunlap House** is a comfortable – and sumptuous – bed-and-breakfast inn patronized by commoners and kings alike.

Samuel Candler Dunlap's ancestors were among the settlers of this community originally called **Mule Camp Springs**. Mr. Dunlap continued his family's prominence in the city, becoming a local banker. He went on to serve as city manager and as mayor.

In 1910, Mr. Dunlap built a home for his bride, **Eva Riley Dunlap**. In this marvelous country residence, the couple found a way to incorporate the relaxed atmosphere of the South with tasteful beauty and grandeur.

The home remained in the Dunlap family until 1985. At that time, **Sam R. Dunlap, Jr.**, an investment banker, along with partners **Don Sigler** and **Carlyle Cox**, bought the property from Sam's father.

After extensive renovations, the doors were opened on "The Dunlap House," an attractive bed-and-breakfast inn. The peaceful ambience and ideal location of the inn soon made it a popular stop for honeymooners, vacationers and corporate travelers.

Today, Dave and Karen Peters own this attractive hostelry. The historic structure is located in the very heart of Gainesville's beautiful Green Street historic district. A drive down Green Street offers travelers an opportunity to admire many very lovely old homes.

Several celebrities have found their way to the door of this attractive inn. Actor **Dennis Weaver**, well-known for his starring roles in television's *Gunsmoke* and *McCloud*, has overnighted at The Dunlap House on several occasions.

A list of other dignitaries and celebrities who have patronized the inn include **Paul Newman**, who overnighted there while racing at nearby **Road Atlanta**, as also has **Tom Cruise** on several occasions. **Jody Powell** (former press secretary to **U.S. President Jimmy Carter**), **Charles Kuralt** and **Shirley Jones** have also overnighted there.

The rooms include all the modern conveniences while maintaining the look and feel of slower, more peaceful times. All are furnished in handsome reproductions of the fine colonial furnishings that would have graced the house in its early days.

A desk and chair are provided in most rooms, as are handy data ports for a computer. The rooms also have individual digital climate controls, and a phone by the bed and in the bath.

The television is tucked away discreetly in a massive pine armoire. Thick terry-cloth robes await guests in the bathroom. Bottled spring water and attractive stemware stand at the ready on the vanity. A hair dryer is tucked away inside the cabinet. All manner of shampoos, lotions and niceties are also nestled in a basket opposite spring water.

Dinner isn't served at The Dunlap House, but there are several nice restaurants around this community, including the very elegant **Rudolph's On Green Street** just across the street.

For breakfast (which is served at the Dunlap House), guests may either be seated at one of the wicker tables on the inn's wide veranda or at a cozy pine table in the main hall. Many guests opt for the veranda on warm days.

The "continental breakfast" of The Dunlap House is a hearty meal which includes a choice of muffins, breads and fresh-baked goods (with jams and jellies), fresh fruit, yogurt, several juices, cereal, coffee and a wonderful assortment of teas. A piping hot casserole rounds out the treats. It is the kind of home cooking one truly appreciates (but which is all too rarely served) at bed & breakfast inns today.

(Room tariffs at the Dunlap House range from $85.00 to $155. For reservations and more information, call (770) 536-0200 or visit the website at www.dunlaphouse.com.)

Helen

Helen, Georgia Getaways

It came to life as a lumber town back in the early 1900s. By the 1960s, the little community of **Helen**, Georgia, had almost withered and died. Today, however, it offers a captivating getaway opportunity, replete with cozy cabins and historic bed and breakfast inns where even the most "uptight" persons can find peaceful solitude.

By the 1960s, the lumber industry in Helen had long since ended, and the town found itself dwindling away, both in population and business opportunities. Then, in 1969, thanks to the ingenuity of a group of local businessmen, this sleepy little burg was transformed into a delightful replica of an Alpine village. Tourists from everywhere began flocking to the new resort to spend time strolling the shops and enjoying the magnificent scenery in and around this pastoral hamlet.

Of course, the great appeal of the Helen area isn't just its scenic beauty, but the ease of access to the resort. Where else can one enjoy the flavor of a Bavarian getaway in only a few hours' driving time? Less than 40 miles from Gainesville and under 90 from Atlanta, Helen affords the great escape to even those with only a day or two to spare.

With this influx of tourists has come a tremendous demand for lodging – the end result of which has been a fevered search for affordable and attractive cabins to rent in the area. From rustic one-room shanties to multi-roomed luxury bungalows, this north Georgia mountains community offers something to suit every taste and budget.

And that doesn't apply just to cabins either. Bed-and-Breakfast inns offering home-cooked meals, historic atmosphere and a surprising variety of inn-keeping styles are popping up all around the sprightly community.

Georgia Highway 356 seems to be the cabin mecca of the region, so we'll begin our "tour de huts" in this vicinity.

Timberloft Cottages is located a few minutes northeast of Helen on Highway 356. Traffic is light, so the cottages' close proximity to the roadway is not a problem. Each unit features a covered front porch, complete with old-fashioned swing. Careful landscaping shrouds each unit and many of the porches offer the added delight of a spa-bath surrounded by full-length draw curtains for additional privacy.

Inside, the cabin's one room includes a queen-size bed and small table and chair set in the carpeted front area. A massive stone fireplace with gas logs adorns one wall and the back section of the room consists of a tiny but fully-equipped kitchenette.

A separately-enclosed bath takes up the rest of the area. A ladder leads up to a sleeping loft containing a queen-size mattress. Rates are $65 to $99. For more information, call (706) 878-2950.

If you travel two miles west of Timberloft you arrive at **Unicoi State Park**. This development offers a 100-room lodge as well as cabins for rent.

Most unique at this park are the "Barrel Cottages," which have been constructed from sections of gigantic pipe. These attractive oddities have room for four people and are nestled into the hillside above the park's 53-acre lake.

Upstairs, each "Barrel" has a bath and a bedroom with two double beds. A complete living room and kitchen are located downstairs. The rustic appeal is enhanced by a wood-burning stove and a tree-canopied deck. Rates are $55 to $95. Two and three bedroom cabins are also available and rent for $65 to $135. For more information on these accommodations, call (706) 878-3982.

Approximately one mile northeast of Unicoi is **Tanglewood Cabins**. Tanglewood offers an exceptional variety of accommodations. All units are relatively new and beautifully maintained.

These facilities range from simple one-bedroom bungalows to sprawling six-bedroom "Ponderosas." Each cabin is tucked into its own wooded setting, giving its guests enjoyable seclusion while affording every modern convenience. Rates vary greatly, depending upon the accommodations and season. For more information on **Tanglewood**, call (706) 878-3286.

Ron and Diane Powell are the owners of three of the area's facilities: **Pine Ridge**,

Moonlight Ridge and Cherokee Ridge (706) 878-3290. These, too, offer travelers a great selection from which to choose. Other cabin accommodations in the area include: (1) **Blue Ridge Cabins** (706) 878-1773; (2) and **Chattahoochee Ridge Lodge and Cabins** (706) 878-3144; (3) **Dukes Creek Cabins** (706) 878-2625; (4) **Georgia Mountain Madness** (706) 878-2851; and **Lazy Bones Mountain Cottages** (706) 219-3630.

If you're looking for sheer scenic beauty and don't mind driving approximately 25 miles to enjoy Helen, some accommodations a little further outside of town like **Blood Mountain Cabins** will probably be more to your liking. Located on U.S. 129 North at 9894 Gainesville Highway, Blood Mountain Cabins are owned and operated by George Case. There is no better authority on the location of scenic waterfalls, cascading mountain streams, historic sites and great picnicking spots than Mr. Case, and the setting for his cabins is breath-taking.

And at 3,000 feet above sea level, Blood Mountain Cabins will get snow on many days when the rest of Georgia is only dreaming of it! Ironically, this property was originally designed as a ski resort many, many years ago.

The are 14 cabins at Blood Mountain Cabins. Each has one bath, a main level bedroom with a queen-size bed and a loft with a queen bed. Each also has a television, VCR and satellite reception for excellent television programming. Costs range from $79 to $99 per night, and $389 to $469 per week.

Approximately 15 miles from Helen on the Richard B. Russell Scenic Highway, Mr. Case also operates **Green Mansions** which is a development of exceptional log cabin rentals, each of which sleeps 2-6 people, and costs approximately $109 per night ($500 per week).

But maybe a cabin outside of town isn't exactly what you're seeking. . . There are a number of attractive inns and motels right in the downtown vicinity of Helen, allowing you to spend all your time right in town.

The downtown area is within walking distance of Helen's most prestigious resort – **Innsbruck**. Villas at this fine hostelry offer guests the opportunity to relax in a quiet atmosphere while having excellent access to additional facilities such as a fine golf course, swimming pool and tennis courts. For more information on this resort, call (800) 204-3536.

Only a couple of blocks off Main Street is **RiverBend Chalets**, cradled on the banks of the Chattahoochee River. Each of these charming cabins includes plenty of room for four adults, and features a spa bath, fireplace, and upstairs and downstairs baths.

After a full day of enjoying the sights, what better way to kick back and relax than to prop your feet on the railing of your own cabin getaway? No wonder there's such a rash of cabins springing up around this scenic little mountain resort deep in the north Georgia mountains. A word of caution while we're on the subject. . . Cabin fever is extremely difficult to get out of your system.

But let's assume a bed-and-breakfast inn is more to your liking. . . In many scenic and historic areas, the bed and breakfast inns are the new kid on the block. Not so here. Within and around the Helen area, B&Bs have been welcoming guests for decades. Many of the B&Bs, in fact, are historic sites themselves!

In the very heart of the little Alpine village is **Black Forest B&B**, a former art gallery. A stay at this inn offers guests the ultimate in convenience to all the downtown area has to offer. It's the perfect place for anyone who wants to park the car and forget about it until time to go home. (706) 878-3995.

Up on Ridge Road, you'll spy a miniature waterfall cascading down an ivy-covered hillside. And as you peer up through the foliage, you'll see **Dutch Cottage Bed and Breakfast**. This tranquil respite belongs to Heidi and Chuck Waldron, and offers three beautifully decorated rooms plus a separate "honeymoon" chalet.

Dutch Cottage is tastefully decorated with plenty of antiques, blue Delft and imported laces. Breakfast is served plentifully and buffet-style.

Hilltop Haus Bed and Breakfast sits high atop Chattahoochee Street. Guests can enjoy a rest on the deck overlooking the river, or stroll the short distance to the village center. Breakfast is served in the inn's plant-filled sunroom. (706) 878-2388.

One of the vicinity's earliest (and most historic) bed and breakfasts belongs to Libby Tucker, and is known as **Grampa's Room**. Located on Highway 17 in the historic **Sautee-Nacoochee Valley**, this faded flower of the past is only four miles from Helen, but worlds away in time.

To be referred to as a "faded flower" may seem uncomplimentary to some individuals, but one look at this grand old house and you'll see just how gracefully this "flower" has faded. To say that this home has character is a massive understatement.

Built around 1872 this aged inn has been serving traveling guests on and off since its earliest days. It was acquired by Mrs. Tucker's ancestors as soon as it was completed, and still has many of its original furnishings. Aside from the addition of electricity and plumbing, the structure seems untouched by time.

A "dog-trot"-style hallway runs the full length of the upper and lower levels. Two spacious bedrooms are available for guests. The Grampa's Room brochure promises guests a full country breakfast and it acknowledges acceptance of most major credit cards. It also states: "Barter is a consideration." (706) 878-2364.

Just down the road in Sautee, you'll find the **Nacoochee Valley Guest House**. An Oriental proverb displayed in the entranceway speaks volumes: "In the mountains we forget to count the days." This 1920s-era beauty helps visitors do just that.

The inn features three well-appointed guest rooms, such as **The Cherub Room** with a canopied king-size bed, fireplace and private entrance. A full and fabulous breakfast is served for guests.

The inn specializes in Country French cuisine and opens to the public for lunch and dinner. The mouth-watering entrees served here include Seafood Bernadette and Beef Wellington. For dessert, diners can feast upon Lemon Apricot Nectar Cake with Sabayon Sauce. (706) 878-3830.

Helen and the surrounding communities are wonderful destinations for any individuals seeking a sanity-saving "great escape." If you're a nature lover, you'll thrill to the area's wildlife (deer, raccoons and opossums abound), much of which is protected in state and national parks and preserves.

Cascading waterfalls and scenic hiking trails add to the natural beauty surrounding Helen. The famous **Appalachian Trail** snakes along the northern border of White County just a few miles from Helen. You'll also find **Amicalola Falls State Park** off Highway 52 west of Dahlonega. This scenic cascade plummets 700 feet and is easily reached by a short trail. Northeast of Helen on Highway 356 is **Unicoi State Park** and **Anna Ruby Falls**. Viewing these lovely twin falls requires only a 0.4 mile walk. Other nearby scenic falls include **Duke's Creek, Raven Cliff, Helton Creek** and **DeSoto Falls**.

Brasstown Bald, Georgia's highest peak is located off Highway 180 northeast of Helen.

At 4,784 feet, this lofty mountain (by eastern U.S. standards) affords magnificent views. The Visitors Center offers a multi-media presentation and a gift shop. And over near the town of Hiawassee, visitors can enjoy the amenities of **Moccasin Creek State Park** and take a tour of the adjacent **Lake Burton Fish Hatchery**.

While you're in the Hiawassee area, don't overlook the opportunity to enjoy the sights and sounds of the **Georgia Mountain Fairgrounds** (seasonal) and the series of country music concerts held there each spring, summer and autumn (Tel.: 706-896-4191).

Art lovers will appreciate the abundance of local galleries. Cleveland's **Mary T's Antiques and Collectibles** offers an excellent selection of goods. And for the discriminating collector, **Artique of Lake Chatague** in Hiawassee features exceptionally fine art and sculpture.

But you really don't have to leave Helen to see most anything mentioned above. Main Street is home to oodles of specialty shops. **Tekakwitha** deals in authentic Native American art. **Carol's Christmas Shop** carries a vast array of decorations, collectibles and gift items. **Kaiser Bill's** claim to fame is as one of the largest beer stein dealers in the world. He also keeps on hand a number of unusual collectibles such as die-cast banks and Lefton and Spencer Collin lighthouses.

There's no shortage of good food around either. Right on Main Street, you have a wide choice of cuisines ranging from **The Wurst Haus**, featuring Schaller & Weber gourmet wursts to **Paul's On The River**, offering steaks and seafood.

During the summer months, tubing is a favorite Helen pastime. The **Chattahoochee River** lazily winds its way through the village, and companies like **Flea Market Tubing** and **Cool River Tubing** provide tubes and transport tubers back to their vehicles after a long refreshing ride downstream.

Whatever your preferences (within reasonable confines), Helen can fill the bill. Shoppers, dining enthusiasts, outdoorsmen, golfers – whatever your interests – Helen and its neighboring communities present a veritable smorgasbord of activities options. Top that with the tranquility of its magnificent forests, clear running streams, majestic mountains, interesting historic sites and much more, and you'll still have only part of the picture.

The best way to describe Helen? You just have to see it for yourself.

Hiawassee

The Fieldstone Inn

Just as described in the best-selling novel *Deliverance* by author **James A. Dickey**, an entire community disappeared beneath the waters of the huge hydroelectric project in north Georgia's Towns County in 1939-40. With it, the land, legacy and way of life for many north Georgia mountaineers were swallowed up as the lake waters rose. One of these individuals, however, was determined to retain a foothold in the vicinity. He returned a number of years later to create the now popular **Fieldstone Inn** in Hiawassee.

Travelers driving down U.S. Highway 76 in extreme north Georgia pass the impressive mountain inn on the edge of Lake Chatuge in Towns County. The founder, **Bob Cloer**, is understandably proud of the Fieldstone, now a popular destination for weekend getaways, summer vacations, conferences, business meetings and family get-togethers. The Cloer family success, however, is tinged with irony.

Early Life

Bessie Cloer, Bob's mother, was interviewed in 1996 at the age of 89. She said that despite "progress," she still yearned for "the good old days, back before the lake came."

Bessie's father had moved his family to Towns County from North Carolina in 1914, seeking something better for his children. The family raised everything they ate. They had a patch of syrup cane; they grew corn and wheat which they took to the local grist mill to be ground into meal and flour, and of course, they had a substantial vegetable garden.

"Mother always kept chickens and we had cows," Bessie continued. "I milked the cows from the time I was big enough to reach them." She says she also churned milk to make butter.

Bessie described both her parents as extremely resourceful. They had to be. Those were hard times, but to Bessie and her family, it was just life.

When she was sixteen, Bessie says she married Wiley Cloer, who was twenty. They lived with his mother at Woods Grove community near the present site of the Fieldstone Inn. The actual spot of their former home is covered today by Lake Chatuge. Had it not been, her son Bob, no doubt would have erected a memorial on the site.

Wylie and Bessie ultimately became the parents of four children – Carl, Bob, Shirley, and George.

Arrival Of The Lake

At first, the residents of Hiawassee didn't understand when they heard all the talk about a dam being built by the Tennessee Valley Authority (TVA) to create a a huge reservoir. Eventually, however, they each were told they had to sell their land and move away. They would be paid for their land, but they had to move away – no exceptions.

The Cloers received $6,500 for forty acres of farm land and ten acres of mountain property. "We had never sold or bought land before, so we knew very little about its value," Bessie lamented.

The Cloers eventually found a little patch of land across U.S. Highway 76 and slightly west of the Fieldstone Inn. A moving company from Greenville, South Carolina, moved the old family home on rollers for the approximate one-mile distance to the new site.

A few years later, the Cloers bought land from Paul Dyer who also lived near the present location of the Fieldstone Inn. When the impounded water from Lake Chatuge didn't completely cover it, an additional tract of land – purchased by TVA from Vernon Kimsey – was later sold by TVA to Wiley Cloer. It was on this piece of property that the Fieldstone Inn would later be built.

Tourism In Towns

Wiley Cloer – as resourceful as ever – apparently decided to take advantage of the situation, even if it had practically destroyed his community. He built a boat dock, as well as the first fishing boats used on the new lake. And he began charging $1.50 a day for boat rentals.

It was then that he realized that people who came to fish for a day needed a place to spend the night. The first visitor over-nighted in the Cloer home one weekend and then asked if there were any public accommodations for the future.

Wiley quickly explained he had a second house with apartments. The Cloers eventually began keeping overnighters, providing 20 beds in all and charging $1.00 per person a night for a room.

Then came the meals. In retrospect, it's kind of difficult to decide who got the best deal – the Cloer family or the fishermen.

"I had never eaten out in my life," Bessie laughed in remembrance, "and I didn't know what would be a fair price, so I asked the fishermen. They suggested fifty cents a meal."

Though fifty cents a meal sounds like rather lean pickings, it must be remembered that the Cloers produced practically everything they needed. And by this point, they were also able to buy a freezer to stockpile perishables.

Bessie's meals included a meat, vegetables, desserts, and biscuits and cornbread. For breakfasts, she served ham, sausage, and red-eye gravy. "Some of the men would have contests to see who could eat the most biscuits," she smiled appreciatively. "I'd take biscuits out of the oven and they were gone before I could turn around."

Approximately 25 to 30 people eventually began arriving for the weekends in season, so Bessie finally had to get some help. She was already doing all the cleaning and washing all the dishes and bed linens (75 sheets at a time) herself.

Idea For An Inn

Bob tried his best to get his father to borrow money to build a motel, saying, "It's going to come," but Wiley had never borrowed a cent in his life, and he wasn't about to begin at that late date.

Bessie was always concerned about her children's education, and the fact that there was no money for that. She always told Bob, "Get an education and get out of here."

Her son eventually heeded her admonitions, obtaining not only an undergraduate degree, but a law degree as well from the University of Georgia. He decided, however, against the law profession, opting instead to become a builder.

In 1987, in the midst of his building career, Bob finally decided to fulfill his dream of a real estate development on Lake Chatuge. Bob built his mountain hotel, naming it the Fieldstone Inn. In February of 2002, Bob Cloer sold The Fieldstone to Richard and Dana Pelham.

Amenities

Under the guidance of the Pelham family, The Fieldstone Inn has been transformed into **The Fieldstone Resort**. Set on the western bank of **Lake Chatuge**, the Fieldstone has 66 well-appointed guest rooms with outstanding views of the mountains and lake. All rooms have walk-out balconies and two double beds or a king-size bed. Some executive suites include personal spa-baths. The main conference center at the resort was expanded to seat over 200, and a new poolside conference room was added.

With over $6.5 million in renovations to the property, The Fieldstone Resort has become one of the premier destination resorts of the southern Appalachians. The improvements include the **Watercrest Restaurant** – a Four-Star fine dining establishment, the new **Yacht Club**, and the **Lakeside Tavern & Grill** located in the marina at Fieldstone. **The Fieldstone Marina** now offers a full line of new boats and services as well as a rental fleet of over 60 pontoons, jet skis, bass boats, canoes, kayaks and sailboats. **Mountain Adventures**, a full-service outfitters which opened in 2003, provides everything from whitewater trips to Appalachian Trail hikes. Over 30 new condominiums which are available for purchase or weekly rentals have been built as well.

Just a few minutes away from The Fieldstone, is the famed **Georgia Mountain Fairgrounds**. This historic mountain music event is held each summer in Hiawassee. The equally popular **Spring** and **Fall Music Festivals** are big attractions at the Fairgrounds as well, as is a fiddler's convention in October. For more information about the dates, times and reservations for these events, call the **Georgia Mountain Fair** at **706-896-4191**.

(The Fieldstone Inn is open year-round, and is located three miles west of Hiawassee on U.S. Highway 76.)

Highlands, NC

A Scenic Travel Route thru NE GA to Highlands

One driving route through north Georgia to Highlands, North Carolina, offers a variety of historic sites along the way – if one knows where to look. And the scenic town of Highlands just across the Georgia state line can offer a bounty of relaxation and entertainment too – in both summer and winter.

North Georgia has many scenic backroads and byways which travelers can enjoy on a drive through the mountains. The trick is deciding which one you can enjoy the most.

One very scenic route through north Georgia to North Carolina is from Dahlonega to Clarkesville to Tallulah Falls, and ultimately, to Highlands, North Carolina. This route is much like the scenic drive through the Sautee-Nacoochee Valley in White County. If you follow the older backroads, you can catch a glimpse of many historic sites from yesteryear, and enjoy scenic vistas not available on the superhighways.

This article is designed for travelers from the Atlanta area, but may be used by visitors from almost any area *south of Lumpkin County*. We'll begin our driving tour at the intersection of Georgia 400 Highway and Georgia Highway 60 in Lumpkin. Press or click your mileage calculator/odometer at this point until it reads "0." I'll be pointing out sites along the way based upon the mileage from the Georgia 400 – Highway 60 intersection, so you'll need to keep track of the miles. Also, you won't be able to venture off the route described in this article. If you do, the mileage calculator in your automobile will not be coordinated with the milemarks described in this article.

If one is headed north on Georgia 400, it dead-ends at Georgia Highway 60. Immediately across this intersection, another smaller road continues on into Lumpkin County. This road has been known for many years as **Longbranch Road.**

Lumpkin County

Very near this beginning of Longbranch (approximately where the large gasoline/quickstop market exists today on the right side of the road), a pioneer home from yesteryear still stood until the late 1990s. This home, built by **Merritt M. London**, was probably constructed sometime in the 1860s. Merritt was 28 years of age when he married 17-year-old **Mary Neisler** in Lumpkin County in 1859.

The old **London home** was quite historic, and it is sad that it had to be lost to new development. It was at this site (actually in the little store which once stood next to the home) that, according to accounts, infamous **Old West outlaw Bill Miner** stopped in 1911 to purchase supplies following his last robbery.

Unbeknownst to the London family, Miner, who was wanted in California and numerous other towns for murder and stagecoach holdups, had robbed Southern Railway's Train Number 36 just north of Gainesville on February 18, 1911, escaping with a cache of valuables. An article in the February, 1911 *Dahlonega Nugget* newspaper recorded that one of Miner's accomplices in the robbery ate breakfast at the home of **W.H. Early** (brother-in-law of Merritt London). The **W.H. Early home** still stands as of this writing at mile-mark 1.3 on the left side of Longbranch Road a short distance from the former site of the London home.

The *Nugget* article goes on to explain the outlaws purchased tobacco and candy at **McGuire's Soda Fountain** and six boxes of snuff in **J.W. Moore's store** in Dahlonega. The determined thieves later put the snuff in their shoes to confuse the dogs they knew would be tracking them.

Miner and his two accomplices reportedly split up at this point. Miner was later captured in the little community of Nimblewill northwest of Dahlonega. More information on the interesting chase and capture of this bandit may be obtained in *A North Georgia Journal of History, Volume I*, available from Legacy Communications.

Continuing on up Longbranch Road, it eventually intersects with Highway 52 East. Turn right onto to Highway 52. On the right side of the road at mile-mark 5.2, you will see historic **Mt. Gilead Church** and the remnants of a community known as "Garland." This portion of Highway 52 is part of the old road between Gainesville and Dahlonega, and many pioneer travelers once passed through this vicinity, some settling to mine gold and farm the rich bottomlands here, and some continuing westward.

At mile-mark 6.8, the old road leading to the **Clermont Hotel** is seen on the right. This historic structure was built in 1911-1912 beside the tracks of the **Gainesville-Northwestern Railroad** which once existed between Gainesville in Hall County and Robertstown in White County. Visit this old hotel on another trip to the mountains, since any departure from our established route today will disorganize our mile-marker calculations. Additional details about the hotel and the town of Clermont can also be found in *Volume I* of the hardbound *A North Georgia Journal of History*.

In the same general vicinity of mile-mark 6.8, Highway 115 to Cleveland branches off to the left. Take this road and continue toward Cleveland.

White County

At mile-mark 16, the turn-off for old **Tesnatee Gap Road** is visible on the left. It was in this general vicinity that another very colorful pioneer of Lumpkin County – **Harrison Riley** – once had a plantation and home in White County. Riley was a fiery businessman and politician who owned – among many other things – the **Eagle Hotel** which once stood on the south side of the town square in Dahlonega.

Because of his great wealth, and because Riley did not believe in keeping his money in a bank, it was believed that a treasure-trove was buried by Riley inside or around his plantation home near Tesnatee Gap. Today, the site is pock-marked with pits and excavations where looters have searched for Riley's buried silver and gold. If such a treasure actually did exist, and if all or part of it were in gold coins minted at the old **U.S. Branch Mint** which once existed in Dahlonega, it would be worth hundreds of thousands, if not millions of dollars today.

At mile-mark 16.8 in Cleveland, Underwood Street branches off (from Highway 115) to the right. (Again, do not venture off onto Underwood Street, since it is not on our planned route. Remain on Highway 115) A short distance up this street, **Babyland General Hospital** stands. It was here that White County native **Xavier Roberts** began his "**Little People**" creations which eventually attracted world-wide attention in the 1970s and '80s, ultimately becoming a pop phenomenon and creating a multi-million dollar business enterprise.

It was also along the vicinity occupied today by Underwood Street, that the original pioneer village of **Mount Yonah** once existed in the years between the 1830s and the 1850s. The early roots of present-day White County are found along this street.

Back on Highway 115 at mile-mark 17.2, **Old White County Courthouse** on the town square in Cleveland is visible on the left. This historic structure, completed in 1860, was built of bricks molded and fired by black slaves somewhere in the vicinity of Mount Yonah. The walls of the courthouse are 16 inches thick at ground level.

This historic hall of justice has witnessed many long years of growth in the county, and has dispensed judgements for many criminals. It continued to be used until 1964, when a more modern facility was constructed a short distance away. During the U.S. Civil War, troops were mustered and practiced close-quarter drills on the grounds immediately surrounding the courthouse.

At mile-mark 18.2, one of the sites at which a convicted criminal was executed is visible on the right. On September 10, 1906, White County resident Bob Moore, a Negro convicted of the rape of a young female, was executed at this spot. Moore was conveyed, under heavy guard, to a gallows which had been erected on the right side of present-day Highway 115 North, a short distance north of the present-day site of Truett-McConnell College.

Clarkesville

At mile-mark 30.2, the highway enters the town square of historic Clarkesville. At this point, turn left and continue northward on "**Historic 441 Highway**." There will be several points at which you will have an opportunity to access the more modern four-lane version of Highway 441, but I encourage you to resist these and remain on "Historic 441," at least until you reach **Tallulah Falls** where you will have no further choice but to join the new route. The old historic route between Clarkesville and Tallulah Falls is much more scenic and enjoyable to travel.

After turning left at the courthouse in Clarkesville, the road makes a sharp turn back to the right and heads north. At this sharp right turn, a small shop – now used for other purposes – once sold mountain crafts, gifts and collectibles. Two strangers once stopped in here on a scenic driving tour of their own. They were **Burt Reynolds** and **Loni Anderson**, headed to Burt's second home (which he later lost to Loni in their divorce settlement) a short distance across the Georgia state line in North Carolina. A photograph of them in happier days in this shop in Clarkesville is still in the possession of the former owner of this business.

Still headed north on Historic 441 Highway, if you look to the left at mile-mark 34.2, you will see an ancient-looking home with a Georgia Historic Commission marker in the front yard. This historic structure reportedly was originally built as the summer home of **Joseph Habersham** of Savannah (1751-1815). Habersham was a Georgia patriot, Revolutionary War hero, and political leader. He was a colonel in the Continental Army, a member of the Continental Congress, and of the Georgia Convention which ratified the U.S. Constitution in 1788. Habersham County, created December 19, 1818, was named in his honor.

Interestingly, though the historic marker in the front yard of this home which identifies it as the summer home of Joseph Habersham was erected by the Georgia Historic Commission, at least one representative of the Georgia Department of Natural Resources, Parks & Historic Sites Division, maintains that this home was not actually Habersham's summer home at all. Therefore, some doubt surrounds the identity of this site today, but it, nevertheless, remains a very historic structure in its own right.

At mile-mark 35.5, a portion of one of the original pioneer trails – the **Unicoi Turnpike** – is visible on the left. This route was an important pedestrian and oxcart trail during the years of the infancy of the state of Georgia. Indians and pioneers alike moved westward along this route.

At mile-mark 38.8, and again at mile-marker 39, a long section of the roadbed of what once was the fabled **Tallulah Falls Railroad** is visible on the right side of the highway. This historic rail line, begun in 1898, was last used in 1961. That same year, the line's insolvency ultimately caused it to be shut down permanently. It had provided transportation for 63 years for the timber, hydro-electric power construction, highway construction and wood products industries. The route once ran from Cornelia, Georgia to Franklin, North Carolina, carrying the U.S. mails and other supplies to inaccessible mountainous areas. It quite likely would still be in use today had it ever been completed to Almond, North Carolina, or another site offering a connection with a major line. Unfortunately, due to its short-line status, it eventually worked itself out of a job.

The Tallulah Falls Railroad was such a scenic line, that it caught the eye of several major Hollywood filmmakers in the 1950s, not the least of which were **Walt Disney** (in 1955 with *The Great Locomotive Chase* starring **Fess Parker**, **Slim Pickens** and others), and **Henry King** (in 1950 with *I'd Climb The Highest Mountain*, starring **Susan Hayward**, **Rory Calhoun**, **William Lundigan**, **Gene Lockhart**, **Barbara Bates**, and **Alexander Knox**).

Tallulah Falls

At mile-mark 42.7, the traveler will finally be forced to access the modern four-lane version of U.S. Highway 441. At mile-mark 43.6, you will see a turn-off (on the right) for another portion of old historic Highway 441. If you take this little loop, you will be able to see some interesting shops (which have existed at this site for at least 50 or 60 years), as well as a breathtaking view of **Tallulah Gorge**.

At mile-mark 44.6, you will enter the little

community of Tallulah Falls. If you look to your left at this point, you will see the old **Tallulah Falls Railroad Depot**. I encourage you to stop at this site, since it contains the products of Co-Op Crafts, a non-profit organization dedicated to the sales of mountain products and crafts items handcrafted by mountain artisans. Items such as quilts, novelties, dolls, books, and myriad other items may be purchased here. (Also, since this site is quite near the highway, you won't badly upset the odometer accuracy of your car as associated with the mile-mark designations I will continue to give you for interesting sites ahead.)

The Tallulah Falls Depot remains today in its original site, and as one drives up Highway 441 toward the depot, he or she is actually driving on the original route of the Tallulah Falls Railroad as it emerged from the brow of Tallulah Gorge. The historic little town of Tallulah Falls was once a very popular tourist resort from the 1890s to the 1920s, with scores of huge hotels along the gorge. Unfortunately, in 1921, a horrendous fire – spread by cyclonic winds – destroyed most of the town. Since the thunderous falls which once had attracted tourists had already been choked off in 1911 by the large hydro-electric dam on the Tallulah River, there no longer was a great attraction to the site, and after the fire, the little town simply was never re-built.

Clayton / Rabun Gap

At mile-mark 55.6, you will enter the town of Clayton. This community gradually grew up over the years at this point due to several Indian and pioneer trails which intersected in this vicinity.

At mile-mark 58.7, the nationally-acclaimed *Foxfire* Museum and headquarters building is visible on the left. Also at this same general site at the junction of Highway 441 with Black Rock Mountain Road, an aged hotel once stood. Portions of the acclaimed major motion picture *Deliverance*, starring **Burt Reynolds, Jon Voight** and **Ned Beatty**, were filmed in this structure, now long gone.

At mile-mark 59.9, additional remnants of the Tallulah Falls Railroad – as well as the turn-off to the historic **York House** – may be seen on the right side of the road. Immediately opposite this site, on the left side of U.S. Highway 441, the old Fisher home, with its aged cylindrical

farm silo, may be seen. It was in the Fisher home on July 19, 1983, that a horrible double-murder was committed. The circumstances surrounding this heinous crime were never completely solved.

At mile-mark 61.8, teacher-historian **Dess Oliver** has – with the help of others – constructed a museum (right side of the road) with relics and information concerning the Tallulah Falls Railroad. Oliver operates a very interesting shop full of memorabilia involving the historic line, and is happy to answer questions on the history of the area. When he's not operating the shop, he teaches at **Rabun Gap-Nacoochee School**, a private educational facility across the highway up on the beautiful hills visible in the distance.

Rabun Gap-Nacoochee School, historic in its own right, was also the birthplace of the famed *Foxfire* program, having been started there by Eliot Wigginton in the 1960s. The organization later found a new student body at nearby Rabun County High School, where the well-known magazine is still produced today.

A short distance beyond the turn-off for the famed **Dillard House Restaurant**, Georgia Highway 246 (later Carolina 106) turns off to the right and heads steeply up into the Appalachian Mountains. At this point, you're really headed up into the high country (at least for the eastern United States) toward Highlands, North Carolina.

Highlands, NC

Highlands is enjoyable almost any time of the year. In the colder months, you will avoid the crowds and still be able to enjoy a cozy bed and breakfast inn with a cheery fire in the hearth, good restaurants, some moderate snow skiing opportunities, and interesting shops and scenery. In the summer months, there are more people, but there are also more open shops, activities, Jeep four-wheel driving tours, fishing opportunities, scenic swimming holes at any number of waterfalls and lakes in the area, camping sites, and much more.

The temperature extremes at this higher altitude (over 4,000 feet) can be surprising too. Even on a hot 88-degree summer day in the lowlands of Georgia, the daytime temperature in Highlands may drop as low as 59 degrees Fahrenheit.

The Highlands area also enjoys an abundance of rainfall. The annual average rainfall in Highlands is 79.47 inches, which, in itself, isn't an excessive amount. However, the area often gets considerably more rainfall. In 1916, 120 inches inundated the area; in 1949, 107 inches fell; in 1979, 116 inches soaked the town, and as recently as 1982, 92 inches of precipitation were recorded. In just a ten-day period in 1964, 26 inches of rain fell in Highlands. The downfall was so overwhelming that there was much concern as to whether the Lake Sequoyah dam would hold if either the Mirror Lake or the **Highlands Country Club** dams gave way. Fortunately, both dams held.

Conversely, Highlands can also get a lot of snow in the wintertime too. In January of 1887, snow fell to a depth of 36 inches and the temperature dropped to 19 degrees below zero. In the winter of 1959-60, an amazing 68 inches of snow fell on the town.

It is the cozy quaintness of Highlands which attracts most visitors to this little burg. Most of the early settlers in the town arrived in the 1870s and 1880s. The site, however, had been inhabited long before these pioneers. In 1981, when a farm field was plowed in the vicinity, hundreds of arrowheads and other relics from Native Americans of long ago were unearthed. Native Americans apparently also enjoyed the cool climes of this vicinity in the summers of long ago.

Over the years, the beauty of Highlands has attracted the wealthy and renowned to its heights. Some of the more well-known individuals who have either visited or purchased homes in Highlands have included **Clark Howell**, a well-known early editor of the *Atlanta Constitution*; **Norman Rockwell**; baseball legend **Tyrus "Ty" Cobb**; early golfing star **Bobby Jones**; **Robert W. Woodruff** of Coca Cola and philanthropic fame; author **Stephen Vincent Benet**, and many others.

The **Highlands Country Club** was built in the 1920s, as were its very scenic golfing links. This enhanced the town's reputation as a spot for refined leisure entertainment. In the 1920s and '30s, golfing great Bobby Jones owned a summer home near the club.

Today, there are a number of attractive country inns and B&Bs for guests. These include the **Kelsey-Hutchinson Inn** and the **Main Street Inn**, both of which would be suitable for most travelers interested in quiet, clean, and well-appointed accommodations.

Built in 1885, the Main Street Inn, is both scenic and historic. It was recently renovated, and offers spacious, airy rooms with large comfortable beds, clean baths, stone fireplaces, as well as cable television and telephones in the rooms.

Main Street Inn also offers meals in a nice dining room and a comfortable reading area with a warm fire in the lobby. Outside, it has large trees shading a well-kept lawn with attractive flowers and shrubs. It is also near the middle of the downtown area, offering easy access to shops, restaurants and attractions. Take your wife or sweetheart to this spot. You'll be glad you did.

The many restaurants in Highlands are too numerous to mention. Suffice it to say there are more than enough to please almost any palate – whether one has expensive or inexpensive tastes.

A word to the uninitiated. . . Don't drive to Highlands looking for shopping bargains. Opportunities do exist, but they are few and far between. Highlands isn't necessarily an expensive travel destination, but in the words of a wise old sage – "It ain't cheap, either." The designers and town fathers have intentionally maintained the community in this fashion, in order to discourage what many people refer to as "riff-raff." There are, however, a smattering of attractive spots for inexpensive meals and entertainment.

The many scenic waterfalls in the Highlands vicinity offer a wide array of eye-candy. One particularly captivating drive is out Highway 64 West, where Bridal Veil Falls, Dry Falls, Kalakalaeskies Falls, Lower Cullasaja Falls, and others decorate the mountainsides.

In the wintertime, nearby Scaly Mountain offers snow-tubing and snow-skiing for beginners. Farther up in North Carolina, better skiing accommodations are available.

Highlands can be a very restful spot to pass time. If you have a summer home or rental on Mirror Lake, you could probably spend each summer in this environment. It can be that appealing as a getaway opportunity. However, if you're staying in a bed & breakfast inn or one of the other accommodations in town, you'll probably be ready to move on in three or four days.

Have a great time, and as an old friend of mine says, "Keep the wind at your back."

Homer

Before dawn each **Easter Sunday**, family and friends of the late Homer Mayor M.E. "Buster" Garrison, start bringing the water in huge black cast-iron pots to 212 degrees Fahrenheit in temperature. For several hours, they boil thousands of eggs for the annual Easter Egg hunt held there. This event, has been listed in the **Guinness Book of World Records** as "the *world's largest and longest-running egg hunt.*"

The World's Largest Easter Egg Hunt

The Garrison family provides the event free of charge to the public. This year, members of the Garrison family maintain they will once again boil around 70,000 eggs.

Volunteers dye the eggs a wide range of colors, while others continue to boil the little objects. "Carriers" run with colanders filled with freshly cooked eggs to supply the dyers. By the time the dyers have finished, they have bright coloring all over their arms and spattered on their faces and clothing.

The dyed eggs are then placed in cartons and packed in huge boxes. More volunteers later pack trucks with the boxes and drive them out to the two large fields in front of the Garrison homes.

At the same time, another truck filled with youngsters eases through the rolling fields. The children throw out huge handfuls of cellophane-wrapped candied eggs into the grass (a total of 80,000) yelling "Happy Easter" as they throw. They don't try to hide these eggs – just provide a tasty treat for participants.

Another truck drives more slowly through the fields as two men set out boxes of boiled eggs every few feet. These eggs are more carefully distributed and hidden in the fields. Some of them (approximately 125) are "prize eggs" which can be exchanged for a live bunny, a stuffed bunny, or an Easter basket.

Members of the Garrison family maintain they have no idea what the event costs. They do know, however, that it generates a lot of fun and goodwill. Just as was stated by Mr. Garrison many times over the years, the family maintains that "Whatever it costs, it's worth it. We don't keep up with the cost. We just pay as we go along."

At noon on the day of the storied event, the Garrisons provide a lunch for the weary volunteers at the Garrison homes. There, the volunteers also receive gift T-shirts that read, *"I was a worker at the World's Largest Easter Egg Hunt"* on the back.

Shortly thereafter, the crowds begin arriving, parking at nearby schools and wherever they can find space. Kids, many dressed in their Easter finery, find a spot to wait for the exciting hunt to begin. Thousands of local residents participate in the event, but visitors from far and wide often arrive too. In the past, people from as far away as Pennsylvania and California have participated.

At exactly 2:00 p.m., a Garrison family member takes a loud speaker and explains the rules of the event to everyone. He points out that children of all ages (right up to adults) will scavenge one field, but that the other field is reserved for children six and under. At a given signal (usually a siren) thousands of people will race out to search for and scoop up eggs in their baskets.

John Faulkner, 35, of Homer, says "Hey, I've been here every year since I can remember. I'll bet I've found a hundred dozen eggs over the years." He says he continues to come so that his kids "can have just as much enjoyment as I did when I was their age."

Needless to say, the Garrisons plan to continue the tradition.

(To reach the Easter Egg Hunt site from Atlanta, take Interstate 85 north to Exit 149, and take Hwy 441 North to Homer. Turn left onto GA 51 W and the Garrison home is on the left, across from Banks County Primary School. No reservations are required for this event. For further information, call the Banks County Chamber of Commerce at 800-638-5004 or 706-677-2108.)

Lake Lanier

Lake Lanier Outdoor Adventure

If power and majesty best characterize **Lake Sidney Lanier**, then peace and tranquility must also be considered hallmarks of this impressive body of water in northeast Georgia. With a landscape so beautiful and inviting, it's not surprising that more and more visitors and residents alike take every opportunity to enjoy the recreational opportunities afforded here. From hot boating, fishing, and swimming to picnicking, camping, and pleasure-cruising, Lanier is one of America's favorite lakes today. . . . the most visited in the nation.

It is a lake with vast scenic vistas reached by boat, where even the silence has a sound of its own. There are 38,000 acres of water with 540 miles of shoreline that extend into five Georgia counties: Dawson, Forsyth, Hall, Gwinnett and Lumpkin.

But Lake Sidney Lanier has not always existed. In fact, it is a relatively new man-made body of water with a very interesting background.

The lake was named in honor of the 19th century native Georgian poet, **Sidney Clopton Lanier**. He was so inspired by Georgia's beauty, he composed the well-known *Song of the Chattahoochee*. It is the mighty **Chattahoochee River** which gives life to Lanier.

It wasn't until 1946, that the Georgia state legislature authorized the development program which would put the Chattahoochee River basin to work for the new and growing population of the region. The project was assigned to the **United States Army Corps of Engineers**. It became their responsibility to design, develop and build a series of five dams and lakes in company with the Chattahoochee River.

During 1950, approximately 58,000 acres were acquired and set aside after painstaking negotiations with thousands of landowners. To develop the 540 miles of shoreline of Lanier, the Army engineers had to clear some 14,000 acres of forest land. As they progressed, obstacles such as grave sites and buildings had to be relocated to other areas. However, natural impediments such as trees, etc., were left as they were and remain today beneath the shimmering waters of the huge impoundment.

Construction Of The Dam

In 1953, construction was begun on Buford Dam and the three "saddle dikes" which impound the waters of Lanier. Little did anyone know, that the soon-to-be-completed lake would shortly be providing not only water and electricity for the region, but recreational pursuits as well .

The 192-feet-high by 2,360-feet-long dam was constructed across the original river channel and on top of raw earth instead of concrete, to control construction costs. The total length of the saddle dike system is 6,600 feet.

Just west of the dam and within an excavated depression in solid rock, construction of a large concrete electrical powerhouse was completed in 1956. It is in this powerhouse that the machinery for electrical generation is housed and operated. Three powerful generators have the capability of producing up to 86,000 kilowatts of hydroelectricity – clean, non-polluting power for some 25,000 homes.

Although power can be generated at this site at the flick of a switch, the energy which is created is not storable. It, therefore, must be utilized at the time of production, and as such, is mainly produced during the peak usage periods of summer afternoons. To generate this power, water enters the gated in-take structure and flows through penstocks (tunnels) to the powerhouse. There, the force of the water rotates huge turbines which are connected to generators. After its power is spent, the water is then returned back into the riverbed downstream.

Static water-flow from the lake back into the Chattahoochee is regulated from the powerhouse as well. The dam's giant valves can easily release water through its 100-feet-wide spillway chute, an action which can quickly raise the water-level of the Chattahoochee. Before any release takes place at **Buford Dam**, a powerful horn is sounded to warn fishermen and others on the river of the impending deluge. Once the chute is opened, the river rises suddenly and dramatically. Caution must be exercised when fishing below the dam.

Not only was the dam created to provide a source of electrical generation and drinking water in the area, it was also designed to support the tremendous anticipated industrial growth of Georgia and to become the primary source of water for Atlanta.

Preceding the dedication of Buford Dam, another dam – **Morgan Falls Dam** – a short distance downstream was constructed as a means of impounding and re-regulating the flow of river-water from Buford Dam. It also helps to provide Atlanta with water during the periods of time when it is most needed.

A North Georgia Playground

Recreational opportunities, fishing, and wildlife management are major features which were eventually included as public benefits for the millions of visitors to this huge man-made project. Management of these natural resources requires the joint efforts of the very dedicated persons employed by the **Georgia Department of Natural Resources** (DNR) and the **U.S. Army Corps of Engineers** (Mobile District), with assistance provided by the **U.S. Fish and Wildlife Service.** From these organizations, biologists, law enforcement officials, engineers, park rangers and many others keep the lake safe and in peak condition. They also control the lake level for proper fish reproduction, enforce wildlife regulations, and assist in the maintenance of nesting habitat for wildfowl.

Lake Lanier has become a major refuge for now-abundant species of wildlife, fish and plant life. Endangered species such as the Southern bald eagle and the peregrin falcon have taken refuge within the protected confines of the forests surrounding the lake. Their protection is just one of the many reasons the Corps of Engineers is so quick to cite developers and owners around the lake for any rules infractions.

The Corps' park rangers enforce Title 36

of the Code of Federal Regulations which governs how the public is allowed to use the lake. These rules and regulations were enacted with the intent of ensuring public safety and the protection of the lake's environment. Boating regulations are a joint effort of the Corps and the Georgia Department of Natural Resources.

When the 45 million dollar Buford Dam and Lake Lanier were officially opened during 1957, it was estimated that approximately a quarter of a million people visited this wonderland. And a wonderland it is, with approximately 20 million visitors a year today. Of some 76 recreational areas, the Corps oversees 49 park areas, including nine campgrounds, 40 day-time parks and 54 boat launching areas. Corps officials also constantly review the development and operation of parks operated by state, county and city governments. Because of serious environmental concerns, they routinely test the water and maintain a constant vigil for pollution.

Lake Lanier Islands (LLI) includes the acclaimed one-and-one-half-mile white sand beach – reportedly the longest inland man-made white sand beach in the nation. The water park at LLI offers more thrills than anyone can imagine.

For avid boaters and game fishermen, the lake offers a rich harvest of trout and bass. The 12 to 14-inch spotted bass are very abundant and largemouth bass are increasing in number, averaging from one and one-half pounds to five pounds or more in the upper third region of the lake. There have been eight-pound spotted bass, 16-pound largemouth and one lucky angler landed a whopping 46-pound striped bass.

For the past several years, Lake Lanier has held the title of being the most visited federally operated lake in the nation. In fairness, it could also easily be called "Hotlanta's Hot Boat Playground."

{For additional information, call: Lake Lanier and Buford Dam (770)-945-1467. Information on Lake Lanier Islands Beach & Water Park may be obtained at (770)-932-7200 or (800)-840-LAKE.}

The aged building which today houses Louie Caro's Italian restaurant on **Lake Rabun** in **Lakemont** is so old, it actually leans a bit to one side. The sturdy structure, however, has a lot of life left in it, and Louie's Italian dishes are generating renewed interest in this historic lakefront community.

The structure, in fact, was originally built as a cafe. Back in the 1920s after Mr. M.E. Crowe had built his **Lake Rabun Hotel** on the rise across the road, he knew he needed an additional building in which to serve meals to his patrons.

Louie's On The Lake

The little building doubled as a dance-hall in the 1920s and '30s too. On Saturday nights, the tables and chairs would be moved to one side and an honest-to-goodness mountain square dance would be held in the middle of the big room.

All of this has done nothing but add character to the structure in which Louie Caro is serving up some delicious meals today.

"I bought this building after it had been abandoned a couple of years," Caro explains with a smile. He has painted the structure a deep green with a rust-brown trim to "to resemble the changing of the leaves in the fall," he adds.

Atlanta magazine named Louie's pizza as *"the best"* two years in a row. In a rustic, casual family setting, he and his family prepare all the dishes at Louie's On The Lake themselves.

After hiring a young lady as a waitress, Louie wound up marrying her. Today, Stacy does a bit of everything – making up menus, keeping the books, etc. Caro's cousin, Anna Maria, is a talented Italian cook as well, and she helps in the kitchen.

Louie's dishes bear no resemblance to mass-produced items sold by chain pizza-makers. "Everything I have is fresh," he repeats. "My pizzas aren't made and then frozen in another city and shipped in here," he adds emphatically. He says he specializes in hand-tossed thin crusts.

Louie also makes all his desserts himself. These range from old fashioned ricotta cheese and cream cheese cheesecake to ice cream.

When his customers began asking him about the recipe for his Italian dressing, Louie knew he was on to something. He soon began selling it in supermarkets.

Wine – especially Italian wines – and beer are served at Louie's On The Lake. Louie says he also does catering too.

Fresh flowers on the tables and counter reinforce the freshness theme Louie maintains.

The building, located in heavy shade, has no need for air-conditioning during the summer months. Ceiling fans add an additional cooling element, as do the open windows. "This building has 800 wall-to-wall windowpanes," Louie laughs. "I know. I painted the trim on all of them myself."

In cool (and cold) months, two large ovens which can range up to 1100 degrees Fahrenheit, keep the restaurant toasty warm. A wood-burning stove at the fireplace hearth provides additional heat.

After you have eaten one of Louie's delicious treats, stroll across the street and explore the historic Lake Rabun Hotel (if you don't already have accommodations there). This structure, built by hotelier M.E. Crowe, offered accommodations to travelers on the Tallulah Falls Railroad and lumbermen back in the 1920s and '30s. Today, it is little-changed, and provides a cozy, romantic getaway for couples interested in enjoying the Tallulah Falls area.

And if you have accommodations anywhere else on Lake Rabun, give Louie Caro a call. He says he occasionally delivers his creations to residents around the lake. But he does it by going "across" the lake, not "around" it. He delivers by boat!

(Louie's On The Lake is open March thru November, Tuesdays and Fridays, from 5:00 P.M. to 10 P.M.; and on Saturdays and Sundays from 12:00 Noon to 10:00 P.M. For further information or to make reservations, call (706) 782-3276. Prices range from $4.95 to $12.95. If you would like a rustic but comfy place to overnight, the historic Lake Rabun Hotel right across the road is an excellent choice.)

Old Lake Rabun Hotel

Chances are, you won't have a private bath at the **Lake Rabun Hotel,** and your bedroom will be air-conditioned with little more than a cool mountain breeze thru your screened window, and furnished with little more than a comfortable bed with quilts and a dresser. But if you're seeking peaceful solitude, scenic beauty, and a taste of what life was like in a mountain hotel in the early 1900s, then the Lake Rabun Hotel is a stop you need to make.

Built in 1922, when lumber was still king in north Georgia, this treasure from a bygone era has experienced few, if any, alterations since its original construction.

It was built by a Mr. **M.E. Crowe,** to take advantage of the travelers on the **Tallulah Falls Railroad** who were vacationers on **Lake Rabun,** and others involved with the lumber industry which was very active in northeast Georgia in the 1920s. However, Mr. Crowe lost possession of the unique little inn after **Augustus Andreae** – who had financed the inn's construction – was forced to foreclose on Mr. Crowe after the innkeeper was unable to maintain payments on the debt.

After the foreclosure, Mr. Andreae, a German immigrant, decided to try the innkeeping business himself. He operated the Lake Rabun Hotel for approximately 15 years, giving it the charm and quaintness which make it so special today.

Interestingly, the inn is literally a Rabun County historic landmark, although no such proclamation or designation marks the spot. It remains almost exactly as it was constructed in the 1920s when Mr. Crowe built it approximately 80 years ago.

The chairs, benches, coffee tables, lamps – even the rockers – in this hostelry are all uniquely constructed of mountain laurel. Andreae commissioned a mountain craftsman to build them for the hotel. They remain as a part of this quiet German's unusual legacy to this area.

A huge fieldstone chimney and hearth (now blackened from decades of use) beckon warmly from a corner of the roomy and yet cozy lobby. No telephones, room service, ice machines, or any other "modern" conveniences will disturb your sleep at this peaceful stop (although unin-sulated inner walls don't permit total silence from adjoining rooms. This, admittedly, is a slight drawback, but then, this is the way the old mountain inns were built!).

Aside from the lobby phone and television, and a nice old refrigerator on the second floor which is "community property," there are no other conveniences, and quite frankly, none are needed. There are a total of 16 guestrooms (six with semi-private baths, one with a private half-bath, and one with a king-size bed). A "**Honeymoon Suite**" has its own fieldstone fireplace, and undoubtedly remains a fond memory for all who have experienced it.

The pervasive peaceful atmosphere and quiet beauty of the hotel are the elements that now attract customers. A television in the 2nd floor lobby area also offers an opportunity to keep up with your favorite television programs and weekend football games – if that's your reason for driving all the way to the north Georgia mountains.

One recent addition to the hotel – **Bill's Boar's Head Saloon and Grill** – was built in 1996. It is open Friday and Saturday nights and on special occasions. Gourmet dinners, appetizers and specialty items as well as your favorite beverage are available, as are both inside and outside seating.

Lake Rabun has long been a place of escape for Atlanta's (and Georgia's) wealthy. It was created circa 1913 by the Georgia Power Company, to generate electricity. The tiny community of **Lakemont** grew up around the site.

Across the street from the hotel, **Louie's On The Lake** is a nice little pizza restaurant which occupies the structure also built by Mr. Crowe as a restaurant to feed his guests in the 1920s. Next door, a business called **The Lake House** occupies another historic structure and offers antiques and an assortment of oddities for sale.

{The Lake Rabun Hotel is open from April to Thanksgiving weekend. It is located 4 miles west of U.S. 441 (2 miles north of Tallulah Falls) near Lakemont. A full breakfast on weekends and a continental breakfast on weekdays is included in the room tariff. Children are welcome and can sleep on regular beds. For reservations and additional information, call 706-782-4946.}

Lula

Lula
Covered Bridge

It had been abandoned and ignored for years, and finally succumbed to Mother Nature, collapsing into the creek over which it had provided safe passage for so many years. It might have rotted away completely, had not one concerned citizen gotten involved to save this historic landmark.

The year was 1975. It was an all too familiar sight in Georgia. The **1910 King Post covered bridge** built across a small tributary to **Oak Grove Creek** in northeast Georgia's Banks County lay in ruins. It had collapsed into the creek. It was a sad testimony for the once-proud, historic little structure.

The old tin roof lay among the broken planks of the flooring and the far end of the bridge no longer even existed. Only one side stood, supported by the sturdy basic King Post trusses. The floorboards sagged under the invisible weight of the horses and carriages of yesteryear, and decay had sapped the strength of the strongest beams.

Andrew Walker of **Georgia First Bank of Gainesville**, decided enough was enough. He was going to take on the sizeable task himself of reconstructing the bridge as a bicentennial project. Though the tiny community of Lula is in Hall County, the old bridge actually lay in Banks County.

Walker went to the county commissioners who agreed to help with some of the purchases necessary for the reconstruction. The local **Chamber of Commerce**, the **County Historical Society**, and the county schools also joined the team.

It almost seemed like the renovation might become a reality until Walker learned the cost of the repairs could total $10,000.

Then the dream was suddenly shattered – just like the rotted planks of the old bridge.

But at about this same time, a bridge builder from Marietta offered to reconstruct the old bridge for free. And then the Banks County Commission offered to reconstruct a road to the bridge and to supply trees, labor, landscaping and picnic tables. An architectural firm drew up free detailed plans to develop a small area around the bridge. More free help came, and the owner of the acreage in the vicinity donated the land around the structure. Suddenly, the dream was looking like it might become a reality again.

Today, the restored wooden bridge stands proudly on the original slab and has been refurbished with as much of the original materials as possible.

The sides and roof have been shingled with cedar shakes to keep out the weather once again. Most of the bridge was built on the side of the creek, then lifted by crane onto its foundations.

What was accomplished here may seem insignificant to many people, but to others it was an important milestone for the county. It means another historic item in Banks County's legacy has been saved for posterity. It's just another way that tomorrow's children may see – up close and personal – how the children of yesteryear lived.

(For more information about this or other historic sites in Banks County, contact the Banks County Chamber of Commerce at 800-677-2108 or 706-677-2108.)

The Foxfire Center

I was visiting the quaint community of Mountain City, Georgia, recently, when my curiosity got the best of me and I decided to visit what has become a nationally-recognized institution – the **Foxfire** organization. I'd always thought of this place as one of those "back-to-the-good-ole-days" attractions. . . I had no idea there was so much more to the story of this place.

Robert Murray, conservator at Foxfire, explained to me the ideas behind the creation of the program.

"Years ago, families, by necessity, lived in close-knit units or communities," he said. "Families like *The Waltons* of television fame were typical. Three generations under one roof was not uncommon.

"Because of this, grandparents and even great-grandparents were a valuable part of the everyday lives of their families," Robert continued. "Skills, wisdom, and training were passed along as adult children and younger ones drew upon the knowledge of their older relatives. Today, this process is almost (nonexistent)."

Robert went on to point out to me that this is what the people who founded Foxfire ultimately recognized. Think about it this way: Imagine a person who has never heard of a jigsaw puzzle. Would it be easier for you to give this individual written instructions to follow in order to assemble a puzzle, or would it be simpler if you just sat down and showed the person how to put the puzzle together?

Of course the hands-on experience would be far better and more effective. And even though we've known for years that interactive learning has always been the fastest way to teach a skill, this approach, strangely enough, has rarely been a part of the teaching methods used in our schools.

The Foxfire organizers also recognized the importance of sharing new information. What's the first thing you want to do when you learn a new skill or an easier way of accomplishing a task? You want to tell someone about it, right?

Hands-on learning and a means of sharing new skills and knowledge were the foundation of Foxfire's "new" approach to learning. Of course, in actuality, it was merely a return to a centuries-old method of passing along knowledge.

With its roots in the **Appalachian Mountains** culture, Foxfire was begun in 1966 when a local Rabun County teacher embarked upon an innovative way of teaching a group of high school students who had very short attention spans. The teacher decided to teach his students the basics of journalism and then send them out to interview relatives and neighbors who were familiar with many of the "old ways" that were rapidly disappearing from modern society.

Most of the students quickly became enamored with this new method of earning a grade in the class. They began recording the life stories of people who recalled things like "house raisings" – a time when whole communities would come together to rough-in or complete a family's home – and a multitude of other "old-time" family practices.

The teacher then taught the students how to compile the interviews into magazine form and *Foxfire* **magazine** was born. The approach was an instant success. More and more schools invited Foxfire's staff to present this amazing new teaching method to their faculty.

In the process, the students learned a greater respect for older adults and the wisdom with which they were so richly endowed. The students also became enthusiastic about putting together the information they had learned and being able to share it with others.

Today, most everyone has read – or at least has heard of – many of the *Foxfire* **books** that have been published since 1972. Each book is an anthology of articles taken from the student-published Foxfire magazine.

"The organization itself is over three

decades old," Robert relates. "There have been twelve *Foxfire* books so far, and the first eleven's sales have totaled over eight and one-half million copies."

Robert offered to serve as my personal tour-guide of the Foxfire grounds, so I took him up on his offer. We began with the museum, which held its own story.

In 1982-83, students from **Rabun County High School** actually built the museum cabin themselves, having spent one short week in a special class taught by log cabin builder Peter Gott of Marshall, North Carolina. Every bit of its construction was done on-site at the school's property.

Then, in 1989, the building was completely disassembled by another group of students and moved to its present location at the Foxfire facility grounds in nearby **Mountain City**. The following summer, another group of students reassembled the building. Finally, in 1991, the year the museum was opened, a third student force added a fieldstone chimney onto the structure.

Today, the museum houses over 150 artifacts, many from the stories the students have written over the years. There are handcrafted toys – climbing bears, ox yoke puzzles, and delightful "limberjacks" (wooden dancing toys) – and much more. Primitive tools include a shaving horse and a froe (used for splitting wood into shingles).

My favorite of all the old-time gadgets was the traveler. This little device was used to measure the circumference of a wagon wheel so that the blacksmith could determine the length of iron needed for the rim of the wheel.

A wagon built by Judd Nelson (Yes, that's his real name.) of Sugar Valley, Georgia, was also on display. When Mr. Nelson built the wagon for Foxfire, he was one of only a handful of blacksmiths who still knew how to construct one from start to finish.

Ever heard the expression, *"Keep your nose to the grindstone?"* Well, at the Foxfire museum, I found out just how that phrase was born. Robert Murray explained it to me as he showed me the grist mill workings on display in the museum.

The task of keeping the tension adjusted between the bed stone and the top or "runner"

stone was critical in any gristmill. Too much pressure between the two large grindstones could easily cause one of them to crack and break apart, possibly causing severe if not devastating damage to the mill or the operator. If the stones were compressed too tightly, the friction also produced too much heat, causing the grinding corn to become scorched. A cautious worker stayed alert for the tell-tale odor of scorched corn by – you guessed it – keeping his nose attuned to the grindstones.

Anyone who grew up in the country will also remember the big black iron washpots that once graced the front lawns of many homes. By the time I came along, most of these had been converted to use as planters and thus were filled with flowers.

In earlier days, however, these big black pots were each family's washing machine. Foxfire's washpot was complete with a paddle (used to stir and lift the clothes) and a "battlin' board." A pounding with one of these devices barely allowed the fabric to survive, let alone any dirt to remain.

I viewed a cross-cut saw, a "calf-weaner" (Talk about an unpleasant-looking nose ring!), a home-made shoe and any number of other items and implements once used in domestic life in the mountains. There were traps for all manner of game, a churn, and a rope bed.

The rope bed was another eye-opener. Here was the basis for the old adage – *"Sleep tight."* The ropes forming the mattress had to be periodically tightened with a wooden key-like instrument called a bed wrench; otherwise, the bed would sag and become uncomfortable to sleep on.

My Foxfire experience didn't end at the museum. Just up the road is the **Foxfire Center,** known affectionately as **"The Land."** It is 110 wooded acres of land with a collection of historic log cabins and realistic reproductions. Many of the authentic structures were destined for destruction at their original sites; the relocation spared them from extinction.

Robert offered to drive me in his pickup truck, and I gladly accepted. Climbing over an array of parts, tools and equipment, I cleared a space on the truck seat and resigned myself to resting my feet on what looked like the remains of a well-worn alternator.

As we wandered the property, Robert identified every twig, weed and shrub along the way, as well as the medicinal or other use of each one. He amazed me with his knowledge of the land, its history, and its people. I was introduced to the wonders of butterfly weed (finding out that this plant's roots were once believed to be a cure for pleurisy). Plant life had been utilized by early settlers for everything from mad dog bites to childbirth complications.

And the shelters and outbuildings around us showed the ingenuity of the spirited mountain people. I discovered that a rock structure resembling a barbecue pit with a built-in iron pot was actually a hog-scalder. I'll spare you the details on this one. . . Suffice it to say, it brought back memories of the major motion picture, *Fried Green Tomatoes.*

The **Savannah House** was a wonderful old cabin. This home, built around 1820 in the Savannah Creek vicinity of what came to be Jackson County, North Carolina, served as home to **the Richard Wilsons**, a family of Irish immigrants. This solemn 21' by 21' building housed several generations of the Wilsons, a number of whom raised as many as ten children within its modest walls.

In the real communities of Appalachia, the church was the core of the community's activities. Students of Foxfire constructed **The Land's Chapel**, modeling it after the design of a church that once stood near Waynesville, North Carolina. Split log benches served as pews and the interior walls were paneled in a beautiful wood known as wormy chestnut.

I asked Robert about the wooden coffins displayed in the church. "Death was a constant reality in those days," he informed me. I was astounded to learn that the infant mortality rate was frequently as high as one out of two. Besides serving as the area's schoolhouse, the church was used all too often for funerals.

And speaking of deaths, has anyone around you ever referred to something as being *"dead as a doornail?"* Robert Murray had the explanation for that expression too. . . Showing me a nail that had been driven through the door of one of the cabins, he explained that these protruding nails were bent or "deadened" intentionally, to prevent people from being stuck or from tearing their clothing as they entered and departed the cabins.

Since nails were valuable and nothing was ever wasted, nails accidentally bent during construction work would always be straightened for re-use. But a doornail, having been intentionally bent to a severe degree, was not reusable. Even if it could be removed, any attempt to straighten one would usually just result in a broken nail – making it "dead."

We also took a tour of an authentic **blacksmith shop**, and a wonderful garden surrounded by handmade paling fence. Other outbuildings included a **gristmill**, a **root cellar**, a **mule barn** and **wagon shed**. A wonderful treat was tucked inside one of the sheds – a freight wagon from the late 1700s which had been donated to the Center by Mrs. Retta Zuraw.

There were at least twenty structures on the property and each one's actual history or historical relevance had been carefully documented. Somehow, Robert Murray seemed to have stored all this documentation inside his head. Time after time, he was able to relate a cabin's entire family history.

By the time Robert drove me back to my car, my head was swimming with newly-discovered information and my citified bones ached from all the hiking we had done. The most incredible thing was that I had not only had a fantastic time, I had received a wealth of information in the process. And that night, I knew without a doubt that I would "sleep tight," because I was so tired, I was as "dead as a doornail."

(The Foxfire Museum is currently located in Mountain City, Georgia, on Highway 441. The Museum's gift shop includes an excellent collection of books on Appalachia, including all the Foxfire series books, plus handcrafted items, toys and folk art. For more information: (706) 746-5828 or visit their internet site at www.foxfire.org.)

Rutledge

Yesterday Cafe

"The previous owner of this restaurant named it, and it was so fitting, we just couldn't bring ourselves to change it," says Teri Bragg, of **Yesterday Cafe** in Rutledge, Georgia. This interesting eatery, owned by Teri and her husband, Alan, exists in a turn-of-the-century pharmacy. The Braggs say they once visited Rutledge from Florida, loved it, and subsequently moved there. Today, they serve up delicious food to grateful guests.

Rutledge was incorporated in 1871 on the old road from Atlanta to Augusta, and was once known as the trains' "turn-around town." The small community has a charming downtown area with period storefront businesses, and is becoming known as an antique-lovers village.

Upon entering the restaurant, one of the first things guests see is the 1893-vintage tile floors, laid when the structure was built. A 1903-vintage brass cash register (not the original) rests on the counter. The original skylight and tin ceiling, however, have been carefully preserved.

To conform to the traditional drugstore look, Teri uses no tablecloths. Tommy Dorsey and other orchestras of the big bands era emanate from speakers, adding to the nostalgic ambience of the business.

Period photos depicting bygone years in Rutledge, line the walls. "All the photos came from local residents," Teri explains. "It started when one person donated one. We hung it up and the donor bragged about it, and we've been getting 'new' old photos ever since."

A banquet room in an adjacent area was once part of a general store. It is available for wedding receptions, as well as for evening dining.

At breakfast – which is served seven days a week, 8:00 a.m. to 11:00 a.m. – guests can choose between cat-head biscuits with gravy, blueberry pancakes or western omelets, just to name a few of the delicious items on the menu. Prices range from $1.50 up to $5.25.

Lunchtime is usually a lively affair, and includes two meats and seven vegetables. A variety of salads and delicious sandwiches are also offered. Lunch is served seven days a week 11:00 a.m. to 2:00 p.m., and prices range from $3.99 to $6.99.

At night, the lights go down, and the pace of business slows somewhat. The menu becomes more sophisticated, with chicken dijon, herbed catfish, filet mignon and other tasty treats. Specials include prime rib, grilled grouper and baby-back ribs. The dinner meal is served Thursdays from 5:00 p.m. to 9:00 p.m., and Fridays and Saturdays from 5:00 p.m. to 9:30 p.m. Prices range from $6.99 to $14.99. A selection of beers and wines is also available.

Stop by and enjoy this little eatery from yesteryear, and as you're doing so, just remember, the sun never sets on you at Yesterday Café!

(Yesterday Cafe is located at 120 Fairplay Road in historic Rutledge, Georgia. The drugstore area of the restaurant seats 60. An additional 40 people can be seated in the banquet room. For further information, call 706-557-9337.)

Sautee

Nacoochee Indian Mound

The prehistoric mounds known as **Chota (Nacoochee) Mound** in northeast Georgia's White County is one of the state's most scenic and historic landmarks. Its origin and purpose, however, have puzzled mankind for centuries.

Visitors to the mound often speculate that it was built to serve as a refuge during floods. Since the mound stands well above the surrounding Chattahoochee River bottomlands, this is a reasonable assumption. However, it is also incorrect. Visitors to the site have been making the same mistake for more than two centuries.

William Bartram, a noted botanist and explorer, jumped to the same conclusion during a 1776 expedition into the wilderness north of Augusta, Georgia. He accompanied a surgeon from the garrison at Fort Dartmouth to the ruins of an ancient village beside the Savannah River. Within the ruins he discovered several "remarkable Indian monuments" including an earthen mound that stood fifty feet high with a circumference of 200 to 300 yards. Bartram speculated about its purpose:

"It is altogether unknown to us, what could have induced the Indians to raise such a heap of earth in this place, the ground for a great space around being subject to inundations, at least once a year. . . We may however hazard a conjecture;. . . . this mount (was) raised for a retreat and refuge in case of inundations, which are unforeseen and surprise them very suddenly, spring and autumn."

Continuing his travels through the mountains of Georgia and North Carolina, Bartram soon arrived at the Cherokee village of **Cowe**. He discovered that the Cherokees there had erected a meeting house on an ancient mound in the center of this village. But Bartram found that the Indians too were ignorant about *"what people or for what purpose these*

artificial hills were raised."* They told Bartram that the mounds were there when *"their forefathers arrived from the West and possessed themselves of the country, after vanquishing the nations of red men who then inhabited it, who themselves had found these mounts when they took possession of the country. . ."* After further consideration, Bartram decided that the mounds might have been designed *"to some religious purpose, as great altars and temples similar to the high places and sacred groves amongst the canaanites and other nations of Palestine and Judea."*

It turns out that Bartram's speculation, quite possibly, was "right on the money" this time. After more than a century of excavations and study, archaeologists today believe that mounds of the type found in north Georgia were constructed by an early culture of Native Americans called **Mississippians** whose religion centered around the worship of the sun. The abode of the village chieftain – who was believed to be a descendant of the sun – was erected atop an earthen mound which served as a village's political and religious center.

Like the **Etowah Indian Mounds State Historic Site** near present-day Cartersville, Georgia, Mississippian villagers erected the picturesque mound at Chota (commonly known today as Nacoochee Mound and topped with a gazebo). This mound is on private property and has not been excavated since the 1920s. It, too, is a temple mound. The excavation, conducted by the **Smithsonian Institute** in Washington, D.C., recovered a number of artifacts, including pottery, pipes, wooden ear ornaments, bone pins, a copper celt, copper arm bands and beads. **Hernando de DeSoto**, who reportedly visited this village in May of 1540, referred to it as **Guaxule**.

Another misconception about Indian

mounds is the widely-held belief that they were used for mass burials. In most of the north Georgia villages the only time remains were laid to rest within a mound was in the event of the death of a chieftain. The Mississippians customarily buried their dead beneath the floors of their homes and, since the home of the chieftain happened to be atop a mound, his body would be buried in the mound.

The Mississippians had a stratified society. The houses of the leaders occupied places of prominence and some were built on the smaller mounds. The houses were wood post structures plastered with clay and covered by a grass or cane thatch roof. Each had a clay-lined fireplace in the center of the floor and smoke escaped through a hole in the roof.

The arrival of European explorers possibly led to the demise of the Mississippian villages. According to University of Georgia archaeologist Dr. Mark Williams, the Indians were decimated when they were exposed to diseases to which they had no natural immunity.

When the Cherokees and Creeks arrived in north Georgia in the late 17th century, they apparently did not attach any religious significance to the mounds. There was a much greater Cherokee presence in the Chattahoochee River valley in the vicinity of the Chota or Nacoochee mound. There were three Cherokee villages in this valley – Chota, Nacoochee, and Sauta. In 1716, Colonel George Chicken referred to Chota as a "town of peace." Later, a Colonel Willet described Sauta as the "first of the Indian towns" with 16 or 18 houses.

These towns suffered greatly during the **American Revolution**. The Cherokees, who were allies of the British, engaged in a series of bloody raids and reprisals against the Americans. In 1781, a force of Georgia and South Carolina militia descended upon the Cherokee towns. Beginning with Sauta at dawn, and ending up at Chota at noon, the militia reportedly killed 77 Indians and one British sympathizer.

Soon after the close of the Revolution, the Cherokee presence in the Chattahoochee River valley ended. By 1795, the Indians had abandoned Sauta and Chota. Nacoochee endured until 1815, but it too was abandoned when the Cherokees ceded the lands east of the Blue Ridge Mountains and Chestatee River to Georgia by treaties signed in 1817 and 1819.

Surprisingly, the greatest threat to Indian mounds in modern times has not been posed by relic hunters. Most of the damage – at least in the more recent past – has been caused by modern development. Hundreds of Indian mounds which once stood beside Georgia's rivers have succumbed to "progress." Another big culprit may have been farmers who wished to fully cultivate their rich river bottom-lands which were obstructed by the odd raised mounds. Fortunately, a few north Georgia mounds – notably those at Etowah and Chota – have escaped this fate.

{The Chota (Nacoochee) Indian Mound is located near the intersection of Georgia Highways 75 and 17 in the Nacoochee Valley, and can be viewed from the highway. The mound, however, is located on private property and therefore is not open for visitation by the public.}

Sautee

The Stovall House

Built in 1837, when this part of Georgia was still largely a frontier with Cherokee Indians clinging desperately to what remained of their homeland, the **Stovall House** was the pioneer home of **Moses Harshaw**, a man colorfully etched in the history of the valley as "the meanest man who ever lived." Today, the dwelling carries the name of the William Stovall family which resided in the house from 1893 to the late 1940s. This site is a popular bed and breakfast destination for travelers to the very scenic **Sautee-Nacoochee Valley**.

The Stovalls were saw-millers, drawn to the community in the days when the **Gainesville & Northwestern Railroad** extended to nearby **Helen** and **Robertstown** for the purpose of hauling the wood products produced by the huge lumbermill which existed in Helen in the early 1900s.

If ever a bed-and-breakfast inn offered a peaceful "country" experience, it would be the Stovall House. It exudes a wealth of charm in the scenic Sautee-Nacoochee Valley, and in the winter months, you'll encounter much less competition for access to this mountain hideaway.

Helen observes the traditional German **"Fasching"** season in January and February with lively masquerades and parties, and the Stovall House is just a few minutes away.

The restaurant at The Stovall House is open to the public (not just the Inn guests) and features a mix of continental and gourmet foods, made on-site, with a fresh difference.

The *A La Carte* menu for dinner includes soup, salad and pasta appetizers, and entrees of baked or sauteed trout, stuffed chicken, stuffed phyllo pastry, pork scallopine, lamb chops, and daily specials. Entrees range from $10.00 to $15.00.

The restaurant hours are Thursday through Saturday from 5:30 P.M. to 8:30 P.M. Reservations are always recommended.

As a travel tip, if you would like to dine at The Stovall House but find the date you'd like to patronize the inn is on a day the restaurant is normally closed, call ahead and check on availability anyway. You might just find that owner Hamilton Schwartz has opened the restaurant up anyway for a special group, and if so, he usually will serve other diners on those days too.

The inn offers five guest rooms, all with a private bath and furnished in antiques. The rooms, particularly the upstairs quarters, offer a cozy warmth one would expect from a mountain inn. They have cheerful skylights and hand-stenciled embroidery around the walls.

Two of the rooms have a connecting bed/sitting room with brass day-bed. A unique "pinned-beam" construction technique is visible around the walls of the upstairs rooms.

The Stovall House carries the unique classification of a "bed-and-breakfast inn," and as such, a continental breakfast is included in the cost of the room tariff. A single-occupancy costs $60.00. A double costs $92.00.

Special rates are available for stays of four or more nights, and cribs and roll-away beds are available.

{The Stovall House is located on Georgia Highway 255, just one and one-half miles north of its intersection with Georgia 17. The address of the Stovall House is 1526 Highway 255 N, Sautee, Georgia, 30571. For reservations and more information, contact the Stovall House.}

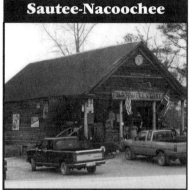

Sautee-Nacoochee

Sautee-Nacoochee Valley

Some knowledgeable travelers and native north Georgians are aware of the special place known as the **Sautee-Nacoochee Valley**. It is a quiet rural area only a few hours drive from Atlanta in the foothills of the **Blue Ridge Mountains**, nestled between the towns of Clarkesville, Cleveland and Helen. The beauty of this vicinity has attracted wanderers for as long as there has been human inhabitation in the Americas, and for an autumn driving tour, this area is hard to beat.

Today, Sautee-Nacoochee is best known for one particular landmark – an Indian mound topped with a gazebo near the vicinity where GA Highway 75 crosses the Chattahoochee River. This rather mysterious earthen marker, the creation of an ancient culture with a 19th Century addition, is but one of the many scenic landmarks that make up the unique history of this area. There are many, many others.

For thousands of years, these valleys have been routes of migration, trade and habitation. Grazing prehistoric mastodons, primitive hunters, and more recently even buffalo, Cherokee Indians, settlers and gold miners all have been drawn to this vicinity.

Nacoochee Community Center

The best way to learn about this fascinating place is to visit the local museum at the **Sautee-Nacoochee Arts and Community Center**. From the Indian mound, head south on GA Highway 17 through the Nacoochee Valley. Turn north (left) onto GA 255 and you'll see the Center on your left, just past the post office and fire department. It's located in the old red brick schoolhouse.

This charming old building was known as **Nacoochee School** until 1974, when county consolidation forced its closure. It was recently converted to use as the Arts and Community Center and is operated by the Sautee-Nacoochee Community Association, a non-profit organization dedicated to the preservation of the cultural, environmental and historical resources of the area. Art shows, musical events, theater and dance performances, workshops, classes, and of course, a fine museum are all available at "The Center."

First Residents

From maps and written materials we learn that as long ago as 15,000 B.C., the valleys of Sautee and Nacoochee were an intersection for two major routes of early travel. The earliest travelers were migrating animals. Indians followed. Then came the trappers and hunters. Eventually, the trail became a road and ox-drawn carts and wagons followed.

From this introductory section at the museum, one moves into "Indian History" and to some of the museum's most prized treasures. A fish-shaped stone about 2 inches in length called a **Clovis point** is of great archaeological significance. It was found in Nacoochee Valley and is proof that humans were in this area around 15,000 B.C.

Although to the uninitiated the Clovis point may be confused with an arrowhead, it actually pre-dates the arrowhead by thousands of years. It is a projectile point fashioned by its creator (a Paleo-Indian) to be strapped onto a staff and used like a javelin (rather than onto an arrow shaft to be used with a bow). It is named for Clovis, New Mexico, where the first such point was found embedded in the vertebra of an extinct buffalo. Two Clovis points have actually been found in the Sautee-Nacoochee valleys and the museum committee is delighted to have this "scarce as hen's teeth" relic in their collection.

Another treasure, a 1,500-pound rock with bowl-shaped indentations in it, is a special find also. It has been identified as a prehistoric stone mortar. It is believed that native people, as early as 8,000 B.C., created the cavities in this rock, either to create materials for religious ceremonies, or to grind acorns, hickory nuts and chestnuts into edible foodstuffs.. The rock was discovered by a **Georgia Department of Transportation** worker during the widening of the bridge near the **Nacoochee mound**. The mound itself is believed to have pre-dated the Cherokees by at least 2,500 years, having been created by the Mississippians, a much more ancient culture.

Early Educational Institutions

One of the primary aims of the museum has been the documentation and collection of items pertaining to the educational history of the valleys' children. There is an area dedicated to the Nacoochee Institute (forerunner of Nacoochee School) with lots of photographs of graduating classes.

Up until the opening of the Institute in 1903, many of the mountain children were educated in one-room school houses. The Institute introduced an era of extremely successful education that drew boarders as well as local children. To the great dismay of the community, however, fire destroyed the Institute in 1926.

Meanwhile, back in the Sautee Valley, another educational facility – Nacoochee School – was built on the site of the old Institute two years after the fire. Classes were small, with the first graduating class in the Spring of 1928 being made up of only one student. The school, however, remained in operation as a public facility for forty-six years.

Other Historic Sites

Back out on the highway, there are many, many more historic sites to be explored and enjoyed in the Sautee-Nacoochee valleys. About a mile away from The Center on

GA Highway 255, you'll find historic **Stovall Mill Bridge,** famous for being the shortest historic covered bridge in Georgia. Stay on this route and you'll pass many of the homes of the prosperous settlers and old-moneyed families who have given this area its reputation for significant American architecture.

Or, you can head back to Highway 17 and visit the **Old Sautee Store**, formerly the post office for the valleys and now a combination museum and gift shop. Northward on GA 17, you'll see several **Georgia Historic Commission** markers explaining sites of historic significance along the road. You'll also get a great view of the Nacoochee Valley.

Across from the Indian mound is the former estate of **Confederate Captain James Nichols**, known today as the **Nichols-Hunnicutt-Hardman House.** Nichols was responsible for the construction of the gazebo which graces the mound today and the nearby **Crescent Hill Baptist Church**. Both structures were built around 1870 in a Gothic style similar to that of his home.

Just around the corner from the old Nichols estate on Highway 75 North, you'll find historic **Nora Mill**. This structure on the Chattahoochee River still grinds flour and meal just as it did over a hundred years ago, and was the site of a portion of the filming for the major motion picture *I'd Climb The Highest Mountain* filmed in 1950. It starred **Susan Hayward, Bill Lundigan** and **Rory Calhoun**, with a bit part by a struggling young actor named **John Kollock**, who today is a highly-respected artist and author still living in the area.

(For more information on the sites above, contact the White County Chamber of Commerce.)

Tallulah Falls

Historic Tallulah Falls Communnity

The once surging and roaring falls are silent today – victims of the need for hydroelectric power. The scenic **Tallulah Falls Railroad** and the huge resort hotels which once hugged the mountainside along the rim of the gorge have also disappeared – victims of progress and natural disasters. Yet life continues to stir in this resort community which once rivaled Niagara Falls as a travel destination.

So heavy was the flow of traffic from vacationers traveling the rough mountain trail to Tallulah Falls by the mid-1800s, that settlers in the area began taking in and feeding wayfarers for a fee. The practice had become such a success by 1870, that the **Shirley Hotel** was built about one mile from the falls. The resort era of **Tallulah Falls** had begun.

The completion of the Tallulah Falls Railroad to Tallulah Falls in 1882 meant transportation to the rapidly growing resort was "a given." One round trip daily from Cornelia, serviced connections from Athens and Atlanta. Weekend excursion fares from Atlanta were $3.35 and $2.50 from Athens.

News accounts of the resort attracted travelers from far and wide to Tallulah Falls, reinforced all the more by the dependable availability of rail transportation. As the railroad increased the flow of tourists to the site, grand Victorian hotels began to appear along the rim of the gorge. At its peak, there were seventeen hotels and boarding houses in and around the town.

The romance of this very scenic resort made it a favorite site for honeymoon destinations. Romantic names were gradually assigned to favorite overlooks and rock formations: Witch's Head; Devil's Pulpit; Vulcan's Forge; and many more. Any interesting spot was acclaimed as Lover's Squeeze, Chimney Rock, Needle's Eye, Trysting Rock, and such.

It wasn't long, however, before early organizers of what later became the **Georgia Power Company**, realized that the immense hydroelectric resources in the region of Tallulah Falls could answer the growing shortage of electrical power in Atlanta to the south. In 1912, construction began on a dam at the head of the gorge. It was to be 116 feet high, and 400 feet across the top. In 1913, the damming of the

river was completed, and the raging falls were silenced for the first time in thousands, possibly millions of years.

Despite the impact of the dam (which choked off the mighty falls) on the Tallulah River, it was actually a couple of even more disastrous events which sounded the death knell for Tallulah Falls. The most important of these occurred on a cold December night in 1921.

On that night, an extremely strong wind whipped through the streets of Tallulah Falls. Residents and tourists awakened to find the town ablaze around them. The fire, aided by the growing windstorm, quickly spread up and down River Street, the town's main thoroughfare, and eventually engulfed the entire town.

As was the case in many small towns in the mountains in those days, there was no fire-fighting equipment. Residents could do nothing but watch their town burn. In the end, the heart of Tallulah Falls was destroyed by the horrendous fire, and without insurance, few if any of the owners of the property rebuilt their businesses.

Today, however, a new Georgia facility – **Tallulah Gorge State Park** – has been established in the gorge to protect the site and provide camping, hiking, and canoeing opportunities for campers and vacationers. Other accommodations include **Terrora Park Visitors Center** (a facility developed by the Georgia Power Company), as well as a few vestiges of the historic community. These include the old **Tallulah Falls Railroad Depot** (which today houses an interesting craft shop of mountain products).

U.S. Highway 23-441 leading through Tallulah Falls was once little more than a mountain trail. Today, traffic continues at a brisk pace during peak travel seasons, much of it headed for the higher mountains of northeast Georgia, Tennessee, and North Carolina. Some of these visitors however, stop to visit the scenic little community of Tallulah Falls, impressed with the awe-inspiring Tallulah Gorge, and no doubt imagining what life was like in the little community when the falls still roared.

(For more information about Tallulah Falls, call the Habersham Chamber of Commerce at 706-778-7970.)

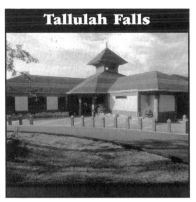
Tallulah Falls

Tallulah Gorge Interpretive Center

A century ago, newly-weds regularly flocked to **Tallulah Falls.** Well-dressed gentlemen and ladies in lace dresses summered there. It was one of the most popular resorts in the South and one of the most heavily photographed spots in the Southeast. Victorian Tallulah Falls was a "dreamland of romance."

In those days, the **Tallulah Falls Brass Band** greeted train travelers who were coming to enjoy the town's many offerings. There were grand hotels, cottages and boarding houses in which to stay. Wonderful restaurants for the enjoyment of fresh country cuisine were numerous, and there were guided tours of the natural wonders of the area. Winding stairs, walkways and even a rope bridge allowed tourists to immerse themselves in the world of the gorge and the awe-inspiring waterfalls for which the town was named. Tallulah Falls was heralded by newspapers regularly as *"the Niagara of the South."*

Yet, there is much more to the story of Tallulah Falls and **Tallulah Gorge** than these few short decades of immense popularity and prosperity. You see, primitive man inhabited this area as far back as 12,000 years ago. And after that, various cultures of **Native Americans**, and still later, waves of European settlers moved through this idyllic spot.

The gorge itself is a portion of the oldest of the great mountain chains of North America. Time, good soil and a temperate climate have collectively spawned a tremendous variety of plants and animals. Some of this flora and fauna are found no where else in the world today. There is a rich history to tell.

The **Jane Hurt Yarn Interpretive Center** at **Tallulah Gorge State Park** came into being as a result of a partnership between the **Georgia Department of Natural Resources** and **Georgia Power Company.** This link-up between the state and the private sector is the first of its kind. The wonderful facility that this teamwork has produced is evidence that such a liaison can work.

With the help of generous donations, the Interpretive Center now houses many treasures of bygone days. The collection includes archaeological artifacts, written and oral histories, photographs, etchings, paintings, mounted specimens, interactive exhibits and much more. The displays are divided between two floors and tell two main stories. Upstairs, the human story is detailed. Downstairs, the story of the gorge itself is chronicled.

As visitors enter the main entrance to the Interpretive Center, one and all are treated to "A Walk Through Time." It starts with the American Indian culture of northeast Georgia, and includes displays of stone tools and quartz arrow and spear points. These stone-age findings are the type used by big-game hunters of the **Paleo Period** and hunter-gatherers from the **Archaic Period** who were the first-known humans in the gorge. The **Cherokees** are believed to have evolved from these earlier cultures. Cherokee baskets and replica pottery are on display.

Additional displays describe the ways of early European traders of the late 1600s and early 1700s. We learn that more than a million deerskins were shipped to England from Charleston during this period – many of them transported out of remote areas like Tallulah to South Carolina where they were put on ships sailing across the Atlantic. Some of the hunted animals, such as the American Bison, disappeared from these areas forever.

From the early to mid-1800s, Tallulah Falls was a travel destination for adventurers, writers and artists who risked life and limb to get there. Many traveled by boat and stagecoach, on horseback and on foot, coming from places all over the country.

This all changed in 1882, when a railway line to Tallulah Falls was completed. First chartered as the **Northeastern Railroad**, the line was owned by the **Richmond & Danville System** when it was completed into Tallulah Falls. In 1897, the line was sold to a new company called **Tallulah Falls Railway Company.** Exhibits in the Interpretive Center detail the many challenges overcome to construct the railroad and the dangers of traveling on these early trains.

The Victorian period in the history of Tallulah Falls is well documented in the Center. Lots of photography and items of luxury – fans, picnic baskets, umbrellas and walking sticks – tell the story. In a section called "The Image-makers," items on exhibit include cameras, a tripod and a stereographic viewer.

Much of the photographic documentation of turn-of-the-century Tallulah Falls was created by a native of the town, Walter Hunnicutt. This well-known, prolific photographer was also the publisher of the town's first newspaper – *The Tallulah Spray.*

On July 12, 1909, a momentous event occurred in Tallulah Falls. The **Tallulah Falls Industrial School** was opened for elementary students. No longer did the mountain children have to go to school in a single room over the town jail. And in addition to the educational basics, they also began to learn weaving, basketry, stone masonry, animal husbandry, woodworking and more.

This new school was founded by the **Georgia Federation of Women's Clubs** and is still operating today. It is now known simply as **Tallulah Falls School** and has expanded from its original five acres to five hundred acres, and welcomes students in grades six through twelve. An elementary school speller and two table runners woven by early students are some of the items on display.

With the dawn of the 20th Century and increased industrialism came the need for more electrical power. Today's Georgia Power Company, then doing business as Georgia Railway and Power Company, harnessed the Tallulah River with a hydroelectric dam. Electricity transmitted to Atlanta, 90 miles away, ran streetcars and enabled the city to double its manufacturing capacity. This engineering feat included the blasting out of a tunnel (over a year in the making) and the building of an incline railway. These and other challenges of working in the gorge are explained and illustrated in this portion of the exhibit.

Tallulah Gorge has attracted many famous visitors in its long human history. Among them is German-born trapeze artist **Karl Wallenda**. In celebration of his 50th anniversary as an aerial artist in 1970, he walked across Tallulah Gorge on a high-wire in 93-degree heat for an audience of some 35,000 onlookers. He began his walk at a point known today as **"Wallenda Overlook," formerly known as "Inspiration Point."** Photos, memorabilia and a Wallenda performance costume permanently memorialize this event for visitors to the Interpretive Center. It was only few years later that the famed Wallenda died in a tragic fall from the high wire in a death-defying feat in San Juan, Puerto Rico.

Another well-known individual commemorated at the Interpretive Center is fourth-generation northeast Georgian, **John Kollock**. Kollock is an artist, author and historian who has dedicated much of the past 40 years to the preservation of the region he calls "home." Kollock's original watercolor paintings entitled The Tallulah Falls Collection are on display in the Center. They depict four historical periods: Land of Legends (prehistory); Hunters and Hermits (1820); The First Tourists (1856); and The Grand Era (1900).

A photo of Kollock as a young actor with **Fess Parker** and **Slim Pickens** in the **Walt Disney** feature-length movie *The Great Locomotive Chase*, is included in the "Hollywood Comes To Tallulah" display. This 1955 production was filmed at various sites along the Tallulah Falls Railroad, because it was the only site Disney deemed appropriate in the entire United States for this Civil War-era movie.

After you complete the "cultural tour," take some time to enjoy the views from the large windows in the atrium area in the Center. Soak up the landscape. Take a closer look with one of the half dozen pairs of binoculars placed by the windows exclusively for your use. See if you can spot some native birds.

While you are communing with nature from inside the Center, you may hear birds calling, crickets chirping and frogs croaking. Don't worry. Your imagination isn't playing tricks on you. . . What you are actually hearing is a digital soundtrack that has been playing quietly in the background throughout your visit. It's part of the rich experience of a visit to the Interpretive Center.

Before descending to the lower level to learn the story of the gorge itself, take note of the information near the entryway that introduces you to **Jane Hurt Yarn** for whom the **Interpretive Center** is named. Georgia Governor **Zell Miller** has described her as the state's most precious resource and says she inspired all that he has accomplished for Georgia in the environmental arena. Yarn devoted three decades of her life to the preservation and wise stewardship of Georgia's natural resources. She gained national prominence for her good works.

Downstairs, there's a lot to see and do once again. In the "Take A Closer Look" section, there are microscopes where you can really check out the plant life. Then there's the "Test Your Knowledge" quiz. What animal likes to play dead? What is the highest waterfall in Tallulah Gorge? There are thirty questions to stump you.

Also on this level, a rock and mineral collection provides samples of mica, quartz, pyrite, semi-precious stones like garnets, and more – all of which are found naturally in the gorge. Written material and illustrations explain how rock and water have sculpted the gorge to make it look the way it does today.

Moving on to the "Ecosystems" display, we learn about herbivores, omnivores and carnivores, just to name a few. Push one of the twelve buttons to see what lights up. There, the seven worlds that make up the natural environment of Tallulah Gorge are explained. They are Lake, River, Stream, Lower Slope, Dry Rim and Cliff, Moist Rim and Cliff, and Upper Slope. Each of these natural communities has its own distinct geography, animals and plant life, and each is explained with large photographs and easy to read copy.

The aquarium is a two hundred-gallon tank of fresh water with lake and stream species of north Georgia fish. A continually running video of wildflowers will alternately show you the spring and autumn varieties. Interpretive Center staff say that more exhibits are planned and that the Center is a work in progress.

There is one more stop on the "indoor tour" of Tallulah Gorge. It is the Center's theater. Here, one can enjoy a twenty-minute award-winning presentation that will leave you breathless. It conveys the excitement and incredible force of the gorge when the Tallulah lake-water is released from the upriver dam.

In this presentation, one can also see wildlife and plant life, including an endangered species – persistent trillium – found nowhere else in the world. We learn that the gorge is the deepest natural crevasse east of the Mississippi River – close to 1,200 feet deep (almost one-quarter of a mile), 1,000 feet wide and two miles long. It drops sharply in the first mile of its down-river route (over 500 feet). We also see dramatic views of each of the five waterfalls at Tallulah – Hurricane, Tempesta, Oceana, Bridal Veil and L'Eau d'Or (also known as LaDore). At this point, it's time to venture outdoors where you'll see some of these sites in person.

Just outside the theater are outdoor exits and in little more than a hundred yards, one can find a fantastic overlook of the gorge. Hard-packed, easy to walk trails lead off in several directions. Take a short walk to the next overlook or check them all out. You can spend a few minutes or a leisurely hour to explore the trails and overlooks along the rim of the gorge. Sneakers are all that's needed to enjoy this sightseers paradise which is also maneuverable in a wheelchair.

While you're here, don't forget that from the 1880s to the 1930s, the rim of the gorge was lined with comfortable mountain hotels, inns and restaurants. Imagine the Tallulah Falls Railroad train chugging around the rim of the gorge (as it actually did) and into town to the depot, and the sights and sounds of that day long past.

A suspension bridge sways 80 feet above the rocky bottom of the gorge at one spot, providing spectacular views of the river and waterfalls. It is 200 feet long and is suspended near the top of historic "Hurricane Falls."

In order to get to the suspension bridge, a somewhat strenuous hike is required, since the visitor must hike down approximately 350 stairs (and then back up). The bridge connects both sides of the gorge via the Hurricane Falls Trail which is actually two sets of stairs that descend from the North Rim Trail at Overlook #2 and from the South Rim Trail at Overlooks #7 and #8. There are nearly 850 steps on the two staircase systems. Individuals who are unaccustomed to strenuous physical activity are discouraged from hiking the stairs or any of the gorge floor.

If you decide to hike into the gorge, be sure to arrive early and be prepared with the proper footwear and clothing. You'll need a permit, and they are only issued "in person" to the recipient and only on the day the permit is to be used to access the gorge, weather permitting.

The park service ranks safety as its top priority, and therefore limits the number of people allowed into the gorge on a daily basis. They not only want to protect the visitors to the gorge, but also the gorge itself from being overwhelmed by visitors. Currently, only 120 permits are issued per day – 100 for hikers and 20 for rock climbers.

If you wish to coordinate your visit with a "water release day" (a day when the gates on the dam are opened allowing the water to thunder once again through the gorge), you should know that all of the permits for those days are officially reserved for kayakers. Not a good day for hiking! However, don't be dismayed. . . You can still enjoy the thundering water from the gorge rim. The water releases are currently scheduled each year for the first two weekends in April and the first three weekends in November. Happy hiking!

{The Jane Hurt Yarn Interpretive Center at Tallulah Gorge State Park is located in Tallulah Falls, Georgia. For more information, call (706) 754-7970. Email: tallulah@alltel.net}

Tallulah Falls

Tallulah Gorge State Park

On June 22, 1996, a group of individuals with The **Georgia Conservancy** participated in a hike down into amazing Tallulah Gorge. The participants signed in at the **Georgia Power Company** facility just beyond Lake Tallulah, and after they had acquired the necessary permits, they were accompanied down the "**Sliding Rock Trail**" by Bill Tanner, superintendent of the Tallulah Gorge State Park, Georgia's newest state-sponsored facility.

There currently are two trails into the Gorge. Sliding Rock Trail is about one-quarter of a mile in length – straight down.

Good hiking boots, as well as a supply of water are necessary for this trek. Hiking sticks are invaluable for balance when climbing over rocks and as a brake during the climb down into the gorge.

It is anticipated that Tallulah Gorge will be the most patronized state park in Georgia within a short time. "Hikes such as this are now possible on a regular basis, except when the full flow of the Tallulah River is periodically released back into the gorge," Tanner said.

The Georgia Power Company (which owns the property), in conjunction with the **Georgia Department of Natural Resources** (which manages the park and leases the acreage) periodically allows an amount of lake water to be released into the gorge once again so that the natural power of the river can be felt and enjoyed at the gorge rim. It is a concept which has excited naturalists and nature enthusiasts across the state.

Much of the area around Tallulah Falls is still a remote wilderness area. Prior to white settlement, the Cherokee Indians inhabited this region.

As a result of the new management program, the mighty falls periodically thunder once again with raw power. Current plans call for the river flow to be increased enough for kayaking on two weekends in April and two in November, according to Tanner.

Park officials say the present ecology of the gorge is approximately 100 years old (begun when the Tallulah Dam was completed circa 1917), and is well established. They believe it should be maintained as is, with the exception of the occasional releases of water.

As a result, permits for only 100 persons per day are granted for hikes down into the gorge, and no overnighting is allowed whatsoever. "In the past, many campers found it too much of an effort to carry tents, coolers and empty bottles back up the 600-foot trail out of the gorge," Tanner added. The river gorge was becoming a dumping ground for debris and discarded equipment.

After the group of hikers reached the bottom of the gorge, they were allowed roughly an hour for the participants to eat a snack, rest or try their hand at sliding down the smooth rock into the pool at the bottom. It was quite near this spot that some of the strategic scenes from the feature-length movie *Deliverance*, starring **Burt Reynolds, Jon Voight** and **Ned Beatty** were filmed in the 1970s.

After this break, the group hiked on up the gorge to see more of the falls. Anchor pins were still embedded into the rocks in many spots where guy-wires for the Wallenda walk cable were once anchored.

As the participants continued their hike, Tanner explained how in prehistoric times, the **Tallulah** and **Chattooga** rivers once flowed into the **Chattahoochee River**. Eventually, however – over eons of time – the swifter-moving waters of the **Savannah River** captured the Tallulah and Chattooga rivers. Today, the bed of **Deep Creek** southwest of Tallulah Falls shows evidence of having once been a much larger river, and is quite likely the former route of the Tallulah when it flowed into the Chattahoochee.

The Tallulah Gorge is a fascinating and historic natural wonder.

{For more information on Tallulah Gorge, contact Tallulah Gorge State Park at (706) 754-7970.}

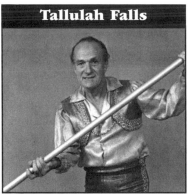

Tallulah Falls

Tallulah Gorge Tight-Rope Walkers

Tallulah Falls and Gorge in northeast Georgia are considered one of the major natural wonders of the state, and indeed the Southeast. And two dare-devils, one in the 19th Century and one in the 20th, only added to the awe inspired by this amazing site.

The unusual natural wonder of the huge gorge near these falls first impressed the Native Americans – the **Cherokee Indians** and their predecessors – in the region. Then came the fur traders and pioneers in the 17th and 18th Centuries who were equally amazed by the site. But in the 19th and 20th Centuries, a new wonder appeared – tight rope walking – and it involved two of the best in the business.

Travelers and tourists had been flocking to the falls for over a century when the first of these "aerialists" staged his act. By 1819 and thereafter, residents near the falls had begun to keep guests in their homes. Tallulah Falls was becoming quite a destination for vacationers and honeymooners, and thus also was a prime destination for performers.

As the years went by, elaborate hotels opened. The **Tallulah Lodge** was called *"one of the finest hotels in the entire South."* By 1882, the railroad (called the **Northeastern Railroad** at that time, then later the **Blue Ridge & Atlantic** and still later the **Tallulah Falls Railroad**) had even made its way around the rim of the gorge and into the mountain community, offering the most scenic ride in the state.

Many of the early hotel owners began inevitably to devise attractions to draw still more customers. In 1886, one owner – Colonel **Frank Young** – witnessed a young performer tight-rope-walking between two buildings above Peachtree Street in Atlanta. The performer **J. A. St. John**, used the professional name of "**Professor Leon**." Col. Young was able to hire St. John to perform the previously unheard of stunt of walking a tight-rope across the Tallulah Gorge. It not only would be the longest such walk ever attempted, but the highest. Colonel Young, no doubt, was very pleased with his success at promoting this stunt.

Following a strong marketing program in area newspapers and through flyers, approximately 3,000 to 6,000 people (the largest crowd ever assembled in the little community up to that time) were attracted via excursion trains from communities in Georgia, South Carolina, Alabama and Florida, to view the death-defying feat.

Professor Leon, then in his thirties, was sponsored by the Young Men's Library Association. He brought his own 20,000 pounds of hemp rope which he, amazingly, stretched across the huge gorge himself. It included a main strand hundreds of feet above the gorge and the churning waters below, and 14 guy-ropes attached to various spots across the gorge to stabilize the main rope.

Needless to say, this was a very dangerous stunt, one which had never been attempted before. It is important to note that it was performed on a "rope," not heavy wire (as used today), and it was done at a time when the roaring waters of the Tallulah River rushed and thundered down the gorge unimpeded. The dam across the Tallulah River which restricts the water flow today did not exist in 1886.

Professor Leon reportedly started his walk near the spot long known as "Inspiration Point" on the Rabun County side of the gorge, and concluded the stunt at the spot known as "Lover's Leap" on the Habersham County side.

St. John's walk was not without some excitement and intrigue. When he had gone one-fourth of the 1,449-foot distance, one of the principal guy lines either gave way or was cut by a saboteur. The main rope jerked violently when the guy line came free.

As St. John tried desperately to collect himself, the rope swayed from side to side, reportedly in as much as a ten-foot span. The de-stabilization very nearly toppled St. John into the gorge.

Apparently realizing disaster was imminent, St. John quickly sat down upon the rope, but he was able to do so without losing his grip on the important 46-pound balancing pole he carried. This quick action quite likely saved the young man's life.

St. John remained in this position until the guy-lines could be re-tightened, a feverish effort which took some 20 minutes. He then regained his composure and continued his walk.

According to one account of the incident, St. John, prior to his walk, had indicated he would dive head-first into the Tallulah River from another rope which hung straight down from the main rope in the center of the gorge. This stunt was billed as *"The Most Terrific Athletic Feat Ever Attempted By Man."* However, after the breath-taking partial collapse of the rope from the lost guy-line, St. John wanted nothing more than to reach the safety of the gorge rim once again.

St. John's contract with the hotel, however, did call for him to make a return trip across the gorge following a successful first trip, but his nerves were shot, and he refused even to honor that. Many onlookers had placed bets upon the successful completion versus a failure in the walk. It was rumored at the time that gamblers who had bet that St. John would be unsuccessful had cut the guy-wire as insurance.

For the performance of this amazing stunt, J.A. St. John received a grand total of $250. Judging from the lack of other aerialists willing to perform this feat, St. John should have charged much more.

Nearly 84 years to the day later, **Karl Wallenda**, the most famous high-wire artist of all time, again crossed the gorge on July 18, 1970. Karl, then 65, had been performing for 50 years, and had promised his wife, Helen, that he would slow down.

A Miss Maxwell, a daughter of then-Mayor Sam Maxwell of Tallulah Falls, had met the famous Wallenda at a Shrine Circus in New Orleans, Louisiana. She asked him if he'd ever thought of walking Tallulah Gorge in Georgia. Karl later said that she had approached him from his slightly deaf side, and although he responded "Ja!" immediately, he later said he hadn't known what a "gorge" was.

Sometime later, Maxwell's sister, Peggy Maxwell Cliffs, reportedly called Wallenda and renewed the proposal with him. He subsequently flew to Atlanta and Peggy drove him to the gorge on a wet misty day to meet her father. As the three of them stood looking over the rim of the gorge where swirling fog blocked out the bottom, Wallenda reportedly shook his head

in disbelief. He later said it looked like the edge of the world itself.

Despite his reservations, he surprisingly offered to perform a highwire walk across the chasm without a net for a fee of $10,000. His employers agreed to the deal, and the stage was set for yet another dramatic feat at the gorge.

When the Georgia Power Company dammed the Tallulah River at Tallulah Falls in 1913, it converted what was once a huge thundering waterfall into a mere trickle. With the demise of the falls, the resort community lost most of its former appeal, and following a disastrous fire which destroyed the community in 1921, the fate of the city had been sealed. The Maxwell family wanted to try to regenerate some of the former appeal of the little community as a tourism destination, and they were hoping Wallenda would be a catalyst.

Karl Wallenda was walking much the same precipitous route taken across the gorge by Professor Leon back in 1886. There were several big differences, however. The mighty Tallulah River and the falls no longer thundered in the huge gorge below. It was a much quieter and non-misty walk. However, Wallenda would also be walking across a much heavier "steel" cable which, as a result, would have a severe bow in the middle, requiring Wallenda to walk both downhill and uphill – a dangerous feat. Professor Leon had walked on a simple hemp rope which had much less of a bow in it.

For his purposes, Wallenda stipulated the 997-foot cable be rigged to meet his brother Herman's satisfaction. Peggy organized a team of structural and landscape engineers, plus workmen, who labored 14 hours a day for three weeks to erect two gleaming silver towers, one more than five stories tall at a cost of $60,000.

The cable was stretched some 700 feet above the gorge, and erected similar to a suspension bridge. It was composed of a one and eleven-sixteenths-inch main cable pulled at a tension of 90,000 pounds. It was anchored to solid rock at the gorge's bottom by 56 guy wires spaced 30 feet apart using 35,000 feet of wire. Four 54-foot-long pre-stressed steel bars were also set in solid rock and 22 cubic yards of concrete weighing 75,000 pounds anchored the three-ton cable (christened Yo-Yo) on each side. The cable ran from a bright yellow ten-foot tower on the south rim to a forty-foot tower on the north rim.

Stringing the wire across the gorge proved

to be more difficult than anticipated. The riggers first shot three harpoons with the cable attached across the gorge, but all three got lost below. Finally, after a number of attempts via another method, the efforts were successful.

On the sunny morning of July 18, an estimated 35,000 attendees showed up. Many undoubtedly sneaked in without paying, since it was difficult to control the crowd. Twenty mounted police and 100 law enforcement officers on foot patrolled the area.

Forty-five shuttle buses drove spectators up and down the gorge. More than 200 reporters, broadcasters and photographers turned out, some even from the **BBC** in London. A Karl Wallenda walk was a major feat indeed, because it was almost always death-defying.

Lloyds of London charged one million dollars to insure the event (if adequate crowd-control was provided), but would not insure Wallenda. Two hundred Boy Scouts patrolled the area picking up litter. Several first-aid stations stood ready if needed, and 175 portable toilets dotted the landscape.

The late Georgia Governor **Lester G. Maddox** and his wife attended the event, and greeted Wallenda at his trailer prior to the feat. To the governor's amazement, "Wallenda drank some hard liquor," he recalled. "He said he never went out without it."

At 3:00 p.m., Karl allowed medics to check his vital signs, especially his heart rate.

"Are you worried about the wind up there, Mr. Wallenda?" asked one newscaster. Karl shook his head. "It doesn't seem so bad. The wind never bothers me. . ."

Karl wore an outfit Helen had sewn for him: a gold satin shirt under a maroon bolero jacket and matching pants with a gold stripe. A bandanna would keep sweat out of his eyes on that blistering 93-degree afternoon.

Herman Wallenda conducted his final inspection of the rigging prior to the walk. A nervous woman asked the county sheriff who stood by the rim about rescue plans should Wallenda lose his footing. The lawman reportedly squinted into the sun, spat a stream of tobacco juice into the gorge, then bluntly replied, "Lady, ain't no plan in hell gonna bring that fellah back alive."

Karl felt concerned mainly about the handling of the balancing pole. He estimated the walk would take him about 16 minutes.

As Governor Maddox wished him "Bon Voyage," Karl said to the waiting crowd, "Now I see the wire, I must try and do it."

The wire's extreme length caused a fearful 60-foot bow in the center of the span, causing Karl to walk downhill for eight minutes. Balancing one's self on a high-wire while walking at a downward slant is the most dangerous action for an aerialist to attempt. Wallenda, however, made it look easy.

When Karl reached the center of the wire, he knelt slowly, laid the pole at a right angle to the wire, and amazingly, lifted his body up into a handstand. He lowered himself back to a standing position and continued walking, then stopped again (at the request of a group of Vietnam War veterans), did another handstand and semaphored with his feet. He was a consummate performer and the crowds loved him, roaring their approval of his feats.

As he approached the catwalk at the end of the feat, he was heard saying, "That catwalk. . . it's the hardest thing to catch." Strangely, stepping from the steel cable to the safety of the wooden platform worried him. He made the step however, then moved to the safety of solid ground.

The walk had taken a total of 17.7 minutes. "It was the most peaceful moment of my life," he later told his biographer.

Years later, however, Karl confessed in a magazine article, "I tell you the truth, the only time I was ever really frightened was at Tallulah Gorge in Georgia."

Wallenda continued performing his amazing feats even into his seventies. Then, in 1974 at age 73, fate finally caught up with him. While performing another high-wire act on a cable strung between two buildings in Puerto Rico, he lost his balance as high winds buffeted the wire. He fell and was killed instantly as he struck the concrete.

Today, remnants of the supports for Wallenda's cable across Tallulah Gorge can still be seen if one knows where to look. Ironically, despite the amazing feat, the famed aerialist did not have the tourism impact on Tallulah Falls that had been anticipated by the Maxwell family. However, a new state park established in the gorge in 1995 quite likely will.

{For more information on the walks of these two tightrope artists across Tallulah Gorge, contact the Tallulah Gorge State Park at Tallulah Falls, Georgia (706-754-7970).

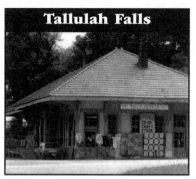

Tallulah Falls

The Co-op Crafts Store

Born in the 1960s out of President Lyndon B. Johnson's "New Society Program," the **Co-Op Craft Store** (officially known as the "Georgia Mountain Arts Products Association, Inc." has persevered through good times and bad, helping to stimulate commerce in the mountains region of north Georgia. Today, this unique shop in northeast Georgia provides an opportunity to purchase authentic mountain crafts items, and help preserve a heritage from yesteryear.

Located on historic Highway 441 in Habersham and Rabun counties, this "cooperative" specializes in the sale of unique items made by mountain craftspersons. The shop (located in the historic old depot of the **Tallulah Falls Railroad** in Tallulah Falls) is only closed, amazingly, for three days during the entire year: Easter, Thanksgiving and Christmas. So if you're thinking about a drive up into the mountains to check out this captivating little mountain crafts store, you don't have to worry whether or not the shop will be open.

The vibrant little enterprise is certainly no "fly-by-night business" either. The year 2003 marked its 35th year of buying handmade creations from local craftspersons and reselling them to other locals and tourists. Some 100 mountain craftspeople regularly sell their wares to the Co-Op Craft Store.

Unique items retailed in the store include walking canes made from twisted hickory saplings, delicate dolls, pottery (from several local artists) in every enticing shape and design, breath-taking quilts of every design and color, books, barn-wood frames, delicious eatables, and a large selection of wooden toys. And these items barely scratch the surface of the inventory in this shop. Other items include baby items, hand-painted items such as saws, mailboxes, buckets, etc., T-shirts painted with all manner of scenic north Georgia subjects; jars of pickles, jams, and jellies; aprons; bonnets; birdhouses and much, much more. Even pine knots from tree limbs have been cut into unusual "whatnots" in the shape of birds.

This eye-catching stop-off in scenic northeast Georgia has attracted its share of tourist traffic, including an occasional celebrity. Such notables as **Kenny Rogers**, **Burt Reynolds** and **Loni Anderson** have visited the Co-op Craft Store.

In 1965, the Appalachian Regional Commission was created to serve the 13 Appalachian states. The commission was the first major step of President Lyndon Johnson's "New Society" program, to stimulate the economies in poverty-stricken areas such as Appalachia.

The commission started the wheels turning for better access to these areas, and another New Society program – Volunteers In Service To America (VISTA) – scattered business organizers throughout the 13 states to facilitate the sales of locally-produced handcrafted products and artwork.

Pretty soon, Appalachian quilts were being sought for stores such as Bloomingdale's in New York City. Country crafts began appearing in cosmopolitan settings. Sophisticates began seeking home-making skills which for centuries had been used almost solely by isolated mountain families.

In 1969, these same VISTA volunteers came to northeast Georgia where they formed the Georgia Mountains Arts Products, Inc., known locally as the Co-Op Craft Store.

It was at this time that area native Lassie Bradshaw, who had been raised in the Persimmon Community of Rabun County, was working with Ninth District Opportunity in Clayton. When time allowed, Lassie enjoyed crocheting, quilting and making corn-shuck dolls. One day, one of the VISTA volunteers asked her if she would like to work in the Co-Op and she agreed, helping with the organization for many years.

Today, interest in mountain crafts and artwork remains strong, and new ribbons of highway have threaded their way back into the mountains to provide access to these sites. But in order to enjoy the true flavor of this slice of cultural and historic Americana, one must drive the original historic back-roads, where the pockets of mountain natives and their wares are found. The Co-Op Craft Store is a good example – located on historic (Old) U.S. 441 which winds from Cornelia to Mountain City, Georgia and beyond.

Today, the business is managed by longtime guiding light Jean Williams. It has a nine-member board of directors which meets quarterly to make policy decisions.

{The Co-Op Craft Store locations are open year-round from 10:00 a.m. to 5:00 p.m. Monday thru Saturday, and from 1:00 to 5:00 p.m. on Sundays. The store is in Tallulah Falls (Telephone toll-free: 888-766-5965) in the historic former Tallulah Falls Railroad Depot. WEB site: www.co-opcraftstores.com}

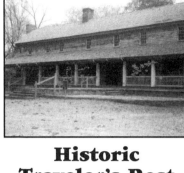

Toccoa

While traveling the Unicoi Turnpike in north Georgia in 1836, Englishman **G.W. Featherstonenaugh** overnighted at Traveler's Rest inn. The next day, he recorded, "I got an excellent breakfast of coffee, ham, chicken, good bread and butter, honey and plenty of new milk for a quarter of a dollar. What a charming country this would be to travel in if one was sure of meeting with such nice clean quarters once a day."

Historic Traveler's Rest

The place to which Mr. Featherstonenaugh referred is located near present-day Toccoa, Georgia. It began life as an inn in the early 1800s before Toccoa even existed as a town, providing accommodations to the growing number of stagecoach travelers involved in the great migration of Manifest Destiny, moving ever westward as European immigrants settled the American Midwest and West. On the way, many of these travelers overnighted at Traveler's Rest.

Today, the 6,000-square-foot landmark is preserved in nearly authentic condition by the State of Georgia. Visitors may enjoy not only the exterior architecture of this remarkable structure, but its still-furnished interior as well. In the process, interested individuals may obtain a very personal look at the furnishings and way of life of the frontier settlers which once inhabited it.

The first white settler to see the potential of this rich land located near the Tugaloo River, was **Major Jesse Walton**. He had fought heroically in the American Revolution and had petitioned **Governor George Walton** for a land grant not far from the Cherokee village of **Old Tugaloo Town**. After receiving the grant, he brought his wife and child and his dreams to north Georgia in 1784.

Since the 16th century, there had been friction between the native Cherokees and white European immigrant settlers. Jesse Walton no doubt breathed a sigh of relief when he witnessed the signing of the **Treaty of Hopewell** on November 28, 1775. However, since the white settlers continued to violate the terms of the treaty, tensions between the Native Americans and the settlers continued to erupt into violence.

In July of 1789, the Indians killed Major Walton as he was working his land one day. His distraught widow subsequently sold the land to a brother-in-law, **Joseph Martin**, who promptly re-sold it to **James Wyly** for $2,000.00.

Wyly is believed to have been the first man to have operated the large log house as an inn. It was he who added on the southern end of the house in 1815 and then enlarged it a second time.

In the midst of the development of his inn, Wyly was appointed as chief contractor for the Unicoi Turnpike. This toll road, interestingly, was built directly past Wyly's house and rapidly became the chief migratory route for settlers from South Carolina who were traveling westward across north Georgia.

Despite Wyly's development of the inn and the road, it was an individual by the name of **Deveraux Jarrett** who was chiefly responsible for creating the overall plantation and inn viewed by patrons today. Jarrett purchased the Traveler's Rest property from Wyly for $6,000.00 in 1833. He continued the inn, but also added numerous other functions to the property, including service as a tavern and post office. He added a blacksmith forge, a cotton gin, a tanyard and a sawmill to the property as well.

Jarrett continued to acquire land adjoining the original tract too. At his death in 1852, he had accumulated 14,400 acres and was considered one of the richest men in north Georgia. He had made the inn a comfortable and very hospitable stop along the Unicoi.

Many notable guests enjoyed the inn's hospitality in the 18th and 19th centuries. Among them were **John C. Calhoun**, vice president of the United States who used the inn as he traveled from his home in South Carolina to his gold mining interests in Auraria, Georgia, and **Joseph Emerson Brown**, destined later to become Georgia's Confederate governor.

Many of the wealthy guests must have engendered some envy among the locals judging from one amusing comment made to a prominent doctor. The physician apparently had several hatboxes, and was being helped to his room by a neighborhood sharecropper. The worker reportedly informed the doctor, "Sir, God only gave us one head. Surely he only intended for us to have one hat."

Charles Kennedy Jarrett, the youngest of the Jarrett's four children, inherited the inn from the elder Jarrett. The winds of change were blowing across the South by this time. The War Between The States had called Jarrett to fight for the South. Charles enlisted in the Cherokee Van Guards, Company A, 43rd P Regiment of Cherokee County on March 10, 1862, but he was released later that same year due to "weak eyes."

After the war, societal trends and travel advances gradually were causing way-stations such as Traveler's Rest to become obsolete. Along with the changes in plantation life, the railroad had become the main method of transportation, and the inn traffic, already severely impacted by the devastation of the South, had been reduced even more by the new mode of transportation. Charles Jarrett, nevertheless, continued to maintain Traveler's Rest as an inn and as his residence until his death in 1877.

Ironically, it was the railroad which eventually brought renewed life to the inn. After the war, the **Airline Railroad** was constructed a short distance from the inn, and a passenger station was built at the crossroads there. As normally happened in these instances, a community grew up at the site.

During the rainy winter months, a low area in the vicinity filled up with runoff water to become a pond, but in the summer's heat, the water evaporated. The town at the site was thus named "Dry Pond," but in the early 1870s, the name was changed to Toccoa, reportedly a Cherokee word for "beautiful." The town grew and prospered until it was larger even than Clarkesville, the nearby Habersham County seat.

This increase in the population of the vicinity and the traffic from the railroad meant renewed life for Traveler's Rest. Patrons came and went, overnighting at the inn. Life for the inn's owners continued unimpaired.

Mary Jarrett White's portrait still hangs in her room at Traveler's Rest. She was Charles' daughter. Mary was somewhat of a rebel for her time. She was the first woman to vote in Georgia. It is unknown today how her name was able to appear on the voting rolls of the county, and even more surprising that she was allowed to vote. Whatever the circumstances, she did indeed cast a ballot in the May, 1920 election, three months before Georgia ratified the 19th Amendment to the Constitution giving women the right to vote.

In 1955, its acreage shrunk to a pittance of its former grandeur, Mary sold historic Traveler's Rest and three acres around it to the State of Georgia, in order that it might be preserved as a national treasure. Throughout her life, she maintained a youthful outlook. Upon being asked her age shortly before her death, she reportedly replied, "It's not polite to ask a lady's age, but if you must know, I'm seventeen."

When one visits Traveler's Rest today, he or she may trace the stages of the building's additions through the years. It is preserved in the style of a mid-19th century inn and plantation home.

The inn was constructed of numbered, foot-thick, squared logs. In some of the rooms, the original numbers on the rafters can still be seen. The building rises a remarkable three stories in height, and is built over a cobblestoned basement.

The kitchen, wine cellar and storerooms were built in the basement of the inn. Much of the construction is remarkably well-preserved. A huge open fireplace served many purposes. It was used for cooking and many other functions requiring heat. The adjacent area doubled as a bath area, and the family bathing apparatus still exists there, since the large fireplace was used to heat the water for the baths in pioneer days. The tub resembles a sitz-bath type tub with an additional foot bath.

Each of the front downstairs rooms opens to the expansive front porch which runs the hundred-foot length of the building. Three separate staircases to the upper level rooms were arranged to afford easy access and egress. The third level attic rooms are much less luxurious than the second floor and main level rooms.

If the inn appears small compared to today's hotels, one must remember that in 19th century pioneer Georgia, travelers did not expect – or receive – private rooms. Many individuals slept in a room at one time, oftentimes two or more to a bed. There were no sanitary facilities either, save a chamber pot for toiletry, and a bowl and pitcher for washing up. At that time, bathing wasn't an especially important function, and deodorant hadn't even been invented, so strong bodily odors were an accepted condition.

Along with the main structure, there are many outbuildings which offer a further glimpse of life at the inn/plantation in the 19th century.

A slave cabin on the grounds, once occupied by a nanny for the Charles Kennedy Jarrett family, is the original structure built in the 1850s.

One of the most interesting outbuildings is the dairy house. This original edifice – beyond its former use for dairy products – was once used experimentally in a silk production enterprise of the family. It served as a cocoonery for imported silkworms. The upstairs slave quarters still has two looms, one of which was actually used by the servants to weave silk.

An large black cast-iron antique wash-pot on the grounds reminds us how laborious once was the chore of cleaning soiled clothing, prior to the advent of washing machines.

The meat house, the only other log structure besides the inn itself, is a reproduction of the original, but maintains the feel of authenticity of the inn outbuildings.

The well-house is a reproduction as well (no pun intended), but is also a *working* replica of the original.

When determining the oldest artifact on the property, that qualification goes to an ancient stone which was inscribed with petroglyphs in prehistory by Native Americans. Local lore maintains that Deveraux Jarrett hauled the rock from the Tugaloo River nearby. It is believed to pre-date the Cherokee Indians which once inhabited the area.

When visiting Traveler's Rest, one almost invariably must venture also to the nearby quaint town of Toccoa. Here, Tugaloo State Park offers camping, cottages, swimming, boating, fishing, water skiing, nature trails and many other activities.

Nearby, beautiful **Toccoa Falls** on the campus of **Toccoa Falls College** offers a look at a sparkling cascade of mountain water that amazingly falls 29 feet further than Niagara Falls. This ribbon of white froth drops 136 feet over weathered rock.

The **Gate Cottage Restaurant** on the campus is also open to the public for Sunday brunch, and the school will arrange tours for interested parties. It is difficult to believe that this peaceful beautiful campus was the scene of unimaginable devastation in November of 1977, when the dam holding back the lake waters burst open. The resulting flood took 39 lives as the furious waters consumed the campus. The tragedy, however, can never be repeated – at least not without an act of God – since the waters of the lake which once existed above the beautiful falls have been permanently drained.

Another historic home in downtown Toccoa – the **Whitmire-Davis House** – was built in 1898 for the Whitmire-Carter family. It was purchased in 1912 by **Judge John H. Davis**. Today, it is a well-maintained Victorian cottage which houses the museum of the Stephens County Historical Society. It proudly displays many historic items, artifacts and much memorabilia, including that of **Olympic Gold Medalist and one-time "World's Strongest Man" Paul Anderson**, who was a Toccoa native.

Another well-visited spot in Toccoa is the historic Belk Building. Built in 1903 across from the Stephens County Courthouse, it was occupied by Belk Department Store for almost 60 years. In 1998, Belk deeded its portion to the city and the city purchased the remainder. The city then renovated and opened the Cornerstone Antique Market, providing a great place for the serious antique shopper to browse.

Toccoa-Stephens County offers a number of festivals and events throughout the year. **Earthfest** provides a "Taste Of Toccoa" in April. **Confederate Memorial Day** is also celebrated in April with a two-day schedule of activities at Traveler's Rest. The **Toccoa Harvest and the Martin Fall Festival** celebrate the traditional harvest season with handmade crafts, foods and antiques.

With all it has to offer, it's no wonder this quiet foothills town is still drawing visitors just as it did in yesteryear, when Traveler's Rest was the only place in the vicinity to offer a bed and hot food on the old Unicoi Turnpike.

(Traveler's Rest State Historic Site is located at 8162 Riverdale Road, Toccoa, Georgia, 30577. It is open Thursday through Saturday, 9 a.m. to 5 p.m., and Sundays, 2 p.m. to 5 p.m. Admission is $1.50 to $2.50 per person. For more information, call 706-886-2256.)

Winter nights are bone-chilling in the woods of north Georgia, causing one to crave the warmth of a campfire. But on the night of February 13, 1779, when three Whig militia colonels – two Georgians and a South Carolinian – huddled in the forest near the site of present-day **Washington, Georgia**, they chose to shiver in the dark, rather than chance a fire. They were on a mission of great importance.

Washington

Kettle Creek Battle Site

In the Indian uprising of 1776, Clarke served as a captain in the Georgia militia, but without distinction. In early 1778, he led an expedition against the British in south Georgia, but without success or distinction there either.

Clarke had proven himself as a fighter, however, so on January 26, 1779, he had been elected lieutenant colonel of the Georgia militia. With this latest Loyalist incursion threatening to lay waste to the back-country, the best fighters were selected to counter the threat.

Scattered around them, the roughly 340 men they commanded did likewise, no doubt grumbling like soldiers in most wars are want to do, as they wrapped their linens and buckskins tighter around them. They made do with their cold rations of parched corn and dried beef.

To the southwest, the **Whigs** saw the sky aglow from the toasty campfires of the **Loyalist forces** they were stalking. These soldiers – who had remained loyal to the mother-country, England – were camped a scant four miles away, and their numbers were roughly twice that of the Whigs.

Several miles to the south, the Whigs also knew that yet another Loyalist force almost as large waited for this group to join them. Amazingly, neither group of Loyalists seemed aware that the Whig commanders had managed to move their men so near. Faced with only two choices – fight or flee – **Colonels Elijah Clarke, John Dooly** and **Andrew Pickens** saw a glimpse of a desperate chance for victory.

The fiery Clarke likely argued fiercely for a surprise attack. One historian has described the stout, bull-necked Georgian as *"a true rustic. . . rather slow of wit and almost wholly illiterate,"* but he was also known to be courageous almost to the point of foolhardiness. These traits, coupled with his cunning and ruthless approach to warfare, made him a natural at the no-holds-barred fighting in the back-country during the **American Revolution**.

Clarke was 43 years of age at this time. He had settled in north Georgia in 1774, emigrating from his native North Carolina where he is thought to have had a hand in the Regulator uprising.

Clarke probably didn't have to argue very hard to persuade **John Dooly** to strike at the Loyalists. Also a native North Carolinian, the 42-year-old Dooly comes down through history to us as a dark and brooding figure, driven by personal demons. He and his brothers, Thomas and George, had taken up claims in north Georgia in late 1773, coming then from the area of the Ninety-Six District of South Carolina. Early in the **Indian Uprising** of 1776, Thomas was wounded, captured and tortured to death by the Creeks, and from then on, John Dooly seems to have been driven by an unquenchable thirst for revenge.

The heaviest weight of the decision facing the three colonels rested upon the third man, **Colonel Andrew Pickens** of South Carolina. More than half the Whig militiamen shivering in the woods around the colonels were his Carolinians, and he would never throw them into a desperate battle recklessly.

Lean, dour and long-faced, the 40-year-old Pickens was a Presbyterian elder and the quintessential Scotch-Irishman. He rarely smiled and no one ever noted hearing him laugh. He was so deliberate and reticent, an acquaintance once said, that "he would first take the words from his mouth in his fingers, and examine them before uttering them."

Pickens, however, was also one of the most cunning, fearless, experienced, and thoroughly dangerous warriors the frontier ever produced. Pennsylvania-born, he had eventually settled near Long Cane Creek in upper South Carolina and had prospered as a farmer. He also served as a magistrate and as a captain of the militia.

He had fought in the first **Cherokee War of 1760-'61**, and in 1776, he had once again battled the Cherokees in the South Carolina hills, helping to drive the Indians ever westward. In one skirmish, he and 25 of his men had defeated nearly 200 of the natives in hand-to-hand fighting. His bravery and cunning won him the grudging respect of the Cherokees who called him Skyagunsta (the wizard owl).

All three colonels had "smelt powder" in enough back-country scraps to command the respect of the colorful bands of settlers they led, but as the colonels huddled, Pickens' voice reportedly was the one with measured words of wisdom and wider experience. In the past few days, he had come close to bagging one Loyalist force and some of his men had been bloodied by the force he now stalked. He was probably spoiling for a fight but he also knew the odds.

In the end, the colonels agreed: If the Loyalist forces unite, the Whig rebellion in the back-country would be crushed in a matter of days and the Whigs' families and homes would be entirely at the Loyalists' mercy. Retreat, therefore, was not an option, and the advantage of surprise offered the Whigs their only real chance for victory. With Pickens in command, they would move against the Loyalists at first light. . .

Clues To Mysteries

There are many mysteries surrounding the battle of Kettle Creek, and as one delves into the history of the battle and the events leading up to it, other equally-fascinating questions are provoked.

The first historian to write of Kettle Creek in any detail was **Hugh McCall** in his *The History of Georgia*, published in 1811. McCall's father, James, had fought at Kettle Creek under Clarke, so presumably, the younger McCall was heir to a rich lode of first-hand accounts passed on by word of mouth.

The only veteran to actually write of the battle in any detail was Dooly, and his descriptions were tersely constructed at best. The taciturn Pickens and the barely literate Clarke wrote sparingly, and apparently none of the Whig rank-and-file veterans left any scribblings at all.

McCall's account went largely unquestioned. When **Otis Ashmore** and **Charles Olmstead** set out in 1926 to write a definitive account of Kettle Creek for *The Georgia Historical Quarterly*, they borrowed liberally from McCall and carved the traditional story even deeper into stone. More critical eyes, however, might have raised a brow at some of McCall's details.

For one thing, the traditional account is vague, and some of it does not seem to square with the battlefield's geography – especially Clarke's decisive charge across the creek. Read in one light, it might seem that the hill where the Loyalists rallied lies south of the creek, but in fact, it lies to the north.

The crucial detail, overlooked in these early accounts, was that for Dooly and Clarke to be successful in the maneuvers they performed, they would have to have crossed the creek not once, but twice, and would have met their first resistance on the south side of the creek. It would be 1978 before historian **Robert S. Davis, Jr.** would write and privately publish a now-rare monograph giving a more credible depiction to the event, but even there, the detail is given but cursory treatment.

In some stories, the Loyalists even became British regulars (a version perpetuated by at least one congressional candidate stumping in the area in recent years). **Nancy Hart** added notches to her musket there – whether she was actually there or not – while stories such as that of **Austin Dabney**, a free black who fought under Clarke, were pushed into yet another corner to be virtually forgotten.

Dooly, Pickens and Clarke were never placed on white chargers, but one can't help but suspect that this is only because some of the tale-spinners lacked that much imagination. Ironically, as this local folklore took hold, it may have eclipsed the real significance of the battle itself.

The Battlefield Today

The task of actually finding the Kettle Creek battleground today seems only scarcely easier than it was for the Whigs. To reach it, one must drive eight miles southwest out of Washington on GA 44, through rolling farm country, until a historical marker directs a right turn onto Stony Ridge Road, a paved road to the left. A mile and a half through clear-cut barrens and stands of scrub pine brings one to War Hill Road, an unpaved road to the left. This trail is marked only by a roughly one-foot square sign announcing the battlefield and is very easy to miss.

Then, only weathered tire tracks, the sparse gravel and one's own sense of time and place betray that it isn't still the year 1779. The road

– really only a gash through the sandy, red hill country, is narrow enough to have been cut for wagons. It weaves and undulates through the thick mixed woods that pinch in on both sides like the edges of a closing wound. After approximately one and one-quarter miles, you will reach a parking area faced by fieldstone gateposts at the base of War Hill.

The hill rises a good 50% to its crest from this approach. The road continues through the gate and up to the hilltop. Trudging up the steep wooded slope, one can't help but ponder the fact that he or she is traveling over roughly the same ground covered by the Whigs' final charge, when, as Dooly recalled, *"it appeared to me that they fired 200 guns at us in half a Minet [sic].* The hill had been the Loyalists' "Gibraltar." The outnumbered Whigs knew only too well that any repulse and defeat likely meant certain death for most – if not all – of them. Often in the partisan war of the back-country, neither side bothered to give quarter. And even if they did, the prisoners usually faced a hangman's noose at their captors' earliest convenience, so the Whigs fought like madmen.

The other major landmark of the battlefield is Kettle Creek itself, which now isn't easy to find at all. Visitors to the site have to pick their way over a narrow trail down the hill's even steeper and more heavily wooded reverse slope. The tangle of canebrakes that lined the creek banks and slowed the Whigs' attack is still very distinct, but the creek today is only a trickle of its former self, having been diverted in the 1920s so that farmland downstream would be spared the winter flooding that, ironically, had led the Loyalist commander to use the creek as a shield.

If suitably informed on the circumstances of the battle, one can still follow the back and forth fighting over the wooded hillsides, the cane thickets and the creek, easily imagining Dooly's, Pickens' and Clarke's men stealthily moving into position for the momentous clash. They advanced in three wings – Pickens in the center with a small skirmish force about 150 yards in front; Dooly on his right, and Clarke on his left, about 340 men in all.

They pushed forward rapidly over the frosty ground – at least as rapidly as they could through the woods and clearings – while maintaining their rough order. Stealth was their watchword. And the closer they moved to the Loyalists, the more critical the slightest crackling branch became. Just imagine today taking 340 men through a deep woods trying to sneak up on an enemy. It's very difficult for one man to accomplish a feat such as this, let alone over 300. Yet, that's just what the backwoodsmen did.

After the Whigs had covered three or four miles, they heard the Loyalists' drums beat assembly, and they paused to re-prime their weapons before pushing forward at a quickened pace. Pickens sent scouts ahead of his skirmishers.

Boyd too, had been on the move early, but had soon called a halt to his troops, making a fresh camp at the bend of Kettle Creek, near a farm. Since the ambush at the river, he had been driving hard to the rendezvous with Campbell, and his men needed food and their mounts needed frequent rest. The horses were turned loose to graze among the canebrakes along the swollen creek bank. The men parched corn and slaughtered and roasted bullocks taken from the farm.

The Loyalists' camp was in the bend of the shallow U the creek made at that point, and to their rear rose a hill rimmed with the scraps of a rail fence and a few fallen trees. Pickens' scouts reported the lay of it all to their commanders.

Pickens, therefore, decided he would advance straight for the hill. Dooly and Clarke would cross their men at the bends of the creek, right and left, in order to encircle the Loyalists, or at least to be able to undermine any defense of the hill by firing into their rear.

A Ferocious Engagement

McCall's and subsequent accounts maintain that Boyd's pickets spotted the advance and fired first. Dooly's written account maintains that Pickens' skirmishers fired first. It really doesn't matter today. Any notice Boyd received of the attacking Whigs was far too little.

The Whigs erupted from the clearing, Pickens making for the hill and Dooly and Clarke for the creek, all firing as they advanced. Rifles cracked and muskets roared as the men on both sides loaded and fired as rapidly as possible on the move, filling the air with humming balls of lead, buzzing shot and a gray sulfurous, eye-stinging shroud of black powder smoke that telescoped from each man's position on the battlefield.

The wavering lines of Whigs swept forward toward their surprised enemies, pushing do-or-die for the hilltop where the Loyalists had rallied behind rocks and the ragged rail fence. When Pickens' column was within 30 yards, Boyd gave the order to fire, probably first in volleys and then at will. Through the hailstorm of lead, however, Pickens' men pushed for the hilltop.

Muzzle blasts flashed and stabbed through the smoke. Things were not proceeding exactly as Pickens had hoped. He was receiving precious little support from his wings.

Pickens' plan had called for Dooly's and Clarke's columns to cross the frigid, booming creek twice, first on each side of the hill, and then directly behind it where the Loyalists had been camped.

Dooly's account, read in one light, indicates that the first crossings were accomplished without difficulty. They met resistence from the Loyalists – who apparently also had crossed to the south side of the creek:

"In a few Minets it became a General Ingagement and helf for about 15 Minets Vary hot and then thay Retreated a Cross the Creek through a Large Cane Swamp and Imbodied them Selves on the other side of the hill."

The breaking of this Loyalist line south of the creek was a turning point, but Dooly and Clarke still had the main Loyalist camp to assault and after that, the hill where the enemy was reforming. They struggled to move their forces through the dense canebrakes so they could cross the cold, swollen creek – again.

Flying lead found flesh and bone with sickening thumps, and the screams and groans of the wounded and dying fused with the shouts and yells rising in a fevered pitch as the sides closed to hand-to-hand fighting with knives, hatchets, and gun butts amid the swirls of choking, brimstone-reeking smoke.

Meanwhile, Pickens, pressing ahead in what might have seemed then a forlorn hope, managed to overlap the right flank of Boyd's line. Unable to muster reinforcements, Boyd ordered a retreat. Almost immediately thereafter, he fell, mortally wounded, two bullets through his body and one through his thigh. With the Loyalists in retreat, Pickens' men pushed for the crest.

From his position behind the hill, Elijah Clarke glimpsed enough through the smoke to see the Loyalists' camp was in confusion, yet it was still rallying to the hill. Clarke yelled for his men to follow him, then spurred his horse for the creek. As he reached the bank, his mount was shot from under him. Catching another – maybe a Loyalist's – he remounted and plunged into the creek, emerging on the other side charging for the hilltop.

The roar of the battle had muted Clarke's order, so not more than a fourth of his command had followed him immediately, but the others pressed ahead, advancing into the vicious musket fire Dooly later described as seeming *"like 200 bullets in half a minute."* Nevertheless, both Clarke's and Pickens' men gained the hill as Dooly's charged from their side. The Loyalists, shocked and disorganized, broke and ran for their lives. Their mob of troops had been crushed by a Whig force half their size.

Aftermath

Following the battle, seventy Loyalists were either dead or suffering from the effects of mortal wounds. The Whigs took 75 prisoners, some of whom were wounded. The remainder of the Loyalists scattered to the winds, some making their way to Indian territories to the north and 270 to the Loyalist garrison in Augusta.

The Whigs also captured nearly 700 horses and a wealth of weapons and badly-needed ammunition. For all this, they suffered only nine dead and 23 wounded, two mortally.

With McGirth's force still near (a mere six miles away), and the possibility of others as well, the Whigs dared not dally. They collected their dead and wounded, as well as their booty of horses and weapons, and left the field, freeing a few of their Loyalist prisoners in order that they might bury their dead.

Before leaving, Pickens himself attended the dying Boyd. Accounts of this vary too. One story maintains that Boyd told Pickens "Sir, I glory in the cause – I die for my King and Country." Another version, which is decidedly more believable, maintains that Boyd said, "I want none of your damned Rebel's prayers."

Pickens himself never wrote which, if indeed either, story was correct. Both versions, however, have Boyd giving Pickens a brooch, his watch, and his sword, with the request that he make sure they reached his wife. Pickens honored the dying request.

The campaign to Kettle Creek thus ended. Pickens returned to South Carolina, taking with him the Loyalist prisoners. Twenty of them were later tried for treason in the Ninety-Six District and sentenced to hang. All but five, however, were granted reprieves.

Pickens himself had other battles in his future, as did Elijah Clarke. The end of the Revolution would find them both still fighting, and in 1782, they would fight together again against the Indians. For Dooly, however, Kettle Creek was his shining moment. In 1780, he accepted a British parole, but he found no peace. In June of that same year, he was murdered in his own house by Loyalist rangers sent from Augusta by his old enemy, "Burnfoot" Brown.

It would be left to his neighbor, Nancy Hart, to extract a most dramatic revenge for Dooly's murder. Nancy single-handedly captured six of Dooly's murderers, then supervised their hangings.

In the years following the hallowed Battle of Kettle Creek, the battleground was farmed over, and the site was little noted. Plows would sometimes turn up bullets and the occasional relic of a shattered musket. The hilltop was chosen as the site for the local **Revolutionary War Veteran's Cemetery**. In time, the area near the creek became a favorite picnic site.

In 1930, the local chapter of the **Daughters of the American Revolution** was able to set aside the field and erect the monument to the victory. The fieldstone gate was added a short time later. In 1998, the **Georgia Society of The Sons of The American Revolution** held a two-day gala capped by a rededication of the field.

From Kettle Creek To Yorktown

Kettle Creek gets little mention in broad histories of the American Revolution, due quite possibly to the fact that the bulk of the more outstanding battles were fought in Virginia and New England, and most of the histories were written from the perspective of individuals living north of the Mason-Dixon Line. However, even Dr. **Henry Lumpkin**, the late professor emeritus of history at the University of South Carolina, gave it only a cursory mention in his classic *From Savannah To Yorktown*: The American Revolution In The South.

Dr. Lumpkin follows up with the conclusion that any gains for the colonial cause in Georgia were wiped out by the mauling the British handed General John Ashe's Continental force two weeks later at Briar Creek. It seems the consensus maintained the Battle of Kettle Creek is one of those incidents doomed for the dusty corner.

The north Georgia back-country ultimately became a base and refuge for partisans fighting

in other areas. Operating from their home ground, Clarke and his men terrorized the Loyalists and British in Augusta and South Carolina. Clarke himself, was not at the **Battle of King's Mountain** in upstate South Carolina in October of 1780, but his men were. Clarke was responsible for setting in motion the chain of events which led to King's Mountain where Whig militiamen annihilated the Loyalist wing of **Lord Cornwallis**'s British army sent to subdue the South.

King's Mountain itself, set in motion events which ultimately precipitated the nearby **Battle of Cowpens** in January of 1781, where **General Daniel Morgan** annihilated the regular light infantry wing of Cornwallis's army. Once again, Clarke's veterans of Kettle Creek joined Pickens and his South Carolinians to play a critical role.

A Pyrrhic victory later over **General Nathaniel Greene** at Guilford Courthouse nevertheless convinced Cornwallis that the Southern campaign was lost. He abandoned it, and began the long march that led him to his rendezvous with a fellow by the name of George Washington at Yorktown.

More than any two battles, Kings Mountain and Cowpens changed the course of the American Revolution. They, however, were links in a chain which seems to begin at a conflict called Kettle Creek.

Is it possible that without Kettle Creek, neither of the other two would have occurred? It may not have been, as Andrew Pickens described it, *"the severest check and chastisement, the [Loyalists] ever received in South Carolina or Georgia,"* but it quite possibly was the first.

(To reach the Kettle Creek battle site today, drive eight miles southwest out of Washington, Georgia, on GA Highway 44. A historical marker directs a right turn onto Stony Ridge Road. After approximately a mile and a half, War Hill Road will be reached on the left. Follow this rough road approximately one and one-quarter miles until you reach the parking area faced by gateposts at the base of War Hill. For more information, contact the Wilkes County Chamber of Commerce)

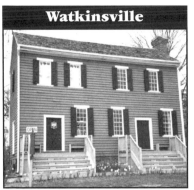

Historic Watkinsville

It was deemed so wicked, that it was rejected as a site for the new university built a short time later in the area. Today, however, the little town of Watkinsville has come a long way since its earliest days some 200 years ago.

In the early 1800s, Watkinsville – a stagecoach stop a short distance from Athens, Georgia – was so rowdy in fact, that it was declared "off limits" to the students at Athens' newly founded **University of Georgia**. The center of this decadent community was the **Eagle Tavern** – a regular stop on the stage route between Milledgeville and Athens.

The Eagle gained notoriety as a place one could obtain a meal, alcoholic beverages, a room for the night, and a lady of the evening if one so desired. Watkinsville is named for **Colonel Robert Watkins**, a prominent attorney and war hero from Augusta.

The earliest known building in Watkinsville may have been a small blockhouse. The first documented evidence refers to "a fort." Interestingly, in the late 1700s, Watkinsville was the farthest frontier outpost for settlers pushing westward from the original thirteen colonies.

The earliest occupation of Watkinsville was recorded in 1789 in the small fort which once existed at the site. Sometime between 1794 and 1801, the Eagle Tavern was built.

Through the years, owners of the tavern added to the original structure to accommodate the growing community. In addition to being a stagecoach stop, Watkinsville was also the county seat of Clarke County.

In 1821 **Richard Richardson** purchased the Eagle and began a series of renovations, ultimately adding six rooms to take care of the town's court proceedings and the growing clientele from the stagecoach business. Richardson's daughter, Martha, married a man named Edward Billups. When they were killed by Indians, their daughter, Belle, took over the business.

Despite the fact that Watkinsville was rejected as a site for the University of Georgia because of the "wicked tavern" located there, the Eagle Tavern, nevertheless, played a part in the life of the early students, becoming an oft-used site for a little drinking and illegal fun.

By the 1840s, the Eagle had achieved a measure of respectability – if only moderately. Harold W. Mann mentioned the tavern in his 1865 biography of 19th century Methodist preacher Rev. Atticus G. Haygood of Watkinsville.

"Most of the liquor was consumed in three established saloons, one of them at Watkinsville in the Eagle Hotel," Mann wrote, "where Athens lawyers stayed during the court sessions. Liquor drinking by respectable gentlemen in the 1840s is not to be confused with the riotous backwoods life of Georgia, especially two and three decades earlier."

Despite its notorious nature – and its connection with the court proceedings of the county – the Eagle escaped destruction when troops under the command of **General William T. Sherman** marched through the area in 1864. In 1959, the old tavern – on its last legs by that time – was deeded to the **Georgia Historical Commission** and later to Oconee County.

Following renovations, the tavern today houses the offices of the **Oconee County Welcome Center**, and Watkinsville has gained a regional reputation as a haven for artists. The scenic little town is also attracting an increasing number of tourists.

Today, the old tavern houses many artifacts from life in 19th century Watkinsville. Halford Lowder, a local resident, loaned one of the newest displays – a large loom and spinning wheel – once used by women of the era to spin cotton into thread and weave cloth.

The downtown area around the Eagle Tavern building was designated as a **Historical**

District in 1979, and houses many shops offering art objects, crafts and antiques today. The entire length of Main Street is faced by old homes and businesses, each with a different story to tell.

Another unique structure in Watkinsville is **Elder Mill Bridge**. This aged conveyance was built in 1880, and is one of the few covered bridges remaining in the state. Once dotted with scores of the colorful covered bridges, the Georgia landscape today now retains only a handful, and due to their scarcity, most of these are now carefully preserved.

No visit to the bridge would be complete without a word about its self-appointed guardian, Al Cumings, who built his home next to the aged structure when it was in serious disrepair. Al successfully lobbied then-Governor **Jimmy Carter** for funds to stabilize and preserve the bridge. He continued with his fundraising efforts for the bridge until the necessary funds were granted and the structure was repaired.

The nearby **Haygood House** which also figured in the early history of Watkinsville was built in 1827, and was the birthplace (1839) of **Bishop Atticus G. Haygood**, and his sister (1845), **Laura Askew Haygood**. The home served as the parsonage of the Methodist Church until 1972.

Atticus Haygood was president of **Emory College** and later Bishop of the diocese. He died in 1899.

Laura Haygood was principal of an early school for girls in Atlanta. She was also one of the first female missionaries to China. Another Haygood brother and sister are buried on the Haygood House property in Watkinsville. The headstones marking their final resting places still remain in the front yard today.

In 1999, Kathy and Jerry Chappelle bought the Haygood House and began a restoration which lasted two and a half years. They recently opened the historic home as **The Chappelle Gallery**, a retail business which features American crafts from artists with a national reputation.

The Chappells are no stranger to the art world of Watkinsville. In 1970 they converted an old farm and created the now renowned **Happy Valley Pottery & Art Colony**. They named the enterprise after a *Walt Disney Studios* production of *Mickey & The Beanstalk*, and like the mythical bean plant, the business grew rapidly.

Jerry Chappelle however, recalls it wasn't all sunshine in the early years. He says he and Kathy moved to the farm and began turning chicken houses into studios, but "from the day we moved in, everybody laughed at us because they didn't know what a potter was. At our first little summer festival we had thirty five people, but in 1999, the festival drew between 2,500 to 3,000 people, and it's still growing."

Jerry says the festival offers an artistic home base for other disciplines as well as pottery. Visitors can watch Jeff Bishoff throw a clay pot on his wheel and Judy Williams create a mosaic in stained glass. Loretta Eby shares the magic of glass-blowing with onlookers as she creates one of her renowned **"Witch Bottles."** She works her magic on a piece of molten glass as she shapes and colors it, and deftly removes it from the long pipe-like blower she handles so skillfully. She and her husband, Jeff Jackson – who works with metal and stained glass – collaborate on many projects.

The Witch Bottle legend began in medieval European glass-blowing studios. Often the craftsmen would be called to war and have to leave their studios. The last object created would be a colorful ornament with a hole left in the center. The evil spirits reportedly would be attracted by the bright colors and find their way inside. When the artist returned, he would throw the bottle into his newly fired furnace, thus destroying the malignant spirit.

Visitors to Watkinsville can find examples of the Jacksons' work, as well as that of other local artists at **Ashford Manor**, another historic home reincarnated into a thriving bed and breakfast inn. Ashford Manor was built in 1893 by **Alexander Woodson "A.W." Ashford** and his wife, **Elizabeth (Loula) Ashford**, who raised their brood of nine children in the structure.

Over the years, Ashford Manor has been witness to both good and bad times. A. W.

Ashford died of a heart attack in the home after what came to be known as "Black Friday" – the **Stock Market crash of 1929**. Ashford's son committed suicide in the family bank nearby when he was unable to cope with financial pressures.

The Victorian style of Ashford Manor lends itself well to the whimsical decorating styles of its current owners, Jim and Dave Shearon and Mario Castro. The trio had become tired of fighting Northern winters and decided to find a house that would lend itself to their idea of a bed and breakfast inn.

Today, Ashford Manor is home to several annual charity events. **Grace's Memorial Birthday Party** is a fundraiser for local animal charities held in June in memory of Jim's canine companion who died several years ago. Another is the annual **Fall Wine Fest** held in October to benefit the arts.

Bishop Haygood preached many a sermon in the Ashford Methodist Church located next door to Ashford Manor. This religious sanctuary from yesteryear enjoys a rich history of its own. During the **U.S. Civil War**, one of **Gen. William T. Sherman**'s officers quartered his troops' horses in the basement of the church.

Today, the church has been expanded to meet the needs of a modern congregation, but one can still observe the original exposed wooden beams overhead, as well as many of the handmade bricks in the walls.

In the late 1700s, huge parcels of land on what then was the western frontier were granted to Revolutionary war heroes as a reward for service. One such grant was made to **William Daniell**.

Built around 1790, the **William Daniell House** is believed to be the oldest house still in existence in Oconee County. This structure, located in **Founders Grove Subdivision** near Watkinsville, is considered a magnificent example of Plantation Plain architecture. The house was once the center of Daniell's 500+ acre plantation in Oconee County.

William Daniell died in 1840 at the age of 97. He lived a full and apparent lusty life, fathering 24 children. His first wife, Rachel Howe, died in childbirth bearing their eleventh child. William then married 17-year-old Mary Melton. Many of the Daniell descendants continue to live in Oconee County today.

Of course, there are other things to see and do in Watkinsville besides the exploration and admiration of the many historic structures. For fine dining mixed with art, the area's newest restaurant, **Le Maison Bleu**, offers exhibits by talented artists as well as food with an artistic touch.

Nearby **Harris Shoals Park** boasts a great nature trail that winds along a secluded creek and crosses a small lake. A picnic area and lots of wooded acreage offer a great place to enjoy nature at its best.

History buff, art connoisseur, or just plain tourist, you'll almost have to agree that though Watkinsville was once known as wild and wicked, it has earned the title today of "**Wonderful Watkinsville**." Plan to spend a day there on your next trip to Athens.

(For more information on Watkinsville and the Athens-Clarke County area, contact the Athens-Clarke County Chamber of Commerce.)

Ball Ground

Stancil's Store

Today's shoppers think nothing of competing with snarled traffic and human congestion in huge malls in order to shop for things they need. At one north Georgia general store from yesteryear, however, nostalgic shoppers may still purchase the merchandise once valued by our forefathers - and they don't have to fight traffic to do it.

Every so often, wandering travelers in north Georgia will pass one of these old general stores which still sparsely exist in the countryside. More often than not, the experience is a pleasant surprise too; a trip back thru time to a much simpler station in life. **Stancil's Store** on Yellow Creek Road in Cherokee County is just such an experience.

In their hey-days, the old general stores were a world without credit cards; a place where goods were bartered as often as they were sold, and a man's word was often good enough for credit. These old-time centers of commerce provided plowshares, horseshoes, sugar, coffee, tobacco, nails, flour and foodstuffs, - all the staples of rural agrarian life.

Precious few of these old bastions of barter have survived the march of time. That's what makes the few which do still exist - such as Broughton Stancil's store - so special. Stancil's still operates in much the same fashion that it did when Broughton's father ran it nearly 80 years ago, seemingly caught in a time-warp of sorts.

The potpourri that exists in the building today is part country store, part museum, and part tourist attraction. At first glimpse, the store appears to be a most disorganized place, but after you've been lost among the piles of merchandise, the uniqueness of it all begins to take on an enchantment that tends to fascinate even the most sublime personality.

And though the structure which houses Stancil's Store maintains an aura of a day long since passed, it, surprisingly, isn't the original Stancil's Store. That building, built by William L. Stancil in 1912, stands across the road, a faded yellow structure, rather smallish and unpretentious – hardly noticed by passing traffic. William did business there for six years until he built the "new" store across the road in 1918, the one still operated by son, Broughton, and his grandson, Mark, today.

In earlier days, Stancil's had a corn mill and a hammer mill to grind feed for livestock. There were hitching posts out front to "park" mules and horses. There was a sugar barrel and a coffee barrel in one corner. Everything was sold in bulk. There was no packaging.

Coffee was two pounds for a quarter, and it was sold in beans, because everybody had their own coffee grinder.

Today, the old store continues to offer old-fashioned butter churns, earthen jars, coal scuttles and slop jars. There is harness and tackle for any rig you'd ever need, and a display of horse collars that is impressive, to say the least. The sizes run from No. 12 to No. 26.

Horseshoes? Stancil's Store offers any size you need, from 000 to No. 2.

It can really become a comical situation for modern-day visitors, because much of what the store offers is from another – perhaps several – generation(s) back. If you need a yoke for a team of oxen, it's here. There are iron wash pots in several sizes. There are wheat "cradles," or scythes. There are wooden pitch forks for pitching hay, and much much more.

The items which seem to be the fastest sellers today are the boots and overalls. The late **Junior Samples** who gained fame on the television sitcom *"Hee-Haw,"* purchased all of his overalls here. He bought them half a dozen at a time. He wore size 60, but anybody bigger wouldn't have had a problem, because Stancil's carries overalls up to size 70!

Today, much of the responsibilities of the old store fall to Broughton's son Mark, 38. Mark says he often wonders what he's going to do about the place when it becomes his.

"I don't know if it'd be easier to just build a new place, or to try to re-organize this one," he laughs.

Some of the locals are more philosophical. *"If Stancil's ain't got it, then you don't need it,"* they quip.

{To get to Stancil's Store, follow GA 400 Highway north to GA 369. Turn left onto GA 369 and continue approximately nine miles to Yellow Creek Road (on right). Follow Yellow Creek Road approximately four miles to Stancil's Store. (Tel.: 770-893-2200.)}

Two Brothers Barbecue

We've all heard the old saying, "When life gives you lemons, make lemonade." Two brothers, Roy and G.E. Jordan, did just that after being laid-off from jobs at Lockheed in 1974. The pair had cooked barbecue which had been warmly-received at many family reunions in the past, so they decided to go into the barbecue restaurant business.

Roy and G.E. opened their fledgling business in their father's abandoned dry-goods store in Ballground, Georgia. They called their enterprise, appropriately enough, "Two Brothers Restaurant." And the rest, as they say, is history.

Since 1973, Two Brothers has served up delicious plates of barbecue to an admiring crowd. Business has never been lacking.

After a time, G.E. had an opportunity to return to Lockheed, so Roy devoted himself full-time to the restaurant which has grown and prospered. Today, Roy and his son, Randy, continue serving delicious pork barbecue and other mouth-watering dishes to a satisfied public.

The basic menu at Two Brothers consists of Brunswick stew, barbecue beans, cole slaw, hand-cut French-fried potatoes and pies. Much of the preparation takes place right on the premises too.

"We use ham a lot," Randy explains, "because it's easier to clean. We take off all the fat so that it's very lean."

A total of 120 hams a week ultimately are used to satisfy the appetites of the customers at Two Brothers. The Jordans are very careful about the way they prepare their meat too. The hams cook 12 to 14 hours, then are hand-cleaned and chopped. Father and son smoke the pork over hickory wood, buying the wood by the truck-load from local suppliers and then splitting it into slats.

The Jordans have learned that variety is the name of the game too. As a result, they serve chicken dishes as well. "Our mild, tomato-based sauce is a secret family recipe," Randy intones.

On Thursdays and Fridays, the restaurant offers lunch specials: green beans, great northern beans, fried okra, squash, fried green tomatoes (in season), sweet potato souffle', pan-fried potatoes, and fruit cobblers. On Fridays and Saturdays, customers consume 20 gallons of cole slaw according to the Jordans.

Roy Jordan's neighbor has been making the home-made pies for Two Brothers for 20 years. The cobblers include chocolate fudge, coconut meringue, egg custard pecan, and lemon chess. And the pies are cut into wedges too, not slices.

Part of what you get at Two Brothers is "atmosphere." The floor isn't your normal restaurant hardwood or linoleum. In fact, it's covered with sawdust. "The floor of the 1952 building was warped and buckled, and this was what I came up with to keep the tables steady," Roy explains with a smile. His customers seem to love it.

Roy is also an avid collector of antiques, and has a marvelous display of period farm tools, old cash registers, period photographs of the area, etc., that he has picked up over the years.

Roy says he is proudest of the old guns hanging on the walls, especially an 1800s-era buffalo gun he found in Idaho. "That had to be a pretty good gun to bring down an elk," he says. He's also proud of an old Montana muzzle-loader.

Lunch and dinner are served at Two Brothers on Thursday, Friday, Saturday and Sunday. It is closed on Monday, Tuesday and Wednesday.

No alcoholic beverages are served at Two Brothers Barbecue, and despite the barbecue smoke, tobacco smoke is strictly forbidden. The basic barbecue plate costs $8.50. Credit cards are not accepted.

(Two Brothers Barbecue is located at 1695 Old Canton Road in Ball Ground, Georgia (Tel.: 770-735-2900). Take Exit 27 off 565 north, continuing through the stop sign, then through a four-way stop. The restaurant is one and one-half miles ahead on the left.)

3 NORTH-CENTRAL GEORGIA

Blue Ridge

Blue Ridge Scenic Railway

The old rails from the **Louisville & Nashville Railroad** (formerly **Marietta & North Georgia Railroad**) had languished for years, and were being threatened with extinction when a group of stockholders in a small north Georgia railroad came up with a plan to revitalize the line.

Today, the **Blue Ridge Scenic Railway** (BRSR) is actually part of the **Georgia Northeastern Railroad** (GNR). The Georgia Northeastern is owned by stockholders of which the majority owner is an individual named **Wilds Pierce**, who is president of the line.

The idea for the scenic passenger service was hatched after a substantial number of Georgia residents made known their desire for a scenic line back into the mountains. Passenger service into the little north Georgia towns was discontinued long ago, and the rails unfortunately have been removed from many of the old railroads such as the famed **Tallulah Falls Railroad**. Former passengers have mourned the loss of this romantic (and useful) form of transportation for decades, and even younger individuals have expressed an interest in rail transportation to the quaint and attractive north Georgia mountain towns from yesteryear.

The old Louisville & Nashville (L&N) line from Marietta to McCaysville, was an exception. It, somehow had managed to survive the years. The rail line itself is owned by the Georgia Department of Transportation and is leased to the **Georgia Northeastern Railroad**. Following a feasibility study and some cooperative efforts with the city of **Blue Ridge**, Georgia, the Blue Ridge Scenic Railway was born, and is fulfilling the dream of travelers who wish to get back to the "good old days" of rail travel. It is fast-becoming a popular weekend activity for Atlanta-area residents.

The train leaves the recently-restored turn-of-the-century **L&N Railroad Depot** in Blue Ridge. As it travels northward through the Fannin County countryside, passengers are treated to some of the most beautiful scenery in the state.

The train is typically composed of a commissary car (where snacks and drinks are available) and a number of coach cars, all pulled by vintage 1960s diesel locomotives. Each coach features traditional upholstered seats (arranged in pairs), and many of the seats face each other, a situation which facilitates and enhances conversations with other passengers.

Each coach also has a restroom, and all the cars have picture windows for unrestricted viewing of the scenic beauty one experiences along the ride. The coaches also all have air-conditioning to keep the cars cool in summer and toasty warm in the fall and winter months.

The coaches were all built in the 1940s and '50s, so they offer a true opportunity to savor a vintage railroad ride. One of the coaches was built in the 1950s for the **Santa Fe Railroad**. It was purchased from a chapter of the **National Railway Historical Society** in Greensboro, North Carolina. The commissary car was built in 1951 for the Northern Pacific Railroad in Washington state. Two of the cars are being leased from the Atlanta Chapter of the **National Railway Historic Society** headquartered in Duluth, Georgia.

There is also one "open air" car which features padded bench seats facing to the outside and running the length of the car. This option provides an even better view of the scenery for riders who prefer the great outdoors.

The trip is particularly popular with individuals and groups who wish to spend a day in the mountains.

Diane Kittendorf, a crew chief who recruits and trains safety volunteers on the line says, "This is meant to be a fun trip." She and her husband, Del, members of the Atlanta Chapter of the National Railroad Historic Society, donate many hours to the excursions.

"We want to run a safe railroad with no chance for injuries," Diane explains. "We help people get onto the train, and make sure kids don't hang out windows since this is a very scenic ride along which tree branches occasionally brush the side of the train."

The BRSR began service in June of 1998, and approximately 17,000 riders made the trip during the inaugural season. Elderly people, especially, who feared they might never have a chance to ride trains again, have expressed appreciation for the experience.

Patrons find themselves in a gently-rocking car, with the sun shining through the windows, and the click-clacking sound as the train moves along the jointed track (in contrast to the continuously-welded rail used on modern lines), and it takes them back in time.

Passengers on the one-hour ride enjoy both scenery and a bit of history along the old rail line. Mile markers (which can still be viewed along the western side of the track) were installed when the L&N Railroad first acquired the track at the turn of the century. The markers all show the mileage from the L&N's corporate headquarters in Louisville, Kentucky.

Approximately three-quarters of a mile north of the historic depot in Blue Ridge, the railroad passes the site of the **old engine shops** which once serviced the trains. This facility (long disappeared) was operated between 1887 and 1906.

Approximately two miles north of Blue Ridge the BRSR passes **Murphy Junction**. In earlier days, the line was split at this point. A branch which continued on into North Carolina (to Murphy) angled off to the right, and the main line (angling off to the left) continued (as it still does today) on to Tennessee (Copperhill).

Today, the old Murphy branch-line ends at **Mineral Bluff**, Georgia. The rails between Mineral Bluff and Murphy, regrettably, were taken up long ago. Had they remained in place, the Blue Ridge Scenic Railroad might have had a direct connection with the **Great Smoky Mountains Railroad** which is so popular with vacationers in North Carolina today.

Also at Murphy Junction, there is a "y" in the tracks – or, in railroading parlance, a "wye" – which allows for a train to turn around or reverse the direction in which it is heading.

On the western side of the wye, an old family home which has long existed on the route can still be viewed today. A family by the name of **Panter** (pronounced "painter") built the home in the 1880s, and helped lay the track of the original rail line. Today, descendants of these railroading pioneers still live in the home.

Part of the route of the scenic line follows the beautiful **Toccoa River**. At one spot in the river near **Curtis Switch Road**, a historic landmark – an ancient fish-trap built by **Native Americans** in prehistory – can sometimes be seen (requires a brief walk across private property). During times of drought or low-water in the river, the large rocks comprising the fish trap become visible.

The fish trap consists of a series of the rocks placed in a "V" formation on the riverbed. When the Indians still inhabited this region, they periodically drove fish into the large opening of the "V" and gradually forced the fish down the length of the "V" until they were forced to pass out through the small end where they were caught in woven baskets.

The scenic train continues northward until it reaches the **Tennessee State Line** (which divides McCaysville, Georgia from Copperhill, Tennessee). The train stops just a few feet short of the state line to allow passengers to disembark.

After leaving the train, all passengers have one hour to browse the many shops in McCaysville. Tourism has replaced copper as a major industry in this scenic mountain town – the county's largest – incorporated in 1902.

One unique aspect of McCaysville has marked it as a fun spot for youngsters for a long time. Smart community promoters have painted a line across the community to mark the boundary between Georgia and Tennessee. And it seems that children just love to straddle the blue boundary. On the Georgia side, the town is called McCaysville. On the Tennessee side, it's known as Copperhill.

The blue-painted boundary line interestingly slices through the Hometown Foods IGA in McCaysville and its adjacent parking lot, then continues diagonally across the street before scaling the yellow brick building which houses the Copper Emporium furniture store. (How do they know who to pay their taxes to?)

Folks in McCaysville like to tell the story of how the boundary line is actually not quite accurate, since the surveyors back in the 1800s reportedly spent too much time sampling from a moonshine still they had chanced upon at the time.

Whether that's the reason for the erroneously-marked boundary or not, the state of Georgia contends its border with Tennessee should actually lie farther north – at the 35th parallel, as specified in the laws of both states. "But if the boundary is corrected, it will shift a mile-wide strip of south Chattanooga and most of Copperhill into Georgia," says Edwin Jackson, co-author with Marion Hemperley of *Georgia's Boundaries: The Shaping Of A State*, "and that's just not likely to happen. Even though a suit could be filed in the U.S. Supreme Court, the rulings of that court in similar situations have suggested that a boundary line which has been recognized and accepted in the past will stand, even if later found to have been drawn in error."

Whatever the circumstances, kids love to stand with one foot in Tennessee and one foot in Georgia and taunt their cohorts.

And as for the adults, most of them are entertained by the interesting shops in McCaysville. Everything from crafts, to antiques, to novelty gifts and tasty treats can be found aplenty!

One group of shops are housed in a large complex called the **Toccoa Center**. These include Mattie's Deli and Ice Cream Dipper where passengers can buy sandwiches, coffee and hand-dipped ice cream; Peach Pit Crafts, a nice crafts shop; Toccoa River Antiques and Gifts, and Bubbles Bath & Gift Shop.

It is noteworthy to point out that the former clinic of **Dr. Thomas J. Hicks** – who quietly operated a baby-selling practice in the 1950s and whose story was recently told in the national media on programs such as *ABC Television's 20-20* – once existed in the space occupied today by the shops in the Toccoa Center complex.

Following the return trip to Blue Ridge, many patrons have an opportunity to discovered there are a number of interesting shops and venues for entertainment there as well. . . and they're located along East and West Main streets on both sides of the railroad tracks. The community itself has changed little since the glory days of passenger travel back in the 1940s, and many of the old store-fronts still survive today.

There is a gift shop in the restored depot. Other establishments include the Fannin County Historical Museum, the Vault Antiques on West First Street, and the Antique Mall in the historic old Lovell Hotel on East Main Street.

{The Blue Ridge Scenic Railway operates from April thru November and departs from Blue Ridge, Georgia. Rates are: adults, $23; children (3-12) $12; and senior citizens (65 or older) $20. Groups are also charged $20 per person. All tickets include tax. Trains depart at 10 a.m. and 2 p.m. on Fridays and Saturdays and at 2 p.m. on Sundays. School charters run on Thursdays. To purchase tickets, call (800) 934-1898 or (706) 632-9833.}

Blue Ridge

Mercier Orchards

They've been grown in and around Gilmer and Fannin Counties for generations, and have become a lure for weekend getaways every year when the colorful leaves of autumn begin appearing on the landscape. Indeed, the apple orchards of north Georgia are an irresistible treat for those who enjoy this tasty fruit, and **Mercier Orchards** near Blue Ridge is one of the best in the business.

Mercier is located in Fannin County, just north of the heart of Georgia's apple-growing region in Gilmer County.

The bakery at this popular business (the largest and oldest orchard in Georgia) has breads – especially a delicious apple bread – donuts, and cinnamon rolls, all freshly-baked every day (as my nose had already told me). This mouth-watering shop also yields apple pies of different varieties, including old-fashioned fried pies (fried in vegetable oil); and some baked the modern way to avoid fat.

Some of the pies are made from fresh apples and some are made with dried apples (the latter is my favorite). Other tasty fried pie treats include peach, apricot, blueberry and pecan pies in season.

"Many of our customers tell us that our flaky pastry makes our pies extra good," explains Tim Mercier who serves as general manager for the business. Many of his guests know exactly what he means. If a pie has a good crust, it's more than half-way there already, when it comes to pleasing a customer.

"We're going to add cherry pies later," Tim adds, "but we'll be using a mix for them, since we don't grow cherries."

This area of Fannin County and its neighbor - Gilmer - have been a mecca for apple treats for many years now, ever since a few growers realized that the vicinity was well-suited for apple-growing. In 1943, **Bill Mercier** bought 25 acres of apple trees that a Blue Ridge pharmacist had planted in 1925. The elder Mercier has steadily enlarged the project ever since, later bringing his son into the business.

"The north Georgia mountains provide four important ingredients needed for the successful cultivation of apple trees and apples," Tim explains. "Those are warm days, cool nights, plenty of sunshine and plenty of moisture."

For that reason, a bonanza of apples are grown annually in Gilmer and surrounding counties. There is an apple growers association, and each year, an annual "**Georgia Apple Festival Arts & Crafts Fair**" to celebrate the abundance of this popular fruit.

The apple festival is sponsored each year by the **Gilmer County Chamber of Commerce** and the **Ellijay Lions Club**, and is held at the **Ellijay Lions Club Fairgrounds** just south of Ellijay on old Highway 5.

Mercier Orchards is a big player in the festival each year, and for good reason. Founder Bill Mercier is a big promoter of the apple industry and believes in it steadfastly. He was well-trained for the profession, earning a degree from the University of Georgia, and serving as a county extension agent for the Georgia Department of Agriculture for many years.

And he's received strong support from his family too. His wife has been actively involved in the business for years. ("But if I'd known he was going to become a farmer, I wouldn't have married him!" she smiles.) His son, Tim, earned a horticulture degree from the University, as well as a Master Degree in plant pathology from Clemson University. Tim joined his dad in the business following graduation.

Other family members are steadily coming on board too. Tim's daughters, Melissa, and husband David Lillard and Mandy and Joe, started working there in August of 1997. Both are graduates of the University of Georgia also, but in other areas of specialization: Melissa has a degree in communications, and David has a degree in chemistry with public health expertise in many areas.

"But no matter," Tim jokes. "We'll train them to do what's necessary here."

"Growers today use complex technology and machinery to bring apple products to consumers that are healthy, tasty and above all, safe," Tim continued. "Farming today is much more technically demanding than ever before because of all the new materials growers have to use. And new government regulations add to the complexity of the profession, controlling what products we can use and how often we can use them."

Tim explained that even the trees of today are vastly different from those grown when he was a child. Back then, climbing an apple tree to retrieve a prized apple was a challenge to the timid-hearted. No longer do growers climb 20 or 30 feet off the ground to pick fruit. Today, dwarf trees grow a maximum of nine feet in height, providing circumstances for easier picking and maintenance.

Mercier Orchards is one of the last apple houses in the state to grow, pack and ship fruit interstate. It has primarily been involved in the wholesale business, but is steadily enlarging its roadside market which has proven lucrative in recent years. Fresh apples, fried apple pies, and cider, etc., are solid sales items.

In recent years, many people have been alarmed to learn that cider may be unsafe if the apples are picked off the ground where they may have come into contact with cattle or horse manure or the feces of wildlife.

At Mercier Orchards, however, this is not a concern. The Merciers do not use manure fertilizer; no apples are picked off the ground; and all fruit is sanitized prior to being crushed.

"Most of our customers have been with us for years," Tim continued, "and they trust us. That's important to us."

And if by chance you're wondering about the special flavor of the cider you find at these apple grower houses, there is a reason. "Sweet cider (government-regulated, untreated natural juice) tastes much better than pasteurized," Tim maintains. He prefers selling sweet cider because he says full pasteurization destroys the taste of the product. (Bottled juice must be pasteurized to give it a long shelf life.) "We blend varieties to get a special flavor and we use top-of-the-line equipment to get an all-natural product."

Tim says he believes the apple-growing business looks bright for the years ahead. "Because of all the growing population and the growing awareness about the importance of eating fresh fruits and vegetables for good health, the consumption of apples will only increase," he says.

Georgia orchards produce perhaps one million bushels of apples a year. That's a lot of sweet and juicy treats, but it's only a small fraction of the total production nationwide (230 million bushels) each year.

After you eat your fill of apples at any one of the many packing houses in northeast Georgia, pack some up to take home with you. You'll want to enjoy them again in the days ahead, and especially over the holidays. Mercier Orchards will ship gift packages anywhere you want via UPS.

(Mercier Orchards, Inc., is open year-round. To reach it, take Highway 5 north at Blue Ridge off of GA Highway 515. For more information, call (706) 632-3411.)

Cartecay

R & A Orchard

Beautiful Apple Alley lies along the route of the rippling Cartecay River in central north Georgia. Here, along Georgia Highway 52 in the Cartecay community, families have been raising apples and operating apple businesses for generations. Andy and Jennifer Futch own one such operation – R&A Orchards – which was once owned by Andy's grandfather.

Andy, in fact, says his earliest memories are of the orchard. "My grandpa Leonard Payne had a slide he pulled behind the tractor that hauled bushel boxes of apples," he says. "My mother would put me in a box and I would get a ride on the slide."

Andy grew up in the world of apples next door to the orchard where his parents still live. Everybody in the area grew apples, and he says all his school friends lived in a similar world.

"There's no better place in the world to live than in Cartecay," he says today, emphasizing the point with a broad smile.

Jennifer – Andy's wife – grew up just five miles east, the daughter of B.J. Reece, one of three brothers who planted orchards there. Her twin brother, John, now operates her family's orchard. Her earliest memories – like her husband's – deal with apples.

"My mother used to put us in apple boxes while she worked in the orchard," she says. "I grew up in apples, then married into apples," she added, enjoying the humor in her comment.

In 1946, at the end of World War II, Andy's grandfather – disabled veteran Leonard Payne – had started a little orchard across the hill from R&A's present location. He sold apples from a truck he drove on a route, calling on grocery store owners.

Leonard Payne's daughter, Ann, married Roger Futch in 1967. After living in Atlanta two years, the couple moved back to the mountains where they bought this orchard, naming it from the initials of their first names.

In 1972, Roger opened his first roadside market. He has worked at the telephone company for many years and has added a few acres at a time to enlarge the orchard to its present size of approximately 60 acres.

Roger and Ann had two children – Andy, born in 1969, and Rhonda, born in 1972.

"Some of our regular customers have been with us as long as we've been here," Roger remembers. "They've watched Andy grow up."

As a 16-year-old high school student, Andy started a Future Farmers Of America project in which he planted 800 apple trees with $5,000 his father loaned him.

"I set up the account, sprayed the trees regularly, and eventually sold the apples," he explains. "Since it takes trees five years to mature, for that stretch of time it was all spending and no income."

Andy says he learned a lot from the project though, and ultimately received the state-sponsored "Star FFA Award" during his senior year in high school.

After high school, Andy had every intention of pursuing a college degree. He attended Abraham Baldwin Agricultural College in Tifton, Georgia, for three weeks, but decided he preferred to learn "on-the-job."

"I had the quickest college education there ever was," he quips with a grin today. "I figured that if I was going to be home farming anyway, I might as well be here learning."

In 1987, Roger made his son a co-owner in the business. That meant Andy would be reaping the rewards of income from the business, but it also meant he'd be taking on more responsibility and paying half of all the expenses.

"Andy knows the business, and he knows how to deal with the public too," Roger explains with pride. "He's also sharp on knowing what to buy. If he weren't in the business, I would have had to give it up or take early retirement from the telephone company."

Andy says he grows mostly semi-dwarf trees that reach a maximum of 25 feet in height. "Those trees require less labor in picking," he adds.

Most of the fruit is picked by hand by Andy himself, but when the trees get really heavy with fruit, he says he occasionally hires extra help. The apples are packed in 20-bushel boxes and the more fragile peaches – which they also grow – are packed in one-bushel boxes.

Andy says the only downside to the business is the occasional bad-crop years which result in low or no income at all. He says he well remembers August 10, 1998, when hail destroyed the entire apple crop in one day.

"We carried over $20,000 we had invested, and we had no return for that investment," he said, still downcast in the memory. He says some late cold weather snaps continue to worry him each spring, but the blooms usually survive, forecasting another good crop year.

Andy has learned that, like woman's work, an apple grower's work is never done. "My daddy always said that someone in the apple business can always find something to do," he continues.

Since the selling of the fruit is a seasonal endeavor, outsiders might think that apple growers just take it easy the rest of the year. In fact, the opposite is true.

"The pruning of the trees begins around Thanksgiving and goes through the first of May," he explains. "I start pruning the 10 acres of peaches the last of May, then start picking them about June 20."

The spraying of the trees begins around the last of February, and Andy says he usually does this 13-hour job at night. "I have to do the whole orchard every seven days," he explains.

Orchard owners must always be on the lookout for new pests too. "A friend of mine lost 75% of his crop one year in mid-August when the ornamental fruit moth from California invaded the orchard," Andy said.

Andy says he has never seen one of the one-inch-long worms that evolve from the moth, but he has certainly witnessed the damage from the worms' feeding. "One year, worms had eaten nine-tenths of the apples in each box," he adds. Andy puts out traps to catch the moths before they can complete their growth stages into the worms.

To equip himself to stay ahead of the pests, Andy took a course entitled "Integrated Pest Management" at the University of Georgia. "I learned how to save the beneficial pests such as honeybees, ladybugs, and black ants, and to destroy the harmful pests."

To keep up with trends in the industry and to learn of new developments, Andy says he belongs to the North Georgia Apple Growers Association and to the Southeastern Apple Growers Association.

Ideally, one needs to swap out trees every 20 to 30 years. Andy says their newest apples are the Gold Rush, Pink Lady, and Sinshu - a Japanese variety.

Changes in the market sometimes force changes on the growers too. "In the 1960s and '70s, when my grandpa ran the orchard, he raised Red Delicious apples because they shipped well," Andy explains. "In the late '70s and early '80s, shipping declined when Washington state growers developed a storage technique that kept apples fresh for 12 months. For Georgia growers, the market became seasonal and people now buy fresh fruit."

In recent years, Andy and Jennifer have begun turning their excess apples into apple butter and jelly, and excess peaches into peach preserves. Jennifer stirs pots in her kitchen in the apple house, using her grandmother's and Ann's recipes. She also makes grape jelly from vines around the farm.

R&A Orchards also offers dried apples, canned goods, sweet potatoes, and apple-related products, such as apple peelers. The Futches contract with a cider mill to furnish pasteurized apple cider, using several varieties of apples.

"A blend makes the best cider," Andy says. "We dry some apples, but get most of our dried apples from a specialty business in New York State."

Jennifer has run the apple house almost since the day the couple was married. "This is all I've ever known," she says. "I do whatever Andy needs me to do. I deal with the public, and I love it. People I met at Daddy's years ago come by, and we have new customers over here. There's no better life than this."

R&A Orchards raises 25 varieties of apples, 22 varieties of peaches, and nectarines. The season starts in late June with 12 varieties of peaches – freestone, mostly red meat peaches and a few white-meat varieties. They are staggered to ripen until mid-August.

The Lodi – an early thin-skinned tart apple that is good for drying, applesauce, and pies – ripens in July. "I have only 10 Lodi trees, and I plant them mainly for pollination," Andy explains. "Certain varieties of apples are sterile, so we growers have to plant different varieties to serve as pollinators."

Apples like the Detroit Reds and Ozark Golds start coming in around August 1. Red and Golden Delicious varieties start ripening in late August and go through early September. Rome Beauties, Stamen, Winesap, Mutzu and Jonagold last all season till early December, which is the closing date of the apple house.

And lest you think Andy doesn't work hard enough. . . in addition to the orchard work, he also raises a flock of 30,000 pullets for Gold Kist. He starts a new flock every 21 weeks. He also raises beef cattle and Holstein heifers.

(For further information and the best times to visit R&A Orchards, call 706-273-3821.)

Cherry Log

Pink Pig Barbecue

Mention the name "Pink Pig," and many folks think of a once-famous ride in the old downtown Rich's department store building in Atlanta. But up in the north Georgia mountains in a quiet little community called Cherry Log, another Pink Pig has been attracting patrons for approximately 30 years now, including some very famous individuals.

You never know what you'll find at one of those word-of-mouth low-profile back-road barbecue joints. Much to our pleasant surprise, however, we found the Pink Pig in tiny **Cherry Log** to be a delightful dining experience, and the list of regular patrons reads like a "Who's Who" in Georgia.

The Pink Pig is a simple eating establishment in appearance: a log cabin which backs right up to the hill. It's about as long as half a football field, with a small wooden sign simply stating "*Holloway's Pink Pig Bar-B-Que.*"

Inside, guests are welcomed and promptly seated. On cool mornings, a crackling fire radiates warmth and ambiance at one end of the building. The long dining room is furnished with rustic pine tables and pink wooden pig-shaped place mats.

The fireplace is a massive stone structure with pig andirons. Pigs, of the wooden, porcelain, and cast-iron variety, adorn most of the thick log walls, as well as an entire shelf along one side of the long room. A comparable shelf on the other side holds a collection of earthenware jugs – the kind in which folks in these parts once kept their moonshine.

It will take a few minutes to look over the menu. The specialty, as one might expect, is the pork barbecue, with the usual side orders of baked beans and slaw. The menu however, also unexpectedly includes such fare as steaks "cut to order," grilled chicken, fried chicken livers, and a house special – garlic salad.

Bud Holloway has owned and managed the Pink Pig for roughly 30 years now. He takes great pride in offering the finest, the freshest and the best.

"We make everything we can here – all our own sauces and seasonings," Bud tells us. "We don't get in a hurry about it. Good food takes time," he adds.

The pork is tender, tasty and lean. It's made from fresh pork hams, cooked patiently with indirect heat and hickory smoke in a pit for about 24 hours, or until the meat is falling off the bone. It took ten years for Bud to perfect the tangy and mellow sauce which so effectively complements the meat.

The Brunswick stew is thick with generous portions of meat. It has simmered all day in an iron kettle by the time patrons are allowed to enjoy it.

Bud's special garlic salad dressing has aged for several weeks before it is served. French fries are freshly cut; onion rings are home-made. The food is presented on casual and homey blue enamelware plates, and the beverages are served in generously-sized canning jars.

Photographs of some of the many prominent Georgians and public figures who have dined at the Pink Pig in years past are hung on the walls. On the fireplace mantle is a signed portrait of former **President Jimmy** and **First Lady Rosalynn Carter**.

Also included are pictures of television personalities, writers, sports figures, politicians, and, most notably, the former governor of Georgia and now U.S. Senator – the honorable **Zell Miller** – a long-time patron and fan of the Pink Pig.

As the oldest continuously-operating restaurant in Gilmer County, the Pink Pig is the only thriving business in the historic community of Cherry Log. And you have to watch closely for the side road off GA 515 onto State Road 5, or you'll miss both it and the Pink Pig, and breeze right on up the road to Blue Ridge!

{The Pink Pig is located 8 miles north of Ellijay just off Highway 515 (Zell Miller Mountain Parkway) on State Road 5. For hours of operation and other information, call 706-276-3311.}

3 NORTH-CENTRAL GEORGIA

Ellijay

Ellijay Wildlife Sanctuary

The rain is falling steadily on Debbie Cylke's long brown hair, and even though her rain jacket has a hood, she's so preoccupied with her lecture she doesn't think to cover her head. A group of students from Gordon Central High School in Calhoun listen attentively as she describes – just as she has done countless other times – the many fascinating aspects of the animal kingdom at Ellijay Wildlife Rehabilitation Sanctuary.

Debbie – who has been bitten by cougar, bear, bobcats, raccoons and snakes – does not consider simple rain to be a matter of concern. Her passion for her mission in life overrides any minor inconveniences regarding her personal comfort.

She continues the tour, leading the group to the cougars' lair. "This animal actually has 57 different names," she informs the group, "depending upon the location. Here [in north Georgia], they are usually referred to as 'panthers' or 'painters.' In the western United States, they are called 'mountain lions.'"

Debbie describes in detail the physical differences between the eastern and western breeds, then quizzes the students as she points to different animals.

Five years ago, Debbie and her husband Craig "Grizzly" Cylke initiated Georgia's only captive breeding program for the eastern panther. Less than 50 documented eastern panthers exist today, so the Cylkes feel that time is running out for the breed to reestablish itself.

The Cylkes have six western panthers that were rescued from illegal owners and canned hunt operators. Until 1978, cougar pelts brought $50 each from the government which encouraged the killing of these animals. The six panthers being maintained by the Cylkes offer new bloodlines to strengthen the dangerously-small gene pool of the breed's eastern cousins. Today [as of this writing], the sanctuary has five eastern and 13 western panthers

ready to mate.

"We feed them white meat to encourage a docile temperament," Debbie says. "Red meat creates chemical reactions which encourage a more aggressive nature."

The group gets a brief reprieve from the drizzle as they go indoors into the snake house. "This California mountain king snake is an endangered species," Debbie explains, as she points out the creature. She goes down the line in the snake house, describing the various species housed here.

It is in the snake house that Debbie likes to tell one slightly shocking story concerning her husband.

"Grizzly can't seem to turn away any animal in need of a home," Debbie begins, describing her husband. "He'll bring in the absolute ugliest creatures," she adds with a laugh. "One day, he told me he wanted to bring in a large rock python. I didn't like the idea because, judging from the almost-desperate tone of the donor, I was afraid the snake had become aggressive.

"But Grizzly just said 'Aw Baby, he needs a home,' so I gave in, and we isolated it for 90 days. After the isolation period – which we thought would calm the snake – my 16-year-old son, Jonathan, and I opened the cage door to take the python out. That snake leapt at least two feet and bit Jonathan twice before we could restrain it."

Animals are wild creatures, and it's easy to forget that fact. Most of them – if they feel threatened, discomfited or hungry – have the capacity to lash out, even if they seem tame. They are not the same as domesticated animals, and they'll prove it time and time again if given the chance.

Back outdoors, the group meets three young black bears that were orphaned when a Pickens County man shot their mother who had climbed into an apple tree on his property.

"We hope they [the bear cubs] can be

returned to the wild," Debbie says.

As the tour continues, Debbie explains the medical records they keep on each animal. She also explains some of the sacrifices which must sometimes be made to maintain a healthy rehab sanctuary.

"The animals come first," she adds. "We don't eat until they do."

Ellijay Wildlife Sanctuary is an accredited nonprofit scholastic organization the Cylkes started 32 years ago on 50 acres in the rolling hills of Gilmer County. Alongside that work, Craig designed, built and developed a similar sanctuary in Cohutta Springs for another group.

"I always loved animals as a youngster and young adult," he explains somewhat wistfully. "I always had my pockets full of injured 'critters.' Since my parents were nature lovers, they encouraged my interests."

Craig's parents – Ed and Charlotte – have remained close to their roots and early leanings too. They even live on the wildlife sanctuary property where Ed runs a machine shop.

For the first 15 years of the existence of their wildlife sanctuary, the Cylkes operated it on an amateur basis. Local people knew they could bring injured wildlife there for treatment.

Finally, the Georgia Department of Natural Resources (DNR) informed them they needed to obtain a license if they wanted to continue the endeavor. Since that time, the Cylkes have been regularly assisted and the Ellijay Wildlife Sanctuary facilities have been regularly inspected by DNR. The facilities are also regularly inspected by the U.S. Department of Agriculture (USDA).

"The two sanctuaries I've started were the first in Georgia to receive a 100% rating from USDA," Craig says proudly, "and this is the only center certified by DNR to deal with wildlife with rabies."

Craig is quick to praise Debbie and her work. "I met this beautiful country woman, and one look was all it took," he says with a quick smile. "For the past 23 years, she's been my right- and left-hand woman. She has helped this facility to be the best of its type in Georgia.

"Our program mainly involves two areas,"

Craig continues, "wildlife rehabilitation and public awareness education. Our main focus is directed toward the treatment and rehabilitation of injured animals. We take orphaned or injured indigenous wild animals and raise or rehabilitate them back to health. Whenever possible, we will release these animals back into the wild.

"A wonderful by-product of the rehabilitation process is education," Craig adds. "We take the non-releasable animals – such as wildlife which have imprinted upon a human or animals which have been in contact with humans for so long that it would be hazardous to release them back into the wild – and create a habitat in which they can spend the rest of their lives in comfort and safety. We then incorporate each of these animals and their problems into a complete education experience for our visitors."

In order to provide the utmost protection for their rehabilitated animals, the Cylkes do not allow others to know of the release date of their rehabilitated animals. "It would be a great shame for us to rehabilitate an animal at great cost, only to have it shot immediately after it left us," Craig explains.

Before the animals are released, they have to go through a "hazing" period during which they are isolated away from any human contact. The process can last six to 12 months, and the Georgia Department of Natural Resources must supervise the release.

Until the eastern cougar recovers in justifiable numbers, Craig says he won't be releasing any of them into the wild. His western cougars aren't indigenous to north Georgia and will always be captive animals.

One way Craig hopes to ensure preservation – and successful releases – is with natural release areas where bears and cougars can get used to living on their own before they are completely released.

Craig says he would create three-acre plots – enclosed habitat where the animals would have a chance to develop or regain the skills necessary for survival. "Once a wild animal becomes used to human contact, it loses its fear of man and poses a serious danger if released," Craig explains. "To prevent this, we plan to place an expectant panther mom in the five-acre natural habitat for two years, during which time we would provide her with live prey to teach her cubs survival in the wild. Once mature, the cubs would be released into appropriate wilderness areas throughout the eastern United States."

Despite his organization's best efforts, Craig says the release process can backfire. For example, through their contact with humans, bears learn that where there are people, there also is food. Released bears are tagged, and if they become a nuisance and have to be moved more than three times, they are euthanized.

"These animals are not pets," Craig warns. "They will 'bite' you."

One of the ways Craig assures that his message of preservation will reach the public is through education. He is an accredited outdoor educator in several curricula and Debbie has taken college coursework in biology, zoology and pre-vet technology. Between the two of them, they conduct classes at several sites.

A 300-seat amphitheater in the sanctuary was recently completed. Youngsters from schools and other organizations throughout the north Georgia area come to spend an hour, a day, and even longer on camping trips in the sanctuary.

With an annual operating budget of over $250,000, the nonprofit, fully-licensed facility receives no government funding according to the Cylkes, and depends entirely upon donations and proceeds from its education and camping programs to finance operations.

Many of the animals at Ellijay Wildlife Sanctuary have big appetites. The cougars, black bears, bobcats, lynx, deer, birds of prey, reptiles, raccoons and other creatures consume two tons of meat and one ton of dog food each month. The food bill currently totals $1,000.00 weekly, say the Cylkes.

With the assistance of Dr. Francis Cipullo, veterinarian at the Appalachian Animals Hospital in Ellijay, and other volunteer veterinarians, the Cylkes say they have rehabilitated and released tens of thousands of indigenous animals to the wild. Through their wildlife conservation programs, they have educated more than half a million people.

The Cylkes say they would love to have a wildlife hospital; a vet-tech training and research center to allow on-going studies of the survival of the eastern panther; a small apartments building for vet-tech students; and a complete wildlife library. Those things, however, will obviously have to wait until funding may be obtained.

"Our hope is that by teaching young and old alike, we can make a difference in our world," Craig states. And as he is constantly reminding his students, "Let us not forget that if too much of our wildlife ceases to exist, so also may you and I."

(For more information on the Ellijay Wildlife Rehabilitation Sanctuary, call 706-276-2980 or visit the website: www.wildliferehabsanctuary.org.)

Ellijay

Hillcrest Orchards

L ooking for an inter-esting day-trip this autumn? Try one of the apple growing farms in north Georgia's Gilmer County. You absolutely will not be disappointed, and your children will be snacking on one of the healthiest foods available.

Ellijay, in northeast Georgia has been the heart of the apple industry in the southeastern United States since the early 1900s. Apple farms and sales outlets can be found along almost every thoroughfare and visitors travel from all over the state every fall to "get their apples" in Gilmer County.

One of these businesses – **Hillcrest Apple Market** – is a thriving enterprise today, but things weren't always so "apple pie-ish." In fact, in 1991, the endeavor almost collapsed completely.

In 1991, Hillcrest owner and operator **Jerry Smith** passed away. Though only in his late 30s, he was the victim of a fatal brain aneurysm. It was a tragic loss.

Smith's wife, Janice, was left with a family to raise and a lot of unanswered questions. How in the world was she going to keep the business going by herself?

Janice's parents, Hayward and Ellen Reece, urged her to sell the business. "It's too much for you to handle alone," they told her, especially since she was now a single parent as well.

The Reeces were natives of the Ellijay area though, and knew all about orchards. Hayward, in fact, had started Hillcrest on 75 acres of prime Ellijay apple growing land nearly 50 years earlier in 1947, just after he returned from serving in World War II.

Hayward and Ellen had worked hard to build up the orchard. It, practically, was a life-long investment. They retired when Janice married Jerry Smith and the couple took over the management of the orchards.

"Jerry was a very hard worker and he loved the orchards a lot, but we just didn't think

Janice could handle the business on her own," Hayward explains. To her credit, however, the Reece's daughter proved to be a determined survivor.

"I just couldn't bear to give up the place," Janice says. "It's always been a part of my life and Jerry loved it too much for me to just abandon it. I also knew Mom and Dad didn't like retirement all that much, we all just went back to work in the orchards."

Today, the family looks back upon that decision as a momentous one. What was a successful family business before Jerry died is even more so today.

The enterprise is tightly managed by Janice. Her college training and work experience in business and accounting, along with some innovative ideas, have paid off handsomely.

All one has to do is pay a visit to Hillcrest Orchards to view this success story first-hand. And if you do, Janice and her parents will welcome you.

Plan to spend the better part of a day if you make the trek to Hillcrest, especially if you're taking the kids along. All children visiting Hillcrest are guaranteed to sleep all the way home.

The first thing to do when you get to Hillcrest is to watch a ten-minute video production. This nice little presentation is gladly provided upon request, and it's worth your time, due to the background information it provides on the apple production business. For instance, where do you think all the bees come from that are necessary to pollinate those millions of buds on the trees each spring? Though we'd like to think they abound naturally, the fact of the matter is – they don't.

The bees are rented, of course. Beekeepers from all over the mountains bring their bees to Ellijay and rent them to apple growers each spring.

The video also explains about the training

3

NORTH-CENTRAL GEORGIA

and grooming necessary for the trees. Pruning, for instance, is the exact science of removing only those branches necessary to allow maximum sunshine to reach the fruit while keeping the height of the branches low enough for easy fruit-picking.

And yes, you heard correctly. Young trees must be "trained," just like young children. I won't spoil your fun by explaining every detail of the film, but weights and rubber bands are involved in the training process.

One primary area of interest to youngsters and oldsters alike is the **Hillcrest Petting Farm**. All the favorites are found here, including goats, pigs, lambs, chickens, calves, rabbits, geese, ducks, and more. Bring plenty of film and be ready for lots of photo opportunities of the children holding and petting the animals to their hearts' content. However, there is a fee for access to the petting farm.

A tractor-drawn wagon ride follows a path through the orchard and ends at the **Nature Trail** which leads to the **Petting Farm and Play Area** with its 50-foot slide. Guided tours for groups are available by appointment.

A special exhibit includes a **Moonshine Museum** complete with a copper still.

Inside the **Farm Market** there is a gift shop and many crafts items. There is no charge for admission to the Farm Market, bakery and ice cream parlor . An ice-cold "cider slushy" is almost guaranteed to "hit the spot" while you're browsing.

Also in this shop are any number of fascinating apple-oriented tools. There are wedgers, corers, dryers, and that most amazing machine of all, the peeler. It does everything imaginable to an apple.

Just jab a big juicy apple on the peeler, turn the crank, and watch in fascination as a colorful ribbon of red or green apple peel shoots out one opening in the machine. The apple, peeled, cored and sliced into one continuous delicious strip, pops out another opening. It can then be dried, baked, or simply eaten as it is.

It's also here at the Farm Market that you'll find all the apples. Believe it or not, there are 22 varieties of this delicious fruit at Hillcrest. Most are time-tested old favorites, but there are also several brand-new varieties. From Sweet Red, Golden Delicious and Granny Smiths to Jonathans, Arkansas Blacks, Rome Beauties and Stayman Winesaps, you'll have a wide selection from which to choose your favorite. A new variety called "Mutsu" (and also known as "Crispin") is fast becoming Hillcrest's best seller.

Hundreds of colorful canned goods – from chow-chow to pepper jelly – fill the market's shelves. Mountain honey and sorghum syrup are lined up beside the apple butter and pickled cling peaches. I have to control myself or I'd take home one or two of each every time I visit.

Homemade individual apple pies (baked, not fried) are Ellen Reece's specialty. Dried apples and the famous Hillcrest Apple Cider Doughnuts are also available.

{Hillcrest is open August through November seven days a week, but most entertainment opportunities are only offered on weekends. To book a tour or for more information, call (706) 273-3838 (www.hillcrestorchards.net). To reach Hillcrest from Atlanta, take Interstate 75 north to Kennesaw where Interstate 575 branches off to the right. Continue northward on I-575. The interstate shortly becomes Georgia Highway 515. Continue northward to the East Ellijay exit. Turn left on GA Highway 52 East. Continue for nine miles. The orchard is on the right.)

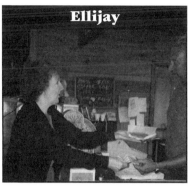

Panorama Orchards

Have you ever seen one million apples packed into one room? Count them. . . 10,000 bushels. That's how many of the delicious round treats the **Panorama Orchards Apple House** stores in its cold-storage facility just south of Ellijay in Gilmer County - the apple-growing capital of Georgia.

Panorama Orchards has its own cold-storage facility, as well as the largest retail (and wholesale) square footage for sales of any apple grower in the county.

All this sales space makes for a lot of room for delicious goodies, and owner **Gene Stembridge** doesn't waste a single inch. Visitors can enjoy fried apple and peach pies, regular dish apple pies, home-made apple brandy cake, caramel apples, and coffee – just to get started.

One of the many very popular items at Panorama is the fried apple pies. Gene has developed his own special – and secret – recipe which he will not divulge.

As with the apple brandy cakes for which Panorama has become known, Gene also helps with the production of the pies. In the busy season (the autumn months), customers reportedly eat several thousand fried apple pies a week. Fried peach pies are available as well. All the fried pies are now produced in commercial frying equipment which has reduced the grease content.

A new dining area was recently added to the complex at Panorama Orchards. There, a full menu offers barbecue, slaw, and baked beans. Visitors can also buy homemade jams and jellies, mountain sorghum and honey, homemade ice cream, fall squash, pumpkins, Indian corn, nuts in season, and bird houses.

Those curious about the apple industry can watch a packing line where apples are cleaned, sorted, graded, and packed for shipping. Guests can also view apple butter being made and poured into jars. An elevated second-floor viewing area offers a unique vantage point.

And if you want to do it yourself, Panorama Orchards even offers a **Pick Your Own area**. Monday through Saturday (and Sundays after 1:00 p.m.), participants can pick all the apples and peaches they want – for a fee – till dusk.

And lest the reader think Panorama Orchards is a "Johnny Come Lately," Gene Stembridge says he is carrying on a business begun by his father and uncle nearly 70 years ago. Those brothers harvested apples from orchards in the Ella Gap region of the county near where Panorama Orchards stands today. The men shipped their apples by train from the siding at Ella Gap.

{Panorama Orchards is open year-round, seven days a week, 9:00 a.m. to 6:00 p.m. The facility is located off GA 515 (Interstate 575) three miles south of Ellijay. For more information, call (706) 276-3813.}

3 NORTH-CENTRAL GEORGIA

Ellijay

"Pick Your Own" Apples

When the autumn season arrives each year, one of the first things signaling its presence in Georgia is the ripening of the state's apple trees. According to the **Gilmer County Chamber of Commerce**, Ellijay produces the first apple crop in the nation every year, and lots of area residents like to just go out and "pick their own!"

Gilmer County boasts a wide variety of apple farms – the most in the state. Many of these businesses offer **"Pick Your Own Apples"** privileges to interested individuals. There are also a number of other fine orchards in Fannin, Lumpkin, Union and Towns counties too.

As a result, individuals wishing to pick their own apples have a number of choices for this adventure. We checked out three apple growers to see what they had to offer. Here's what we discovered:

Panorama Orchards

Jennifer Kirby hosts visitors at the "Pick-Your-Own" sections of Panorama Orchards in East Ellijay. Many pickers come back regularly – some returning every year.

The pickers don't just come from Georgia either. "We get pickers quite often from a variety of places in the U.S., and sometimes from other locales as well," Jennifer adds.

The apple-picking season in Ellijay runs from late August into December, and produces approximately 70% of all of Georgia's apples. The season at Panorama Orchards usually starts sometime around Labor Day weekend.

The red and golden delicious varieties usually ripen first. The Rome beauties are ready by mid-September, and the Granny Smiths ripen in October.

Panorama charges $7 for a one-half bushel bag of fruit.

(Panorama Orchards is located on Georgia Highway 575, approximately three and one-half miles south of Ellijay. To get a map to the "Pick Your Own" section, stop at the Panorama apple house. To find out when apples are ripe for picking, call (706) 276-3849 each August. Groups need to make reservations.)

Mountain View Orchard

Two thousand trees sounds like a lot of hardwood, but Joe Dickey thinks his orchard – Mountain View – in McCaysville, may be the smallest in north Georgia.

Dickey says he has no cold storage, so his apples go directly from the tree to the buyer. He also sells fried apple pies, caramel apples, candy apples, apple cider, apple butter and homemade jellies.

"Pick Your Own" privileges at Mountain View last from August 1 to October 31. The apples cost the same per bushel picked from the trees as they do purchased right off the apple house floor. That comes to right around $13 per bushel.

Mountain View Orchard is open from 9:00 a.m. to 6:00 p.m., Monday thru Saturday, and from 12:30 p.m. to 6:00 p.m. on Sundays.

(To get to Mountain View from Atlanta, travel north on GA Highway 515. Turn left onto Georgia Highway 5 at the first traffic light in Blue Ridge. Travel approximately 10 miles to McCaysville. Turn left at the first traffic light in town and continue on for approximately three miles. The orchard is on the right on Mobile Road. For more information, call (706) 492-7753.)

Hillcrest Orchards

Hillcrest has 80 acres of apple trees. Much of this farm begins a celebration on September 19 and 20 from 9:00 a.m. to 11:00 p.m. when an annual "Apple Pickin' Jubilee" is observed. This special event is always held the last two weekends in September, and is a great time for participants to "Pick Their Own" apples.

Nineteen orchards at Hillcrest produce 22 varieties of apples – enough to satisfy most anyone's palate. The Golden Delicious apples usually are the most popular variety.

Live entertainment is provided throughout the Jubilee. A mountain barbecue and other "vittles," (including home-made fried apple pies, ice cream, apple cider, doughnuts, and more) are available for sale. And of course, the main event - pickin' your own apples right from the trees - is the major attraction at this festival. "Pick Your Own" apples at this farm cost $2.00 for one-quarter of a peck; $3.00 for one-half a peck; $5.00 for a peck; and $7.00 for one-half a bushel. (Note: There are four pecks to a bushel.). Admission to the festival is free.

(Hillcrest Orchard is open Monday thru Saturday, from 9:00 a.m. to 6:00 p.m., and on Sundays from 1:00 p.m to 6:00 p.m. To reach Hillcrest from Atlanta (while traveling north on Georgia Highway 515), turn left onto Highway 52 in Ellijay. Travel approximately nine miles. For more information, call (706) 273-3838.)

Historic Trippe-Simmons-Nelson Tavern

Pickens County's first historical society was formed years ago with the specific goal of preserving an aged structure in private ownership just outside Jasper known as the **Trippe-Simmons-Nelson House**. That mission, however, was never allowed to be accomplished – until 1997. That year, the old structure – probably the most historic in the county – was finally donated to the Society for preservation and restoration.

This donation is a remarkable gift in itself, in view of the unique history of this home and its former occupants. Pickens has always been a small county in size and population, and every loss of any historic structure or site is a special tragedy. The Trippe-Simmons-Nelson House had been heavily vandalized in recent years and appeared headed for the same demise.

Descendants of the Trippe family, however, realized the important structure was in a perilous situation. Thankfully, they decided that enough was enough..

Though there have been many losses of historic structures in Pickens over the years, its residents are quite fortunate to a large degree. Such wonderful old buildings as the aged hotels at Talking Rock, the **Pink Marble Mansion** at Tate, the **Lee Cape House** in Hinton, the old **Philadelphia school/church** near Jasper, Jasper's **Woodbridge Inn**, and the Indian cabins at **Hill City** are unique reminders of the former existence of Native Americans and pioneer settlers at these sites. Structures of this historic quality and value disappeared long ago in many other Georgia communities.

What has survived – all things considered – is impressive, but undoubtedly, the Trippe-Simmons-Nelson House deserves credit as Pickens County's most historic structure, with the most links to the county's history. The former occupants are historically unique in many

regards, and the structure's location on the old Federal Road in Pickens lends even more historic value to the site.

In 1804, the United States government persuaded a reluctant **Cherokee Nation** to allow the state of Georgia to survey the **Federal Road** through what today is northwest Georgia. This simple wagon path, which wound along the crests of numerous mountain ridges, became the region's major thoroughfare as well as **Georgia's first official state highway**.

The old road is still visible in many places today, especially in Pickens, where more of it exists than in any other county. It was after the road was opened in 1805, that a simple, one-story log tavern/inn was built to take advantage of the road's traffic. Many other taverns/inns were built along the route during pioneer days. **Vann's Tavern** near the present-day Hall/Forsyth County lines (moved and preserved today at **New Echota State Historic Site** in Calhoun) and the **James Vann House** at Spring Place in present-day Murray County are two good examples which still survive intact today.

By 1832, **General Charles Haney Nelson** (1796-1848) of the Georgia Militia was occupying the tavern. (Trippe-Simmons-Nelson House). He lived there with a Cherokee woman that "he had taken up with."

This was during the unfortunate period of the Cherokee Indians Removal from what was fast becoming an ever-growing state of Georgia. Nelson and his troops represented "law and order" in that part of Georgia, fighting running battles with greedy whites who were attempting to illegally operate gold mines on Indian lands and to seize lands which the Indians had not yet vacated.

Nelson's family was an old-time military family. His ancestor, **John Nelson**, had been involved with the Revolutionary War **Battle of Kettle Creek** in Wilkes County, Georgia. Charles won his rank in the Seminole Indian wars and later served with distinction in the war with Mexico. Nelson's family also claimed kinship to British admiral **Lord Horatio Nelson**.

Charles Nelson eventually moved to Calhoun, giving up the tavern/inn to Indian trader **James Simmons** (1803-1894) of nearby Sanderstown (Talking Rock). Simmons expanded the log structure with new wings, porches, and an additional half story with gables. This completed structure is the building known today as the Trippe-Simmons-Nelson house.

Across the road from his house, Simmons operated a log trading post (long disappeared). One of his store account books from the 1850s is preserved on microfilm at the **Georgia Department of Archives and History** in Atlanta, and also at the Pickens County Public Library in Jasper.

Simmons himself enjoyed a long and colorful political career. During the 1850s, he headed Pickens County's local "**American Know Nothing Party**," a radical third political party that tried to unite a country which was fast coming apart at the seams over the issue of slavery.

The Democratic Party, led by local representatives **Lemuel Allred** and **Stephen Tate**, stopped the progress of the "Know Nothings." Simmons, however, was just getting started. He subsequently was elected to the Georgia Secession Convention of 1860 as a "pro-Union man."

The Convention eventually voted in favor of secession, but Simmons refused to support the move, even as a sign of unity after the issue had obviously been settled. He and the other four hold-outs did, however, sign a document stating they would defend the state of Georgia against all enemies.

Simmons apparently was good to his word too. During the **War Between The States**, Simmons served in the Georgia Confederate State Senate, and wrote to Georgia's Governor Brown about a critical shortage of salt in Pickens County. When a group of Unionists tried to kidnap Simmons, the local Confederate Home Guard under the command of **Benjamin Jordan** came to his rescue.

Because of his political affiliation, James Simmons had been appointed to the financially-lucrative political position of federal postmaster. His house served as the **Talking Rock Post Office** from January 18, 1832 to July 15, 1833. It also later became the **Marblehead Post Office** on July 5, 1850, and was renamed the **Jasper Post Office** (for the newly-created county seat of the new county of Pickens) on June 3, 1854.

Today, the aged Dutch doors, common to all old post offices, are still functional in the home. This is just one of the many architectural elements of the home which make it invaluable to historians today.

Among James Simmons' descendants were prominent politician **Philip Rice Simmons**, as well as astronaut **Gordon Cooper**. James is buried in the Jasper City Cemetery.

The last family to occupy the historic home was the Trippe family. The most recent Trippe descendant, fearing further vandalism of the old house, was the individual who donated the aged structure to the Marble Valley Historical Society, an organization known for successfully saving and restoring the 1906 Pickens County Jail.

In his 1934 seminal volume of history on Pickens, Luke Tate included a drawing of the home, referring to it as "one of the oldest houses in northwest Georgia." The Marble Valley Historical Society has never forgotten that of all that remains of Pickens' past, nothing manmade holds so much historical significance as the Trippe-Simmons-Nelson House.

Today, despite the ravages of missionaries and Indians, politics, the War Between The States, tornadoes and the elements, Pickens County's most valuable historic treasure will be around when all of us have been reduced to mere lines in a book of census data.

(For more information on the Trippe-Simmons-Nelson House, contact the Pickens County Historic Society or the Pickens County Chamber of Commerce.)

Jasper

The Woodbridge Inn

It was built as an inn where two major thoroughfares – the **Old Federal Road** and the **Marietta & North Georgia Railroad** – provided a steady supply of customers. Today, the charm of this century-old structure and especially the tasty meals served there keep guests returning year after year.

The excellent food at this interesting site has almost always been its drawing card, all the way back to the days when the old railroad depot was once located down the hill and to the right of the aged bridge in front of the inn from which its name is drawn. At that time, the Marietta & North Georgia Railroad (or the **L&N Railroad**, depending upon the timeframe), offered both passenger and freight service. Upon arrival in Jasper, travelers would automatically trudge up the hill for food and accommodations at the inn.

On June 4, 1877, **Edmond E. Lenning** purchased seventeen acres with a two-room log cabin divided by a dog-trot in Jasper. Around 1880, he replaced his cabin with a two-story heart-pine frame building - the same structure which today is known as the Woodbridge Inn.

According to Luke E. Tate's *History Of Pickens County*, Lenning had been among the stampede of miners in the **California Gold Rush** of 1849. *"Before leaving home, Ed Lenning had made the statement that he was going out there and make ten thousand dollars in gold, then come back to the 'red hills of Georgia,' marry, and not work any more. He kept his word all the way through,"* wrote Tate.

On July 16, 1919, Lenning passed away, leaving the *"Lenning House"* to his two widowed daughters. By the 1930s, the sisters had moved from Jasper and the building was all but abandoned.

Edmond's son – **James E. Lenning** – purchased the property on February 4, 1937. His wife, Mary, became the manager of what came to be known as the Lenning Hotel. She continued to operate the business after her husband's death in 1942. In 1950, having no children, she bequeathed the hotel to her sister – **Ora Cox Little.**

Ora Little operated the business until 1970. By 1971, however, the work had become too much for the spry little lady, and she decided to retire. Her sale of the inn began a rapid succession of owners and a dramatic decline in the property.

Finally, on December 27, 1976, **Jochem** (Joe) and **Brenda S. Rueffert** began a new era for the aging edifice. They also began a dramatic facelift of the historic structure, and its star slowly began to ascend once again.

In 1991, in an effort to satisfy the many individuals seeking overnight accommodations in the area, the Ruefferts built a **lodge** adjacent to the restaurant.

The dining fare in the restaurant is Continental American with such mouth-watering treats as filet mignon forestiere, roast Long Island duckling a l'orange, veal oscar, fresh ostrich filet, shiitake mushrooms, tournedoes a la maison, twin medallions of fresh venison, wiener schnitzel, and a host of tasteful seafood delicacies such filet of flounder imperial, and fresh rainbow trout.

Prices for entrees range from $13.95 to $18.95. Desserts such as bananas foster, flaming peaches and hot fudge cake never cease to delight diners.

Take the time to visit the Woodbridge Inn and sample the delicious fare served up by the Ruefferts. You'll be glad you did.

{The Woodbridge Inn is located at 44 Chambers Street, Jasper, Georgia, 30143. Reservations at the Woodbridge Inn are strongly recommended, especially during the late summer and Autumn months (high season). A wait of an hour or so is not uncommon for drop-in guests, but guests with reservations many times are luckier. For directions and additional information, call 706-253-6293. Email: info@woodbridgeinn.net.}

3

NORTH-CENTRAL GEORGIA

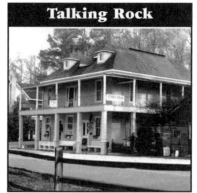

Historic Talking Rock Community

They say General Sherman was careless with matches, and Atlanta rose like a phoenix from the ashes. In a similar fashion, the little town of Talking Rock, Georgia, has shaken off years of dust, rust and inactivity while preserving its historic downtown area. Today, the fresh-faced hamlet is heading its own resurgence as a budding antiques district in north Georgia's Pickens County.

While Atlanta, over the years, has all too often torn down the old to create the new, her mountain cousin has not followed this lead. Talking Rock is being reborn as a place in love with its past. The old commercial district – through much of which can only be described as sheer luck - has been preserved much as it appeared a century ago. The buildings have been restored and rejuvenated as a variety of antique shops.

A number of the structures which have survived were saved after reaching the brink of demise. Prior to their restoration, many of them were well on the way toward implosion from sheer termite infestations.

"In the teens and 20s, this was a terrific cotton market," said lifelong resident N.C. Low. Mr. Low served as mayor of the town for 30-plus years.

The elder statesman of the town said he remembered when the rail siding through the town was lined with bales of cotton, chestnut-oak tanning bark, and stacks of pulpwood. Rural people, short of cash, traded the pulpwood and tanning bark to storekeepers for store goods. In turn, the merchants sold the bark to leather tanneries, and the pulpwood to paper companies. The raw materials were all transported to buyers by the railroad.

"I've seen 75 to 100 cotton wagons on the street in the fall," Low continued. "(There were) so many that there was no room to turn around." He described how four men would grab hold of the corners of a mule-drawn wagon and rotate it in place to reverse its direction.

The autumn season marked the cotton harvest and ginning time. The Cagle family operated a steam-powered cotton gin on Talking Rock Creek, just west of town. There, cotton was ginned, weighed, and baled.

Many farmers operated throughout the year on credit, drawing food and supplies from a storekeeper against the day their crop came in. The day it was ginned and baled, these farmers hauled their crop into town to settle up. Once the debts were paid, the farmers received the remaining value of their cotton crop in goods and cash. The merchant, in turn, sold the cotton bales to other buyers and shipped it via the railroad.

In the heydays of Talking Rock, two Louisville & Nashville (L&N) Railroad freight trains and four passenger trains arrived in town daily. The little community was abuzz with activity. The boom-times, however, did not last.

"The boll weevil and the Depression put people out of the cotton business," Low said. "I remember the Depression days. The people in this community didn't have one thin dime in their pockets. No cash money. They lived off the land. Some survived on cooked apples, lard gravy, and biscuits."

Mr. Low said he grew up in a white house just up the hill behind Times Past, an antique store on Main Street.

Mrs. Low grew up in this same building when it was a general store and the residence of her parents. Her husband purchased the store from his future in-laws in 1952, not long after he had returned from World War II.

In 1952, as new storekeeper of N.C. Low General Merchandise, Low still bought pulpwood from local citizens. The barter system, however, had been discontinued. Low said he wrote a check for each transaction. In time, he said he began buying saw-timber too, shipping it to sawmills on the L&N Railroad.

By that time, the freight trains were still running regularly through Talking Rock, but the passenger trains had virtually disappeared. Freight crews "laid-over" at Talking Rock. They waited while large trains of marble chips were being put together just up the line at Whitestone. Low said he befriended many of the trainmen who killed time at his store.

By that point, the town of Talking Rock was beginning to die. It happened to many communities all across the United States as the passenger trains were discontinued. The railroad was the lifeblood of these communities. As it disappeared, so also did the commercial heart of the towns. During the years he operated his store, Mr. Low was able to purchase a number of buildings in the downtown area.

In Talking Rock, the L&N line eventually was completely abandoned. The death knell for the town had been sounded. Mr. Low said supermarkets in other more vibrant towns nearby lured away his grocery customers.

"I hung on, operating as a convenience store until there was no money in it," Low added. He closed the store in 1982.

Retired, Low described how he indulged an obsession with auctions and antiques. While commercial Talking Rock acquired the look of a ghost town, Mr. Low said he frequented auctions where he was able to purchase a variety of antiques which he then stored in his empty buildings along Main Street.

And then a stranger blew into town. Two strangers, actually. They were Paulette and Mark Grizzle. Veteran antique dealers, the Grizzles ran a shop near Lost Mountain in Cobb County. They arrived in Talking Rock to attend an auction. N.C. Low was selling off some antiques.

The Grizzles, however, were disappointed. "That narrow building was absolutely full of old tools," Ms. Grizzle explained. The Grizzles were looking for furniture. As the couple was leaving, the auctioneer – an individual named McDonald – sniffed an opportunity.

Aside from his auctioneer profession, McDonald was also a real estate agent. He led the Grizzles down the street to have a look at the old J.R. Allen house. Years earlier, the Reverend J.R. Allen – a Baptist minister – had been a prominent citizen in Talking Rock. His two-story home fronted on Main Street. Verandas graced both levels of the spacious structure. The reverend had left town long ago – presumably for heaven – and the old house had been steadily declining in condition. Mr. McDonald suggested the building to the Grizzles as a prime location for a new antiques shop.

At the time, the old Allen house, to say the least, was a poor excuse for a home. Half of its lower story gaped empty from a previous attempt at restoration. Vines cloaked its other side. The Grizzles, however, smelled the potential of the spot. They thought about it for 24 hours then bought the place.

The restoration of the Allen home took the Grizzles a year to complete. Mark, however, had grown up in the construction and cabinet making businesses, so he was able to trim away some of the costs. By 1995, Hollyhocks Of Talking Rock was open for business.

Unwilling to sit back idly and watch the Grizzles go it alone, N.C. Low reopened his store just across the street. Low and his wife, Helen, re-christened the place Times Past, and began selling off Low's extensive antiques collection.

Other entrepreneurs saw good things happening too, and decided to join the parade. Richard Willey and his wife opened Creekside Antiques in October of 1995. Their building formerly housed a convenience store, a laundromat, a restaurant, a motorcycle shop, a church, a tractor business, and an auction house.

Pete Cagle and his wife are owners of an antique shop they call The Talking Rock Country Store. Formerly Atlantans, the Cagles first visited Talking Rock in 1997. They bought an old two-story house in town, restored it, and retired there a few years back.

Mary Ann Manzel opened her consignment shop – The Talking Rock Exchange – three years ago. A native of Cherokee County, Ms. Manzel ran a shop in Woodstock for eight years. She said she discovered Talking Rock while driving through north Georgia.

Ms. Manzel purchased a total of 11 acres of real estate in Talking Rock. He parcel includes the original house (dating from 1845) and the old country store of the Darnells, a family once prominent in Talking Rock. Ms. Manzel renovated the store to house her shop.

Partners Donna Jenkins, Deb Gill, and Doreen Clyatt opened The Tea Garden in May of 2001. It offers tasty treats pleasing to the palate on Thursday, Friday and Saturday, and reservations are required.

The Hat House opened in October of 2001. Lauri Pinkard is the proud owner of this enterprise. Her father, Mark Grizzle of the Hollyhocks shop, restored and improved the building. Stock includes antiques and cabin furnishings.

Many shops are coming back to life in Talking Rock, but most are only open Thursday through Sunday. "A number of old-timers have stopped by," Linville continued. "They say, 'Sure is good to see that building coming back.'"

That kind of sentiment could well be applied to the entire town. Talking Rock is on the mend.

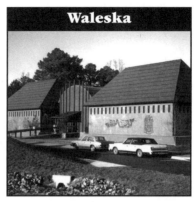

Waleska

The F. James and Florrie Guy **Funk Heritage Center** at **Reinhardt College** in Waleska is unique in Georgia. According to the management of the Center, there are few comparable museums in the Southeast.

"We fit beautifully into Georgia's Native American story," says Dr. Joseph Kitchens, executive director of the Center. "There is a rising interest in that culture, due partly to our own rising awareness of ecological issues related to the preservation of our planet."

Like many ventures, the Center started with a dream, with different people making contributions toward bringing the dream to fruition.

Several years ago, **Dr. James Funk** of Atlanta, a long-time Reinhardt trustee and prominent retired orthopedic surgeon, discovered an authentic 1830s-era log cabin on his farm in Cherokee County. He donated it to Reinhardt, putting into motion the work which ultimately resulted in the Center.

A second event was also instrumental in the creation of the Center. The **Wal-mart Corporation** wanted to build a store in Canton, Georgia, and prior to construction, the retail giant conducted the required archaeological dig at the construction site, expecting to turn up only a few artifacts. The dig eventually cost $600,000 and revealed over 100,000 artifacts from prehistoric settlements which extended back 10,000 years.

After the dig, Dr. Funk said, "We ought to do something." Some of the trustees of the college asked, "What does this have to do with education?" The archaeologist at the Wal-mart dig explained there is a growing need for archeologists in the nation. "Maybe this can serve to develop an interest in this profession by undergraduates," Dr. Funk added.

Funk Heritage Center

A tour of this excellent facility usually begins at the cathedral-like lobby of the "Longhouse" in the **Bennett History Museum**, named for John and Ethel C. Bennett, Sr. who had once operated a general store (a mid-1800s trading post in the Salacoa Valley area of Cherokee County).

Visitors are next shown into the high-definition image theater to watch a captivating film entitled "The Southeastern Indians." The production was a cooperative project between the Funk Heritage Center / Reinhardt College and the Georgia Department of Natural Resources. To date, this documentary has won 11 awards, and is a wonderful introduction to the Heritage Center.

Two permanent exhibits inside the museum include the **Rogers Gallery of Contemporary Native American Art**, and the **Sellars Collection of Tools of the Trades**. Donated by Mrs. Margaret Rogers who spent decades collecting native art from all over the country, the collection contains more than 400 paintings, sculptures, and other artworks. Rotating exhibits from this collection are always on display.

The Sellars tool collection is literally astonishing. Donated by Mrs. Louise Sellars in memory of her late husband, Alan Sellars, owner/operator of Marietta Hardware for several decades, this gallery contains thousands of beautifully-displayed historic hand tools. The tool collection and associated Appalachian settlement allow visitors to understand how European settlers and their technology helped to transform North America from a nation of hunter-gatherers to the most powerful nation on earth.

In the "**Hall of the Ancients**," local Native American history is featured. This exhibit spans the period beginning with the first nomadic

Indian tribes to the Salacoa Valley settlers. The room mimics a Mississippian culture lodge where a council of Native Americans would have met.

Matt McCoy – who does what he calls "edutainment" – designed the interior of this room in a fashion which allows it to tell a story. "I create exhibits that use all the senses for family education and entertainment," he says. "The work shocks, educates and entertains visitors."

McCoy oversaw the fabrication of exhibits, using murals, 3-dimensional props, theatrical lighting, and graphically-interactive computer touch stations. These exhibits lead visitors through a time-line and story-line.

Visitors initially enter the hall on the east side where a life-size reproduction of a **Paleo man** (13,000 – 9,000 B.C. time-period) is situated. Children can see the clothing these prehistoric residents wore, and how they killed a mammoth (a relative of the modern-day elephant which once lived in what today is North America) for food. A touch station at this point has three touch-screen computers which can be used to research more information about Native cultures and time-lines, and there are four additional monitors situated at other points in the Hall.

Video clips of primitive skills provide examples of how the ancients survived. A historical map shows each phase of the nomadic tribal migrations, and a star chart shows how the ancient stars would have looked.

The north wall has two more dioramas. One shows how **Archaic man** lived from 9,000 to 3,000 B.C. It includes a family scene near a river, explaining how the ancients used the waterway for travel, trade, fishing, and to quench their thirst. Another scene shows the life of the **Woodland-era** people who lived from 3,000 to 900 B.C., the era in which agriculture first emerged.

A fourth diorama shows the **Mississippian culture** which existed from 900 B.C. to approximately 1540 A.D. A final diorama demonstrates how the Indians tried to conform to the white man's culture during the Historic era.

State archaeologist/naturalist Scott Jones helped design exhibits in the Hall of the Ancients, and replicated prehistoric tools and artifacts to illustrate how they were used.

A huge stone covered with petroglyphs in the center of the room was discovered near the Etowah River approximately 40 years ago and donated to the college by the Cline family. The symbols engraved in this large boulder have been studied, but continue to perplex researchers even today.

A short trail connects the museum to the **Appalachian Settlement**. Visitors to this exhibit learn about frontier and Indian life of the mid-1800s. This facility currently contains two authentic log cabins of the period - the one donated by Dr. Funk, and another donated by the Cline family, long-time residents of Cherokee County. The settlement has open-air structures for workshops, gardens, trails, and ponds, as well as a blacksmith shop and sorghum mill.

The Center is a popular site for elementary school field trips. When the Funk Heritage Center opened in November of 1999, then-Reinhardt President **William Nevious** said "The Center is the campus community giving something back to the region. The college will subsidize this creditable education facility, and we hope the north Georgia community will come and use it."

In 2002, the Georgia State Legislature recognized the Funk Heritage Center by naming it "**Georgia's Official Frontier and Southeastern Indian Interpretive Center**." The Funk is also host to lectures, special presentations, festivals, workshops, and other activities.

{For more information on Funk Heritage Center, contact the Cherokee County Chamber of Commerce.}

Adairsville

1902 Stock Exchange

In 1994, **Newt Freeman** – then 92 years of age – amazingly drove himself to **Adairsville**, Georgia. He had a date with an old love, and he wouldn't have missed it for the world.

Several years earlier, **Rita Pritchard** "just happened upon Adairsville," as she was driving some of the sleepy back-roads of north Georgia. She was looking for a place to relocate her Cobb County antiques shop. As she drove through the town, she remembers thinking, "this is a jewel waiting to be discovered." She knew instinctively this was where she needed to relocate her business.

At that time, the old downtown area of Adairsville had definitely seen better days. Many of the downtown buildings were abandoned - a classic sign of downtown flight - as shops and businesses moved to higher traffic areas elsewhere.

An old two-story building on the corner of the town square caught Mrs. Pritchard's eye. It was the largest on the square and had been a showplace in its day, but now it just looked desolate. Rita, however, apparently saw potential where others saw waste.

As it turned out, she was right, and better yet, she was just in time to save the old building. The city of Adairsville had actually planned to tear down the landmark building. Water damage had added to the unattractive appearance of the building. Inside, the staircase was gone and the upstairs floor was considered unsafe. Most people just thought it was beyond reclamation.

"I looked at the building's ornate wood and pressed-metal features, its cast-iron columns, and its 1902 construction date still emblazoned on top," she smiles in remembrance, "and I just couldn't walk away from it." In her mind, the old structure was a classic turn-of-the-century shopping emporium, and she was determined to bring it back to life.

"When I spoke to my husband, DeWitt, about buying the building," she adds, "he just shook his head doubtfully and said, 'Are you sure it can ever look like anything?'"

Rita, to her credit, never gave up on her dream. She was almost as interested in the history of the old building as she was in the business potential. The structure has indeed weathered its share of historic events.

A Kentucky native, Pritchard says she learned additional information about the U.S. Civil War after moving to Georgia with her husband some years ago. "I now love anything to do with history," she says.

First known as **Oothcalooga Village**, the community known today as Adairsville was founded by pioneer settlers of Scottish descent in the 1820s. They lived peacefully with native Cherokee Indians, intermarrying with them.

By the time of the Civil War, Adairsville had achieved strategic importance as a stop on the **Western & Atlantic Railroad** which provided arms, munitions, and other supplies from Atlanta which were destined for the front lines in Virginia. Following the ravages of the war, and still later, the poverty brought on by the boll weevil which devastated "King Cotton" all across the South, Adairsville began making a come-back.

The Civil War had brought John Schmitz to Adairsville. He had been a soldier in General William T. Sherman's army. After the war, Schmitz decided he could make a living helping to rebuild the Adairsville area. He had been trained as an architect-builder, and ultimately constructed a number of the local houses and buildings in the town.

Schmitz lived in Adairsville from 1901 to 1917, and designed a building downtown which was owned and built by **Newt C. Anderson**. It was this building – in which

Anderson had operated a general mercantile business for many years – that intrigued Rita Pritchard in 1991, despite its forlorn appearance.

It took Rita a year to buy the structure, so she first rented the old drugstore on the square for her antiques shop. "I realized it would take more than antiques to draw people to the downtown area," she explains.

She became involved with a group of local women who organized a historical commission. She then began working with state and national preservation offices as she bought her 1902 vintage building which was actually three buildings in one.

Choosing the name "**1902 Stock Exchange**" for her building, Rita says she wanted a name that would describe a site where people had exchanged their cash for goods. "The original business had sold dry goods, hardware, and groceries and things," she states. "It was an upscale place where a man could get a good suit or a woman a good dress."

Rita had never been involved in the restoration of a building before - let alone a historic structure - so she knew she needed some professional help to bring her property to life. She secured the services of Bobby McElwee who had been instrumental in the restoration of nearby historic **Barnsley Gardens**.

McElwee put together a specialized team of workmen, including a master carpenter for the project. "It was he who actually preserved the authenticity of the building," she smiles gratefully. "He took the time and patience to figure out ways to save the details of the building."

The renovation ultimately proved to be far more extensive than Rita ever imagined. "When you're working on old buildings, you never know what you're going to run into," she says. And she did indeed run into a lot more time and expenses than she expected, but she never quit.

Rita had the plaster removed from the bricks and then resealed them, leaving the native building blocks exposed. A local mill cut 38 beams of varying sizes to reinforce and stabilize the upstairs floor to make it safe.

The original stairway (now gone) had been a strictly functional piece of work –

straight and narrow. McElwee suggested they put in something with a little more elegance – more suited for the function this building would now provide. Rita agreed, and the present dramatic, curved staircase with its wide steps and two landings adds grace and charm to the building.

Four turn-of-the-century chandeliers that have iron-and-gold-painted wood which resembles metal, now hang throughout the building. A kitchen sink found upstairs in the drugstore now enjoys renewed life in a downstairs restroom.

The dividers in the upstairs restroom are the original beaded board, and the period doors came from the master carpenter's collection. Most of the stained glass windows are original. A final touch came when the building was painted in a sumptuous hunter green and gold.

When it was completed, it was obvious to all that the hard work had paid off handsomely. The building had gone from being a derelict to being a showpiece in downtown Adairsville.

Today, the spacious building has 9,000 square feet of floor space, and high ceilings which lend it an air of grandeur. In 1995, Rita was honored with an award for *Outstanding Rehabilitation Project* from the **Georgia Trust For Historic Preservation**. The award, one of seven given that year, was the only one given to a project in northwest Georgia.

The grand opening of the modern version of the historic building took place in April of 1994. Newt Freeman – all 92 years of him – surprised almost everyone by his presence, and made a startling revelation to those gathered at the event. He explained that his father had worked for Newt Anderson (builder of the structure in 1902), and that his father had named him after Mr. Anderson.

"When I was seven years old," Freeman explained, smiling, "Mr. Anderson told me 'Because you're my namesake, I'm going to give you a suit.' I picked out my first suit of clothes in this store."

Mrs. Maurine McDonald also attended the opening. She said she had shopped in Anderson's store as a little girl with her mother.

"I never thought I'd see life in this building again," she said, amazed. She later celebrated her 85th birthday at the Dinner Theater upstairs.

The theater presents period plays in keeping with the atmosphere of the building. "I want people to feel as if they're stepping back in time," she explains. "We have good wholesome family entertainment, suitable for everyone – plays like *"Little Women," "Abe Lincoln's America," Mark Twain's "The Diaries Of Adam And Eve,"* and an original musical taken from Twain's *"Tom Sawyer."*

Costumed waiters serve period-themed dinners. The menu consists of two entrees, vegetables, salads, bread, coffee, tea and dessert. The cost of the dinner and theater is $35.00 to $40.00 per person.

And just as big as the dinner theater is the antiques shop downstairs. There, in the scintillating air of the turn-of-the-century building, a dozen vendors provide Victorian collectibles and accessories, Heritage Lace curtains and fine table lace, baby christening outfits, crystal, silverware, antique wedding dresses, furniture, china, glassware, lamps, antique toys, antique furniture and reproductions, dried-flower-and-herb arrangements, shops offering handmade items, *Coca-Cola* memorabilia, new gift items, home accessories, a variety of prints and a few paintings, and much more.

The **Corra Harris Bookstore** – named after the famed Pine Log novelist – offers used, rare and new books by Georgia and other authors. Mrs. Harris's works include *A Circuit Rider's Wife*, later made into a major motion picture entitled *I'd Climb The Highest Mountain*, starring **Susan Hayward, Rory Calhoun, Bill Lundigan, Barbara Bates,** **Alexander Knox** and **Gene Lockhart**.

Maggie Mae's Tea Room/cafe which seats 30 is located in the center of the 1902 Stock Exchange complex. It opens onto a courtyard that has the original brick floor and wall, and is decorated with statues, greenery, lights and a fountain. When weather permits, diners are served outdoors.

The menu offers a chicken salad plate, three kinds of quiche, sandwiches and two hot "special of the day" dishes, such as vegetable lasagna and chicken pasta. Specialty desserts include hummingbird cake, white chocolate and turtle cheesecake, and specialty coffees and teas.

Coffee, tea and desserts are served during all open hours. "People stop in after they visit Barnsley Gardens sometimes," Rita says.

The second floor dinner theater can seat 150 people for buffet-style meals, and up to 300 can be accommodated for weddings and receptions. A wedding consultant and coordinator can help brides and grooms plan meaningful ceremonies, and the attractive staircase offers an excellent background for bridal portraits.

Newt Anderson would be glad to know his old building lives on in such grace and charm.

{The 1902 Stock Exchange is located at 124 Public Square, and is open Tuesday thru Saturday, 10:00 a.m. to 5:00 p.m. and Sundays from 1:00 p.m. to 3:00 p.m. Lunch is served Tuesday thru Saturday, 11:30 a.m. to 2:30 p.m. Coffee, tea, and dessert are served during store hours. To reach Adairsville, take Georgia Highway 140 West off U.S. Interstate 75. Cross U.S. Highway 41 and turn left onto Main Street. For further information or to secure a schedule of events or dinner-theater tickets, call (770) 773-1902.}

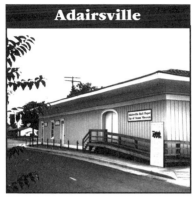

Adairsville

Historic Adairsville

North Georgia boasts a wide variety of unique communities with attractive historic downtown districts, but not many of them offer the same quality as a little community in Bartow County known as Adairsville. Many people living in this area all their lives have not realized this little treasure in their own back yard.

On December 4, 1987, the entire town of Adairsville was listed on the *National Register of Historic Places*. This unique town has more than 130 homes and businesses designated as historic properties, including many unique sites such as the home in which notorious gangster **Charles Arthur "Pretty Boy" Floyd** was born and lived for a number of years.

Julia Witherington has been a resident of Adairsville for more than sixty years. She knew J.M. and Marguerite Veach personally prior to their deaths. The Veachs were the owners and long-time residents of the home in Adairsville which is currently operated as the Adairsville Inn, a popular restaurant. As far as Adairsville is concerned, all roads in the early history of the town led to the Veach family.

J.M. Veach was one of the original land purchasers in Adairsville. This community is a town with deep roots in Cherokee history. The settlement at this site was originally known as Oothcalooga Village, after the stream running through the valley. It was home to the Adairs, Scottish settlers who intermarried with the Cherokee Indians.

After the Cherokees were removed, a small settlement with a store or two arose about two miles north of the present-day town of Adairsville. This settlement was the first to be called "Adairsville" in honor of the prominent Adair family. Today, a historical marker at the edge of the highway indicates the original site of this town.

In 1832, Hubbard Williams won Land Lot 168 which consisted of 160 acres, much of which comprises the present-day downtown area of Adairsville. This land was later sold to William Watts in 1836 for $1,200. Watts is credited with founding what today is known as Adairsville.

Between 1836 and 1846, a momentous event occurred which literally put Adairsville on the map. The town was destined to grow in importance because it was on the direct path of the state-owned **Western & Atlantic (W&A) Railroad** from Atlanta to Chattanooga, Tennessee.

The railroad began construction in 1838, and Mr. Watts deeded to the W&A land for the rail line through Adairsville in 1840. In 1846, Watts sold the State of Georgia three additional acres of land for a depot – completed in 1847 – in the center of town. This original depot still exists today in downtown Adairsville, and has been renovated for use as a history museum.

Mr. Watts first called his new town, "Adair Station," but the little town appears on Bonner's 1847 *Map of Georgia* as "Williams," probably in deference to the original land owner.

As with other railroad towns, it wasn't long before the small village two miles northward known as "Adairsville" began merging with the commerce springing up around the new depot at "Adair Station," causing the two sites to be merged into one township known as Adairsville.

Two of the earliest purchasers of property for businesses in town were Jonathan H. Whitesides (1849) and the firm of Veach and Lawrence (1850). The Veach family appears in the history of Adairsville from its earliest days.

James Madison Veach was born and educated in Virginia. He worked in New York for a time, but found he liked the milder climate of Georgia. After moving to the South, he finally settled at Adairsville.

In 1868, Veach built a flour and gristmill which grew into the J.M. Veach Milling Company. The factory housed the most advanced technology of that day, using rollers to process the flour.

According to the 1883-1884 *Directory of Cherokee & Cartersville*, "Mr. Veach is one of the proudest diadems in the circlet of Georgia's commercial brilliancy. He came to Adairsville in the spring of the year 1847, commenced merchandising, and by paying liberal cash prices, bought the grain product of the whole surrounding country, and was engaged in shipping it till he erected his mill. By degrees he has risen to be the largest tax-payer in Bartow County. He has about 700 acres of land in and around Adairsville, and he has built most of the best houses in town. He has recently given a church site to the people. He has himself an attractive residence, surrounded by every convenience in the way of stables, barns, orchards, dairies, etc. He is a gentleman of genial grace and wonderful popularity. Intelligence and force are written in his face. He is a fine example of what may be attained by honest intention and liberality combined with strict business principles."

The Veach family was not only first on the scene in commerce, they also were the first in Adairsville to own one of the new-fangled "automobiles," purchasing their car in 1910.

J.M. was the grandson of James Madison Veach who was the owner of the Veach Milling Company. George Veach was J.M.'s father.

In the 1860s during the U.S. Civil War, with its location on the W&A Railroad, Adairsville was a swiftly-growing town, and a community very important to the Confederate war effort. Plans called for the town to become a terminus for the railroad, with a roundhouse, machine shops, and other railroad necessities.

The W&A was used to transport arms, munitions and other war supplies being shipped from Atlanta factories to the front lines in Virginia. A gun and powder factory near Adairsville also aided the war effort. Mr. Veach, with his experience in commerce, became a purchasing agent for the Confederacy.

Adairsville is famous for its role in an incident known as "**The Great Locomotive Chase**" during the war. This chase occurred when Union Army spy James Andrews, hijacked a Confederate locomotive – "**General**" – in Kennesaw, Georgia, and proceeded up the railroad line through Adairsville. Andrews' mission was to destroy and interrupt the railroad supplying the Confederates in Chattanooga, but his plan was thwarted when the locomotive "Texas" set out in pursuit of the spy in Adairsville.

Today, the town of Adairsville hosts an annual event called **The Great Locomotive Festival** during the months of September/October, in observance of *The Great Locomotive Chase* which occurred on April 12, 1862.

During the Civil War, Adairsville was severely damaged and its resources depleted. The Austin Rifle factory was hastily removed to South Georgia before the impending invasion of the federal army.

Later, after the town had recovered somewhat from the effects of the war, the business section of Adairsville was destroyed by fire in the 1890s. Despite these catastrophes, the town somehow managed to persevere and grow.

During the early 1900s, peach and cotton farms in the Adairsville area formed the nucleus of a booming business for the town. It was also about this time that Adairsville became known for its good private schools, churches and cultured family life.

Carolyn and Derrell Adams are the present-day owners of the Adairsville Inn. She will readily share the history of the Inn – formerly the Veach home – with visitors.

It is unknown today when this fine historic structure was actually built, but it is believed the Veach house was constructed sometime in the late 1800s or early 1900s. J.M. Veach purchased the home in 1927 from an earlier owner. J.M. died in the home in 1947, and Marguerite passed away there in 1981.

After the Veachs, the home was acquired and used as office space by the Bank of Adairsville. It was also used as a community center until 1990, when Jim and Sharon Southerland purchased it and opened the Adairsville Inn.

During their renovation of the home, Sharon and Jim discovered square nails and wooden pegs which had been used in the original construction, indicating the home may have been built prior to the turn of the century.

Carolyn and Derrell bought the Inn in July of 2000. Derrell had retired from Delta Airlines, and when he learned that the Inn might be available, he felt it was an opportunity he could not pass up. Carolyn said that despite some early reservations about the acquisition, their perseverance has paid off in the rewards of seeing everything come together under their ownership.

The main dining room of the restaurant is elegant and cozy. Lunch entrees include a variety of crepes, sandwiches, salads and delicious home-made desserts. For dinner, choices include steaks, seafood, chicken, or pasta and crepes.

The portions are more than adequate, so be sure to leave room for the delicious desserts such as peach cobbler, pecan delight, strawberry crepe, coconut cream pie, and numerous other treats.

After you have enjoyed a meal at the Adairsville Inn, a leisurely walk to the old town square and its numerous interesting shops offers excellent opportunities for gift-buying or just browsing. Enjoy your trip!

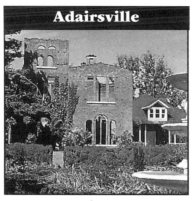

Adairsville

Barnsley Gardens

Looking for a getaway opportunity that offers history, breath-taking floral beauty, excellent dining opportunities, excellent accommodations and an extraordinary golf course – all in the foothills of north Georgia? If you are, then look no further than the completely renovated and upgraded Barnsley Gardens at Adairsville, Georgia.

This unique attraction is built around the manor house ruins (built in 1842) and formal English gardens once owned by **Godfrey Barnsley**, a successful cotton broker of the mid-19th century. **Prince Hubertus Fugger** of Germany purchased the property in 1988, paying $1.5 million for it "as is," and has developed it into an outstanding getaway opportunity.

Since the purchase, another $3.5 million was spent stabilizing the manor house ruins, and reclaiming the gardens and grounds from years of weather, neglect, and vandalism. Today, a brick shell of the house stands in mute testimony to the family which once lived and struggled on this property.

When Prince Fugger bought the property, wild trees were growing inside the once-elegant manor house. The walls had to be stabilized and a floor added to allow visitors an opportunity to walk around inside the home and view the rooms where the Barnsley family had once lived.

Elsewhere on the grounds, the boxwood parterre had to be nurtured and restored to its former glory. The formal English gardens were planted in keeping with the ideas of Andrew Jackson Downing, a well-known landscape architect of that day. Many of the plants and breath-taking flowers were nurtured back to health or replaced with duplicates. And in 1994, the historic Rice House Restaurant was added to provide dining accommodations on the grounds.

Still, Prince Fugger felt that he could do more to create an atmosphere for enjoyment and relaxation at his Barnsley property. He envisioned an expansion which would include accommodations in a reproduction 19th century English village, an 18-hole golf course, an inn, a beer garden, and a steakhouse-style restaurant.

His idea of an English village of homes was developed from house sketches done by Andrew Jackson Downing. This expansion into a full-scale resort necessitated the closure of Barnsley Gardens during all of 1998. The resort reopened in the summer of 1999.

Today, thirty-three English cottages, designed in the weathered colors reminiscent of the mother country are eye-catching and serene in their surroundings. If the streets had been dirt, one might almost expect to see a horse-drawn carriage on the lanes at any moment.

Maturing trees, well-placed flowers and other expensive landscaping designs complete the finished look of the tidy village. Gables, cornices, lattice porch-work and other Victorian architectural details abound.

Approximately 70 elegant guest suites in this village have been created as accommodations for golfing and relaxation getaways. The offerings – **Garden Cottage Suite**, **Meadow Cottage Suite**, **Arbor Cottage Manor** and **Woodlands Jr. Suites** – beckon enticingly. In the style of the long-departed Godfrey Barnsley, each cottage is surrounded by flowers and attractive shrubs, soothing the spirit with something always in bloom.

Guests will enjoy the comfort and luxury of king-sized four-poster or sleigh beds, dressed in attractive comforters, and sewn from fine fabrics in historic colors. Each guest suite features barnwood front doors, wood flooring, a sitting bay or window box, a porch overlooking the gardens, a wet bar, armoire, pedestal sink, and an antique free-standing tub and shower enclosure.

Upon entering one of the cottages, one can't help but have the feeling of having walked into a gracious country home from a century past. One, however, is not deprived of modern conveniences either. Telephones, voice-mail, and televisions bridge the gap between the centuries. Room rates begin at $250 per night and packages start at $425.

For dining, guests may choose between **The Woodlands Grill** and the historic **Rice House Restaurant**. The Woodlands – a newly-constructed restaurant – is a steakhouse-type restaurant. The Rice House serves New South cuisine in a circa-1854 farm home which has been relocated and converted into a restaurant filled both with excellent food and nostalgic memorabilia.

The Woodlands Grill is open from 7:00 A.M. to 10:00 P.M. Guests may walk from their cottages. This dining option is light and airy inside with open twelve-foot ceilings. The atmosphere is soft and relaxed – no hustle and bustle here – just pure quiet time to relax and ponder the pretty surroundings. Many mementos of Prince Fugger's world travels fill curios which may be admired by guests.

Breakfast at Woodlands may be light fare or hearty. For the smaller appetite, there are breads, muffins, pastries, Georgia peaches and Creme Friache, or granola with yogurt and berries and dried fruits. For those planning an active day, there are gourmet pancakes, waffles, omelets, eggs Benedict, country ham and sausages.

Lunch choices include grilled chicken with shiitake mushrooms, pear tomatoes, snow peas over penne pasta, seared sea bass, sandwiches and daily specials. Dinner entrees become more dramatic: Herb-broiled free range chicken breast, sauteed rainbow trout, bourbon-glazed salmon medallions, sauteed shrimp, grilled prime center-cut filet mignon and pan-seared veal chops.

Godfrey Barnsley loved Georgia peaches. He reportedly tended orchards, and kept a storehouse of peach brandy. Legend has it that Union soldiers also shared his enjoyment of the peach brandy, becoming rowdy and drunk as they pillaged the elegant estate in 1864.

Today, guests may be soothed by ginger peach tea that is served at Woodlands. It is a delightful thirst-quencher with a hint of sweet peach juices and ginger. Guests may also admire the fine China on which their meals are served – all bearing the historic Barnsley crest.

The Rice House Restaurant is a quaint, gabled country home. It is the former homeplace of the Fleming Rice family, and was moved from nearby Floyd County to the Barnsley property in 1993. Floor to ceiling windows allow the wonder and freshness of the outdoors to spill inside. The restaurant is arranged in four rooms: The Civil War Room, The Bavarian Room, The Sunporch, and the Main Dining Room.

A trip to the Rice House offers a taste of Civil War history as well as gourmet food. The Rice farmland was the scene of a Civil War skirmish and bullet holes still visible in the front of the home attest to this fact. Dining selections include bourbon-glazed salmon filet, grilled free range chicken breast, grilled pork tenderloins, grilled petite filet mignon, roast Colorado rack of lamb with rosemary mint pest crust and other delectable entrees are available. An a la carte menu is also offered when fewer courses are desired.

The historic district includes the Manor House ruins and a museum. Standing gaunt on a hill is the brick shell of the Italianate-style manor house. A visit to the ruins might lead to some soul searching, as there is time to ponder what might have been had the Godfrey Barnsley venture – which ended in ruin – been successful.

Barnsley made a fortune in brokering cotton in Savannah, but he lost it all during the disastrous War Between The States.

Godfrey suffered tragedy in his marriage too. His wife, Julia, was his romantic dream. He had built the elegant mansion and gardens in north Georgia for her. The couple had eight children, but Julia was constantly ill.

Godfrey purchased the 3,680-acre estate, began construction of the home and the lovely gardens - all to impress his beloved wife- but she, tragically, died before she ever saw any of it.

Barnsley kept up his cotton brokerage business and remained at Woodlands (his name for his north Georgia estate) throughout the war. Wartime activity at Woodlands took a heavy toll, particularly as involved the stragglers and looters who ransacked the fine home, taking everything of value, right down to the silver latches on the windows.

By the end of the war, Barnsley had lost his fortune. He spent his remaining years at his only remaining cotton brokerage office which was in New Orleans, trying to recoup some of his losses. He died there in 1873, a virtual pauper. His body was returned to Woodlands where he was buried.

Although some of Godfrey's children did their best to keep up the estate in the ensuing years, a tornado blew off the roof of the manor house in 1906, and Godfrey's granddaughter, Addie Saylor, could not afford to repair it. She and her family moved into the right wing of the house (which had escaped damage and which is a museum today), and continued living there thru the years. The other portion of the house with no roof was abandoned, and fell into disrepair.

Admission to the gardens at Barnsley is $10 for adults, $8 for seniors, and $5 for children. Guests pay at the entrance gatehouse facility and receive armbands there.

The 18-hole golf course was designed by Jim Fazio. The course was planned with as little disruption to the woodland setting as possible. It meanders through the property and is built where the land dictates. Green fees and cart fees are around $100 per player.

In a day of ultimate pampering and rejuvenation, the spa packages are sure to please even the most demanding guests. The names themselves are soothing. The Barnsley Rose Package (6 hours) costs $395. A Half-Day Package (3 hours) costs $180, and a Full-Day Package (5 hours) costs $320.

After you visit Barnsley, you may not be eager to leave. The resort is a unique hospitality experience. A wide variety of offerings await guests to this captivating and intriguing getaway from yesteryear.

(For more information, call (770) 773-7480, or visit the resort's internet page at www.barnsleyinngolf.com.)

The Rice House Restaurant

When **Prince Hubertus Fugger** of Germany acquired the **Barnsley Gardens** property in 1988, it was estimated that the restoration of the manor house ruins and gardens would cost in the neighborhood of $2,000,000. Weather, time, general neglect, and vandalism had taken a heavy toll, and additional historic structures would be needed to complement the planned tourist development. In particular, a restaurant which would blend with the garden attractions was highly desired.

Raspberry fudge pie and a history involving the **War Between The States** seem like unlikely bedfellows, but a structure known as the **Rice House** entertains both of these subjects nicely today. Known as the Rice House Restaurant at Barnsley Gardens, this homey eatery offers Southern food for guests in a two-story farmhouse which once existed on a battlefield of the War Between The States.

The Rice House was built in 1854 by Fleming Rice on the Alabama Road in Floyd County. Fleming was a wheat and corn farmer - a departure from the norm in a region known for cotton farming in the mid-1800s. Rice was also a wine-maker. One family legend maintains that he prevented the torching of his house during the Civil War by bribing Union soldiers with whiskey.

Mrs. Elsie Gunn Stokes, the granddaughter of Fleming Rice lived in the house much of her life. The farm as Fleming knew it began as 100 acres of land for which he paid $1,800 in 1855, and was later enlarged to some 800 acres. Today, however, only 100 of the original acres remain in the family. Bill Rose, Sr., of New York (Mrs. Stokes's nephew) inherited the property following her death in 1990.

A few years later, Mr. Rose placed the old home on the market for sale. Despite his interest in the sale, he was fearful that the house might be demolished by its new owner, and he wanted to do what he could to preserve it.

It was around this same time that Gilbert Smith, a local historian, was researching a Civil War skirmish that was fought west of Rome. He was able to pinpoint the battle site as the Rice Springs Farm.

To confirm his theory about the location of the battle, Mr. Smith asked the present residents in the vicinity for permission to walk the land with a metal detector to search for bullets and other metal relics from the engagement. To his delight, Smith recovered one pistol bullet, one Spencer rifle bullet, one expended Spencer brass cartridge, and a U.S. 23rd Corpsman's badge. He later learned the Rose family had found their share of relics on the property too. Two cannon balls and five or six bullets had been family possessions for years, and had been passed down to relatives.

At about this same time, the developers of Barnsley Gardens were looking for a historic home to convert into a restaurant. Through conversations between Rose, Clent Coker (a historian affiliated with Barnsley Gardens) and ultimately Prince Fugger himself, the old Rice farmhouse was purchased for use as a restaurant at Barnsley and plans were made to move the home.

In March of 1994, the T-shaped house was cut into four sections and moved from Floyd County to Barnsley Gardens about 25 miles away. According to Coker, "Every board was numbered (for precise reconstruction later)." One year later, the Rice House opened to its first noon-time diners. Today, the planter-style house sparkles cleanly in white, with green shutters and three gables.

The culinary offerings of Chef Charles Vosberg are described as "contemporary Southern food." The abundant buffet features chicken, beef or pork, and seafood, two vegetables, one starch, homemade breads, beverages, salads and a dessert bar. Some of the featured specialties are: roasted pork loin, herb roasted chicken, barbecue seasoned chicken, lentil stew, oven-roasted red potatoes, parsley rice, and summer squash and zucchini with herb butter.

As one enters the restaurant, the first room to the left is the Rice Room, where Rice family mementos, a Civil War musket, and bullets are displayed on the walls. Across from the Rice Room is the Bavarian Room, where the decor reflects Prince Fugger's homeland.

The **K.O. Dugan Tavern** area evokes a feeling of the Depression era. K.O. Dugan is the fighting name of Godfrey Barnsley's prize-fighting great-grandson, **Preston Saylor**, who killed his brother, Harry, in a family dispute in 1935. The tale of the feuding brothers is one of the many intriguing aspects of the legacy of Barnsley Gardens. Preston's boxing gloves are displayed in the tavern, as are framed articles detailing his career as a boxer.

The long room to the rear of the restaurant is Godfrey's Hall. This is actually an extension of the original dwelling and is constructed of new materials. The wide-plank floors came from an old warehouse in Rome.

Recently, a contented diner was seen out front munching a macadamia nut cookie and examining the bullet holes on the front of the house. The bullet holes were made by bullets fired from Union rifles on October 13, 1864, when a skirmish was fought at Rice Springs.

Research conducted by Gilbert Smith and Stacy McCain of Rome, Georgia, brought the little-known battle to light. According to a diary kept by Rome resident Reuben Norton who watched the Union troops as they headed toward the Coosa River that morning, *"At half past four this morning, the Army commenced moving until 9:00 a.m., numbering probably 20,000. The cavalry crossed the Etowah, a few cannon were heard in the fore part of the day, nothing more."*

The next entry in Mr. Norton's diary was at 4:00 p.m. on October 13, 1864. *"The Army are returning, and report having met the Confederates near Rice's, about 5 or 6 miles on the Alabama Road; the fight continued several hours, resulting in the capture of about 60 men and 2 pieces of cannon from the Confederates."*

There were over 70 Confederate casualties and 14 Union soldiers killed or wounded. The Rice House stopped at least four bullets too, as the holes in the structure quickly attest today.

Also viewable from the porch are the ruins of the old **Barnsley manor house**. Standing both proud and forlorn, only the bare brick walls remain from the once-grand home that Godfrey Barnsley built in the 1840s. A 1906 tornado tore off the roof, and family members did not have the funds to repair the structure. They were forced to move into an undamaged wing of the large home which is a museum today.

When the property was acquired by Prince Fugger in 1987, the walls were covered in kudzu and wild trees grew inside the structure. The walls were stabilized and a sturdy wooden floor was built. Julia Barnsley's dream house now stands gaunt and silent. It seems to look skyward as winds whip through it. Visitors may walk the plank floors of the ruins and ponder the lives of those who passed here before them.

{The Rice House Restaurant can seat 150 people. It is open Fridays and Saturdays from 5:00 P.M. to 10:00 P.M. and on Sundays for brunch from 11:00 A.M. to 2:00 P.M. For more information, call (770) 773-7480, Ext. 2500.}

Historic Banning Mills Resort

The historic ruins had lain abandoned and forgotten for years until an enterprising couple saw the potential of the remote site in the west Georgia hinterlands.

The first thing one notices about Banning Mills (now known as "**Historic Banning Mills**") is the sheer quietness and serenity of this place. The peacefulness here wraps itself around you like a warm blanket, but even then it's difficult to define exactly from whence it springs. Perhaps it's from the gentle sounds of crystal-clear **Snake Creek** as it ripples over the rocks just below the main lodge, or perhaps it's from the lullabies of scores of songbirds flitting among the towering trees.

Some say it comes from the echoes of the past, for there is a harmonious atmosphere here, almost as if all its ghosts – of which there are a gracious plenty – are quite happy living among the vast forests that are dappled with the stonework of old mills and all the sun-ribboned colors of a stained glass window.

Historic Banning Mills – now at its heart a country inn – located just outside Whitesburg in Carroll County (less than an hour's drive west of Atlanta), is exactly the kind of place that evokes images of what a true mountain escape should be, but there is more to it than that – much more. It includes an inn, a resort, a historic masterpiece from yesteryear, and nature's showcase all clustered among some of the prettiest scenery in all of Georgia.

The foundations of Historic Banning Mills spring mostly from its distinctive history. It begins with the Creek and Cherokee Indians, moves to the U.S. Civil War, makes its way to the turn of the century as a mill town, eventually experiences virtual abandonment by its townspeople, and then finally evolves into the captivating getaway at the site today. Along the path of its history, Historic Banning Mills has transformed itself from Indian hunting grounds into a modern day resort that somehow still manages to hold tight to images of its sometimes rocky yet colorful past.

For Mike and Donna Holder, who own this historic property today, it was the peacefulness that drew them into its spell in the first place. Mike, a pilot with American Airlines, and Donna, a registered nurse now retired from Kennesaw Hospital, purchased a portion of the abandoned mill property approximately six years ago with aspirations of turning the site into a church retreat. Convinced that they had made the right choice in their new investment, the young couple and their children packed up everything they owned and moved from Marietta, their hometown.

The Holders soon discovered that not only had they obtained a site that would eventually evolve into their delightful inn and retreat, but also a place so steeped in history that each day became a new adventure into the background of this intriguing property.

Stunning Scenery

The natural beauty of Banning Mills is as important as its history, as both intertwine with and become a sort of stepping stone for the other. Banning Mills, at a higher elevation than most of the other terrain in this region of west Georgia, is a mélange of steep hills, deep gorges, verdant forests, and gurgling creeks and streams. The heavily wooded knolls and valleys, brimming with whitetail deer, grey fox, raccoon, bobcat, snakes and other wildlife, offered an ideal hunting ground for the Creeks and Cherokees before the white settlers eventually came along and drove them away. And, like most of the South, coyotes and armadillos eventually drifted eastward into this area from the High Plains states, settling in among the other wildlife as if they were native to the region. The birding here is no less than spectacular, and in the spring, migratory birds of prey – including bald and golden eagles – soar high above the treetops.

The wooded hiking trails – some quite demanding – crisscross Snake Creek as it tumbles downstream to its intersection with the Chattahoochee River, polishing boulders and rocks along the way almost as smooth as tempered glass. Hiking is good in any season, as the hillsides simmer with spectacular color all year 'round.

The natural landscape of steep inclines and gaping gorges – all carved from ancient rock by wind and water – ultimately became a unique part of the history of Banning Mill. In the 1860s, this remote location saved the town from certain disaster (there's more on that later), and its biological diversity is so rich that even the Nature Conservancy stood and took notice, for the acreage around it will soon become part of a nature preserve.

A Creek & Cherokee Connection

Yes, it's pretty in Banning Mills, and it's easy to see why a town eventually emerged at this spot. The fact remains, however, that Banning Mills simply oozes history.

"When we originally bought Banning," begins Mike, "We didn't realize how extensive the history of this area was. We did research and found some older neighbors who still had pictures of the town. We're still learning things about the history even today."

Banning's origins are much like the rest of Georgia. Up until the early 1800s, most of the area was home to the Creek and Cherokee nations. The Creek Nation, divided into the Upper and Lower Creeks, was probably the more dominant of the two. The Lower Creeks lived in the area of Snake Creek and the Chattahoochee River, enjoying their lives as farmers and hunters and taking advantage of the fertile land and abundant wildlife.

When the white man moved westward from the coastal regions in the early 1800s, this part of Carroll County was considered the western frontier – and even a part of the Wild West to some.

Chief William McIntosh

In the 1820s, this vicinity was also the home of **Chief William McIntosh**, one of the most intriguing characters in all of Georgia history. McIntosh was a "half-breed" who was born about 1775 near Tuetumpla in what today is Alabama. His father, a Scotsman who was also named William, was a Tory officer who served in the American Revolution. His mother was Senoia Henneha of the Coweta-Cussitta Towns of the Lower Creeks. She was a member of the influential Wind Clan of the Lower Creeks; it is from this clan that the leaders were usually chosen. As a young man, McIntosh himself soon became a "Micco" or king of the Lower Creek villages when he was elected as chief spokesman for the smattering of villages in the area.

McIntosh also enjoyed a stellar military career. He fought with **Andrew Jackson** and the American forces during the War of 1812, seeing action in the battles at **Autossee, Horseshoe Bend**, and in the **Florida campaign**. With his extensive military background, he was even appointed to the rank of brigadier general, becoming the only Indian to reach such status. Over the course of his career, he rubbed elbows with the likes of **Thomas Jefferson** in the White House, and he met with Presidents **James Monroe** and **James Madison**. He was also first cousin to **George Troup**, who served as governor of Georgia. It would be fair to say this Creek Indian enjoyed friends in high places.

Chief McIntosh also was a wealthy and astute businessman, eventually owning considerable acreage in Georgia and Alabama. His main plantation, known as **Lockchau Talofau** or "**Acorn Town**," was located a few miles from Banning in the rolling terrain between the Chattahoochee River and present-day Highway 5. With much of his land under cultivation, McIntosh was considered a plantation owner, and had nearly a hundred slaves. Additionally, both white men and Indians worked for him and helped him run the plantation as well as a number of businesses, including taverns, a trading post, and an overnight lodge. He married three times, first to a Cherokee named Peggy, later to a woman named Eliza, and then finally to a Creek named Susanna.

By 1823, when the first land treaties were being signed in Georgia, McIntosh appreciated the tremendous longing that white men had for the ownership of land, but he knew that his own people, the Creeks, wouldn't part with it easily. McIntosh also understood how aggressive the white man was in obtaining land and how great were their numbers. He knew the Creeks must adapt to the white man's ways or be vanquished as a race. Only after the Creeks were promised great sums of money and vast acreage in the West did they ultimately give up their lands in Georgia.

McIntosh Assassination

As an important leader of the Creeks, McIntosh was one of the signers of the **Treaty of Indian Springs** on February 2, 1825. It deeded approximately 20 million acres of Creek lands to the U.S. government in return for a substantial sum of money and a new "reservation" in the western United States. Even as he signed the treaty, McIntosh still had not been able to convince the leaders of the Upper Creek villages to give up their lands and move hundreds of miles away to a totally new life.

Many leaders of the Upper Creeks in fact were enraged with him for "selling out" to the government. Even as the ink was drying on the newly-signed treaty at the Indian Spring Hotel (which still stands today in Butts County, Georgia), these angry Creek leaders stood outside the hotel and swore vengeance upon the men they felt were traitors for signing away their lands. For his part in the signing, McIntosh sealed his own death warrant that day, and he would soon pay the ultimate price for that action.

Several months later, on May 1, 1825, a party of approximately 200 Upper Creeks, led by **Chief Menawa** (Manowei/Munnawwa) and **Chief Tuskehadja** (Tuckeehadjo) came to McIntosh's home with a singular purpose: to kill the man they felt had betrayed them. The Creeks set the plantation ablaze, ran off the slaves, burned the crops, and slaughtered the livestock. McIntosh was driven from inside the two-story log home by the heat of the fire which was fast consuming the structure. As he stepped into the doorway, his body was pierced by at least a half-dozen musket balls.

According to a report of the incident a day later by two of McIntosh's wives and his daughter, the wounded chief was dragged by his feet from the burning house. With his lifeblood flowing from him, he was offered no solace. One of the attacking Creeks suddenly stepped forward and unmercifully stabbed the dying chief in the breast, then scalped him.

As a further indignity, McIntosh's wives were not allowed to bury his body. It was left lying in the front yard of his home. Later, after the assassins had departed, the chief's loved ones returned and interred his body in the yard of Lockchau Talofau quite near where he died. His grave is maintained there today.

McIntosh "Treasure"

Many legends surround the fate of McIntosh and the rewards he received for his participation in the Treaty at Indian Spring. One of these maintains that he was paid the hefty sum of $400,000 in gold coin, and that this treasure is still buried someplace on his former property. In actuality, the entire Creek Nation was "paid" $400,000, of which $200,000 was advanced when the United States Congress ratified the treaty. The remainder was to be paid in annual installments over five years. In return, the greatest part of the remaining Creek territory in Georgia and Alabama was ceded to the United States.

Though he was accused of personally profiting greatly from the treaty, McIntosh almost certainly received far less than was suspected by his jealous tribesmen. According to official records, he was granted $25,000 for his home and property on the Chattahoochee and his **Indian Spring hotel** (which were a portion of the cessation to the U.S. government) and given a reservation of new land in the western United States. He, however, also received a smaller sum of money from the U.S. government (as was customary at the time) for signing the Treaty.

Though many treasure hunters still search for McIntosh's presumed buried riches (not far from where Banning Mills later was built), they almost certainly search in vain. Small sums were paid in gold coin at that time, but larger payments – such as the $25,000 for McIntosh's home and hotel – almost always were paid in what was known as "scrip" and/or bank drafts. Though he was an Indian, McIntosh was educated and refined and likely would not have kept large sums of money at his home.

The next year after McIntosh's death, Governor George Troup ordered a survey be conducted of the chief's former property so that it could be divided into land lots. On December 11, 1826, Carroll County was created from much of that land, and one of the new developments that eventually grew in this general vicinity was Banning Mills.

The Mills & The War

After Carroll County was created, large scale industry was slow to develop in this area because there were so few sites that offered water power. In fact, it wasn't until 1846 that manufacturing communities came to Carroll County; and the earliest – a textile mill located on Snake Creek – was about two miles from present-day Whitesburg, Georgia.

The mill, begun by **William Bowen** and his brothers John, Thomas, and Kit, contained five hundred spindles that produced yarn. From that mill grew a tiny town originally named **Bowenville** after the Bowen brothers. Bowenville even had the distinction of having its own post office in 1849, but by the next year this mill tragically burned to the ground.

Refusing to be defeated by fire, the brothers built another mill and named it **Bowenville Manufacturing Company**. This new mill also produced yarn as well as osnaburg, a type of heavy cloth from which sacks and work clothes were made. This mill was productive for a few years, but by 1855, it had ceased to be a profitable venture and was put up for sale. At that time, a gentleman by the name of William Amis bought the property.

Around the beginning of the U.S. Civil War in 1861, Amis, along with local businessmen John Moyers, William Chilton, and Jet Miller, built **Carroll Manufacturing Company** – a masonry mill – and a stone dam at the site of the old Bowen textile mill on Snake Creek. **Kellog & Company**, another local company, established a paper mill nearby. The little town that grew from the two mills began to prosper, and eventually other goods such as lumber products, meal, and flour were also produced.

Over the next four years – the height of the U.S. Civil War – the mills managed to stay in business, although the South in general was in great turmoil at that time. **General William T.**

Sherman soon learned of the mills and their assistance to the Southern war effort. Sherman ordered his troops to find Bowenville and destroy it.

Interestingly enough, when the Yankees, under the direction of General John Croxton, set out on their mission, they couldn't find the town because it was so well camouflaged in the remote heavily wooded Snake Creek gorge. By that time, the troops, angry and frustrated, marched into Carrollton, where they burned most of the homes and businesses. Without a doubt, the remote lush landscape around Banning Mills helped save it from destruction.

Banning Is Born

After the Civil War, Reconstruction didn't come easily to towns like Bowenville. Many of the small mill communities watched their once successful businesses dwindle away, and Bowenville was no exception. It wasn't until 1878, when Arthur Hutcheson bought the textile mill and U.B. Wilkinson purchased the paper mill, that the economy of Bowenville began to turn around. Records reflect that Wilkinson spent more than $50,000 refurbishing the mill, which eventually employed more than twenty workers and produced twelve tons of wrapping paper a week. The textile mill, now called Hutcheson Manufacturing Company, manufactured warp and bunch yarn.

More changes were on the way when the name of town was changed to "**Banning**." Due to confusion in the postal system (the Bowenville mail was often mixed up with two other nearby communities named Bowersville and Brownsville), Bowenville was renamed Banning (after Frank Banning, a wealthy citizen of the community) in 1882. A new post office was established in 1893, and it seemed as if Banning's future was very bright indeed.

First Electricity

Banning eventually grew to include a gristmill and sawmill. All of the mills were within a mile of each other along Snake Creek. With the escalation of so much industry, Banning had the distinction of becoming one of the first towns in Georgia to produce its own electricity – even in advance of the more progressive Atlanta. Electricity was such a rarity that folks from all around took daylong horse-and-buggy rides just to see the lights come on in Banning each night.

With its mills and electrical power, Banning was thriving. Tiny Whitesburg even had had the privilege of becoming the first rail center in Carroll County in 1873, so it became the shipping point for Banning Mills. Whitesburg's population grew to more than a thousand people; the town seemed as if it were about to become even larger than Carrollton, the county seat.

When the rail line was extended into Carrollton in the late 1800s, Whitesburg surprisingly began to decline, causing a shift of growth away from Banning. The true downfall of Banning, however, began in 1892, when Wilkinson's paper mill burned and was never rebuilt. Jobs disappeared and people began to move away. After Hutcheson passed away in 1895, Colonel C.S. Reid took over and successfully ran the textile mill until 1920, when a group from Akron, Ohio, took it over and operated it until 1971 when it was permanently closed.

The Inn/Modern Times

Once a bustling village, the abandoned mills and their dams either crumbled away or were torn down over the ensuing years, but much of the beautiful old collection of stone dams and mill ruins is part of the scenic beauty of Banning Mills today. Mike and Donna Holder, visionaries in every sense of the word, transformed the old decaying bones of the mills into a four-star country inn and corporate retreat. For the Holders, the opening of Historic Banning Mills was the culmination of imagination, sheer determination, and a dream come true.

"The property, for the most part, had been neglected for over ten years," explains Mike. "The facilities were in a state of disrepair, and the trails and roads were very overgrown, but we could see the great beauty and uniqueness shining through."

"This property is sort of a lost jewel in that it reflects the mill town life of the 1800s," says Donna, "and we're learning more about it as we go along."

In the three years it took to clear the land, renovate the main lodge – which Donna says was "completely black with mold and had ani-mals living inside" – and build additional cottages and cabins, the Holders' aspirations grew even larger. Instead of adhering to their plan of constructing a simple church retreat, Historic Banning Mills slowly metamorphosed into the homey yet elegant inn it is today. It has become a favored retreat for such clients as employees of The Coca-Cola Company and Georgia Tech. Even Georgia Governor Sonny Perdue has visited the property on occasion.

The inn sits smack-dab in the middle of 700 forested acres, high on a hill overlooking the cold, sweet waters of Snake Creek and the mill ruins. An immense stone fireplace and wrap-around porch highlight the main lodge, and its timbered exterior blends seamlessly with the surrounding woodlands. With cottages, cabins, and Jacuzzi suites, there is something for everyone here, from honeymooners to families to groups to just flat-out adventurers. With lots of high-beamed ceilings, wooden floors, spacious rooms, and rocking chairs, one of the primary themes here is pure relaxation.

Some people, however, find that relaxation is way down on their list of things to do in this high energy resort simply because they enjoy the great outdoors. If that describes your attitude, then Historic Banning Mills is about as good as it gets. There is an Olympic-size swimming pool, an archery range, an 18-hole putting green, basketball courts, volleyball fields, a pistol range, and even a "low ropes" course that offers challenging rope exercises. And you can even pamper yourself in the full service day spa with packages offering facials, massages, and manicures.

From the ghosts of the Creek Indians and the soldiers of the Civil War to its naturally breath-taking landscape and world-class inn, Historic Banning Mills is not only an intriguing adventure, but also a heck of a lot of fun. The only difficult part about a visit to this gem is accepting the fact that you ultimately have to leave!

(For more information on Historic Banning Mills, call toll-free (866) 447-8688. The website is www.historicbanningmills.com, and the e-mail address is info@historicbanningmills.com.)

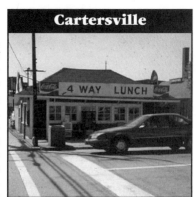

Cartersville

4-Way Lunch

Ernie Garrison, owner of Cartersville's 4-**Way Lunch** starts out his day early. He checks in about 3:00 a.m. Monday through Saturday to start making some 250 biscuits that his customers will have devoured by 10:00 a.m. that day. You might say Ernie's habit is deeply ingrained, because he has maintained the routine at the little diner since he was eight years old, working for his father who founded the business in that same building in 1931.

Ernie's father – **Fred Garrison** – operated a meat market and a grocery store across the street in the late 1920s. By 1931, the nation had found itself firmly in the grips of economic depression, "Locally, the mine and lumber mill had closed," Ernie says emphatically. "Our customers had no money and no one could afford to buy anything from my father."

The depression, however, was only a minor set-back for the enterprising Fred Garrison. He just took his hamburger buns and meat across the street and opened a hamburger stand in a little building there. "He charged a nickel apiece for hot dogs, cokes, and hamburgers," Ernie explained. People could practically buy a whole meal from him for ten or fifteen cents!

After the elder Garrison died, Ernie worked for the **U.S. Army Corps of Engineers** who were building nearby **Allatoona Lake and Dam**. "I wasn't pleased with my paycheck, though," he adds, "so I started operating the restaurant here." He says he's been at it ever since, working until about mid-day Monday through Friday, and staying all day on Saturdays.

The square squat brick building, now painted barn red, was built in the late 1800s, so it's a genuine piece of Southern history. "It started out as an open-front fruit stand," Ernie explains.

Downtown diners have been going the way of the dinosaurs now for a number of years, but 4-Way just keeps on thriving. And that's in spite of a location on a traffic-clogged Main Street with limited parking space and with several fast-food franchises nearby.

To 4-Way's credit, however, it is the ultimate fast-food place and much more. Hundreds of people come every day to stand in a cramped space, chatting while waiting for a seat at one of the 11 vintage black-vinyl stools at the red-topped formica counter. During peak hours, the diners order quickly when they sit down, and then eat quickly to make space for other customers.

4-Way attracts diners from all walks of life too. A judge might be sitting next to a brick-layer. **Joe Frank Harris**, former governor of Georgia and other members of his family have been regulars over the years. **George "Buddy" Darden**, former U.S. congressman, likes to eat there too. And over the years, even a movie star or two has occupied a seat occasionally in the comfy little diner. **Harrison Ford**, **Robert Duvall** and **Ricky Schroeder** reportedly have all enjoyed meals there while starring in movies being filmed in the area.

Diners can order eggs, meat and biscuits for breakfast. Two eggs with meat (bacon, sausage, ham, or fried bologna biscuits are big favorites) cost $3.00. One egg and meat costs only $2.50. There's delicious sorghum syrup for sopping up with the biscuits or grape jelly for spreading.

For lunch, the standards are beef stew, steak sandwich (unbelievably tender) served on a hamburger roll, or a bacon-lettuce-tomato sandwich for $2.75 each. Hot dogs cost $1.50. Chili, slaw or gravy can top any order. A grilled cheese sandwich costs only $1.25. Slaw is available as a side order.

Drinks – milk, tea, lemonade, or soft

drinks – cost a dollar. That's a long way from the nickel Ernie's dad used to charge, but still a bargain by today's standards.

The mission statement – propped on top of the coffee pot – reads: *"This is not Burger King. You don't get it your way. You get it our way, or you don't get the damn thing."* For over 70 years now, customers have gotten it 4-Way's way and liked it, and they keep coming back.

Although service comes with a smile, another sign reads, *"I Can Only Please One Person A Day – And Today Ain't Your Day."* The messages don't offend the customers, because they really are pleased – both with the food and the service.

The staff at 4-Way have worked together now for many years and have a genuine fondness for each other, not to mention a knack for serving up delicious food. Sue Brockman had lived in Adairsville all her life until she and her husband moved to Alabama in 1981.

"I thought I'd drop back to working here two days a week," she says, following the move to Alabama. The new routine, however, didn't "take," and she resumed her four-day workweek at 4-Way a short time later.

Sue's sister, "Pete" Starnes, started working at 4-Way when she was 13. That was 33 years ago. What keeps these sisters at the historic little landmark? "The people," Pete says immediately. "I don't meet a stranger."

It's obvious the 4-Way staff feel a genuine fondness for their customers. They claim they have some diners who travel regularly from as far away as Athens, Rome and Chattanooga.

John Long, an octogenarian from LaGrange, had been dropping by for lunch since 1938. His sales route required him to travel throughout the Southeast, and he said he liked to get off the highway to eat. He might make it to 4-Way once a week, or only once a month, but he definitely returned as often as he could. "I can't understand how they've been able to get the food to taste the same all these years," he said with a broad smile.

Buddy Pruitt, who lives in Rome, makes a point of dropping in at 4-Way four days a week. He said he has been enjoying the food there "since I was a little bittie kid growing up in Pine Log (just outside Cartersville)."

A few years ago, the local historical society started talking about the possibility of buying 4-Way Lunch with a view of getting the structure placed on the **National Register of Historic Places**. Well. . . why not. . . . The building is well over a hundred years old.

Sue says she recently gave Ernie an "Ernie" puppet (from Sesame Street). It sits atop the soft drink dispenser and constantly surveys the scene in the little diner with its beady little eyes. The gift wasn't prompted by any special occasion. "I just gave it to him 'cause I like him," she grinned.

It seems that's the case with a lot of the people who patronize 4-Way Lunch. It, the food, and the regulars who work and dine there are all just a bunch of likeable characters. That's probably what has kept the little diner going all these years.

{4-Way Lunch is located on the corner of Main and Gilmer streets in Cartersville, Georgia. It is open Monday through Saturday, from 5:30 a.m. to 3:00 p.m. For more information, call (770) 382-2016.}

4 NORTHWEST GEORGIA

Cartersville

Euharlee Covered Bridge

Travelers to the little burg known as **Euharlee** eight miles west of Cartersville in Bartow County cross Euharlee Creek without ever noticing the sturdy but featureless concrete bridge. This stream crossing, however, was not always so uneventful.

Fifty yards upstream, an old covered bridge - one of the last such historic structures remaining in Georgia – has been permanently preserved. It is one of several covered bridges which have existed on this site over the past 140 years. Before it was closed to transportation in 1978, the tired old structure on the site today rattled and groaned with the weight of traffic, threatening to collapse at any moment. It was not an empty threat – as Euharlee residents of the 19th century could easily attest if they were still alive.

Indeed, the citizens of this tiny historic community still tell many stories about the old bridge, including the one about the day it turned killer. That incident occurred on March 5th, 1871, a day when the creek was swollen with the torrents of a spring "freshet."

The aging structure on the site at that time was a surprising survivor of the U.S. Civil War (as far as can be determined), struggling to hang on to the creek banks. Seven years earlier, a Union captain of an artillery unit advancing through "**Euharleeville**" reported that *"the bridge across Euharlee Creek is in such a deteriorated condition I doubt I can get my cannon across, but I will make every effort to do so."*

This uncertain condition seems to have been the norm for the bridge at Euharlee in the early days. After years of wear and tear, one took his or her chances when using it.

Such was the case with **Elihu G. Nelson** in 1871. On that fateful March day, he may have been accustomed to the threatening squeaks and groans as he drove his buggy over the span. Villagers going about their work that day were keenly aware of the decrepit bridge weakened even further by the battering current. Anyone using the structure suddenly became an object of attention, and Elihu Nelson, no doubt, was watched closely as he attempted his crossing.

The account was carried in the *Cartersville Semi-Weekly Express* on Tuesday, March 7th. *"We are pained to learn that Mr. E.G. Nelson of Euharlee, with his two little boys met with a very fatal accident on Sunday last, while crossing the bridge over Euharlee Creek at Tumlin's Mills. The particulars as we learned them are as follows: Mr. Nelson and his little boys were crossing the bridge in a two-horse spring buggy, drawn by a horse and a mule, and when near the end of the bridge it gave way, and the vehicle, animals, Mr. Nelson and sons were tumbled into the stream beneath, killing one of the animals, smashing up the buggy and so seriously injuring Mr. Nelson that he has since died, but strange to say, the little boys escaped uninjured."*

One can only imagine today the terror of that moment, as old timbers screeched, splintered, and finally crashed into the stream, carrying away Nelson and his small companions, along with the buggy and thrashing animals. In an attempt to save the victims and recover the buggy, another man was swept away in the swift water and drowned. Onlookers could do nothing else but stand on the creek bank, powerless to help, horrified as they watched the tragic events unfolding before them.

The account of the incident from the Cartersville newspaper continued by explaining, *"This sad accident should teach the parties whose duty it is to look into these things, the great importance of having bridges perfectly secure - human lives are at stake, and are hazarded every time a person crosses one which is not secure."*

Ironically, a report from the commissioners to the county ordinary shortly after the tragedy noted that, *"Mr. Tumlin only a week before the accident occurred carried Clim a practical mechanic with him under the bridge to examine it."*

Despite the collapse of the bridge, old records indicate a full five years passed before the county contracted for a replacement. In the interim, the wreckage from the collapse, no doubt, was rebuilt as a makeshift span.

4

NORTHWEST GEORGIA

180

In 1876, the Bartow County commissioners contracted with Thomas Tumlin to build a bridge across the Euharlee for $590.00. Whether or not it was completed immediately is unknown. At the end of another five years, the Bartow County commissioners were soliciting bids for a new bridge at *"Euharlee Mills at or near the old bridge."*

In 1881, the commissioners awarded the low bidders, John J. Calhoun and N.C. Sayre, a contract for the project for $999.00. It specified there would be seven spans, four over the creek, with a total length of 260 feet, braced with one and one-half inch round iron. The spans would be supported by wooden trestles *"as high as practicable and the height to be determined by the Board of Commissioners."*

Three years later, another flood allowed this new bridge to sail away on a brief voyage downstream. After only a few yards, it came to rest on the west bank of the creek, jammed up against **Lowry Mill**. Another contract was awarded, this time to H.J. McCormick, the low bidder at $195.00. This low cost seems to suggest that the contractor was simply to recover the original structure and replace it on repaired trestles.

If built shoddily or improperly, the old covered bridges usually did not weather many years. Such seems to have been the case with the Euharlee Bridge. Just two years after H.J. McCormick's repairs, yet another bridge was needed over the unpredictable stream.

By this time in 1886, the Bartow County commissioners no doubt felt they were following a blueprint for failure, and indeed, they were. First, the contractors were Euharlee residents – leading citizens, but not bridge-builders. Second, the "design" sketched in the 1881 specification shows an old-style truss which was a simple triangle with a horizontal span surmounted by two diagonal braces reinforced with a vertical iron rod. It was not a design with durability in mind. And finally, the wooden trestles supporting the structure simply could not withstand the force of the floods which periodically swept through the area.

In most places in the 1800s (and even today), there were good bridges and there were bad bridges. If you wanted a good one, a fellow by the name of Horace King was the man to see. By 1886, he had 60 years of experience as a bridge builder, and was respected throughout the South for his successful projects.

Today, Euharlee townsfolk are fiercely proud of their covered bridge and especially the unusual history of its builder. They had always heard that the builder was Horace King, a freed slave, and he was the builder. . . almost.

King's history is a fascinating account of a nineteenth century success story. According to *Covered Bridges Of Georgia* by Thomas L. French, Jr. and Edward L. French, **Horace King** *"was born a slave in the Chesterfield District of South Carolina on September 8, 1807. His father was a mulatto named Edmund King; his mother, Susan (or Lucky), was the daughter of a full-blood Catawba Indian and a black female slave. In the winter of 1829, Horace King's master died, and King and his mother became the property of John Godwin, a South Carolina house builder and bridge contractor."*

Though he did not know it at the time, Horace's lifestyle – in one single stroke of fate – was transformed from that of servility to that of tremendous opportunity. Under Godwin's tutelage, King steadily learned the home and bridge-building trades. He advanced to the position of construction foreman despite the fact he was a slave.

A close bond developed between King and Godwin. In 1832, the Godwin enterprises moved to Girard, which later became Phenix City, Alabama. Later, when John Godwin – due to misfortune - lost nearly all of his property, he successfully petitioned the Alabama General Assembly to emancipate Horace King in 1846, long before the War Between The States was even a sparkle in Jeff Davis' eye.

As the years passed and King's stature as a bridge contractor was growing, Euharlee's need for a reliable span was growing in almost equal proportion. According to local folklore, Horace King came to Euharlee to build the bridge. Well . . . not quite, and this, no doubt, was a surprise to many current residents of Bartow County.

Although King was certainly the acknowledged master of covered bridge building in Georgia and perhaps even the South, it is unlikely that he visited Euharlee in 1886. At that time, King was living in LaGrange and his health was failing. At age 79, he had less than a year left to live.

However, prior to his ill health, King had taught his sons the crafts of construction and bridge-building, and they reportedly were as gifted as was their father. Their contracting business, "Bridge Company," was flourishing. Horace's eldest son, **Washington**, was building structures under his own name, and in 1883, he and his brother, George, submitted the successful bid for a span over the Etowah River at Howard's Shoals.

A *"Notice To Bridge Builders"* was duly published in the **Cartersville Courant** on August 12, 1886, requesting bids for *"a wooden bridge across Euharlee creek, at Euharlee mills in said county. Said bridge will be about 300 feet long and should be completed within 30 days from date of letting."*

On September 28, 1886, the commissioners of Bartow County accepted the *"best bid"* of $1,300.00 from Jno. H. Burke and W.W. King for *"a Lattice bridge across Euharlee Creek at Lowry's Mills."*

The bridge completed by Burke and King was a sturdy piece of construction, and making it even more durable was the fact that King - contrary to his predecessors in this project – did not use the wooden trestles in the creek waters. Instead, he used heavy stone piers, well elevated to allow for even the highest of floods.

Daniel Lowry, according to his descendants, donated field stone from his farm for the project. And since the stone piers were not included in Burke and King's contract, Lowry and his crew quite possibly also built the piers.

Today – well over 100 years from the date it was constructed - the Town lattice truss of the Euharlee/Lowry Covered Bridge can be examined at close range. The carefully-painted white numbers, from #1 to #79, are still clearly visible at the lower end of each diagonal (Each piece was preassembled and numbered prior to construction). Most of the pieces also carry clear mallet marks where the workers apparently pounded the timbers snugly together with large wooden pegs.

Except for the dust accumulated over the years, the round treenails (pronounced "trunnels") might have been pounded into place yesterday. They reveal the careful craftsmanship of Washington King and Jonathan Burke's crew: Each pair of these pegs is exactly five inches apart.

Today, one can see a covered bridge, well elevated above floods, built by an accomplished contractor using a proven design. Bartow's commissioners of roads and bridges had finally struck the right combination of the elements needed for a successful bridge project. They had solved their problem – or, more correctly, W.W. King had.

After a century, the stately structure is weathered and battered, but still stands firmly above Euharlee Creek. Its endurance has been tested many many times over the years. When Georgia Power was constructing the massive Plant Bowen power plant nearby, it was old Euharlee Covered Bridge that supported the immense weight of truckload after truckload of crushed stone used in construction of the plant. The weight of these trucks was far, far more than the weight for which the bridge had originally been designed.

Finally, in 1978, after appeals to the state, yet another bridge was built over Euharlee Creek – this time a modern concrete affair. Traffic over the creek is now carried by the new structure and no longer threatens Euharlee's treasured landmark.

At one time, Georgia had some 250 of the barn-like wooden structures, roofed and enclosed to shield the timbers from the weather. Today, Georgia's collection of historic covered bridges has been reduced to a mere ten now carried on the **National Register of Historic Places**.

Today, the historic community of Euharlee still includes a number of interesting 100-year-old structures, many of which were preserved with a recently enacted preservation program. The plan includes numerous historic buildings restored by volunteers, as well as recreation and picnic facilities in a park-like setting.

Historical old covered bridges remind many an old-timer of the days when folks traveled by horse and buggy when a "courting couple" could stop in the privacy of the bridge for a treasured embrace. Today, Euharlee Covered Bridge also reminds us of Horace King, a freed slave who had the inner resolve to learn a craft and, against the odds, profit by his excellence. Henceforth, this century-old bridge hopefully will also be remembered not as the product of Horace, but as that of his son, Washington W. King.

{Directions: To reach the community of Euharlee, travel west on GA Highway 113 to the towering twin stacks of Plant Bowen near Stilesboro. Turn right onto Covered Bridge Road which passes the power plant. For more information, contact the Bartow County Chamber of Commerce or the Etowah Foundation's History Center at (770) 382-3818}

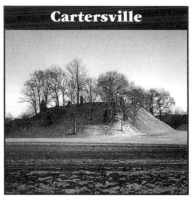
Cartersville

Etowah Indian Mounds

The prehistoric mounds known as **Etowah Indian Mounds** in northwest Georgia's Bartow County are one of the state's most historic landmarks. The origin and purpose of this site, however, has puzzled mankind for centuries.

Visitors to **Etowah Indian Mounds State Historic Site** have often asked Site Manager Libby Bell if the mounds were built to serve as a refuge during floods. Since the tallest mound stands 63 feet over the surrounding Etowah River bottom-lands, this is a reasonable assumption. However, it is also incorrect. Visitors to the site have been making the same mistake for more than two centuries.

William Bartram, a noted botanist and explorer, jumped to the same conclusion during a 1776 expedition into the wilderness north of Augusta, Georgia. He accompanied a surgeon from the garrison at Fort Dartmouth to the ruins of an ancient village beside the Savannah River. Within the ruins he discovered several *"remarkable Indian monuments"* including an earthen mound that stood fifty feet high with a circumference of 200 to 300 yards. Bartram speculated about its purpose:

"It is altogether unknown to us, what could have induced the Indians to raise such a heap of earth in this place, the ground for a great space around being subject to inundations, at least once a year. . . We may however hazard a conjecture;. . . . this mount (was) raised for a retreat and refuge in case of inundations, which are unforeseen and surprise them very suddenly, spring and autumn."

Continuing his travels through the mountains of Georgia and North Carolina, Bartram soon arrived at the Cherokee village of **Cowe**. He discovered that the Cherokees there had erected a meeting house on an ancient mound in the center of this village. At the same time, however, he learned that these same Cherokees were ignorant about *"what people or for what*

purpose these artificial hills were raised." They told Bartram that the mounds were there when *"their forefathers arrived from the West and possessed themselves of the country, after vanquishing the nations of red men who then inhabited it, who themselves had found these mounts when they took possession of the country. . ."* After further consideration, Bartram decided that the mounds might have been designed *"to some religious purpose, as great altars and temples similar to the high places and sacred groves amongst the canaanites and other nations of Palestine and Judea."*

It turns out that Bartram's speculation, quite possibly, was "right on the money" this time. After more than a century of excavations and study, archaeologists today believe that mounds of the type found at Etowah Indian Mounds were constructed by an early culture of Native Americans – labeled by researchers as "Mississippians," whose religion centered around the worship of the sun. They built and occupied the Etowah Indians Mounds village site between 950 and 1560 A.D. The abode of the village chieftain – who was believed to be a descendant of the sun – was erected atop an earthen mound which served as a village's political and religious center.

The Mississippians were an agricultural people whose principal crops included corn, beans, squash, pumpkins, and tobacco. With their primitive tools, they could work only the loose, alluvial soil of river bottoms. Thus they habitually built their villages beside large rivers.

Another misconception about Indian mounds is the widely-held belief that they were used for mass burials. In most of the north Georgia villages the only time remains were laid to rest within a mound was in the event of the death of a chieftain and other members of the ruling class. The commoners among the natives customarily buried their dead beneath the floor of their home.

In a puzzling departure from this norm, however, more than 350 bodies were buried at Etowah Indian Mounds in Mound C. This 19-foot high mound was completely excavated and rebuilt in the 1960s. Within the mound, archaeologists discovered a wealth of artifacts, including two remarkable marble effigies which are now displayed in the visitors center. These artifacts reveal much about the religious practices, social structure, dress, diet, diseases and trade patterns of the villagers.

The Mississippians were hunters and gatherers. Game generally included deer, bear, turkey and fish, but possibly elk and buffalo (which inhabited this region well into the 18th century) as well. There was also an abundant supply of hickory nuts, acorns, walnuts, chestnuts, plums, muscadines, persimmons and other foods.

The Mississippians were also traders who obtained goods from surprisingly distant locations. Excavators discovered flint blades made in Tennessee, shells from the Gulf coast, copper from the Great Lakes area, pottery from the Mississippi River region and obsidian from the Pacific coast. Archaeological discoveries in the area lend credence to the possibility that the village may also have been visited by 16th century Spanish explorers – perhaps even by **Hernando de Soto** himself. Sword hilts, beads and an iron celt have been recovered at the site. Today, many of these artifacts are on display at the park museum.

At its peak in 1200 A.D., the Etowah village occupied more than 50 acres and had a population of 2,000 to 3,000 inhabitants. "Etowah," Bell notes, "served as the capitol of an area within a 50 to 100-mile radius."

The Etowah village was protected by elaborate defensive works, including a 10 to 15-foot-deep ditch that stretched in a semi-circle around the village. An imposing palisade of upright, 12-foot-high logs was placed just inside the ditch.

The village consisted of two temple mounds (Mounds A and B), a burial mound (Mound C), several smaller mounds, and a plaza (a large, flat area raised about a foot-and-a-half above the village floor). The plaza was sprinkled with red ochre and it was the location of trading activities and of ball games.

Bell notes that the Mississippians had a stratified society. The houses of the leaders occupied places of prominence and some were built on the smaller mounds. The houses were wood post structures plastered with clay and covered by a grass or cane thatch roof. Each had a clay-lined fireplace in the center of the floor and smoke escaped through a hole in the roof.

Bell says that much of what is known about the Etowah villagers' living quarters and conditions was learned from an excavation near Mound D. About two to three feet below the soil surface, archaeologists unearthed the floor, hearth and benches of a house built about 1540 A.D. Based upon the size and arrangement of the elements of the house, archaeologists surmised that it was occupied by a small family and was used primarily for sleeping, food storage and shelter during periods of intense cold. This house had been destroyed by a fire.

The arrival of European explorers possibly led to the demise of Etowah and other Mississippian villages. According to University of Georgia archaeologist Dr. Mark Williams, the Indians were decimated when they were exposed to diseases to which they had no natural immunity. By the mid-16th century, the Etowah village site was uninhabited and abandoned.

(The Etowah Indian Mounds State Historic Site is located at 813 Indian Mound Road, SE, Cartersville, Georgia, 30120. For more information, call (770) 387-3747, or check the WEB site www.gastateparks.org}

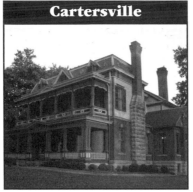

Historic Cartersville

The tracks that divide Cartersville's old downtown district brought life to this historic northwest Georgia community in the late 1800s. Today, this vicinity represents a microcosm of the history of this corner of the state and can provide an interesting weekend getaway.

Colonel Farrish Carter undoubtedly was just joking when, circa 1850s, he suggested the town be named after him due to the frequency of his visits. But Carter carried wealth and influence, and the folks of what then was called "**Birmingham**," Georgia, must have believed (or at least hoped) that his name would bring some of that fortune their way.

In the early 1870s, most of Georgia was still recovering from the devastating effects of the War Between The States, and the re-routed tracks of the **Western & Atlantic Railroad** were beginning to bring business into the little town of Cartersville, while taking commerce away from the original county seat of Cassville. Store-keepers set up shop, churches were erected, and new houses began to surround the downtown district.

Downtown Cartersville is only 40 miles northwest of Atlanta, but today, visitors have a variety of ways to step quickly back in time in this northwest Georgia community. Ancient Indian habitation sites, old country stores, pre-Civil War structures and more are still scattered about the community. Most of the historic structures in this town today, however, were built just after the war.

From the railroad tracks - which still experience 45 trains a day - one can see the world's first outdoor painted-wall advertisement for **Coca-Cola**, a depot built in 1854 and occupied by Confederate troops ten years later, and a theatre that began with opera prior to World War I and which today again serves up live performances.

The historic Coca-Cola sign was painted in 1894, and then painted over and forgotten for perhaps 80 or 90 years. Dean Cox, the owner of the building (**Young Brothers Pharmacy**) on which the sign had been painted eventually discovered the historic artwork beneath some 25 layers of paint. In 1988, he commissioned a tedious stripping and restoration project, revealing the sign as it had been brushed on the wall nearly 100 years earlier.

Inside Young Brothers Pharmacy, photographs on the wall explain the story of how the original sign was revealed. Visitors often note that the paint job is far from perfect. It seems that an industrious Coca-Cola syrup salesman (and not a professional artist) did the brushwork.

The old railroad depot, which has become the centerpiece of a Cartersville downtown park, was originally built of locally-made brick, using slave labor. It was at this depot that General William T. Sherman cut the telegraph wire before launching his now infamous "March To The Sea."

Today, the depot does not resemble the structure as it existed when Sherman paused at the site. Confederate troops knocked out bricks for gun ports and burned the roof and floor. Additions to the building were made in 1902, and portions of the building were demolished in 1972. It, however, is still a very historic structure, and is well-worth a visit.

The **Grand Threatre** is another landmark in Cartersville's downtown district. Grand in both size and design, it was originally built as an opera house, but was destroyed by fire in the 1920s. Rebuilt as a movie house and showing silent films under the name of "**Greenwood Theatre**," it remained in operation until 1978. Today, one can catch live theater or operatic performances at the Grand, which is listed on the National Register Of Historic Places.

The **Bartow History Center and Museum** Store at 13 Wall Street (Tel.: 770-387-2774 or 770-382-3818) are just down the block from the Grand, and offer a wealth of interesting historic information on the town. For a suggested donation of a single dollar, visitors can view a variety of historic relics and photographs. You can also purchase interesting gifts here, as well as publications which can serve as a guide to the historic treasures of the town and county.

Back outside and just a block or two away, the home and other structures are all that remain from a famed evangelist of the late 1800s. Known for his outspoken denouncement of the evils of his day, **Rev. Sam Jones** rose to national acclaim with his ministries.

Following Captain Tom Ryman's conversion by Jones in Tennessee in the late 1800s, the riverboat gambler vowed to build a tabernacle "so that Sam Jones will never have to preach in a tent again." Ryman, builder of Ryman Auditorium in Nashville (which became the home of the Grand Ole Opry), was the owner and operator of a fleet of pleasure boats plying the Cumberland River in Tennessee.

According to an article published in *Echoes Of The Grand Old Opry* on the 60th anniversary of Ryman Auditorium, *"(Ryman) . . . the operator of a fleet of pleasure boats. . . dedicated to dancing, gambling and drinking. . . a rough fellow was Captain Ryman, a man of the world. It is part of the legend that Tom and members of his rowdy crew went to a tent revival service in Nashville intent upon disrupting it. They meant to make sport of the evangelist Sam Jones. Reverend Jones, however, was a preacher of considerable power. In the course of the evening's revival service* (on the subject of motherhood). . .*the rough Tom Ryman was brought to his knees, converted in the ways of Christ. It is said that Captain Ryman led his crewmen back to his boat to throw gaming tables and teakwood bars overboard."*

Sam Jones continued his evangelical journey throughout the nation for years. Both men and women by the scores responded to his message by going forward to embrace a new-found faith. Jones was invited to conduct ministries abroad on a number of occasions, but with the exception of Canada, he always chose not to leave the country.

One of Jones' most cherished responsibilities was that of agent in 1890 for the **Decatur, Georgia Orphan's Home**. He raised over $60,000 in contributions, freeing the home

from debt. He supported the home thereafter from his own funds.

Jones' career ended abruptly on October 15, 1906, when he passed away on a train enroute to Georgia from Oklahoma City, Oklahoma. And, when his body was returned to Atlanta to lie in state in the rotunda of the state Capitol building, it was guarded there by 16 girls from the Decatur Orphans' Home, as thousands paid tribute to him for the final time.

Jones' impressive Victorian mansion called "Roselawn," (Tel.: 770-387-5162) is owned today by Bartow County, and is maintained as a historic museum. The grounds still include the original smoke house, the school house where the Jones children began their education and the carriage house.

The second and third floors of Roselawn are occupied by museums remembering Sam Jones, the **United Daughters of the Confederacy** and **Rebecca Felton**. Felton was the first female U.S. senator and was once a teacher of Sam Jones.

Before straying too far from downtown, you'll find history and lunch just a few steps down Main Street from the railroad tracks. The **4-Way Lunch**, with its 14 barstools, has been grilling hamburgers for folks in Cartersville since 1931, and reportedly has served the likes of actors **Robert Duval, Ricky Schroeder** and **Harrison Ford** who enjoyed meals there while filming movies in the area.

After lunch, walk or drive down some of the streets which spread out from downtown, especially on the west side of town. Dozens of homes in this area have historical significance, including some that are antebellum homes. Many of the most significant structures are so designated by markers from the **Etowah Valley Historical Society**. You'll also find two of Cartersville's oldest churches (both still active) – the **First Presbyterian Church**, established in 1843 and the **Episcopal Church of the Ascension**, built in 1870 – in this area of town.

As you exit the Presbyterian Church, you can drive on up the street for three or four miles to a really captivating historic site built in prehistory by ancient native Americans. Few historic events have been better documented than General Sherman's devastating Civil War campaign through Georgia and his stop at the Cartersville Railroad Depot. Interestingly,

Sherman had been to Cartersville long before the war on a visit to the Etowah Indian Mounds. Glencove, the home where he stayed during this 1848 visit, still stands in Cartersville.

And long before Sherman's visit, the mounds are believed by some to have attracted an even more famous traveler – **Hernando De Soto** – who, in 1540, led some 600 Spanish soldiers, entrepreneurs and priests on a tour through the area known today as Georgia. Prospecting for gold and other treasures, De Soto and his crew explored the riverside mounds, which at the time, still no doubt were inhabited by an active Mississippian Culture of Native Americans.

According to research, this culture began to lose strength shortly after De Soto's departure, and many historians attribute the demise of this ancient culture to visits by European explorers. In addition to the wounds and dismemberments suffered from skirmishes with the Spanish, the natives apparently had no natural immunity with which to ward off European diseases which were introduced by the Spaniards. The Mississippian Culture Native Americans abandoned the mounds and village site by 1600.

At the **Etowah Indian Mounds State Historic Site** today, visitors can step back hundreds of years into the past, learning what occurred on the very ground upon which the visitors stand. A self-guided walking tour takes the visitor to many of this site's remaining features, including ancient Indian fish traps built of large rocks which can still be seen on the river bottom, borrow pits from which dirt was removed to construct the mounds, and the visible edge of a ceremonial plaza.

A 9- to 10-foot-deep ditch, (crossed by a bridge today as one enters the site) was once connected to the Etowah River on each end, providing a defensive moat around the 52 acres of the site. A 12-foot-high palisade flanked the moat on the inside. These barriers protected the largest and most important Indian settlement in the Etowah River valley from approximately 1000 to 1500 A.D.

But it is the mounds themselves which draw the most attention. These earthen structures were used as platforms for the home of the priest/chief, temples and for mortuary houses.

Mound A, the largest, is 63 feet high, the height of a six-story building, and a set of stairs leads to the top. Atop the mound, one can get a great perspective of the plaza area, the other mounds, and the entire historic site.

A museum at the Etowah Indian Mounds' entrance displays over 400 artifacts discovered at the mounds, and provides plenty of interpretive information, as well as a good, 10-minute introductory video.

When you're ready to depart Etowah Indian Mounds, one final side trip is well worth taking, although the destination is seven miles outside of Cartersville. Located just up GA Highway 113 in the tiny hamlet of Euharlee, an old covered bridge spans an Etowah River feeder-creek. Rustic and beautiful, **Lowry** (or **Euharlee**) **Covered Bridge** was constructed in 1886 by African-American bridge builder Horace King's company, with King's son, Washington, probably actually doing the construction.

The little community of **Euharlee** is quite historic and interesting in its own right. The ruins of an old grist mill may be viewed near the covered bridge at this well-manicured community. And the little town boasts an old general store, a small museum and other sites. A popular "**Covered Bridge Festival**" is conducted every autumn at this site and features fine arts and crafts, foods, a Civil War encampment and re-enactment, live entertainment, children's activities and much more. For more information, call (770) 386-1542.

To reach Euharlee, travel west on Highway 113 to the towering twin stacks of Plant Bowen electrical generation plant (you can't miss it.). Turn right on Covered Bridge Road and follow it into the countryside until you reach the bridge and town.

(Cartersville is located just off Interstate 75 (take the Highway 113/Main Street Exit). Main Street goes straight down to the historic downtown district. For more information on Cartersville, including recommended dining sites and overnight accommodations, call the Cartersville-Bartow County Convention and Visitors Bureau at (770) 387-1357.)

Cartersville

Here's a very interesting, quick and easy trip Atlanta-area history buffs can take into the north Georgia hinterlands. It involves the abandoned railroad grade of the historic **Western & Atlantic Railroad** (W&A RR) in the vicinity of **Allatoona Lake** on the **Etowah River** near the Emerson/Cartersville area in Bartow County.

To reach the site, drive up Interstate 75 north to Acworth, then up old Highway 41. Turn right onto Old Sandtown Road, then follow Allatoona Pass Road until you reach the railroad tracks (present-day C.S.X. Railroad).

Old Allatoona Pass

At this point, stop to examine a very historic item – the grave of *The Unknown Hero*. This grave is located approximately one-half mile south of the entrance to **Allatoona Pass**, and contains the last remains of a **Confederate soldier** who fell in battle.

Today, the identity of this fallen soldier – or even the site at which he died – cannot be positively confirmed. One story maintains the remains are those of a young man whose lifeless body was being shipped home by rail in a box labeled simply as "Allatoona, Georgia." No mark showed the origin of the box. The body supposedly reached its destination days after a battle, and had understandably reached a high state of decay.

Six young women, as the story goes, took over a job normally reserved for men. In what could only be interpreted as an attempt to ascertain identity, they reportedly pried off the lid of the box with a crowbar. Inside, they found only a young man dressed in Confederate grey. With him lay a rolled-up, broad-brimmed black hat. Since there was no cemetery nearby, the women dug a grave and buried the soldier on the spot. They placed a crude marker at the spot to mark it for posterity.

Though the above explanation for the grave sounds plausible, some area residents disagree with it. They believe the correct explanation is that offered by Robert White, former stationmaster of the **Cartersville** (Georgia) **Depot**, and the late Colonel Thomas Spencer, a journalist and historian. According to these two men, there are TWO unknown soldier graves at Allatoona Pass, not just one, and the bodies were originally buried on opposite sides of the

W&A tracks near the northern entrance to the pass.

A partial reference to these two grave sites can even be obtained from the publication **The Western & Atlantic Railroad / Marietta**, written in 1887 by former Georgia Governor **Joseph M. Brown**, an ardent student of history. According to Brown, *"The most characteristic memorial of this bloody and famous struggle which now salutes the eye of the tourist, as the train darts through the deep, fern-lined (Allatoona) pass, is a lone grave at its northwestern end, immediately by the track on the west side. This is the resting-place of a Confederate soldier, who was buried on the spot where he fell. For years past, the track-hands of the Western & Atlantic Railroad held this grave under their special charge . . . A neat marble headstone has ben placed there on which is the following inscription: 'An Unknown Hero. He Died For The Cause He Thought Was Right.'"*

According to an article published in the July 4, 1948 issue of **The Atlanta Journal**, historians at that time believed the soldier *"probably fell about 8:30 a.m. on the morning of October 5, 1864, in the Battle of Allatoona. He likely was in Confederate Brig. General Claudius W. Sears' brigade. A member of the Ninety-third Illinois killed him, perhaps. Those two units clashed in the vicinity of the present grave site."*

For many years after the war, the grave site was improved and regularly maintained by track-workers of the W&A RR (and later, the N.C. & St. L. RR). In the 1940s, when Allatoona Lake was under construction, the railroad line was relocated from Allatoona Pass, so the remains in the grave were moved to the relocated line, so that track workers could continue to care for the grave site. The passage of time, unfortunately, has erased the loyalty of the railroad workers to the grave, so a nearby resident maintains the site as of this writing.

This is just one of the many historic aspects of the old W&A Railroad at Allatoona Pass which make it so interesting today. Several of the roads north of Acworth actually exist on the original W&A roadbed which was abandoned during the 1940s when the line was relocated to avoid the new lake. After looking over the grave site and nearby historical markers, you can follow the Emerson-Allatoona Road a very short distance to Allatoona Pass.

There is a parking area here for visitors to park their cars. It's right across the road from the historic (circa 1830) **Clayton House**, which still has bullet holes in it from the battle so long ago.

From this point, you can hike down the old roadbed into the historic pass. At the end of the pass, you will find a set of stairs and a trail to the top of the hill. There, you will be standing in the remains of the **Civil War "Star Fort"** on the left or western side of the pass. This fortified position was used by both Union and Confederate forces to defend the rail line. The earthworks here are still visible from the battle which took place in 1864. A state historic marker explains the fort and the battle which occurred here between Union and Confederate forces.

When the cut (the route where the railroad-bed was graded into the mountain to create the pass) is viewed (looking down into the pass) from the old Civil War Star Fort, one can get a true idea (and perspective) of the immensity of this excavation which created the pass The lower part of the cut, dug largely through rock, has steep sides, but above that point (vertically up the wall of the cut) the soil was much looser, and the wall slopes back out of view. From the track level, visitors to this site can't see the actual top of the cut. Apparently, a terrace was created at this point in the 1860s, and a footbridge was built across the cut (above the railroad) to allow easy movement between two forts - one on either side of the railroad cut.

After exploring this unique site, visitors can return to track level and climb the trail up to the peak on the opposite (eastern) side of the pass. Yet another Civil War fort was once located on this peak.

This second, smaller fort is a good bit east of the railroad cut. And interestingly, inbetween is the original **Allatoona Pass Wagon Road** which dates back to pioneer days in the region. The second fort was actually built to allow defense of this pioneer roadway. Historical markers at this point indicate Civil War trenches and the location of the stables for the horses. Other modern trails lead down to the lake shore.

After exploring this vicinity, most visitors usually return to the old W&A railroad grade in the pass. Here, at the north end of the pass on the western side of the former railroad bed, the original grave site of **"The Unknown Hero"** (described earlier) was once located. As explained earlier, the grave was moved from this site after the railroad was relocated.

Some visitors continue hiking on the old grade until they reach the point at which further progress is blocked by a "plug dam." This is a railroad cut filled with dirt to prevent water from the lake from flowing down the old grade during extreme flood conditions.

There are other interesting sites in this vicinity too. If you hike back to your car, you can drive on through Emerson to the Etowah River. There, sightseers may turn onto the road which parallels the river. After only a short distance, you will come to the sturdy stone bridge piers from the 1848 bridge at Etowah Crossing. This bridge was destroyed and rebuilt several times by both sides during the War Between The States. It was here that **William Fuller** commandeered the **Cooper Ironworks'** locomotive *Yonah* during his pursuit of **James Andrews** and the locomotive *General* during what has become known in folklore as *The Great Locomotive Chase*.

Also in this vicinity is the historic **Cooper Furnace Day Use Area** (a historic park) where you can enjoy your lunch (if you packed it) and the old furnace from this 1800s-era pig-iron smelting plant. The U.S. Army Corps of Engineers has placed grilles on all four sides of the furnace in an attempt to keep explorers out of the huge old stone furnace for safety purposes, but vandals have broken down one of them.

Following lunch, drive the short distance to the **Allatoona Dam Powerhouse**. If you call in advance to the **Etowah Dam Visitors Center**, you can schedule a very interesting tour of the dam and powerhouse..

By the end of that tour, you ought to be ready for a tour of old downtown **Cartersville**. There, you can take in the old depot where **Gen. William T. Sherman** cut the telegraph lines as he began his infamous "**March To The Sea**," and visit the many other historic sites in this antebellum north Georgia town. After that, you ought to be exhausted and ready for the comforts of home once again.

{Admission to the historic Allatoona Pass is free. The pass, the forts at the top of the pass and the grave of the Unknown Soldier are considered a self-guided tour. Visitors are reminded that this is a closely-protected area under the management of the U.S. Army Corps of Engineers. Any use of metal detectors or relic hunting in general is strictly forbidden. High fines can and will be levied upon violators. Also, there is poison ivy in the vicinity of Allatoona Pass, and insect hitch-hikers are prevalent, so don't forget the bug repellent. For more information, contact the U.S. Army Corps of Engineer's Lake Allatoona Visitor Center (east of Interstate 75 on GA 20 Spur) at 770-382-4700.}

Cartersville

Weinman Mineral Museum

Cars speeding along Interstate 75 near Cartersville, Georgia, might catch a fleeting glimpse of the white marble building with antique mining equipment standing nearby. Both casual explorers and ardent "rockhounds" find their way to the **Weinman Mineral Museum**, one of Georgia's best-kept secrets.

Georgia's mining industry totals 1.5 billion dollars per year, and Bartow County, situated as it is in the center of an ancient mineral belt, has produced 43 of the state's 198 minerals – more than any other comparable area in the nation.

For the last hundred years, Cartersville's economy has benefited greatly from mining and limestone quarrying. So, when the **Cartersville Tourism Council** began casting about for a tourist attraction in 1980, they "discovered" their mineral fame and decided that a mineral museum could bring them tourism fame.

A fine building was completed in 1983, funded by – what else – one of the family fortunes made from mining one of Cartersville's minerals – barite. Barium sulfate, a bluish crystalline mineral, is used in a variety of paint, paper, and rubber products, and until World War I, was imported from Germany.

The **Thompson-Weinman Company** began operations in 1914, and when German imports of barium sulfate ceased shortly thereafter, production of the product soared at Thompson-Weinman. Appropriately, the massive silver-painted mill which produced the first minerals and helped to build the fortune of William J. Weinman, stands at the museum's entryway.

As visitors enter the museum complex, the exhibits are located in three exhibit halls: The Neil McNitt Family Room displays some of the rich geology history of the state. The Mayo Wing houses international collections of minerals and gemstones. Another section – The Fossil Room – contains ancient fossils, and includes a life-sized replica of a triceratops skull that the public can touch.

It is the variety and scope of the fossils at Weinman which make it the favorite – hands down – of visiting school children. One stop on the tour – a display of coprolite or "dinosaur doo-doo" always produces a guaranteed reaction from the kids, and tour guides seem to delight in pointing it out.

This unlikely lump is a genuine fossilized dinosaur dropping which was actually found in Oregon. Scientists have been able to determine what the prehistoric beast had for lunch millions of years ago by examining the specimen.

Among displays of more than 2,000 rocks, fossils, artifacts and minerals – many of which are breathtakingly beautiful – the keen eye discovers many more surprises.

Drawing upon their large stock of minerals and fossilized remains in storage, Weinman staffers frequently make new exhibits and improve old ones. Sometimes, the museum temporarily exchanges materials with other museums to obtain new and exciting exhibit items: A jewelry collection from the **Smithsonian Institute** in Washington, D.C., a moon rock from the **Marshall Space Center** in Huntsville, Alabama, and gold from the **Dahlonega Gold Museum** in Dahlonega.

"We are the largest (museum) with the most specimens south of the Smithsonian and east of the Mississippi," says Weinman director Jose Santamaria. Despite this fact, many Georgians are unaware of the uniqueness of Weinman Mineral Museum, and are even surprised to learn of its existence.

Upon entering the museum, the visitor first passes a trickling waterfall and then advances to a simulated mine tunnel where minerals glow with bright eerie colors under ultraviolet illumination ("blacklights").

Beyond the cave is a display of birthstones: diamond for April, ruby for July – one for every month of the year. Then on to a saber-toothed tiger skull and a six-inch shark's tooth, the state fossil. One favorite is a three-foot-high geode from Brazil, half of a rock shell lined with glistening crystals of purple amethyst.

Next, large samples of minerals such as chilly quartz and silky talc are provided for the visitor to "touch-and-feel." All of the exhibits are accessible to the handicapped.

In one corner of the museum, a curious replica of a rustic cabin with an owl perched above it quickly catches the roving eye. "Bartow," the talking owl is set in motion by a pushbutton which activates the opening and closing of the bird's beak. Bartow first hoots, then begins a description of the history of mining in the county.

Seemingly pausing on the cabin's front porch, a replica of an early miner lounges next to the simple, low-tech mining tools of yesteryear – a pick, shovel, and wheelbarrow. These tools were the basic instruments used to mine ocher – colorful combinations of iron oxides. This mineral has been collected since 1877 in a narrow eighty-mile-long belt of deposits nearby. Once used as a pigment for linoleum, ocher is now used for coloring concrete.

"We're very rich in Georgia in mineral resources, both for the mining industries and for the collectors," continues Mr. Santamaria.

The collection of rocks, minerals and fossils is a fun hobby for many individuals – both young and old. Rockhounds are travelers by necessity, and the museum's annual "**RockFest**" (2nd Saturday in June) attracts these enthusiasts from locations miles away.

In the Weinman gift shop, even the most jaded of visitors can usually find an item of interest. Some can

be displayed in a rock collection, and others can be finished into fine jewelry.

One day each year, Weinman holds a "**Mineral I.D. Day**," for visitors to the museum. Everyone is invited to bring anything that they have ever collected, and a panel of experts do their best to identify any and all finds.

On other days, when amateurs visit with an unidentified discovery, Weinman staffmembers say they never know what to expect. Some collectors find worthwhile fossils at road-building sites. Other excited participants are convinced they have discovered gold, or sometimes, a stray meteorite fragment. To date, however, not one supposed gold or meteorite sample supplied by a visitor has turned out to be the real thing. But the amateur prospectors and rockhounds keep searching and bringing their samples to Weinman.

The museum has, over the years, attracted visitors from around the world, but surprisingly, remains relatively unknown among Georgians. "You'd be surprised at how many people who live in Bartow County don't know about it," Santamaria adds.

To be sure, the Weinman Mineral Museum is no simple mineral collection. It is chock full of historic items, geographic lessons on the mineralogy of the area, breath-taking exhibits, displays of prehistoric fossils (and yes, even dinosaur doo-doo).

{To reach Weinman Mineral Museum, take Interstate 75 to the exit for U.S. 411 towards Rome. Take the first left onto Mineral Museum Drive. Admission is $4 for adults, $3.50 for seniors, and $3 for children over the age of six. Hours are Tuesday through Saturday, 10:00 a.m. to 5:00 p.m. and Sunday, 1:00 p.m. to 5:00 p.m. For more information, call (770) 386-0576.}

4 NORTHWEST GEORGIA

Chatsworth

The Overlook Bed & Breakfast Inn

High on a ridgetop with a commanding view of the **Chattahoochee National Forest** and the Blue Ridge Mountains, a new inn offers a special opportunity for travelers and romantics who enjoy communing with nature. As one of Georgia's newest B&Bs, the Overlook Inn is ideally located for travelers in the north Georgia mountains.

Opened in the Fall of 2002, the Overlook was designed and situated to take full advantage of its magnificent surroundings. Its rustic exterior blends naturally with the environment, concealing the elegant accommodations within.

Each guest room offers richly appointed queen and king-size beds, all with exquisite mountain views. In addition to the plush accommodations within, the rooms also offer either a private porch, gas fireplaces or private whirlpool tubs, and some offer all three. All accommodations are complemented by a Southern gourmet morning breakfast and complimentary wine and cheese in the evening.

The **Fieldstone Room** sports a unique rock wall of natural fieldstone. The Moon Eye and Grand Gahuti rooms offer a screened porch and outdoor hot tub.

The **Council Room**, the inn's main gathering room is noted for its floor to ceiling windows commanding a sweeping view of the Blue Ridge Mountains. This room's lustrous hardwood floors, rich leather furnishings, plush Oriental rugs, and wood-burning fireplace create not only a sumptuous, but a cozy atmosphere.

With seating for 24, the Overlook Inn's lobby and Council Room offer ideal options for corporate off-site retreats or family functions and weddings. The Inn's special events facilities can accommodate up to 30 individuals, and five exceptional guestrooms can accommodate up to ten guests.

Experienced in the hosting of weddings and other social functions, innkeeper Alma Wynn works closely with groups, offering expert advice on catering, flowers, photography and more.

And for those seeking the perfect honeymoon spot, the Overlook Inn caters to romance and couples. Honeymoon packages include everything from breakfast in bed to roses, champagne, private picnics and special desserts!

For those who seek adventure and activity by day, antique shopping or browsing through either the on-site gift shop or shops in nearby Ellijay are popular options. There's also a variety of biking, golfing, river rafting and hiking opportunities nearby. In fact, the famed **Appalachian Trail** begins within a few miles of the Overlook.

A trip to **Lake Conasauga**, Georgia's highest lake, or **Civil War battlefields** which preceded Sherman's march through Georgia, are also only a short drive away. A stroll through the surrounding woods can reveal this area's Native American heritage, especially when the casual stroller happens upon an ancient stone arrow point or other artifact.

The Overlook Inn is located between the towns of Ellijay and Chatsworth, near the top of historic **Fort Mountain** in Murray County. It is within one hour of Atlanta, 30 minutes from Chattanooga, Tennessee, and an eternity from the cares and concerns of everyday life outside this idyllic spot.

Room rates begin at $129 to $229, and include a full three-course gourmet country breakfast. There is no extra charge for the delights of Mother Nature all around the Inn.

(For more information, contact Robert or Liz Coleman at 706-517-8810, or visit the website www.theoverlookinn.com.)

Chickamauga

Gordon-Lee Mansion Bed & Breakfast

This historic mansion around which a portion of the **U.S. Civil War** raged in 1863, has been converted into an attractive bed and breakfast inn.

As you mount the steps to the sprawling front porch, you'd never guess that the **Gordon-Lee Bed and Breakfast Inn** was once the headquarters for some of the most grisly surgical procedures of the Civil War. Nestled deep in the heart of Chickamauga, this antebellum mansion is the only structure that survived the historic (and very bloody) Battle Of Chickamauga.

Originally, the land rising above the lush banks of Crawfish Springs was home to the Cherokee Indians, and a Cherokee log courthouse once existed at the site. But when U.S. **President Andrew Jackson** drove the Indians from their homes during the now infamous **Trail of Tears**, the site was taken over by white settlers.

In 1836, James Gordon, a Scotsman, bought 2,500 acres-worth of lottery tracts near the springs, with funds he had acquired through his thriving business – **Gordon's Mill**. By 1860, James most likely was a millionaire by today's standards. He had built the imposing brick house known locally as "**The Mansion**" which was a plantation home and the envy of much of north Georgia.

When James died in 1863, just months before the Battle of Chickamauga, his daughter Elizabeth and her husband **James Morgan Lee** took over the house, and the property grew to 5,000 acres. The mansion became home to the Lees and their six children – Gordon, Tom, Clarkie, Sarah, Molly and Pearl. It also was the home of 29 to 30 slaves.

During the fierce Battle of Chickamauga, some 37,000 men became casualties during a 40-hour period over the days of September 19-20. Union soldiers evicted the Lees to convert the home into a command headquarters for **General William Rosecrans**, leader of the Union Army of the Cumberland. **Chief of Staff James A. Garfield**, who would later go on to become the nation's 20th president, also moved into the home. The structure was later converted into a main hospital for the Union troops.

James Lee died in 1889. His wife, Elizabeth, died 14 years later, in 1903, and their son – Gordon Lee – became a U.S. congressman the next year.

Gordon, who married **Olivia Berry** of Newnan, Georgia, enjoyed close personal friendships with four U.S. presidents – **Theodore Roosevelt, William H. Taft, Calvin Coolidge** and **Woodrow Wilson**.

Gordon Lee died in 1927. In 1947, his spinster nieces – **Sarah** and **Pauline Gaskill** – came to live in the house. The last one died in 1971.

In 1974, after the death of the last family member (the Lees had no children), Dr. Frank Green, a Chattanooga dentist, purchased the structure and restored it.

Today, guests at the Gordon-Lee B&B are treated to a full breakfast served with genuine silver, china, and crystal.

Honeymoon couples are likely to find gifts of soft music and chilled champagne in the private sitting room overlooking the garden. Guests are invited to sip tea in the parlor where Rosecrans is said to have plotted the strategy for the Battle of Chickamauga.

Upstairs, a museum always has an impact upon guests. There, a room is filled with such Civil War artifacts as the breastplate of a Union soldier with a bullet still lodged in the emblem; a tree limb hammered with bullets and missiles from all directions; and an artificial arm which serves as a striking reminder of one of the bloodiest chapters in the history of our nation.

{To get to Gordon-Lee B&B from Atlanta, take Interstate 75 north to Exit 350 (Highway 2). Go to Chickamauga Battlefield Park. Continue following GA 2 approximately 6 miles to Old Lafayette Road. Turn south onto Old Lafayette Road and continue thru the battlefield, turning right at the first traffic light after the park. Turn left at the next light, then left again at the following light. For more information, contact the Gordon-Lee Bed and Breakfast Inn at (706) 375-4728.}

4
NORTHWEST GEORGIA

Lee & Gordon's Mills

Today, there is a historic marker on the road at **Lee & Gordon's Mill** located in Chickamauga, Georgia. From this same vantage point in 1863, an observer would have witnessed the full panoply of one of the major battles of the **War Between The States**. Lee & Gordon's Mill stood at the southern flanks of the Union and Confederate lines during the **Battle at Chickamauga**. For two days, these armies surged across the landscape, plunging through tangled forests and across verdant farm fields. In the end, the battle, with casualties second only to Gettysburg, reaped a grim harvest of more than 37,000 dead and wounded.

Union troops seized Lee & Gordon's Mill several days before the battle after the Confederate army had withdrawn from Chattanooga to Lafayette, Georgia. According to one Southern account of the federal advance, the mill's proprietor, **James Lee**, did his best to prevent the enemy from capturing the water-powered facility intact.

"Mr. Lee, the senior partner of the firm of Lee & Gordon who owned the mill on the Chickamauga close to which the battle was fought, destroyed his mill dam in order to keep the Yankees from using the mill," the **Memphis Daily Appeal** newspaper reported on September 23, 1863. Unfortunately for Lee, however, the federal government failed to appreciate his selfless act of patriotism. *"For this offense against Abraham (Lincoln),"* the **Appeal** continued, *"Lee was hanged by his minions on last Thursday on a tree in front of his own door."*

In actuality, the **Daily Appeal** may have embellished this story (or concocted it entirely) to cast the Yankee invaders in a bad light. In the first place, Lee survived the war and continued operation of the mill until his death in 1889. Secondly, at least one eyewitness account confirms that the dam still stood during the battle.

"As we began the advance," John A. Wyeth of the 4th Alabama Cavalry reminisced after the war, *"our regiment was on the extreme left of our line, and when we struck the Chickamauga we waded the stream just below the Lee & Gordon mill dam."* Some of the Alabamians then took a brief and dangerous detour.

"Hoping to get over dry, a number of us started to run across the dam; but an officer shouted: 'Get off! They're going to rake you with grapeshot.' And we leaped into the water like so many bullfrogs."

This would seem to indicate that Lee hadn't destroyed the dam prior to Wyeth's arrival as had been reported, and it is unlikely that he did so afterwards, either. The Battle of Chickamauga ended in a Confederate victory and Lee would have had no reason to sabotage his property at that point since the Union army had retreated to Chattanooga, leaving the mill safely behind Confederate lines.

If Lee had actually been hung by angry blue-coated soldiers as reported in the **Appeal**, it would not have been the only time that this dam has gotten an owner of Lee & Gordon's Mill into hot water with **Uncle Sam**. Indeed, some 130 years after Lee's purported travails, a later owner – **Frank Pierce** – also found himself at odds with the government. Ironically, Pierce's troubles stemmed not from his efforts to destroy the dam, but from a substantial attempt to save it.

When Pierce – who died in 2003 – purchased the rotting remains of Lee & Gordon's Mill in 1993, he was confronted with a monumental renovation project. The tottering 50-foot-tall structure was perched precariously upon the crumbling bank of Chickamauga Creek. Decay and erosion had weakened the foundation and support beams so much that a corner of the building extending over the creek sagged dangerously.

The mill timbers and boarding and the

ancient wooden dam were in deplorable condition as well. No one could say how long it might take to get the mill machinery – idle since 1969 – running again. And a thicket of weeds, brush and trees concealed the building almost entirely from view. Despite this sad state of affairs, Pierce was undaunted.

A throwback to earlier times when rugged self-reliant individuals simply accomplished a task themselves, Pierce forged ahead with the project, eschewing any government assistance. He embarked on what proved to be a five-year labor of love.

In the first stage of renovation, Pierce's work crews cleared and grubbed the land. Next, 450 truck loads of dirt were dumped around the mill in order to raise the ground level three feet to protect the building from the flood waters that occasionally inundate the site.

Next, using a crane and cables, the sagging northeast corner of the structure was raised and stabilized. The building itself underwent extensive renovations and, inside, salvageable mill machinery was reconditioned while the rest was junked and replaced. In fact, by the time the project was complete in 1998, nearly the entire building had been renovated and repaired.

The replacement of the badly-decayed dam, however, required even more ingenuity. Pierce was unable to find anyone who had experience upon which to draw because the wooden dam is one of only two known to exist in Georgia. Pierce, however, didn't let that stop him. He just figured out how a wooden dam would have been built 150 years ago if the builders had been using modern material and construction equipment.

First, just upstream from the old dam, work crews built a temporary earthen dam that stretched from the bank halfway across the creek creating a dry work area behind it. On the exposed portion of the creek bottom, the workers poured a concrete foundation for the new dam.

"Then we set up a sawmill right there on the property and hauled in black locust logs from Pigeon Mountain," Pierce explained. "We cut 6" by 6" timbers and drove them like posts into the creek bottom at intervals along the length of the dam. Next, we stacked 10" by 10"

timbers horizontally between the posts forming the dam wall." The locust was so hard that the workers had to use sledgehammers to drive nails into the wood.

When the first half of the wooden dam was completed (along with a concrete flume to temporarily handle the waterflow), the temporary earthen dam was removed and the whole laborious process was repeated on the other side of the creek. When completed, the new dam stood nine feet high and 70 feet long. That is exactly the height and length of the original dam built in 1836.

Not everyone, however, applauded Pierce's renovation efforts. The U.S. Army Corps of Engineers stepped in claiming that the project posed a threat to wetlands. Asserting federal jurisdiction over the work site on the rather dubious claim that Chickamauga Creek is a navigable river, the agency threatened to take legal action to halt the work. Apparently, the Corps overlooked the fact that a dam has existed at this site since 1836 and that nothing larger than a canoe can actually navigate the shallow, deadfall-choked waters of the creek anyway.

True to form, Pierce refused to be cowed. "I found out a long time ago that you can get forgiveness a lot easier than you can get permission on certain things," he said during an interview in 1997. He pressed on with the renovations hoping for the best. Eventually, common sense prevailed (after Pierce had spent $2,500 in legal fees and other services to defend himself) and the Corps dropped the matter.

In 1998, after five long years of work and great expense (Pierce said he didn't keep an actual tally and didn't know exactly how much he had spent on the renovations), Lee & Gordon's Mill re-opened for business. For the first time in almost thirty years, the waters of Chickamauga Creek poured through the raceway turning the turbines and powering the machinery for the grinding of corn into meal.

The icing on the cake came when the U.S. Department of the Interior placed the facility on the **National Register of Historic Places** (possibly the first instance in which the federal government and an owner of Lee & Gordon's Mills have seen eye-to-eye on anything.).

The newly-renovated Lee & Gordon's Mill

apparently is, to some degree, the third such mill to have existed on this spot. In 1836, **James Gordon** established the first mill here (two years prior to the time that the **Cherokee Indians** were forcibly removed from the area on the now-infamous **"Trail of Tears."**). That structure, located on the same site at what then was the heavily-traveled road between Chattanooga and Lafayette, served many purposes including those of post office, stagecoach stop, blacksmith shop, general store, sawmill and possibly even as a funeral home of sorts.

The wealthy Gordon owned 29 slaves, 2,500 acres of land stretching for several miles from the mill to sparkling Crawfish Springs. He also owned a magnificent antebellum plantation house (known today as the Gordon-Lee Mansion, a bed and breakfast inn).

According to records, in 1857, the increasingly prosperous Gordon expanded and modernized his facilities by replacing the old gristmill with a new structure and adding a sawmill. Gordon also added a business partner in the late 1850s when his daughter – Elizabeth Mahala – married James Lee. From that point forward, the establishment bore the name of "Lee & Gordon's Mill."

As an aside, **Gordon Lee**, the eldest son of James and Elizabeth Lee, served in the **U.S. Congress** for 22 years shortly after the turn of the 19th century. He and his wife lived in what came to be known as the "Gordon-Lee Mansion."

James Gordon died in February of 1863, leaving his son-in-law James Lee to operate the mill. In 1867, a fire destroyed Lee & Gordon's Mill according to many published sources.

Frank Pierce, however, claimed otherwise.

"We did a lot of work beneath that building and didn't see any evidence of a fire whatsoever," he said. Adding that he believes only a portion of a wing added to the building after the Civil War actually burned. If that is the case, then the current structure (allowing for renovations) is the same building erected by James Gordon in 1857 and featured in the famous 1864 Signal Corps photograph.

Pierce said the differences in the architectural lines of the present building from the structure in the U.S. Civil War photograph stem from his renovations. "We duplicated the building as it appeared (in an 1890s photograph) when it had a wing on the south side," he explained. "The wing served as a general store then and today it houses our gift shop and a display of artifacts and photographs."

Though Pierce passed away in 2003, Lee & Gordon's Mill is again a working gristmill. Unlike the more familiar waterwheel-type mills, it is powered by turbines concealed beneath the ground floor. Operating 19th century machinery in the 21st century, though, comes with its odd moments. When, for instance, it was discovered that the original lubricants used to grease the gears are no longer available, Pierce substituted Crisco brand shortening.

(As of this writing, Lee & Gordon's Mill is a portion of the estate of the late Frank Pierce and is closed to the public. It is located just off U. S. 27 (Old Lafayette Road) two miles south of Chickamauga Battlefield National Military Park on Lee & Gordon's Mill Road.)

Dallas

Pickett's Mill State Historical Site

Pickett's Mill State Historic Site, located about two miles northeast of **New Hope Church** in eastern Paulding County, preserves a battlefield from the War Between The States which was the site of unusually bloody combat one fateful day in May of 1864. Today, the now-peaceful terrain is being rediscovered by history enthusiasts.

In 1864, **Little Pumpkinvine Creek** (known today as **Pickett's Mill Creek**), was the center of a small settlement. The site drew its identity from a grist mill founded by **Benjamin Pickett**.

This relatively new state historic site was opened in May of 1990, and attracted some 4,500 visitors a year its first two years. Considerably larger numbers have visited in subsequent years, due to increased interest in Civil War history, and to improved facilities.

Following fighting at Dallas and at New Hope Church, General William T. Sherman was ready to move in late May. The Union army commander decided to try to maneuver his troops between the Confederates and Atlanta. On May 27, 1864, he committed around 18,000 troops to the fateful venture.

In a heavily-wooded landscape with foliage-choked ravines, the Union troops met with disaster. Although they enjoyed the numerical and weapons superiority, the Federals were no match for the battle-seasoned Confederates in the dense undergrowth of the ravines.

About 5,000 men from Pat Cleburne's Confederate division were waiting atop the Little Pumpkinvine ravine. More than one man termed the lovely little mini-canyon "a hellhole" that day, with the first heavy engagement coming in the late afternoon.

Three times, the Federals stumbled and cursed their way down the steep ravine, only to be pinned down at the bottom by fierce fire. Today, where a quiet little brook flows – one of many small tributaries feeding Pickett's Mill Creek - the dead and wounded piled up in huge numbers in 1864.

The fiercest fighting ended in the early evening, with the surviving Federal troops still pinned down at the bottom of the ravine. The dead and wounded littered the wooded landscape as darkness fell. Federal casualties numbered about 1,600 men. The Confederates lost around 500.

Pickett's Mill, in many ways, was the story of the entire **Atlanta Campaign**. Following fine battlefield performances, the Confederates were forced to withdraw again and again due to Sherman's superior numerical advantage which allowed him to make seemingly endless flanking movements toward Atlanta.

Today, the park's **Visitors Center** offers an excellent multi-media presentation which explains the battle. It also houses related exhibits and a small selection of pertinent books and materials for sale.

Three separate trails of up to 1.5 miles allow visitors an opportunity to hike to the Federal and Confederate positions. Earthworks, thrown up just prior to the battle, are still visible, as are the ruins of the grist mill which jut over the creek. The trails are well-marked, and by reading the *Trail Guide* obtainable at the Visitors Center, a self-guided tour is possible.

Visitors to Pickett's Mill should bring canteens in warm weather and wear shoes suitable for the terrain, since the trail can be steep in spots. None of the trails are handicapped accessible, nor are strollers recommended.

{Directions: To get to Pickett's Mill State Historic Site, travel approximately 12 miles west on Highway 120 from the town square in Marietta. Turn right onto Highway 92 and continue for four miles. Turn left onto Due West Road, continuing for almost two miles to Mt. Tabor Road. After turning right onto Mt. Tabor Road, the entrance to the park will be within half a mile on the right. Park hours are Wednesday through Saturday from 9:00 a.m. to 5:00 p.m., and Sunday from 2:00 to 5:30 p.m. For more information, please call the Pickett's Mill State Historic Site at (770) 443-7850.}

4
NORTHWEST GEORGIA

Dalton

The Blunt House

Ainsworth E. Blunt, who migrated to Dalton, Georgia in 1843, wouldn't recognize the town today if he were still alive. He would, however, feel right at home with the structure at 505 South Thornton Avenue, which has hardly changed at all since he died.

In 1843, Thornton Avenue – which today is a busy city street – was little more than a dirt track, once used by Cherokee Indians for racing their horses.

Blunt built his fine home on Thornton Avenue in 1848. Weathering almost 150 years of use with remarkable stamina - and some tender loving care from the **Whitfield-Murray County Historical Society** – the **Blunt House** today is one of Dalton's historic showpieces.

As the second two-story home built in Dalton, the Blunt House serves as an excellent example of Federal-style architecture. And until the building was deeded to the Whitfield-Murray Historical Society in 1978, Blunt and his direct descendants had been the only occupants of the house for 130 years.

A New Hampshire native, Blunt came to Chattanooga's **Brainerd Mission** in 1822 as a missionary to the Cherokees, a position he held until the **Cherokee Removal** from the area in 1838. After moving to Cross Plains (now Dalton) in 1843, Blunt began a mercantile business, built a home (the Blunt House) and married Elizabeth Ramsey of Tennessee. Their only child - Lillie - was born in 1850.

Blunt played a prominent role in the early development of Dalton, serving as the city's first mayor and first postmaster, as a founder of First Presbyterian Church, and as a leader in the organization of Whitfield County in 1852.

Visiting ministers, travelers and guests were often entertained in the Blunt home. During the Confederate occupation of Dalton in the winter of 1863-64, the Blunts entertained General Joseph E. Johnston and his staff officers.

In 1864, however, as Union forces occupied Dalton, Blunt took his family to a safer haven in Illinois. Returning to Dalton in the summer of 1865, the Blunts discovered their home had been used as a Union hospital. Shrubs had been cut, fences destroyed, and the grounds had been filled with brush arbors as temporary shelters for wounded soldiers.

After Blunt's daughter – Lillie – married Thomas Kirby, the house was expanded to accommodate the needs of a growing family. Between 1875 and 1892, four daughters were born to the Kirbys: Lucy, Carolyn, Alleen and Emery.

The youngest of the four daughters, Emery, lived in the Blunt House her entire life. Upon her death in 1978, she willed the grounds, building, furnishings and contents of the house to the Whitfield-Murray County Historic Society. Having the house placed on the *National Register of Historic Places* was Miss Emery's only stipulation in the agreement – a request which was fulfilled in 1980.

With dreams of restoring the house to its original grandeur, the Society began an extensive renovation in 1988.

"One of the most exciting parts of the renovation was the discovery of the original kitchen fireplace," noted Mary Gene Dykes, the Society's committee chairman for the Blunt House. After removing wall boards in the kitchen, the original fireplace was found intact, complete with the original crane and hooks for holding cookware.

The oldest piece of furniture in the historic home is Blunt's blue "buttermilk" chest, brought from New Hampshire to the Brainerd Mission in 1822. Water-colors appearing throughout the house were painted by Blunt's four granddaughters who were trained in the Victorian traditions of music and art.

In addition to Victorian sofas, chairs and tables, visitors to the Blunt House can view vintage clothing and accessories, first-edition books, antique toys and tools, family linens marked with "B" and "K," antique kitchenware, and hundreds of other items.

{The Blunt House is open for individual and group tours by making arrangements through the Whitfield-Murray County Historical Society, Crown Gardens and Archives, 715 Chattanooga Ave., Dalton, Georgia, 30728. Telephone: (706) 278-0217.}

Prater's Mill Country Fair

On the banks of the rushing Coahulla Creek in northwest Georgia's Whitfield County, knowledgeable historians and travelers still admire the fish trap shoals where the Cherokees once caught their meals. They also admire a sturdy red three-story structure which has survived the wrath of wind, rain, floods and fire for nearly 150 years, and which is the focus of one of the most popular annual festivals in Georgia today.

Benjamin Franklin Prater established **Prater's Mill** in 1855. Not much has changed in his structure since the day he built it. Made of virgin pine with hand-hewn mortise-and-peg joints, it was originally designed for the grinding of customers' corn and soft red winter wheat. Most of its original equipment – the bucket elevator, the wheat sacker, the bolter and sifter, etc. – remains intact today, right down to the wooden spouts.

One of the mill's three turbines even still works, and a "signature beam" penned by Prater himself, can still be viewed on a second-floor wall, undisturbed by Union and Confederate soldiers who camped at the mill at different times in 1864.

"We've always wondered what Mr. Prater did when the Union forces arrived here," mused Judy Alderman who, with friend, Jane Harrell, has been instrumental in the renovation of the mill and the development of the annual **Prater's Mill Country Fair** held each year at the site. "We know he was in the 'Home Guard' and was a 'third lieutenant'" she smiles, "but beyond that, we know very little else about where he was or why the mill was not burned by the Yankees."

Its survival of the Civil War aside, Prater's Mill has, with the help of friends and concerned preservationists, also endured several destructive floods as well as a major fire. "It was heavily flooded in 1973," Mrs. Alderman continued. "It literally had five feet of water inside the mill itself, and the Coahulla Creek was like a raging ocean."

The annual Prater's Mill Country Fair is held each fall. On the mill grounds where customers from nearby Dalton once lined up their wagons and camped all night waiting for their corn to be ground into cornmeal, festival goers today are treated to a nostalgic return to yesteryear.

It, however, was a long road between the conception and the implementation of this delightful and popular affair. In early 1971, when Whitfield County volunteers decided to tackle the run-down mill in hopes of hosting craft shows there, they never realized the events would take "14 months a year" to prepare.

Little by little, Foundation members cleaned and cleared, patched and repaired, and by May of 1971, the place was ready for public scrutiny. By that December, the mill was running again for the first time in years, and in 1978, much to the delight of its restorers, the mill was listed on the **National Register of Historic Places**.

The annual Prater's Mill Country Fair now offers a total of 200 art and craft exhibits; authentic Southern meals of cornbread, barbecue, pinto beans, turnip greens and sweet potato cobbler; and entertainment ranging from country bands and gospel singers to canoeing and pony rides for the kids. Visitors can even take home a bag of the mill's fresh, robust cornmeal.

Word of the festival has snowballed in recent years. *Better Homes & Gardens* magazine named the Prater's Mill Country Fair as one of the top-rated family events in the country in 1990. The Southeast Tourism Society lists it as a **"Top 20 Event,"** and the Library of Congress calls it a Local Legacy of American Tradition.

(The Prater's Mill Country Fair is held the second weekend in October each year. The mill is located 25 miles south of Chattanooga near Dalton. For fair dates and more information, call 706-694-6455. See the Fair's website at www.pratersmill.org.)

Ft. Payne, AL

Little River Canyon Scenic Recreation

To my mind, any excuse is reason enough to pack up the suitcases and head for the mountains in the spring or autumn. Throw in the opportunity to hike along and enjoy the scenic beauty of the deepest gorge east of the Mississippi, and the temptation becomes almost irresistible.

Chances are you haven't heard of this natural wonder just a stone's throw from the northwestern Georgia state line. Don't feel bad. You're not alone. Shielded from the world by tree-topped mountains and a mask of anonymity, it basks in a sort of splendid isolation.

Sculpted eons ago by the **Little River** – said to be the only river in North America that forms and flows its entire length atop a mountain – the gorge runs approximately 24 miles between **Little River Falls** and **Canyon Mouth Park**. At its deepest point, **Little River Canyon** nose-dives an incredible 700 feet, and varies from one-half mile to a mile-and-a-half in width.

Surprisingly, the depths of Little River Canyon are virtually unexplored and, until a short time ago, its more accessible points served as hangouts for **moonshiners** and **bootleggers**. For all practical purposes, this place is in its original wilderness state.

Other than natural beauty, what is the particular charm of this stretch of streams and mountain terrain? A variety of things – all with nature or preservation of the natural environment as the principal feature – appealing to young and old alike.

The best way to enjoy this scenic wonderland is to establish a headquarters at one of the numerous lakeside campsites or, if you want the comforts of home, at one of the motels or B&Bs that are situated around nearby **Lookout Mountain**. Leisurely visits can then be made to most of the outstanding sights.

Park Facilities

Little River Falls (near the Route 35 junction) has a 50-vehicle parking lot. Here, you can sight-see, hike or just relax in the nature's boundless beauty.

The **Canyon Rim Scenic Drive** starts atop **Lookout Mountain** and ends at **Canyon Mouth Park**. It is approximately 23 miles long and takes from one to two hours to complete by car. From this point, a narrower, winding county road continues along the rim to the canyon mouth. The rim drive is primarily within the **Little River Canyon National Preserve** boundary, but there are a few sections where the road is outside the Preserve. A number of scenic overlooks which sport such evocative names as Mushroom Rock, Hawk's Glide and Crow Point offer almost incomparable views. The river below appears to be little more than a tiny trickle.

Canyon Mouth Park is a 130-acre day-use area at the end of the River. It is accessible from Route 273/279. This is a popular recreational area that encourages hiking, white water paddling, canoeing, mountain biking, horseback riding and fishing.

Nearby Attractions

Located seven miles northwest of **Valley Head**, Alabama, just off I-59, **Sequoyah Caverns** is considered to be one of the most beautiful caves in the world. The caverns are named (like the giant trees and national park in California by the same name) for the Cherokee leader who developed a written language for his people in the early 1800s – the only such effort ever undertaken by Native Americans.

The **Fort Payne Landmarks Museum** is housed in the old Fort Payne depot that was built by the **Alabama Great Southern Railroad** in 1891. The museum features a collection of Native American Indian pottery, basketry, weapons, tools and clothing. Many of the items on display were discovered in the Fort Payne area, once a portion of the land the Cherokees called home. **Cloudmont Resort**, the southern-most ski facility in the country, is located six miles north of the **DeSoto State Park** Information Center. There are two ski slopes, but they obviously are only available during the winter months. In the same complex is **Saddle Rock Golf Course**, a fine golfing facility which is open seven days a week, weather permitting.

Lake Weiss, renowned for producing three-pound crappie consistently, is known as the "**Crappie Capital of the South**." More out-of-state fishing licenses are sold in the stores and shops around Lake Weiss than at any other lake in Alabama. The best months for crappie fishing are March through May, followed by September, October and November.

How strange it is that so many people live within a few miles of an immense gorge, yet much of it remains unexplored today. Little River forms in northwest Georgia and northeast Alabama, and flows down the middle of Lookout Mountain, leaving the mountain at Little River Canyon Mouth Park before flowing into Lake Weiss.

This region has a quiet but compelling charm that annually attracts thousands of people to its pristine retreats and crystal-clear bluish-green waters, yet it has remained largely free of commercialized tourist attractions.

The appeal of Little River Canyon and the surrounding area lies in its natural beauty and the wide variety of relaxing activities available in the vicinity. The nature lover, the history hound, the water-sports enthusiast, as well as the angler are all equally at home here.

Little River Canyon National Preserve (established in 1992) is located in Cherokee and DeKalb counties east of Fort Payne, Alabama. The Preserve is within a two- to three-hour drive from Birmingham, Alabama and Atlanta.

Access roads into the Preserve include Interstate 59, Alabama State Routes 35, 89, 176 and 275. State Route 89 is the major access road into DeSoto State Park. This road intersects State Route 35 which is the major access road to the Preserve. State Route 176 is a 23-mile scenic drive that begins at the junction of Route 35. Inside the Preserve boundary, there are no paved roads to points north and east of Route 35, this area being served only by a network of dirt and gravel roads.

(For additional information on Little River Canyon National Preserve, contact Bill Springer, Superintendent, Little River Canyon National Preserve, P.O. Box 45, Fort Payne, AL, 35967, or telephone 256-997-9239.)

Oothcaloga Mission

If the **Moravian missionaries** who lived and ministered at historic Oothcaloga Mission in present-day Gordon County, Georgia, could see this hallowed ground today, they would not recognize it. Much has changed in the almost 200 years since the departure of the missionaries and Indians from this site – most of it for the worst.

On this historic ground, the renowned Cherokee Indian families of the **Ridges, Waties** and others once attended church and worshiped from 1822 to 1833. Famed Cherokee **Stand Watie** himself, frequented this site prior to his departure to the Cherokee Indian reservation out West in the late 1830s. The mission building was erected in 1821 by **Joseph Crutchfield** and sold to the Moravians in 1822. The building was an active church and education center for the Cherokees until 1833.

Moravian leaders at the mission included **John Gambold** (1822-1827), **J.R. Schmidt** (1827-1828), **Franz Eder** (1828-1829), and **Henry G. Clauder** (1828-1838). The mission stood for many years, even lasting long enough for a photo to be snapped of it in the 20th century. However, despite its historic stature, the mission building was not permanently protected after the departure of the Cherokees. Over the years, the structure eventually fell into disrepair, finally disappearing completely.

Thankfully, a well-maintained Georgia Historical Marker (GHM) has recently been re-erected on Bellwood Road (opposite the mission site), at least identifying the site for posterity. This historical marker, however, is the original which was erected in 1959 (when the mission building still existed). It (the marker) apparently was temporarily removed from the site sometime thereafter, and then reinstalled in 2002 without updating the language inscribed thereupon.

The marker describes the old mission building in detail as if it still existed today. Present-day readers of the marker may find it confusing if they are not aware that the mission building no longer stands. The wording on the marker should be updated to reflect the current circumstances of the site.

Across Bellwood Road from the historical marker, (and to the right of what appears to be an abandoned mobile home), an overgrown trail (actually a rough path) leads back into the woods to the clearing where the old mission building once stood. This vicinity is now strewn with abandoned car parts and trash, and there are no visible remnants whatsoever of the old mission building today.

The clearing is also overtaken with undergrowth and infested with ticks. Anyone visiting the site would be well-advised to wear high-top boots and carry a snake stick.

Back out on the opposite side of Bellwood – near the historical marker – is a dirt road leading up a hill to the east. Approximately 100 yards up this trail, a small cemetery will be found. In it, John Gambold – the first Moravian missionary at Oothcaloga Mission – is buried.

Gambold taught many Indian children at the mission in the 1800s, building an active Cherokee Indian church congregation. His mortal remains lie buried beneath a large oak tree in the little cemetery.

Interestingly, Gambold was also a **Revolutionary War veteran**, and according to reports, is the only veteran of that war buried in Gordon County. One would think a local historic society or other civic organization in the Gordon County vicinity would assume the responsibility of maintaining a more worthy final resting place for this distinguished American.

Today, if one wishes to visit this very historic grave, he or she must be prepared for a short hike. It currently is not possible to simply drive a vehicle up the road – even one of the four-wheel-drive variety – because the trail is blocked with large fallen trees. Also, sadly, many piles of trash and debris have been dumped in the woods to each side of the road by uncaring individuals, and the cemetery itself has not been maintained for many years.

Gambold's in-laid grave marker, however, is still intact, and even identifies him as a veteran of the Revolutionary War. Small forgotten historic grave sites such as this dot the Georgia countryside, and it is always a somewhat sad reality that they are totally unprotected, neglected and un-maintained.

In 1832, the state of Georgia conducted a lottery to distribute the Cherokee lands to white settlers. By 1833, two white families had moved into the Oothcaloga Mission house. Moravian Henry G. Clauder continued to minister to the Cherokees for six years after whites occupied the two-story mission building in 1833. With the departure of the last Cherokees on the **Trail of Tears** in 1838, the Moravians eventually departed the Oothcaloga area themselves.

Just as do many others, the isolated cemetery with the John Gambold grave begs for the attention and protection of a sponsoring historic society or county or state agency. Perhaps those who would honor the last vestiges of the Cherokees and their acclaimed leaders such as the revered **Stand Watie** will one day see fit to help preserve this spot so that future generations may admire it, and the spirits of John Gambold and the other deceased souls in this cemetery may sleep in eternal peace.

Looking for a quick and inexpensive place for some winter wonderland fun? There's a great little place just across the extreme northwestern Georgia state line in northeastern Alabama.

When autumn becomes winter, the thoughts of many people turn to sports such as snow skiing. But it's often difficult to get accommodations and very expensive if you do. So what do you do? Many people would never consider the prospect of skiing in the mountains of north Georgia or Alabama, but I've got a nice surprise for you!

Alabama's one and only snow skiing facility – **Cloudmont Ski and Golf Resort** – can offer a very adequate basic skiing opportunity (with man-made snow), and on some days, you might even find a few inches of Mother Nature's white powder snow too.

Georgia also has a nice resort in its northeastern corner called **Sky Valley**, but right now, we're going to focus upon Cloudmont. Most people don't realize that Alabama is home to a bigger chunk of **Lookout Mountain** than either Tennessee or Georgia, and Lookout Mountain does offer some altitude. The little hamlet of **Mentone** – where the resort is located – sits right on top of the mountain and affords spectacular views and one heck of a bargain as a snow skiing experience.

Now you're not going to have ten-foot snow drifts here, but there is more than enough man-made snow for an exciting experience. And on those days when northern Alabama has natural snowfall, you can have a whale of a lot of fun.

To accommodate travelers to this resort, Cloudmont offers some nice little A-frame ski chalets for rent. Some of them overlook the Little River. (That's right. . . Lookout Mountain actually has a river flowing across the top of it, a very unusual geographic anomaly.) The front view from many of the chalets takes

Cloudmont Ski & Golf Resort

in the greens of Cloudmont's **Saddle Rock Golf Course**.

The accommodations are clean and comfortable, but more rustic than cushy. The tiny A-frames have a living room / kitchen area – which is compact to say the least – and a small bath fills a cubbyhole in the hallway. Beyond that, a double-size bed pretty much packs out the downstairs bedroom. In the living area, a narrow spiral staircase leads to a second bedroom in the loft.

Though these accommodations are small (six people max), I doubt many other ski resorts can match the price of $65 per night. Chalets without kitchens are $60 per night.

The adjacent Saddle Rock Golf Course at Cloudmont is open seven days a week year-round. Players can try their skills at 18 tees on nine holes, with the first tee uniquely designed atop a 30-foot-high boulder. Green fees are $7 to $10. Cart fees are $10 to $14.

The resort has been owned by the **Olive & Jack Jones Family** for approximately 40 years now. They also own the nearby **Shady Grove Dude Ranch** that adjoins Cloudmont's boundaries.

Shady Grove is dotted with a number of choices of accommodations, all individually named and all rustically designed to fit the "dude ranch" image. The residences all have names such as "The Roundup," "The Farmhouse," and "Batelle Cottage."

From small to whopper, Jack had a place to put up just about any size group. The Round-Up accommodates up to six people for $150. The Farmhouse has room for up to 24 people at $10 per person (minimum charge is $160). Batelle Cottage holds up to five persons for $75. The Way Station sleeps up to 10 people for $150 to $200.

Trail rides at Shady Grove cost $15 to $30. One and two-hour rides are available, with a reservation. The trails may also be used by riders bringing their own horses. Breakfast rides

($30 per person) can be done for groups of eight or more (with a five-day advance notice). Participants may ride on horseback or in the wagon. Dinner rides ($30 to $40 per person) are available for groups of eight or more (with a five-day notice). Rides include horseback or wagon ride, dinner, campfire and a square dance.

Jack will readily tell anyone who asks that he just loves this part of Alabama, and understandably so. Mentone is also a hideaway for a number of highly-exclusive girls' and boys' camps. Some of the town's current residents were introduced to this northeast Alabama getaway after attending these camps in their youth. It's not hard to understand why a number of the former campers came back to live in Mentone permanently.

As far as the skiing facilities at Cloudmont are concerned, there are two pony lifts that take skiers to the tops of two 1,000-foot slopes. According to Jack, the elevation is 1,800 feet, there's a vertical rise of 150 feet, and he considers these slopes to have a level of difficulty ranging from "Beginner" to "Intermediate."

Jack also says, understandably, that his resort's skiing credibility depends entirely upon the quality of his snow-making equipment. "Cloudmont has eight of the very finest snow-making machines available. Some years we're able to ski a week longer than Gatlinburg (a popular resort high in the nearby Great Smoky Mountains in Tennessee) and a whole lot of other ski resorts further north," he smiles.

The staff at Cloudmont start the snow-making equipment every time the temperature drops to 28 degrees Fahrenheit or colder. Their machinery allows them to put on a deep base that will hold even when the daytime temperature reaches well above freezing.

The resort offers personalized instruction, privately or in groups. It also offers skis, boots and poles rentals. A small building at the foot of the slope serves as a lodge and warm-up spot for skiers.

To find out about daily skiing conditions, call (256) 634-4344, or log onto www.cloudmont.com for regular updates. The ski season is from December 15 thru March 15 (weather permitting), from 10:00 a.m. to 4:00 p.m. Night skiing is also offered (from 6:00 p.m. to 10:00 p.m.).

Prices for skiing (which includes equipment rentals, lift tickets, and beginner lessons) are: Adults: $22 per half day (1:00 p.m. to 4:00 p.m.) and $35 for a full day (9:00 a.m. to 4:00 p.m.). Child and student rates are also available.

With snow skiing this close to home and prices far below what most people would expect to pay, Cloudmont opens up a genuine opportunity for enjoyment of the sport by beginners in the deep South.

(Directions To Cloudmont: From Atlanta, head north on Interstate 75 to the exit for GA 140 West, near Adairsville, Georgia. Continue westward on GA 140 to U.S. 27 North. Continue northwestward on U.S. 27 to Summerville, Georgia and Georgia Highway 48. Stay on GA 48, thru the tiny communities of Menlo and Cloudland, Georgia. Shortly thereafter, you will cross the Alabama state line and the highway becomes AL 117. Continue on AL 117 until you reach Mentone. At the caution light in Mentone, turn onto AL 89 and follow the signs to Cloudmont Resort. To reach Shady Grove Dude Ranch, continue straight on AL 117 from the state line. Shortly after passing thru the little hamlet of Mentone, turn at Moon Lake Church and follow the signs to Shady Grove. For more details and info on Cloudmont Ski and Golf Resort or Shady Grove Dude Ranch, call 256-634-4344, or check the WEB sites of www.shadygroveusa.com and www.cloudmont.com).

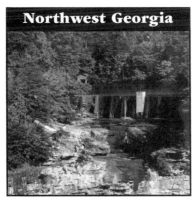

A Northwest Georgia Driving Tour

When the autumn season arrives, the thoughts of many Atlanta-area residents turn to a drive up into the north Georgia mountains where one might enjoy the beauty of the colorful leaves on the trees and the scent of barbecue smoke wafting across the landscape. Most people immediately think the only real opportunities for this lie in the mountains of northeast Georgia, but northwest Georgia can offer an excellent drive too.

In order to enjoy this little outing to the fullest, one must prepare well. Take along enough clothing at least for a couple of days, in case you decide to spend the night someplace. More importantly, take along only comfortable clothing. . . shorts and shirts for the men, and shorts and blouses for the ladies for wearing during the day. Long pants, a flannel shirt or two, etc. should also be included for cool nights. And don't forget a pair of comfortable hiking shoes.

You don't need to bother too much with food, since you should be able to take most of your meals at stops along the way.

Fill up the car with gas, and check all the vital fluids - like engine coolant (engines get really hot climbing the inclines up into the mountains), oil and such. . . and do this before you leave. Don't just plan on getting someone to check it along the way. That strategy invites a break-down. Check also to make certain the spare tire is in good shape.

Finally, don't forget bug repellent (Watch out for those ticks!). It has become a necessity when one is hiking in the woods.

McIntosh Reserve

If you're from the Atlanta area, head west out Interstate 20 toward Carrollton, Georgia. The first stop you'll want to make is at **McIntosh Reserve**, a county-owned park in southwestern Carroll County near Whitesburg.

This historic site was once the home of **William McIntosh**, the half-breed Creek Indian chief who accumulated considerable wealth and standing in the early 1800s, when this part of present-day Georgia was Creek Indian Territory.

McIntosh was born sometime around 1775. He was the son of a Scottish captain in the British army and a full-blooded Creek Indian woman. He was well-educated by his parents and moved easily in both the Creek Indian and white man's worlds.

When he had grown to manhood, William finally became a chief aligned with the **"Lower Creek" Indian Nation**. He had many business enterprises, including **Indian Spring Hotel** in Butts County, and a tavern and ferry service on the Chattahoochee River near his home at McIntosh Reserve.

McIntosh's plantation on the Chattahoochee was known as **Lochau Talofau**, or **Acorn Bluff**. He had lived there for a number of years, but also spent time at another residence he owned at **Indian Spring**, (at present-day Indian Spring State Park) where he represented his tribesmen in the Treaty of 1825.

Unfortunately, it was at this treaty-signing that William McIntosh assured himself of a short life. Though he was acting in the best interest of the Creek Nation in Georgia and Alabama, his actions were perceived by his Creek brethren as a "sell-out" of the Creek Nation and a bid for too much personal gain for McIntosh. On May 30, 1825, a group of Creek warriors traveled to McIntosh's Acorn Bluff home in the McIntosh Reserve. There, they set the home afire, then shot McIntosh to death as he emerged from the burning home. He was then stabbed in the chest and scalped.

A vivid description of this murderous attack was preserved in writing by a white man (the

4

only one on-site), McIntosh's three wives, and several other individuals who were not physically harmed in the slaughter.

Today, the McIntosh Reserve property contains a replica of McIntosh's Acorn Bluff home. The brave leader was buried on the site and his grave is marked today for curious spectators interested in pioneer Georgia Indian history.

An overlook of the river provides a view of the site at which McIntosh's ferry once operated. Displays and signs within the park interpret this period of our state's history for visitors. A program explaining the site, as well as a walking tour can be scheduled in advance.

The 500-acre passive recreation park is a nature preserve as well as a historic park. It offers primitive camping on weekends, picnic shelters and miles of walking trails and horse trails.

Individuals who enjoy canoeing and rafting can put-in four miles upstream in Whitesburg at Georgia Power Company's boat ramp, then drift downstream to McIntosh Reserve. The park does not provide any canoe or raft rentals, but does allow take-outs at the site. Some groups leave a vehicle for pick-up purposes at the park.

For more information about McIntosh Reserve, call (770) 830-5879.

Maple Street Mansion / Carrollton

From McIntosh Reserve, take Georgia Highway 16 north to Carrollton for lunch or dinner. The **Maple Street Mansion** at 401 Maple Street provides nicely for either meal.

In the early 1830s, **Appleton Mandeville** and his wife, Mary, settled in west Georgia and planted maple trees from their native Vermont. A son, **Leroy Clifton (L.C.) Mandeville**, became a prosperous merchant and built a substantial home on Maple Street.

In 1892, L.C. built **Mandeville Mills**, a textile factory which served as the city's largest industry until it was closed in 1954. He also donated the land and helped to build West Georgia College (today's West Georgia State University) in Carrollton.

L.C. Mandeville owned cotton fields that covered much of the land from Carrollton to the Alabama state line. When standing inside the turret on the third floor of his large house, L.C. reportedly could view his cotton fields

which extended as far as the eye could see.

It was in 1889 that L.C. began construction of his fine home which houses the popular Maple Street Mansion restaurant today. The structure took five years to build and is made of heart pine. It has 13 fireplaces and was among the first in the area to have electricity and a telephone.

Today, the first floor of the home has been retained nearly as it was 100 years ago. To enjoy dining in this elegance, call (770) 834-2657.

Maple Street Bed-And-Breakfast Inn

If you're staying overnight, Jim and Marlene Uglam operate the **Maple Street Inn**, a bed-and-breakfast at 338 Maple Street (across the street from the mansion). L.C. Mandeville built this house in 1910 as a gift to the Presbyterian Church in town (which he also helped build).

The inn has four bedrooms. A full breakfast is served. To place reservations, call (770) 214-8950.

John Tanner State Park

After you've had breakfast the next morning, take Highway 16 north for 6 miles to **John Tanner State Park**. It reportedly boasts the largest inland sand beach in Georgia, along with two lakes, picnic tables, and fishing and swimming opportunities. A 6-unit motel can accommodate visitors overnight at this stop too. It is open 7 a.m. to 9 p.m. year-round.

Tally Ho! For Tallapoosa!

If you'd rather skip Tanner Park, take Highway 16 north until it dead-ends into Georgia Highway 100. Then head north to Tallapoosa. This small town has a number of interesting historic sites. The local historical society is actually attempting to get the entire downtown area placed on the **National Register of Historic Places**.

West Georgia Museum in Tallapoosa offers a flashback to the late 1800s and early 1900s, when the town went by its earlier name of **Possum Snout**. Most of the exhibits in this museum depict life in Tallapoosa during the community's hey-days. Tourists flocked to the town to partake of the healing waters in mineral springs there, and to overnight in the 83-room **Lithia Springs Hotel**, reputed to have been the largest wooden building in the South at that time.

In addition to the spirited ingestion of mineral spring water, alcoholic beverages were very popular in the resort too. However, as a result of this association with liquor, the town withered after the onset of "Prohibition."

The museum is located at 21 West Lyon Street, and is open Tuesday thru Friday, 9:00 a.m. to 3:00 p.m., and on Saturdays from 9:00 a.m. to 5:00 p.m. For more information, call (770) 574-3125.

Cave Spring

From Tallapoosa, follow GA Highway 100 north to the scenic little hamlet of **Cave Spring**. This town is a treasure trove of antique shops.

Sample the invigorating natural spring water which bubbles up from a cave in town. Explore **Hearn Academy Inn Bed & Breakfast**, which is a restored dormitory once used as a part of the **Hearn Manual Labor School** begun in 1839.

Many fine old homes (a number of which are on the **National Register of Historic Places**) and shady streets in this sleepy town make it a nice place to visit.

"Sloppy" Floyd State Park

After you've sampled Cave Spring, continue north on GA 100 to **James H. "Sloppy" Floyd State Park**. Nestled among the picturesque surroundings of the **Chattahoochee National Forest**, this park features outstanding seasonal fishing on two managed lakes, and is known for its bluebird population.

Visitors can hike along lake trails or relax in swings along the lake shore. There are cabins, two lakes; 25 tent, trailer, and RV sites; a playground; two boating ramps (for electric trolling motors only); two fishing docks; pedal boat rentals and four picnic shelters.

For more information on Sloppy Floyd State Park, call (706) 857-0826.

Mentone And Lookout Mountain

From Floyd State Park, continue northward on Georgia Highway 100 to **Summerville**. There are a couple of nice little eateries here. Take Georgia Highway 48 out of Summerville and head west up onto **Lookout Mountain**. This is a scenic drive and will take you thru **Menlo** and **Cloudland** before you reach the tiny little Alabama community of **Mentone** on the western crest of Lookout Mountain.

This scenic little mountain crossroads community's name supposedly means "beautiful singing waters."

After years of deterioration, the 1884 Queen Anne Victorian-style **Mentone Springs Hotel** is enjoying a rebirth as a bed-and-breakfast inn on the hill overlooking the little town. The elegant old hotel has claw-footed bathtubs in the baths and Caldwell's Restaurant in the hotel is named for **Dr. Frank Caldwell** who built the structure. For more information, call (256) 634-4040.

Across the highway, the **Mentone Inn Bed & Breakfast** (256-634-4836) also offers historic accommodations.

A short distance away, **Cragsmere Manna** has gained a well-deserved reputation for excellent meals. It, however, is open for dinner only, and only on weekends (Fridays and Saturdays from 5:00 to 9:00 p.m.).

There are several antique shops at the crossroads, including the **White Elephant Galleries** which includes 24 rooms of antiques, collectibles, gifts, arts and crafts. Across the street, a shop called "**Gourdies**" is filled with gourds which have been transformed by an artist into little people replicas with paint and fabric.

DeSoto Falls State Park

Continue down Alabama Highway 89 and take the turn-off for **DeSoto Falls** if you wish to enjoy a truly majestic sight. The 5,000-acre **DeSoto Falls State Park** offers camping sites, a comfortable lodge, mountain chalets, and log cabins for over-nighting.

The centerpiece of this very nice park, however, is a 100-foot waterfall which flows majestically from a horseshoe-shaped prominence. It's amazing that a waterfall as beautiful and large as this could exist *on the top of Lookout Mountain!*

The park complex also includes a pool, bathhouse, picnic and play areas, hiking trails and an extensive network of rhododendron trails that pass by many of the park's 15 waterfalls.

For more information about DeSoto Falls State Park, call 256-845-0051. For reservations at the lodge, call 800-568-8840.

Following a day or two at DeSoto Falls Park, it's probably time to return home. Happy touring.

The Great Locomotive Chase

Many articles have been written over the years which described the famous "Great Locomotive Chase" which occurred on the **Western & Atlantic Railroad** in 1862 in Georgia during the U.S. Civil War. Very few of these articles, however, have taken the reader, step by step, back over this historic route, pointing out the remnants of the historic sites involved in this unusual incident.

The first weekend of every October, Adairsville, Georgia hosts the *Great Locomotive Chase Festival.* As a weekend outing, you may find it interesting to attend this event, and also to retrace the original route of the famous chase.

This will be a very interesting and informative driving tour, so be sure to pack up the kids for this trip too. It will be a great way to have fun, see a lot of the scenic countryside in north Georgia, and make history come alive for the youngsters.

For those of you unfamiliar with the story of this locomotive chase, the following background information is provided: With the U.S. Civil War well underway in 1862, a group of 23 volunteers from the Union Army and one civilian, led by civilian spy **James A. Andrews**, planned to destroy the railroad and disrupt service between Atlanta and Chattanooga.

An account published by the **Louisville & Nashville Railroad (L&N)** summed it up this way:

"The basic plan of the raid was for Andrews and his men to move deep into the Confederacy, take over a locomotive and, en route north, set fire to as many as possible of the several bridges on the W&A. This would put the railroad out of commission for many weeks. Some Federal military strategists felt that such a plan, if successful, could even end the war – or at least shorten it considerably."

On April 10, 1862, the raiders were scheduled to meet in Marietta, but most of them – including Andrews – were held up, and did not arrive until April 11. This forced the men to begin their raid a day later than scheduled. This delay was a harbinger of worse times ahead for the men.

On the night of the 11th, there was a steady rainfall in Marietta. Most of the raiders took quarters at the **Fletcher House**, an imposing brick building which still stands today beside the railroad tracks in downtown Marietta. This structure is known today as the **Kennesaw House**, and we will begin our tour here.

Today, the Kennesaw House provides quarters for the **Marietta Museum of History**, and is an excellent place to see historic items from Civil War days in the Marietta area. This museum is also a great spot to begin piecing together the details surrounding this exciting incident from the war.

On the morning of April 12, 1862, at approximately 5:00 a.m., James Andrews and 19 of the volunteers boarded the passenger car pulled by the Confederate locomotive *General* in Marietta. Including Andrews, there initially were 25 men in the group. However, along the way, two of the men came under suspicion and were forced to join the Confederate army at Chattanooga. Another man never showed up at all, and two others overslept on the morning of their planned departure from Marietta. This reduced the total number of participants to 20.

The first stop after leaving Marietta was **Big Shanty** (present-day Kennesaw), Georgia. It was a miserably wet and rainy day, and the *General* made a scheduled 20-minute stop outside the **Lacy Hotel** at Big Shanty. The trains had no dining cars, so regular stops were necessary so that travelers could take their meals. The Lacy Hotel provided a hearty Southern breakfast which was relished by all the trainmen.

The crew and the passengers trudged inside the hotel – all except for Andrews and his men who remained with the train. **William A. Fuller**, conductor of the *General*, had seated himself by a window with Engineer **Jeff Cain** and machine foreman **Anthony Murphy** when he realized the train was moving! All three men bolted outside where they learned the *General* was being stolen!

Fuller, Cain and Murphy chased the train, but before they could reach it, it had moved too far down the tracks and was gaining momentum. Undeterred, the trio continued running down the tracks for two miles until they reached **Moon's Station**. Here, they commandeered a handcar that a maintenance crew had been using. It was slow going, but it was better than running.

If one wants to see the Lacy Hotel today, he or she will be disappointed. The Lacy was burned to the ground by General William T. Sherman's troops in 1864, and nothing remains of this historic structure today. It was located approximately 100 yards south of the current (circa 1905) railroad depot which exists today on the east side of the tracks.

If one wants to see the *General*, however, this piece of railroad history does still exist. It is housed in the **Southern Museum of Civil War and Locomotive History**, located across Cherokee Street from the depot in Kennesaw.

On to Moon's Station. Nothing, save a lone historic marker, remains of this historic site from the chase. A road named "Moon's Station Road" crossed the tracks at this spot until recent years when it was closed in 1995.

Andrews and his raiders stopped briefly at Moon's Station to obtain tools they needed for their planned demolitions ahead. A "pull-bar," among other things, was taken and later used to pull up rails.

One might wonder how Andrews was able to stop at the many stations along the way without his ruse being uncovered. Andrews has been described as being 6 feet tall with a clear complexion and abundant black hair. He also possessed a confidence which instantly convinced others of his authority. These traits apparently served him well in this venture.

When questioned about his status and destination with the *General*, Andrews reportedly replied, "I'm taking a 'powder train' through to General Beauregard at Corinth." This was a plausible explanation, since the well-known battle at Shiloh in which Beauregard had been involved had occurred only a few days earlier.

Meanwhile, not far behind the *General*, its crew doggedly continued in pursuit. Propelling the little handcar furiously with poles, they made their way down the tracks until they reached the community of Etowah.

Interestingly, a portion of the raiders' plans included the burning of the **Etowah River Bridge**. For reasons unknown today, the demolition of this bridge never occurred. If they had been successful in destroying this bridge, they quite likely would have succeeded beyond their wildest dreams and escaped without detection. This, however, never occurred, and was just one of several fateful decisions which ultimately led to the capture of the raiders.

Today, the massive stone bridge supports of the old Etowah River Bridge still stand in the river. They can be clearly seen from U.S. Highway 41, south of Cartersville. Just two miles from this bridge, visitors may also see remnants of **Cooper's Iron Works**, a large rolling mill and factory which once provided supplies to the Confederacy. One portion of this mill which remains today is an immense stone furnace.

Cooper's Iron Works was an extraordinary complex built by **Jacob Stroup** in the 1830s, and later sold to businessman **Mark David Cooper**. This unusual historic site must be seen first-hand to appreciate the immense size of this pioneer development. It is located in **Cooper's Day Use Area** on **Lake Allatoona** just off U.S. Highway 41. The park has a picnic area and hiking trail, which make it a nice place to stop and take a break during the trip. A number of the old stone buildings from Cooper's Iron Works reportedly still stand today on the bottom of Lake Allatoona.

Cooper's Iron Works also played a significant role in what came to be known as "the Great Locomotive Chase." It was here that Conductor Fuller commandeered the engine *Yonah*, which he used to give further chase to the *General*. By this time, Fuller and his two able assistants were, no doubt, very relieved to trade in the handcar for the locomotive.

Next stop: **Cass Station**. Very little – other than ruins – remains of Cass Station today. The remains of this depot are located north of Cartersville, as was the town which was burned by General Sherman. There is an old warehouse in front of the ruins. In the 1860s, however, Cass Station was an important stop on the Western & Atlantic Railroad – much more important than today's Cartersville.

Andrews and his raiders stopped at Cass to replenish their wood and water supplies for the *General*. While they were at this stop, a tender, William Russell, gave the Union spy a railroad schedule, thinking he was aiding the Confederate war effort. Little did he know he was actually assisting enemy espionage agents.

From Cass Station, the *General* proceeded on to **Kingston**, a busy junction on the W&A. This stop also played a major role in the turn of events which ultimately led to the capture of Andrews and his men.

According to the railroad schedule, the *General* would be side-tracked for only one train. (The W&A was a single-track line which required periodic side tracks to allow scheduled trains to pass each other along the route.) Despite the scheduled one-train wait, Andrews watched frantically as other trains were flagged to resume access to the line ahead of him.

Finally, in desperation, Andrews demanded that any more on-coming trains be held up so he could take his "much needed cargo of ammunition" to General Beauregard at Corinth. The old switch-tender, Uriah Stephens, had reservations about the strangers on Fuller's train, but according to one account, he reluctantly threw the switch that let the *General* pass. (A conflicting report maintains that Andrews was forced to throw the switch himself after Stephens refused.) By the time he was able to depart, Andrews had lost a very precious hour and five minutes at Kingston Station.

The lost time gave Fuller and the *Yonah* just enough time to catch up to Andrews and his men. Fuller later reported the *Yonah* made the 14 miles in 15 minutes at speeds of up to 55 miles per hour. The only thing which saved the capture of Andrews and his men at this point was the fact that trains had been moved to let the *General* pass. These trains on the tracks prevented the *Yonah* from following.

Once again, Fuller, Murphy and Cain applied the only source of transportation left to them – their feet! They took off on foot around the southbound trains and past the station to another northbound train which was about to roll.

With her steam up and wheels ready to turn, the *William R. Smith* was an able locomotive belonging to the Rome Railroad. After hastily explaining the circumstances to conductor Cicero Smith and engineer O. Wiley Harbin, Fuller and his men took over the *William R. Smith* and continued after the raiders. Along the way, several volunteers joined the chase.

Kingston was another of the many cities destroyed by Sherman and his men. According to Emma C. Williams and Martha H. Mullinex, it was a growing and prosperous city on the W&A in 1862.

Emma and Martha are members of the Kingston Women's History Club. The ladies of the club have opened a history museum in Kingston which houses relics and photographs from yesteryear involving this community. This is an interesting place for viewing many historic items, some of which pertain to the Great Locomotive Chase.

The original stone depot in Kingston was destroyed in 1864. Two subsequent depots were built in the same spot, but were likewise destroyed by fire. Today, the foundation of the original depot is the only reminder of the Western & Atlanta Railroad and the Great Locomotive Chase at this spot.

The lovely town of **Adairsville** is the next stop on our tour of the W&A. The *William R. Smith* was forced to stop several times so that the men could remove cross-ties placed on the railroad tracks by the raiders. A short time later, Fuller and his crew had to abandon their train after discovering that a section of the tracks ahead of them had been destroyed.

Without hesitation, Fuller reportedly climbed down from the *William R. Smith* and proceeded once again on foot. When he looked behind him, he discovered that only Murphy was still with him – carrying a shotgun they had acquired sometime during the chase. The other men had abandoned the chase.

Meanwhile, up ahead in Adairsville, Andrews had cunningly convinced Peter Bracken, engineer of the *Texas*, that he must get through to General Beauregard with their cargo of powder. Bracken obligingly sidetracked his train so that Andrews could pass with the *General.*

Having traveled on foot for a couple of miles, Fuller and Murphy were relieved to see the *Texas* steaming down the tracks. They signaled for the train to stop and explained the dire circumstances to Bracken. The engineer immediately put the *Texas* in reverse and backed the 21-car freight train to Adairsville where he sidetracked the cars. The locomotive then continued down the tracks in reverse, chasing feverishly after the *General.* The *Texas* crew now consisted of Fuller, Murphy, Engineer Bracken and his 15-year-old fireman, Henry Haney.

If you visit Adairsville today, you will no doubt enjoy the historic personality of this quaint little town. On December 4, 1987, the entire town was listed on the **National Register of Historic Places**. The original depot which witnessed the Great Locomotive Chase in 1862 still stands on the town square.

Contrary to most other depots which have disappeared from the old route of the W&A, the Adairsville station not only still stands, but has been renovated for use as a history museum. A portion of the museum is dedicated to the history of the Great Locomotive Chase.

According to Col. James Bogle, co-author of the publication *The General & The Texas*, the town of Calhoun was the next stop for the *Texas.*

"The *Texas* made the run, in reverse, to Calhoun in some 12 minutes," Bogle wrote. "Here, the crew picked up valuable reinforcements for their cause. Fleming Cox, an engineer on the Memphis & Charleston Railroad, was on his way to Atlanta. Caught up in the excitement of the day, he climbed aboard the *Texas* and relieved 15-year-old Henry Haney as

Bracken's fireman. Alonzo Martin also climbed on-board and assisted in passing wood to the tender."

Meanwhile, the raiders were approaching their next site of destruction – the Oostanaula River Bridge south of Resaca. They knew the *Texas* was not far behind them, and they realized they must destroy this bridge if they were to elude their pursuers.

To burn the bridge, the men started a fire in the rear car of the train. They intended to use the flames from this car to set the bridge aflame. Unfortunately for them, a steady rain had continued to fall, and the wood was so damp that it would do little more than smolder.

Today, the covered bridge over the Oostanaula no longer exists. The new bridge at this spot, however, uses some of the same stone pilings which once supported the covered bridge. If you stand on the modern-day bridge on Highway 41 and look over to the railroad bridge, you can still see these pilings.

By the time the *Texas* reached the bridge, they had already hooked up with a previous car left behind by the raiders. Now, with the addition of the smoldering car, they were pushing two additional cars up the railroad.

Between **Resaca** and **Dalton**, the *General* had stopped for wood and water, both of which were imperative for operating the large locomotive. However, with the *Texas* hot on their trail, the men were unable to stop long enough to get the amount of wood and water necessary to continue their momentum. Time was running out.

At Dalton, the *General* sped past the depot without stopping. The *Texas*, close behind in pursuit, slowed down just enough to allow a young telegraph operator to jump from the train to telegraph a message ahead. According to a news account of this incident, the raiders cut the telegraph line a few miles beyond the depot, but not before most of the message had been sent ahead to Confederate forces under the command of **General Leadbetter**.

Today, the historic Dalton depot has been renovated and is used as a restaurant appropriately named "**The Depot**". The décor and aura of this historic building transports visitors back in time. As you eat, you can observe trains rushing by large picture windows adjacent to the tracks. The menu is filled with delicious entrees and tasty desserts.

By the time they reached Dalton, the raiders were merely trying to stay ahead of the *Texas* just to prevent their capture. Their plan of destruction had failed. They were fast-approaching **Tunnel Hill**.

Just prior to reaching the tunnel, Fuller slowed down, fearing the raiders might have left their last boxcar inside the dark confines as a trap. Upon reaching the tunnel, he was able to see light from the other end, so he knew it was safe to continue on thru. From this point on, the *General* was in sight most of the time.

Today, Tunnel Hill is boxed between factory buildings, but it is still intact. There are several informative historical markers in this vicinity. Just beyond the Tunnel Hill depot is an old covered bridge. After crossing this bridge, the tunnel comes into sight. The area is closed off with a gate, but can be easily seen. It's hard to imagine this aged tunnel was constructed over 150 years ago.

Ringgold was the last station passed by the *General*. By this time, it was obvious the chase was almost over. In Fuller's words, "About two and a half miles the other side of Ringgold, we saw the engine we were pursuing apparently fagging." In other words, the *General* was running out of steam.

And that is literally what happened. Without an ample supply of wood and water, the mighty engine could not produce the steam necessary to drive it. It finally crawled to a stop, with the raiders scattering in all directions. According to an account at the time, Andrews reportedly said at this point, "Every man take care of himself."

On top of a hill, the old Ringgold Depot still stands today, but it sadly has not been preserved. This, however, in no way diminishes the fun of this trip, nor even a visit to Ringgold.

Just a couple of miles from the depot, a historical marker identifies the spot at which the *General* ultimately came to a stop. Standing at this point, one can feel both a sense of awe and accomplishment.

Unfortunately for them, all of the 22 raiders eventually were caught. Eight of them – including Andrews – were executed in Atlanta, Georgia. Interestingly, eight of the men managed to escape from the Atlanta prison and make their way home. The remaining six were paroled at City Point, Virginia, on March 17, 1863.

Those men who were executed were buried in the National Cemetery in Chattanooga, Tennessee. The "**Ohio Monument**" is a tribute to these men and contains a replica of the *General*. The monument was given to the cemetery by the state of Ohio at a cost of $5,000, and was unveiled at ceremonies on **Decoration Day**, 1891.

Kennesaw House/Marietta Museum of History

From Interstate 75 take exit 263. Go west on loop 120 for approximately 3.3 miles. Turn right onto Mill Street which will take you into the parking lot.

Kennesaw Civil War Museum

From Mill Street, turn right. Continue on Loop 120 for about 1.6 miles, and turn left onto Hwy 41 / Cobb Parkway. Continue for approximately 5.1 miles then angle off to the right onto Old Hwy. 41 just prior to the large Kennesaw Civil War Museum sign. Travel approximately 1.6 miles, then turn right onto

The Great Locomotive Chase Driving Tour

Cherokee Street. After crossing the railroad tracks, the museum will be on the left. The depot and the site at which the Lacy Hotel once existed are on the right.

Moon's Station

From the museum, turn left back onto Cherokee Street and travel approximately two miles to Jiles Road. Turn left onto Jiles for approximately 0.7 of a mile and turn right onto Baker Road (at the traffic light). Travel 0.3 of a mile and the Moon's Station historic marker is on the left.

Etowah River Bridge

Backtrack to Hwy. 41 / Cobb Parkway and turn right onto the highway. Travel approximately 16.4 miles. Take the Highway 293 / Cooper Furnace Day Use Area Exit and then turn right at the stop sign. Continue for approximately 100 yards; turn left onto River Road then go approximately 50 yards and the remains of the old railroad bridge will be visible on the right.

Cooper's Iron Works

Continue on down River Road for approximately 2.5 miles and you will reach a point at which the road dead-ends at the Cooper Day Use Area Park. The remains of Coopers Iron Works at which the locomotive *Yonah* was commandeered by Conductor William Fuller are visible in this vicinity.

Cass Station

Backtrack to Highway 41 and travel north for approximately seven miles to Mac Johnson Road. Turn left at the traffic light. A Texaco service station will be on the left at the light. Turn right onto Highway 293. Turn left onto the first road on the left (Burnt Hickory Road). The remains of Cass Station are approximately 200 yards away on the right, behind an old warehouse just prior to the point at which you reach the railroad tracks.

Kingston

Backtrack back to Highway 41 once again and continue northward. Travel approximately one mile and turn left onto Boyd Morris Road (which is a detour to our objective which is Highway 293). Turn right onto 293 and continue for approximately six miles into Kingston. Turn left at the caution light onto Shaw Street and this will take you into downtown historic Kingston. The foundation of the old depot is on the opposite side of the railroad tracks to the right.

Adairsville Depot

Backtrack to Highway 293. Turn left onto 293 / Howard Street and travel approximately 0.4 of a mile. Turn right onto Hall Station Road. Continue on for approximately ten miles, then turn right onto King Street and travel 0.3 of a mile. Turn right onto Railroad Street and continue on for 0.3 of a mile to the old depot on the left.

Oostanaula River Bridge

Return to King Street and turn right. Go one block then turn left onto Main Street. Travel approximately 0.4 of a mile and turn right onto Highway 140. Continue approximately 1.5 miles to Interstate 75. Turn left onto Interstate 75 North and travel approximately 12.8 miles to Exit 318. Turn right onto Highway 41 and proceed approximately 1.5 miles and the old bridge will be on the right. The stone ramparts at this site date to the Civil War era and the Great Locomotive Chase.

Dalton Depot

Backtrack to Interstate 75 North. Continue 15 miles to Exit 333 / Walnut Avenue. Turn right onto Walnut Avenue and continue for 1.8 miles. Turn left onto Thornton Avenue. Proceed 0.7 of a mile and turn right onto Crawford. Continue for three blocks on Crawford and turn left onto Hamilton Street. Continue for one block and turn right. At this point, you will be in the depot parking lot.

Tunnel Hill

Backtrack to Interstate 75 North and proceed northward for eight miles to Exit 341. Turn left onto Route 201S and proceed for 2.5 miles, continuing straight onto Varnell Street at the point that 201 turns to the right. Turn right onto Main Street. Turn left onto Oak Street and cross the railroad tracks. Turn left onto Clisby-Austin Road. The old depot is on the left. There are several historic markers in this vicinity. Continue on Clisby-Austin Road for approximately 0.3 of a mile and the old tunnel is on the left.

Ringgold Depot

Backtrack to Clisby-Austin and continue straight on Oak Street to Highway 41. Turn right onto Highway 41 and proceed for approximately 7.5 miles. The old depot is on a hill to the right.

Pinelog

Historic Pinelog

It's known as an "eye-blink community" – one that a traveler can pass through and miss at the blink of an eye. Its remote and tranquil location has kept it small in size since its founding by the pioneers, but today, the scenic attractiveness of the community of Pine Log beckons to one and all – even to Hollywood.

Hundreds of people skirt the edge of this tiny Bartow County community on Highway 411 daily. A few stop to photograph the authentic turn-of-the-century general store, or to browse through the antiques sold there. Most folks, however, don't tarry long, because they don't realize just how historic this crossroads community actually is.

In its earliest days – before Georgia was even a colony – Pine Log was an Indian village, established at the intersection of two major Indian trails. One pathway led from **Coosa (Fort Strother, Alabama)** to **Tugaloo (Toccoa)**. The other led from Suwanee Old Town (near present-day Suwanee, Georgia) to the Cherokee capitol of **New Echota** (near present-day Calhoun, Georgia) and continued northward into Tennessee following much of the route of present-day U.S. Highway 411.

It was the Indians, quite possibly, who anointed Pine Log with its name, but several explanations for this naming have evolved through the years.

Mrs. Elizabeth Garrison, a local historian, educator and descendant of the area's earliest pioneers, said that nearly everyone, if they haven't researched it, believes that Pine Log was named for an Indian chief named Pine Log. Others say the area gets its name from Pine Log Creek, named for a well-known pine foot-log that once bridged the stream. Still others maintain the village took its name from the area's mountains, supposedly called Pine Log Mountains by the Indians.

None of these explanations, however, is quite true, according to Mrs. Garrison, co-author of the *History of the Pine Log Methodist Church*, and a school teacher for 32 years in Bartow County.

"If you search back, you'll find that in 1738, a tribe of Indians called the Natchez was driven out of the lower Mississippi Valley area. The Cherokees here allowed them to settle on one bank of the creek and start their own community," Mrs. Garrison explained. "The word 'Natchez' sounded like the Cherokees' word for a pine tree or pine log (after translation into English). It was the custom of the Indians at that time to name the mountains and creeks after the Indians that lived there, so the area came to be known as 'Pine Log.'"

Like many developing pioneer communities in Georgia in the 1830s, Pine Log included a church. Much of pioneer life revolved around religion, and much of that lifestyle is still evident today in the historic **Pine Log Methodist Church**, built by settlers in 1842. The church and grounds, both of which are now listed on the **National Register of Historic Places,** are still in use today.

Gas heaters have replaced the pot-bellied stove as the primary source of heat in **Bradford's General Store**, but the mercantile center is still in business, looking "pretty much the same as it has for nearly a hundred years," according to Willis Bradford, whose father, Sam, opened the store in 1904.

Hollywood too, has been impressed with the unspoiled scenery of the historic community. Several scenes for the **CBS** made-for-TV movie **Shenandoah** were filmed in the community. The location manager for the movie contacted Mrs. Garrison after seeing photos of her family's 150-year-old homeplace – the Mahan homestead – in a Bartow County historical book.

(To get to Pine Log, take Interstate 75 north from Atlanta, continuing beyond Cartersville. Exit onto U.S. 411 north, continuing to the intersection with Georgia Highway 140 west. Turn left and head west.)

4 NORTHWEST GEORGIA

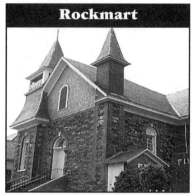

Rockmart

Historic Rockmart

I ts history parallels that of the early development of a tiny community in northwest Georgia. Indeed, the mineral products industry of the town which came to be known as "**Rockmart**" is a unique one – sprinkled with its share of murder, intrigue, sadness and gladness. Today, this unique community in Polk County can be an interesting part of a weekend driving tour.

As a result of the mining of mineral products around Rockmart, the terrain in some spots eventually took on the appearance one might expect from open-pit mining endeavors. It also created some very memorable swimming holes – as well as a convenient place to hide things – like bodies.

In 1959 in southeastern New Mexico, patrolling policemen immediately recognized a vehicle parked in downtown Hobbs. They had been alerted to its description days earlier.

Two men were found asleep inside the car. Following an identification check, the men proved to be young sailors who were "Absent Without Leave" (AWOL) from their base in San Francisco, California. They were "joy-riding" around the country, using the stolen car and credit card of a man who had been missing for two weeks from Meridian, Mississippi.

Following a routine arrest of the two men for automobile theft, the sailors, according to an article in the February 1, 1959 issue of *Rome News Tribune*, were questioned about how they had come into possession of the car. According to statements they gave to Federal Bureau of Investigation (FBI) agents, the two men - George E. Blauvelt and James H. Parkerson - had robbed and murdered 38-year-old William G. Shirley following an argument at a hotel in Livingston, Alabama. They described how they had driven off in the victim's car with the body stuffed in the trunk. Their destination was Rockmart, Georgia, Parkerson's hometown.

According to their confessions, the two sailors described where they had hidden the body of their victim. Present-day Rockmart folklore maintains the men drove around for days searching for a suitable dumpsite for the victim, who by then was growing quite ripe in the trunk. In actuality, however, by the sailors' own admissions, they had arrived in Rockmart the day of the murder and had dumped the corpse the next evening in Blue Hole Lake – an abandoned slate quarry filled with more than fifty feet of water.

When word reached Polk County that a body would probably be found in the quarry, Deputy Sheriff Bob Sproull organized a search. His men put a boat into the water of the quarry and began grappling operations.

The men worked well into the night after lights were brought in to illuminate the area. However, the grisly object of their search eluded them. Operations were suspended until the next day when Georgia Fish and Wildlife Ranger W.E. Murphree found the body and brought it to the surface. The victim's brother and a friend were waiting on shore to identify the remains.

Polk County Sheriff John Redding had expected to find the body in the deepest part of the old quarry, possibly weighted down with a rock. Though the men did not find any stones weighing down the body, they did make a more sinister discovery. The skull of the victim had been crushed. This revelation conflicted with the killers' confessions that they had simply been in a heated argument and had smothered their victim.

The perpetrators' familiarity with their chosen hiding place is understandable. Every red-blooded Rockmart youth from the 1940s through the 1960s had, at one time or another, explored the old slate quarry pits in the area known as "the blue holes." These large abandoned quarries – filled in today - were remnants of Rockmart's oldest industry – slate mining.

The slate mining business in Rockmart began – according to one legend – when slate was accidentally discovered by an individual by the name of Blance, who was staking out the family cow. In 1850, **Joseph G. Blance** recognized the value of the nearly black slate vein and started a quarry beyond the ridge which rises behind Rockmart's **First Baptist Church**.

According to the *Rockmart Journal* of July 20, 1967, *"The Blanceville Slate Mining Company of Georgia was the first of several slate companies, the community around the slate quarries having been called Blanceville at that time."*

One quarry operator who was president of the **Blanceville Slate Mining Company** in the early days was **James F. Dever, Sr.** He was the grandson of company founder **J.G. Blance**. According to Dever's records, *"The first slate quarried in Georgia was taken from lot 923 in 1857, and used in roofing Norton's store in Rome (GA), which is still good."*

Today, the impressive old **Dever homeplace** – a harbinger of days long past – still stands on Plum Street in Rockmart. Mr. and Mrs. Forrest Hutchings inherited and lived in the Dever home for many years. Mr. Hutchings was the grandson of Mr. Dever.

Built in the 1872 by a German architect, the Dever home remained in the possession of descendants of the family until the latter portion of the 20th century, when it was purchased by **Billy and Cherry Clark**. The Clarks completely renovated the home and grounds, restoring the site to its former splendor.

Not long after the Blance family discovery, another quarry was opened and continued slate operations seemed assured when the opening shots of the **War Between The States** were fired. As the turmoil of the war reached the quarries in Rockmart, mining at the slate veins ceased. The men dropped their mining tools and picked up weapons of war.

As the tides of the war pressed in upon the South, many refugees from the devastated towns of north Georgia fled before the attacking Union forces and headed south toward Macon. This city, already crowded with refugees and wounded soldiers, was becoming a manufacturing and distribution center for supplies and military materiel. *"Saddles, harness, shot, cannon, and small weapons were manufactured,"* and to assure the continued production of ordnance, the Confederate Arsenal was moved from Savannah to Macon.

The construction of ordnance buildings, laboratory, and armory required one construction element which only Rockmart could supply. Therefore, in 1863, the mining of slate was begun anew and a third quarry was opened and slate operations were resumed to provide the new facilities at Macon with sturdy roofing.

This third quarry belonged to **Colonel Seaborn Jones,** *"one of the originators of the Rockmart slate industry."* Col. Jones had extensive land holdings and was a major benefactor of the city of Rockmart. He ultimately provided land for churches, a railroad, a town square, and a city park. He eventually sold his slate holdings in the **Georgia Slate Company** to **J.F. Vandeventer**.

Except for the Macon slate order, operations at the Rockmart slate mines remained at a stand-still due to the circumstances of war. Even for as long as 15 years following the war, slate production was nonexistent.

About 1880, the quarries were reopened, and from that year until 1900 was the period of greatest development. During this stretch, Rockmart gained yet another resource for its on-again off-again industry: **Welsh slate workers**. These skilled craftsmen came from northern Wales where slate products have been crafted since the twelfth century.

In the 1880s, Rockmart's growing slate operations were in dire need of experienced workers. The *Cedartown Standard* in April, 1989, described the arrival of one of the first of the Welsh, **Joe Franklin Davis**. According to Rockmart native **Annie Clyde Simpson Russell**, her maternal grandfather sent his son, **Griff Davis**, to see if Rockmart had any substantial quantities of slate. When an affirmative answer reached the Davis patriarch in Wales, the family *"got into a boat and came over."*

Understandably, religion was very important to these laborers. Many of the early Welsh miners in the Rockmart area attended nearby **Van Wert Methodist Church**.

The community of **Van Wert** is little more than a suburb of Rockmart today, but once was the government seat of **Paulding County** when Rockmart did not even exist. The aged graves with the remains of these Welshmen – many marked with simple slate headstones engraved with the sleeping souls' names – can still be seen beneath the undergrowth of the old cemetery on the hillside behind the church.

The old sanctuary, built in 1846, had been vacated by the **North Georgia Methodist Conference** in the mid-1980s, and thereafter stood forlorn and abandoned for many years. It was at this pulpit, in 1872, that an aspiring young evangelist – **Rev. Sam Jones** – had begun a ministry which would eventually take him to the national stage and bring him lasting fame and fortune. Today, this church is one of the most historic structures in Polk County, and is maintained by the **Polk County Historical Society**.

In its day, many uses were found for slate: blackboards and slate tablets used as early education tools; billiard table tops; mantels and hearths; grave vaults and markers; and of course, the use as a roofing material. Today, its uses are more limited, and thus it is mined much more sparingly.

With slate production as a solid industrial foundation, the community became known as a "rock market." In 1872, the name "**Rock Mart**" was chosen to identify the site when the town was officially chartered.

An odd footnote to this circumstance is the fact that one mineral – limestone – was mistakenly identified as marble in the early years of the town, leading to some confusing identities. One of the summits above the community – "**Marble Hill**" – bears this mistaken moniker to this day, and has been the catalyst for innumerable searches over the years by curious individuals looking for the elusive mineral after which the hill was named.

Around 1900, Mr. and Mrs. **B.T. McGarity** built and operated the impressive **Marble Hill Hotel**. This large structure once existed on North Marble Street at the base of Marble Hill. Though its luster was dulled in later years, many Rockmart natives can still remember this big inn which remained a prominent community landmark well into the 1950s. Sadly, it was eventually demolished for the construction of a much-needed supermarket in the community. The new grocery, which has now disappeared itself, didn't last nearly as long as had the old hotel.

Eventually, the slate deposits led to the development of yet another industry for the city of Rockmart: bricks. The **Monarch Brick Company** was organized with the intention of producing slate, and using the waste in brick manufacturing. However, by the time the brick plant was built in 1900, the demand for slate had so declined, that Monarch never produced any slate products at all.

Monarch Brick was soon reorganized, becoming the **Rockmart Shale, Brick and Slate Company**. For about twenty years, the plant manufactured a vitrified paving brick, using in part, weathered slate or shale. These bricks can still be seen in a number of buildings around Rockmart.

Just about the time this brick production factory was begun, concrete was coming into favor for the paving of roads and other uses and it was discovered that Rockmart had a huge natural supply of the materials needed to create cement. The city soon witnessed the construction of its first cement plant. It made a product from the city's excellent limestone and slate deposits. Ironically, despite the availability of all the raw materials for cement in Rockmart, the first street in the city was not paved until 1924.

"The first cement in Polk County, I've always heard, was the cement that was shipped in to (build) the grist mill at **Hightower Falls**," said Rockmart resident Dan Simon, as he recalled some of the stories about the cement business that brought his father to Rockmart. Hightower Falls is also a captivating and unique site with an 80-foot waterfall and historic gristmill. It is located off Morgan Valley Road between Rockmart and Cedartown.

The **Southern States Portland Cement Company** was a financial success, even weathering the disastrous years of the Great Depression. When **Marquette Cement Company** purchased Southern States in 1954, it invested in a thriving enterprise.

Marquette carried on the business for some thirty years, until the mineral resources at its site in Rockmart were depleted. Shortly thereafter, the old plant was closed down.

Interestingly, one of the few stone-based industries remaining in Rockmart today, is the original business – slate – which was begun back before the U.S. Civil War. An idled plant which once had produced lightweight aggregate from expanded shale was revamped in the 1990s by the newly-formed **Rockmart Slate Corporation**.

Meanwhile, throughout the little community of Rockmart, a multitude of homes and commercial buildings constructed of slate and brick, offer mute testimony to this once-vibrant industry. And in the old downtown district, a variety of aged buildings still stand strong and solid, having been constructed of the slate and bricks mined and manufactured nearby.

Over all these years, the financial survival of many families has depended upon this ages-old industry – the mining of minerals and stone. Today, for the most part, the old mills and mining sites around Rockmart are quiet – their destinies fulfilled.

And back in old Van Wert Methodist Church, those first miners – the originators of the industries in Rockmart – sleep the big sleep only a few feet from the stone which once gave meaning and fulfillment to their lives.

Rockmart

The Silver Comet Trail

The historic Seaboard Railroad ceased to exist decades ago, and the tracks of the old line were taken up in Cobb, Paulding and Polk counties and sold for scrap a few years later. However, a growing phenomenon in the great outdoors – the rails to trails hiking and biking paths program – has breathed new life into the old roadbed of the Seaboard rail line, preserving it for future generations.

Called the **Silver Comet Trail** today, much of the renovated and historic trail passes through the little community of **Rockmart**. Outside of a thriving stone products industry, a championship high school football team or two over the years, and a terrible train wreck in 1926, there haven't been many other things to focus regional attention on this little town, but that may be changing, with the growing popularity of this new hiking and biking trail.

To date, approximately 38 miles of the trail have been completed between Smyrna and Rockmart, and the trail has proven to be a big hit among exercise and outdoor enthusiasts. At its completion, the Silver Comet Trail will join other trails to stretch a total of approximately 100 miles as a scenic byway for enjoyment by walkers, bicycle riders, horseback riders and skaters from throughout the state.

On almost any given weekend (and often on weekdays as well), trail users may be seen enjoying this scenic avenue. The trail has not only attracted hikers and bikers, but nature and history enthusiasts as well, since the old railroad bed snakes through some very scenic and historic terrain in northwest Georgia.

The Silver Comet

In 1947, the famous **Silver Comet train** – one of the finest forms of transportation in the southeastern United States at that time – made its maiden journey. Traveling through such major cities as Birmingham, Atlanta, Washington, D.C.; and Philadelphia, this passenger train was unequaled in speed and luxury, and passed through many rural areas such as Polk County along the way.

The Silver Comet consisted of three day coaches, a dining car, a tavern car, and several sleeping cars. Each of the sleeping cars was named after towns along the Comet's route, such as the "Atlantan," or the "Cedartown," and the train flourished for a decade or more.

However, with the growth of interstate highways and increased air travel in the 1960s, rail transportation fell out of vogue, and passengers on the train gradually declined. Eventually, the Silver Comet was unable to generate the revenues necessary to substantiate its existence. In 1969, the Comet made its final run, and passenger service was discontinued. The rail line between Smyrna and Rockmart eventually was abandoned completely.

Luckily for the communities along the old route, however, a movement called "**Rails-To-Trails**" became interested in the road-bed once traveled by the Silver Comet. In 1989, the **Georgia Department of Transportation** purchased the right-of-way of the former line. In 1998, an organization by the name of **PATH** agreed to oversee the construction and completion of what was being called the "Silver Comet Trail" from Smyrna to Rockmart, and the stage was set for a whole new life for the old railroad bed.

The PATH foundation is a non-profit organization dedicated to the conversion of old railways to metro-wide trail systems. In the process, the foundation seeks to enhance community spirit and bring neighborhoods together. The Silver Comet is just one of a number of successful similar projects undertaken by PATH in the foundation's endless pursuit of "Rails-To-Trails" opportunities.

One portion of the Silver Comet Trail – the portion from Rockmart to Cedartown and on to the Alabama state line – remains incomplete as of this writing. When finished, the Silver Comet will connect with the **Chief Ladiga Trail** in Alabama for a combined total of approximately 100 miles of hiking and biking enjoyment.

Stops Along The Trail

From the **Rambo** access point in Dallas, Georgia, the first scenic stop on the trail is the **Pumpkinvine Creek Trestle** at mile marker 23.02. Here, the traveler passes over a 750-foot-long, 126-foot-high historic trestle. Today, this viaduct has been rebuilt with concrete and heavy steel, and, just as did railroad passengers in the late 19th and early 20th centuries, patrons on this route can again admire quite a view from this spot.

The next scenic locale on the trail is **Brushy Mountain Tunnel**. Here, visitors are treated to an 800-foot-long lighted tunnel nestled beneath the beautiful hardwoods and lush waterfalls of Brushy

Mountain. Trail hikers sometimes pause here to explore the adjacent natural environment.

During the **Atlanta Campaign** in the **U.S. Civil War**, the **Battle of Brushy Mountain** occurred not far from this vicinity. **General William T. Sherman** maneuvered **General Joe Johnston**'s Confederate army out of several successive defensive positions in this area. The Confederates had dug in all the way from Brushy Mountain to Lost Mountain.

As a portion of the trail development, a man-made pond with goldfish has been creatively constructed in this vicinity. Frogs and turtles doze along the pond's edge, enjoying the sunlight.

Leaving the coolness of the deep forest at Brushy Mountain, it is approximately three miles to the next stopping point. Along the way, it is not uncommon to encounter abundant wildlife, including deer, turkeys, snakes and other denizens of the forest.

In short order, the traveler will reach the **Coot's Lake Rest Stop**. This local attraction in Polk County includes a lake for swimming and relaxation, a nice beach area, and a snack shop for treats. A fee is charged for admission to the lake and beach.

There is also ample parking at this stop (which is the trailhead just prior to the main **Van Wert Trailhead** a short distance away), and if the snack shop at Coot's Lake is closed, a convenience store at this site offers an additional opportunity for food, refreshments and supplies.

Historic Van Wert

From Coot's Lake, the trail winds down to the historic community of **Van Wert**. Some bikers may wish to take a side trip at this point to visit this tiny town. (Then again, they may not, since there is not a great deal to do here except possibly visit a fragment of history.)

Van Wert originally was the site of a 19th century Indian village and, a little later, an early pioneer community known as "Clean Town." According to folklore, the **Clean Town** name was designed to mock the somewhat uncleanly nature of the trading post and early inhabitants of this town.

As the young state of Georgia was being settled, Van Wert existed within the confines of what then was Paulding County (prior to the creation of Polk County), and as a result, the small but growing town was named as the county seat of Paulding.

At one time, Van Wert boasted a courthouse, several taverns and other mercantile businesses, all of which have burned or been torn down over the years. The only substantial historic public building left in the little community is an aged church – once the town's **Methodist Church** – which includes a very historic adjacent cemetery with aged headstones,

some of which date back to the early 1800s. This church also enjoys the distinction of being the sanctuary at which the once nationally-renowned evangelist **Sam Jones** began his ministry in the late 1800s.

Van Wert remained the county seat for many years until the creation of Polk County in 1851, and the subsequent naming of Cedartown as the county seat of that county. There are a number of historic homes remaining in Van Wert, but the old Methodist church is the most historic *public* structure still in existence.

The Van Wert trailhead a short distance from the Coot's Lake trailhead again includes plenty of parking space. There are also portable toilets, water fountains and picnic tables at this site.

Other Historic Sites

Approximately half a mile from the Van Wert trailhead, Silver Comet Trail patrons will pass a site to which long-time Rockmart locals still refer as "**Ma White's Bottomlands**." Here, visitors will see the lush fertile creek bottomlands which were tilled by Indians in pre-history, and by the owners of a plantation which existed on this site in the 19th and 20th centuries. Numerous Indian artifacts have been discovered in this vicinity over the years by area residents.

The plantation at this site was owned by four previous families before the Whites came into possession of the property. According to records, contingents of **General William T. Sherman**'s troops camped across the road from the plantation home circa 1864, and even fired a cannon round through the length of the home before departing the area. Luckily, the residents of the home had taken refuge in the basement, and escaped harm.

For many years (and indeed until recently), the historic plantation home was still visible across the fields from the Silver Comet Railroad. Unfortunately, the large structure burned to the ground in 1985 during renovations.

A short distance from this spot, travelers on the Silver Comet will pass the historic **Rockmart Slate Quarry** at mile marker 36.8. Here, beside **Thompson/Euharlee Creek**, park benches offer a cool, quiet place to pause for a moment. A historic marker at this spot explains the history of the pre-Civil War slate industry at this site. This vicinity became world-renowned for its bricks, slate and limestone products in the 20th century. Many roofs on the homes in Polk County and elsewhere in the state still contain the original slate shingles installed on these homes, some over 120 years ago.

Also at this spot, the historic **Seaboard Depot** still stands beside the railroad (which continues periodically to be used between this spot and Cedartown, Georgia, by CSX

Railroad). The date of construction of this depot is unknown, but the aged structure appears in very early photos of Rockmart, many of which date back at least to the early 1900s.

Riverwalk

Advancing into downtown Rockmart, many of the historic buildings (with slate shingles) of the town come into view. At this point, you are on the leg of the trail – the **Riverwalk** trailhead – used in Rockmart's annual **Homespun Festival** foot race. Riverwalk ends at **Wayside-Seaborn Jones Memorial Park in downtown Rockmart**. You might wish to take the time here to cool off in the shallow areas of **Euharlee Creek** near the bridge, and to visit the historic downtown section of Rockmart just a few yards away.

If not for pioneer **Seaborn Jones**, the Silver Comet Trail quite likely would never have come into existence. Mr. Jones donated land for the original railroad depot in Rockmart, an event which resulted in the development of the town and subsequently attracted the rail line upon which much of the Silver Comet Trail is built today.

Sometimes known as the "Father of Rockmart," Jones provided land not only for the first railroad depot, but also for several churches, the town square, a city park, and **Rose Hill Cemetery.** Today, his gravestone is still the most prominent in the cemetery.

Also at the Riverwalk trailhead in downtown Rockmart, many other opportunities are available for patrons, including food, picnic tables, pay phones, and commercial items at local businesses. The **Silver Comet Depot** shop offers bike rentals, ice cream, Silver Comet souvenirs and more.

Group activities are often on-going in the park at Riverwalk. Professional photographers are sometimes available here since this trailhead is one of the most beautiful and delightful to visit.

In the middle of the Rockmart town square, **Veterans' Memorial Walk** was recently created. The names of U.S. military veterans – both living and deceased – from the Rockmart area are permanently enshrined here engraved in bricks.

Departing the downtown Rockmart district and heading west, trail patrons encounter an attractive iron bridge with the Silver Comet Trail logo over Euharlee Creek. The view from this bridge back toward Riverwalk offers the opportunity for scenic photos of Euharlee Creek, the bridge and Riverwalk itself.

This short leg of the trail skirts the edge of historic Rose Hill Cemetery, the final resting place of Rockmart's founder, Seaborn Jones, as well as that of a number of other notables. At this vicinity, the trail also intertwines around one of the still active railroads on which freight trains pass daily through Rockmart.

Patrons on the trail next encounter Nathan Dean Sports Complex. Here, many athletic activities take place on well-manicured and maintained baseball and softball fields. When you reach the end of the split-rail fence at the northwestern corner of this complex, you have also reached the current end of the Silver Comet Trail. Construction is underway to continue the trail on to Cedartown, and to the Chief Ladiga Trail in Alabama.

Rockmart Eateries & Events

The slow-paced confines of old downtown Rockmart offer a wholesome area to pass time prior to leaving the trail to depart home. The **Impala Grill,** a 1950s-style diner complete with nostalgic decorations of hotrods and muscle cars from yesteryear is located within easy pedaling distance (a couple of city blocks) of Riverwalk. For the classic automobile enthusiasts, a **Hot Rod Cruiser Show** is periodically held in front of the Impala. **Elvis** has even been known to return from the dead and make an appearance here on occasion.

Other restaurants in the downtown area include **Hometown Pizza, Bar-L Barbecue,** the **Chocolate Café, T's Seafood, Pizza Depot, Sidekicks, House of China** and others. A short distance from the trail end at **Nathan Dean Complex** are fast food franchises such as **McDonalds, Pizza Hut, Hardees,** and **Sonic.** Also in this vicinity is a new **Day's Inn** if you want to overnight in the area.

Rockmart is also home to several local festivals, so plan your trip accordingly. The annual **Homespun Festival** hosted by the local Chamber of Commerce occurs the second week in July each year. Located at Riverwalk and Seaborn Jones Memorial Park, visitors to this event can enjoy a morning parade, a 5-K footrace and other festival activities right on the trail. Also scheduled is a complete lineup of entertainment from morning to night at the gazebo, arts and crafts items for sale, barbecue plates, games and rides for the children and much more. The grand finale is a late evening fireworks celebration which can be seen for miles around.

Other area events include the **Aragon Barbecue** held the last Saturday in June of each year in nearby Aragon, Georgia. A growing event a short distance off the trail after the Coot's Lake trailhead is **"The Rock."** This gathering is held the first weekend in October each year, and is home to a popular arts and crafts festival as well as substantial musical entertainment.

Take advantage of the Silver Comet Trail. You'll be glad you did.

(For more information on the above events and the Silver Comet Trail in Polk County, contact the Polk County Chamber of Commerce at (770) 684-8774.)

John Wisdom's Ride Historic Sites

On a cool spring night in 1863, John Henry Wisdom – out of pure devotion to his mother and the populace of Rome, Georgia – dashed across country to warn them that "the Yankees are coming!" In the process, he earned for himself an honored spot in the history of the South and a footnote in the history of the U.S. Civil War.

Allow me to introduce you to a man not wholly unlike you and me – with two exceptions. He lived during the 1800s in Alabama, and during the U.S. Civil War he made the ride of his life in the middle of the night to warn Georgia residents of the invading Union troops. As a result of his efforts on this night, he is often referred to as the "**Paul Revere of the South.**"

John Henry has been described variously over the years since his famed ride, most often as an honest and hard-working man with a passion for helping anyone in need. This was probably never more evident than on the night of May 2, 1863.

At this time, Wisdom and his family lived in Gadsden, Alabama. He was a mail carrier in Gadsden, but also owned and operated a ferry on the Coosa River. On the afternoon of May 2, he was returning to Gadsden when he discovered to his immense surprise that his ferry had been destroyed.

As he was surveying the damage to his enterprise, three of his friends standing on the opposite side of the river yelled to him, describing the details of what had happened. It was bad enough that his livelihood had suddenly vanished, but when he learned that the destruction had happened at the hands of Yankee soldiers, John Henry could barely contain himself.

As they described the events which had occurred at the ferry that day, his friends told him that the soldiers were on their way to Rome, Georgia, with the mission of destroying the city there.

In the blink of an eye, John Henry realized that someone had to warn the citizens of Rome, so that they might have a chance to avoid at least a portion of the fate he had suffered. He also had another reason for rushing to Rome. His elderly mother lived there and he knew he had to secure her safety.

John Wisdom himself left a description of the events that unfolded that day. Here, in his own words, he details that exciting ride:

"The first lap of the ride was from the east bank of the river at Gadsden to Gnatville, 28 miles, which I drove in my buggy in a little more than two hours. Here, my horse became exhausted and I left him and the buggy with the **Widow Hanks,** who offered me a lame pony on the promise [that I] ride it only five miles to Goshen where I thought I could get another horse.

"On account of the pony's condition, I was obliged to leave him at Goshen, where I found Simpson Johnson coming in from his barn. He saddled two horses and let me ride one and sent his son with me on the other horse to bring both back [home].

"We rode the Johnson horses in a swift gallop eleven miles to the home of Rev. Joel Weems above Spring Garden, Alabama, where I was delayed some time, but finally managed to get a fresh horse.

"On the next lap I stopped several times, trying to get a new animal. At one place I woke up a farmer and told him what I wanted. He replied gruffly that he couldn't [have] any of his horses.

"I rode eleven miles farther to John Baker's, one mile south of Cave Spring. After a short delay, I mounted another horse [there] and asked [Mr. Baker] to keep for the owner the one I had discarded.

"I was now in Georgia, and Cave Spring loomed ahead, then I raced through **Vann's Valley.** While going down a long hill in a sweeping gallop, Mr. Baker's horse stumbled and fell, throwing me in an ungraceful sprawl ahead of him. I got up quickly, remounted and made off [again].

"After proceeding twelve miles to within six miles of Rome, I changed horses for the last time. A gentleman whose name I do not remember loaned me a horse and I lost little time entering the last lap. This horse carried me safely into Rome, where I arrived at four minutes before midnight, May 2, 1863. I thus made the ride of 67 miles in slightly less than eight and a half hours, including delays. Lost time amounted for about an hour and a half.

"On arriving in the city I galloped to the leading hotel, the **Etowah House** – then kept by Mr. G.S. Black – and told him the Yankees were coming. At his request, I rode through the streets, sounding the alarm and waking the people.

"Everybody jumped out of bed, and the excitement was great. The people ran in all directions, but under the command of their leader got down to business piling cotton bales in breastwork style on the Rome ends of the bridges.

"The horses I rode after I left my horse with the Widow Hanks were not trained saddle horses. Every one of them had a rough gait and each one was rougher than the former. I tell you my legs were peeled on the inside and when I got off my horse in Rome, I was so sore I could hardly move.

"After the alarm was given and that was only a mighty few minutes I can tell you, I went to my Mother's, who was living in Rome, and went to bed. If Col. Streight had come into the town then, he would have had a lively time getting me out of bed."

Today, the city of Rome has never forgotten the heroics of John Wisdom. Every October, the town's citizens celebrate the memory of his ride during **Rome's Heritage Holidays**.

Heritage Holidays consists of a week of events that commemorate not only Wisdom's ride, but the entire history of Rome as well. This includes tours of places such as **Myrtle Hill Cemetery**, **Fort Norton**, **Berry College** and **Martha Berry History Museum** to name just a few. Civil War reenactments, musical performances of the dulcimer and an antique car show are a sampling of happenings from past celebrations.

There is also a **Wagon Train Trail Ride** that commemorates John Wisdom's ride. It begins on a Friday with participants gathering at noon to set up camp to spend the night.

In years past, some riders have come from as far away as Texas to enjoy this event. The ride begins on Saturday morning, making a loop around the outskirts of Rome, and culminating with a parade downtown. The entire spectrum of pioneer trail riding is covered by this event, including riders on horseback, in covered wagons and in buggies.

A portion of this event celebrates Rome's successful resistance of the invading Yankees. One citizen describes it this way:

"In the North, they got this wonderful idea of having a raiding party come down and cut the famous **Western & Atlantic Railroad** between Atlanta and Chattanooga. Anybody who could cut that railroad could cut the guts out of the South.

"To do this, they got up a raiding party. They chose a man named **Col. Abel D. Streight** to command the raiding party.

"Streight, working his way across North Alabama, wanted to get to Rome, Georgia where he had heard they had a cannon factory. That was the **Noble Cannon Factory**. One might have thought this factory turned out millions of cannons a year, but it actually only produced some 56 before being destroyed by Union troops. Three of these cannons still exist today.

"Now Col. Streight had some 2,000 troops with him. He made a fateful decision of choosing mules to carry these men because they were sure-footed and hard-working. That's one of the things that slowed him down.

"They asked **Gen. Nathan Bedford Forrest** who came out of the Mississippi area to run a kind of harassment action on Streight as he made his way across country.

"As he approached Gadsden, Streight saw a bridge over what he thought was the Coosa River. So he goes over the bridge with all his men, and as soon as they got over the bridge, they burned it so nobody else could cross.

"When Nathan Bedford Forrest sees the burned bridge, he is perplexed as to a solution to the problem. At that time, there was a little farmhouse and a little girl there about 16 years old. She was standing outside the farmhouse.

"Gen. Forrest probably tipped his hat and said, 'Madam, do you know of a way that my men and horses can get across the river?'

"Who knows how the little girl actually responded, but she probably said something to the effect of 'Well sir, that ain't no river. That's Black Creek.'

"To which Forrest replied, 'Yes, but it looks deep.'

"'Naw, it ain't deep,' she replied. 'I can show you where the cattle are standing in it and it ain't up but to their ankles.'"

This little girl, later identified as **Emma Sansom**, pointed out the way across the creek, and Forrest and his men were able to quickly ford the substantial body of water and continue on to Rome.

"Meanwhile, John Wisdom has made it to Rome and warned the citizens. The town, knowing these 2,000 soldiers were coming, had to do something. All the grown men were already off fighting the war on other battlefields, so the Rome citizens had to come up with a crafty plan.

"They took stovepipes and cotton bales and put them in the streets and positioned the pipes in a way that made them resemble cannons. They gave the old men and boys sticks and broomsticks and they walked up and down the street in close-order drill, just like they were actually Confederate troops.

"In those days, very often, when two big figures met on the battlefield, they would sometimes talk to each other or send people out to talk prior to the battle. The conversation would go something like this:

"'We've got you surrounded. Surrender!'"

"'The hell with you! I'm ready to fight!'" the other would reply.

"Now I am told that Forrest actually only had two cannons with him on the day he met Streight's troops, and Streight's men certainly outnumbered his men. However, Forrest set himself up in a way that allowed him to cleverly deceive Streight.

"As the two sides par-

layed, Forrest would bring up one of his cannons, and each time his men asked 'Where you want me to put this artillery?' Forrest would reply 'We've got four cannons over there already. Just put it over here.'

"His men would then take the cannon away, supposedly to position it according to Forrest's instructions, but instead, they would actually just circle the same cannon around a hillside, bring it back up to Forrest and repeat the ruse all over again. They reportedly performed this device so many times that Streight's men thought they were pretty well surrounded by cannons that were preparing to cut them to pieces.

"Finally, in one of the most amazing feats of the war, Col. Abel D. Streight amazingly surrendered his 2,000 men to Gen. Forrest's 400 to 600 Confederates that day on the outskirts of Rome. For the South, it was one of the great moments of the war."

Today, if one retraces the route of John Wisdom, there are many historic sites along the way to see and enjoy, not to mention some beautiful countryside. You will have views of a number of beautiful Southern homes, some of which undoubtedly were in existence at the time John Wisdom made his historic ride.

In all fairness, I must tell you that this driving tour is a bit of a challenge. There are many twists and turns that take one into the backcountry of Alabama and Georgia, and onto the backroads of yesteryear. However, if you are up to the challenge, you'll know you are following a historic trail, and you'll enjoy plenty of history and scenic sites along the way.

(For more information on this or other incidents concerning U.S. Civil War historic sites in Rome, contact the Rome History Museum or the Floyd County Chamber of Commerce.)

Rome

Gadsden:

From Georgia enter Gadsden from U.S. Highway 411 and turn right onto Walnut Street (near the three bridges). Continue to the second traffic light and turn right onto 2nd Street. Once again, continue to the second traffic light and turn right onto Broad Street. There will be parking available for one block. In front of the Memorial Bridge *(Wisdom's ferry landing and ferryboat were once located in this vicinity)* stands the memorial to heroine **Emma Sansom**. Across the road to the right is a historical marker dedicated to **John Wisdom**. (If you have time, you might wish to ride on the *"Alabama Princess,"* a popular riverboat attraction in Gadsden.)

Hoke's Bluff:

From Broad Street continue across Memorial Bridge and go 0.4 of a mile to the first traffic light. Turn left onto N. Hood Avenue and continue 0.1 of a mile. Turn right onto Elmwood Avenue and go 0.8 of a mile. Turn left onto Hoke Street and go 0.8 of a mile. Turn right onto Megahan Boulevard and continue 0.2 of a mile to the traffic light. Turn left onto Highway 278 E and go 6.3 miles. Turn left onto Alford Bend Road. Continue 0.5 of a mile and Hoke's Bluff City Hall will be on the right. *(Just below the building in the parking lot is a historical marker dedicated to John Wisdom. It was donated by the city of Rome, Georgia.)*

From the parking lot, continue on Alford Bend Road for 0.4 of a mile to the flashing traffic light. Turn left onto Main Street and go 0.3 of a mile. *(John Wisdom's former home – at which he lived at the time of his death – is the second house on the right after you pass Appalachin' Road. It is a brown brick home with red shutters.)*

Retracing John Wisdom's Historic Ride

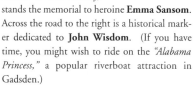

Continue on Main Street for 0.2 of a mile to Ferry Road which forks off to the right. Bearing to the left, continue on this road for 0.3 of a mile. *(This vicinity was once the location of the ferry that carried John Wisdom to Hoke's Bluff.)*

Backtrack to Main Street. Turn right onto Main Street and continue 0.1 of a mile to the cemetery where John Wisdom is buried. Just beyond the church turn right into the cemetery and continue 0.1 of a mile to the rear portion of the cemetery. There, on the left, will be a marker located in front of John Wisdom's grave. *(Wisdom lived in Gadsden at the time of his famed ride. He later moved to Hoke's Bluff.)*

Gnatville:

(John Wisdom borrowed a lame pony from the Widow Nancy Hanks in Gnatville.) From the cemetery in Hoke's Bluff turn left back onto Main Street. Backtrack on Main Street for 1.4 miles crossing Alford Bend Road. Turn right onto Rocky Ford Road and travel 9.3 miles. Turn right onto County Road 19 and continue 2.3 miles. Turn left onto County Road 6 and continue 4.2 miles. (County Road 6 is in the Gnatville area.) Turn left continuing on County Road 6 for 1.4 miles.

Goshen:

From County Road 6 turn right onto County Road 31 and continue for one mile. Turn left onto County Road 2 and continue for 0.2 of a mile. Turn left onto Alabama Highway 9 and continue 0.7 of a mile to County Road 8 and you will be in the Goshen area. *(It was sundown when John Wisdom reached Goshen. Here, he borrowed a horse from Simpson Johnson.)*

Spring Garden:

Turn right onto County Road 8 (You will cross County Road 33) and continue 3.5 miles. Bear right onto County Road 27 and continue

0.4 of a mile. Turn left onto County Road 29. You are now in the Spring Garden vicinity. *(Wisdom, accompanied by Simpson Johnson, stopped at Rev. Joel Weems house at Spring Garden. He ate a quick supper with the reverend before borrowing a horse from him and continuing on his journey.)*

Rock Run Village:

Continue on County Road 29 for 5.5 miles. A white house will be visible on the right which, at the time of this writing, was being renovated. This house was built circa 1830 and was owned by the superintendent of Rock Run Iron Works. You will want to stop and look around in the old store at this site which once housed the Rock Run Commissary. You might possibly find a hidden treasure inside, just as did I. *(This site was not a stop on Wisdom's ride, but these buildings were in existence as he passed by.)*

Cave Spring:

Continue on County Road 29 for an additional 5.3 miles. Turn right onto U.S. Highway 411 and travel 7.4 miles. The Lake House will be on the left. *(The Lake house was built circa 1840. The property on which it stands, and the smaller house to its rear, once belonged to Cherokee David Vann. The property was won by Mr. Lake in one of the Cherokee Land Lotteries.)*

Continue 0.4 of a mile to Cave Spring where Wisdom borrowed a horse from John Baker. You will want to take the time to browse the shops and enjoy lunch at one of the cozy restaurants in this unique little town. In the park just beyond the town square is the famous cave and its abundant spring water from which the town derived its name.

Six Mile:

At the traffic light in Cave Spring, turn left onto U.S. Highway 411 and continue 9.7 miles to Six Mile. *(This community is where John Wisdom borrowed his last horse from Mr. Jones and then rode to Rome.)*

Rome:

Turn left onto Highway 27 and continue 1.3 miles. Turn left onto Walker Mountain Road and immediately turn right onto Cave Spring Road. Continue for 2.1 miles. Turn left onto Park Road and continue for 0.6 of a mile. Turn right onto Black's Bluff Road and continue 1.7 miles. Bear right at the intersection and then turn left onto South Broad Street. Continue for 0.5 of a mile. *(At this point you will see Myrtle Hill Cemetery on the left where many Confederate soldiers are buried. Also on the left on the corner is a statue of Col. Nathan Bedford Forrest and a historical marker dedicated to John Wisdom.)*

Continuing on South Broad, turn right at the traffic light and cross over Broad Street Bridge. This was a covered bridge when John Wisdom made his ride. You are now on Broad Street. *(The Etowah House, John Wisdom's first stop, was once located in the first block to the right, at the approximate spot at which Rome Cleaners is located today.)*

Turn right at the corner of Broad Street and Second Avenue. *(Just beyond the second traffic light, John Wisdom's mother's home once stood on the left at the corner of Second Avenue and 3rd Street. The First Christian Church is now located at this spot.)*

For additional historic details involving the John Wisdom ride and the defense of Rome, Georgia during the U.S. Civil War, be sure to visit the **Rome Area History Museum** on Broad Street in downtown Rome. *(The silver service that was presented to John Wisdom by the City of Rome is displayed at the museum.)*

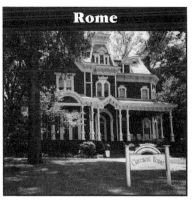

This old-moneyed family's former home in Rome, Georgia, is a unique bed-and-breakfast getaway today, offering more than one intriguing mystery for its guests.

Many times, historic old homes have unsolved mysteries and points of intrigue. For the historic Claremont House, on Second Avenue in East Rome, one such mystery is a huge antique safe built stoutly into the old home's stairwell.

The Claremont House Bed & Breakfast Inn

The Claremont House was built in 1882 by **Colonel Hamilton Yancey**, an attorney and secretary for the Rome Insurance Company. The home became a bed-and-breakfast inn in 1993.

The old safe, which frequently prompts inquiries from guests, is handsomely framed with walnut molding, trimmed with ornate metal detail, and heavily hinged. The old-fashioned lettering on the front of the safe proclaiming "*Macneale & Urban. Cin.,*" is still distinct, as is the word "*Patent*" just below the lock. The door to the safe has handsome artwork upon it, though it is defaced in some spots.

Local accounts maintain Colonel Yancey frequently entertained guests overnight, and offered them the use of the safe's compartments for their valuables – a situation which leads one to wonder what type of guests he entertained. Other explanations maintain that the Colonel kept large reserves of cash hidden away because he did not trust banks.

Whatever the circumstances, the mystery of the huge strongbox has never been solved. In fact, when the house became a B&B, the safe was discovered locked, requiring a locksmith to reveal its hidden contents.

It must have been difficult for the new owners to control their anticipation at what might be found in the vault. After all, it is not uncommon today to find any manner of valuable memorabilia in old antebellum homes, and the Claremont was built only seventeen years following the war.

The owners, however, undoubtedly were disappointed as the locksmith opened the safe. Inside were empty small front compartments. Behind these compartments were two large ones marked separately with Hamilton and Florence Yancey's initials. The only "treasure" found was a drawer of fancy antique keys which were unlabeled.

Another curiosity in the old home is an antique urinal in the downstairs bathroom. According to reports, Colonel Yancey had it installed for himself, and for the use of his male friends. The Yanceys apparently had quite a bit of money to spare. The urinal is made of solid silver, and fits discreetly into the wall.

While pondering the curiosities of the lives of the Claremont's first owners, there are many modern-day trappings to enjoy at the inn. Even with its good state of preservation, the Claremont required over $100,000 in renovations to ready it for service in the innkeeping profession. An internal stairwell, sprinkler system, fire escape, and all new plumbing were added.

Take a trip to the Claremont House and enjoy the good life.

(Breakfast hours at the Claremont are from 6:00 to 9:00 a.m. Visitors may choose from a full breakfast menu seven days a week. Advance notice is required for reservations and there is a 72-hour cancellation polity. Smoking is not allowed in the facility. VISA and MasterCard are accepted. Check-in time is 3:00 p.m. For reservations, call 800-254-4797 or 706-291-0900, or email them at claremonthouse@comcast.net.)

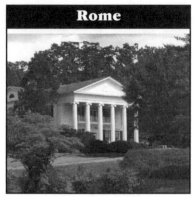

Oak Hill Mansion and Martha Berry Museum

Spread over 30,000 acres, and richly landscaped with fields, forests, mountains, lakes and streams; dotted with buildings that vary in architecture from picturesque Early American log cabins to elegant Gothic-style stone structures (built at an amazing cost), the thriving educational complex at Mount Berry, Georgia, is one of the largest and most beautiful campuses in the world today. It also is a lasting testament to the indomitable will of a woman who insisted on making education possible for the poor mountain children in Georgia's Floyd County at the turn-of-the-century.

Martha Berry was a woman whose life story is the stuff of which motion picture screen writers dream. The "gate of opportunity" that she opened for thousands of boys and girls in the mountains of her native Georgia, originally provided education at a time when it was almost nonexistent for the lower class in that area. And today, **Berry College** and Academy offer an opportunity for thousands more from around the world to enter and prepare for the better life that an outstanding education provides.

Ms. Berry's dream began in her early childhood. Born into Southern plantation wealth near present-day Rome, Georgia, half-way between Atlanta and Chattanooga, Martha's early years were blessed with a governess who provided the youngster with an excellent education. Her domestic life included shining carriages of ornamented woods and glass, servants, and other aspects of the aristocratic lifestyle which dominated the era of her youth. Life at **Oak Hill**, the Berrys' magnificent mansion – with its giant oak trees, formal gardens, and acres of well-groomed lawns – was Southern living at its best.

Martha's venture into education began in earnest at the turn of the century in a log cabin on the grounds of her magnificent home. Her first class consisted of three mountain boys as students. The first lesson she taught was the story of Jonah, and the fish from the *Bible*. It held the boys spell-bound and left them eager to learn more.

The thirst for knowledge from the poor children was greater than even Martha had imagined. She selected an elevated site on her land, bought materials with the $1,000.00 her father had left her in an inheritance, solicited laborers from among the mountain boys to do the work, and began construction on the first school building for the children. The "boys' school" was founded in 1902, on the principle of "educating not only the head, but the hands and heart as well."

As the school grew, more money was needed. The highlanders, all 800 families, gave as much as they could. Their quarters, fifty-cent pieces and dollar bills represented immense sacrifices, and Miss Berry's heart was touched with each one she received. Yet, far more was needed. She explained to "her boys," "I'm going out to get money, so we can continue the school here. Behave while I'm gone, and pray for me."

Her travels led from Rome, Georgia, to Atlanta, to Washington, to Philadelphia, to Baltimore and Hartford, to New York, Chicago, and St. Louis. She crisscrossed half of the United States repeatedly on behalf of Berry School. One person of wealth and concern would refer her to another and more often than not, she was well-received.

Eventually, the governor of Georgia arranged for Martha to meet **Andrew Carnegie**, the great steel production magnate, on one of his visits to Atlanta. Martha's visit with Mr. Carnegie in Atlanta was extremely brief, and she did not have enough time to fully explain her program to him. Never missing a beat, however, she boarded the train (still wearing her party dress) with Carnegie as he was leaving, in order to have more time to describe her school and to seek his support.

Later, a famous magazine editor called the school to the attention of **President Theodore Roosevelt**. So impressed was the President, that he made Martha guest of honor at a White House party where she presented her plan to the distinguished guests and received numerous gifts in return.

Gradually, more buildings were built – a girl's school – and much more. Enrollments grew, bringing with them higher operating costs, and there seemed to be no end to the needs of the endeavor. The task was far from easy.

It was in the early 1920s (on one of her trips to New York) that she met and became a close friend of **Mrs. Thomas Edison**. Through Mrs. Edison, she met **Mrs. Henry Ford**, who was so fascinated by Martha's stories of the Berry schools, that she persuaded her husband to visit them.

Henry Ford, the wealthiest and most famous personage of his day, was not best known for charitable donations. The theme of this school, however, ironically matched so closely his own philosophy, "unity of mind and hands," that it struck a chord in his heart.

Over the next few years, the Fords spent millions adorning the Berry campus with buildings more magnificent than Martha had dared hope for. When they asked Miss Berry just what she would like to have them build, she confessed that for years, she had envisioned a "quadrangle of buildings on the girl's campus – a series of tall stone structures reflecting in an oblong blue pool in the center, and surrounded by a richly landscaped area of trees and shrubs."

In response to this desire, Ford sent the country's foremost architect to see the job through. Built of native Georgia stone, these buildings have been called the nation's best examples of English collegiate Gothic architecture, and their reflections in the blue waters of the pool at the center of the quadrangle add an indefinable beauty to their already picturesque setting.

The 30,000 acres of fields and forests, interspersed with lakes, streams, and trails, offer choice sites for hiking, canoeing, fishing, bicycling and picnicking on the mountainsides, or in the valleys below.

Whatever the season, the beauty of Berry is indescribable, and its environment for living and learning is unsurpassed anywhere.

Martha Berry's heavy travel schedule kept her busy from early morning until late at night, and her exposure to severe weather, and constant stress, eventually took a toll on her health. When asked "What will become of the school when you are gone?," Martha Berry is said to have replied: "My 'children and grandchildren' will carry it on." Her statement proved prophetic. Her end came in February, 1942, and, as she had requested, she was buried under a large tree on the south side of Berry Chapel.

Martha's years of service did not stop with her death. Her spirit, courage and determination live on among her 'heirs' as Berry College continues to grow and prosper under their direction.

At Berry College and Berry Academy today, beauty is not just something to behold, it is a way of life – a way introduced by a beautiful young girl who dreamed of helping others. The legacy of Martha Berry lives on and on.

(Martha Berry Museum is open from 10:00 a.m. to 5:00 p.m., Monday thru Saturday. Admission is $5 for adults, $2.00 for children. A guided tour of the 1847 mansion at Oak Hill is included in the cost, as are walking tours of the carriage house, formal gardens and more. Directions: From Interstate 75, exit onto U.S. 411/20 to Rome. In Rome, take U.S. 27 North (Martha Berry Highway). The entrance is at the corner of U.S. 27 and Loop #1. For more information, telephone 706-291-1883.)

It has witnessed the comings and goings of every U.S. President to date, not to mention an array of other historic events down through the years. This log home – once occupied by a very important chief of the **Cherokee Nation** in what today is Georgia – offers mute testimony to the former existence of Native Americans in our state.

The imposing and yet simple structure sits far from the modern busy thoroughfare, stark in its plainness, and out-of-touch with the twenty-first century. In earlier days, it served as a mountain home, a pioneer trading post, a school, a post office an Indian council meeting house, and as the headquarters for a Union Army general.

It came into existence sometime around 1797. Scottish trader **John McDonald**, a Tory agent living among the **Chickamaugas**, and his half-Cherokee wife, **Anna Shorey**, were its first owners. The land that birthed it belonged to the Cherokee Nation near the presentday Tennessee and Georgia state lines at Poplar Springs on what then was the **Cherokee War Path**.

It was built as a two-story log house with plank floors and rock chimneys. Even today, the entire structure is still held together with nothing more than wooden pegs.

In 1785, a young man was on board a boat from Baltimore taking merchandise to be traded for furs in Tennessee. He was captured by Chickamauga Indians, and quite likely would have been executed had not John McDonald intervened. McDonald reportedly influenced the Chickamaugas to spare the life of **Daniel Ross**, a fellow Scotsman.

In time, Ross and McDonald became partners in the operation of the trading post at **Ross's Landing** (later Rossville). The relationship grew, and Ross later married McDonald's daughter, Mollie.

The Historic John Ross House

The namesake of the historic old home – **John Ross** – was born to Daniel and Mollie on October 3, 1790 in Turkeytown, Alabama, where young John lived until the death of his mother in 1803. At that time, John and his brother Lewis went to live with their grandparents – the McDonalds.

It was during this time-period that the old home became the first school in the northwest Georgia area. John and Lewis were joined by other Cherokee children for instruction in the home.

Following the **War of 1812**, John Ross was married to **Elizabeth Brown Henley**. He brought his new bride to the Poplar Springs house and it wouldn't be too much longer before the community then known as Poplar Springs was to become known as "Rossville."

By 1816, Ross had already made a name for himself. **Colonel Return J. Meigs** had selected him to visit the Cherokee settlement in the west for a report on their welfare. He had also been an outstanding soldier in the **Battle of Horseshoe Bend** under the command of **General Andrew Jackson** – a loyalty Ross no doubt would come to regret later in life.

Ross was one of six Cherokee delegates chosen to visit with **President James Madison** to discuss the Cherokee treaty rights. He was also chairman of the "Committee of Thirteen" who replied to the national request that the Cherokees be forced to leave their lands.

In 1817, Ross was appointed postmaster and mail was delivered to the Poplar Springs house by the Nashville-Augusta stagecoach every two weeks.

In 1824, all rights to the house were turned over to Ross. John then added a twenty-three-foot-long council chamber for meetings of the Cherokees. He served as a senator to the **National Council of the Cherokee Nation** and as president of the senate until 1826.

When John Ross became "**Chief**" **John Ross**, he moved to present-day Rome, Georgia, called "**DeSoto**" at that time. He sold his Rossville house to a relative in 1826. The family of **Thomas Gordon McFarland** subsequently owned the property for over 100 years.

In 1863, long after the terrible and unjust "**Trail Of Tears**" which removed Ross and his family to the west, the old log home at Rossville was still one of the sturdiest and most-admired homes in northwest Georgia. **Major-General Granger** who served under the command of **General William T. Sherman** chose the old home as his headquarters building during the **War Between The States** and **Sherman's** "**March To The Sea.**"

The Union troops were feeling arrogant and invulnerable after the fall of nearby Chattanooga, Tennessee. Little did they know that **General Braxton Bragg** had retreated to LaFayette, Georgia, waiting for **General Longstreet** to arrive from Virginia with 20,000 soldiers.

While both sides waited and nursed their wounds, the Union soldiers headquartered at the Ross house experienced an unusual incident. Their leader, General Granger, was a stern disciplinarian, and was about to demonstrate that to his men.

The troops of the Second Methodist Regiment under the command of **Colonel Jesse H. Moore** had arrived at Rossville ahead of the food wagons, and the men were hungry for food. Rumors had spread that since they were in the Deep South now, unrestrained foraging for food would be permitted. The soldiers took large quantities of fresh beef, veal, pork and poultry, potatoes and honey. Some of the men – dubbed "the Cattle Brigade" – reportedly killed so much cattle that the ruckus sounded like an actual battle.

When he learned of these actions, General Granger became furious. He had his cavalry-men round up over one hundred of the group. He ordered his cavalrymen to dump the foraged foods near the spring in front of the Ross house and to tie the offenders to the fences and trees around the spring. He planned to have them publicly flogged with "black snake" whips.

This scenario, however, didn't set well with Methodist volunteers – many of whom reportedly were ministers – nor with their leader, **Major General Steedman**. When the news spread of their punishment, thousands of sympathetic Union soldiers gathered around the house and spring.

Granger apparently lost his nerve at this point, and, fearing the worst, turned the discipline over to General Steedman who subsequently released the bound soldiers, gave them a slap on the wrist, and a gentle reprimand. Widespread vandalism, destruction, and foraging were commonplace thereafter.

It wasn't long before one of the great battles of the Civil War was fought within ear shot of the house. On the nineteenth of September, the Union and Confederate forces clashed at **Chickamauga**, one of the bloodiest battles of the war.

In 1963, almost a hundred years after the battle, a group of citizens began work on the restoration of the Ross house. They moved it a few hundred feet to a quieter location, collected funds for the patching of its weak spots, and formed the **John Ross Association**.

Today, the John Ross house exists proudly – a testament to the former existence of the Cherokees in northwest Georgia. The site has been designated as a **National Historic Landmark**, receiving a stream of visitors annually.

(For more info on the John Ross House, contact the Walker County Chamber of Commerce at 706-375-7702.)

Spring Place

The Vann House

It was built at the beginning of the 19th century, making it approximately 200 years of age today. It was the site of brutal whippings, beautiful gardens, and a blazing gun-battle. If you're looking for a good way to spend a few hours on a lazy weekend, visit the **Vann House State Historic Site** at the little cross-roads hamlet of **Spring Place**. You can learn the remarkable story of the Vann family.

The federal-style Vann House was built by an individual named Vogt in 1805 for **James Vann II**. Chief Vann wielded considerable influence among the Cherokees of his era, but was somewhat of an enigma to all who knew him. When sober, he was described as friendly, reliable, even-tempered and eminently fair. When intoxicated, however, he was wild and vengeful, often carrying out brutal whippings and other punishments on the grounds of his home. He therefore cultivated his share of enemies.

James Vann II did not live to enjoy his fine home very long. While traveling on the Federal Road in 1809, he was assassinated at a tavern (either **Blackburn's Public House** or **Buffington's Tavern**; historians continue to debate the point) on the old Federal Road somewhere near the present-day Forsyth County – Cherokee County line.

Following James Vann II's death in 1809, his large home was inherited by his son, Joseph Vann, later known as **"Rich Joe" Vann**. It was Joseph who lavished time and money upon the house and grounds to bring it to its ultimate beauty and value. The plantation, comprising hundreds of acres, was worked by scores of slaves, and was an exceedingly prosperous endeavor. It was because of this lucrative property and impressive home that scoundrels and other dregs of society were lured to the scene to wrest it from Vann ownership during the destabilized times of the Cherokee Nation in the early 1830s.

When substantial deposits of gold were discovered in north Georgia in 1828, the region was deluged with white settlers. The state of Georgia coveted the region which was owned at that time by the Cherokees.

In 1834, legislation was enacted by which the property of any Indian could be seized if the Indian was found to be employing a white man. Joseph Vann, unknowledgeable of the law, had employed a white overseer, and as such, was served with an eviction notice. Just that quickly, the home and property which had fostered the Vann family honestly for generations, was taken from the family forever.

The Georgia General Assembly continued the passage of discriminatory legislation against the Indians, going so far as to authorize the creation of a special unit called the "Georgia Guard." Composed loosely of disreputable individuals who "patrolled" Cherokee lands meting out punishments for real or imagined offenses, this group committed numerous outrageous acts.

An account of the incident in which Joseph Vann and his family were dispossessed of their home and possessions at Spring Place was printed in the April 7, 1835 issue of the *Georgia Journal*, published in Milledgeville, which was the capital of Georgia at that time.

According to the article, on March 2, 1835, the captain of the Georgia Guard, **W.N. Bishop**, traveled with his rag-tag group to Spring Place, to seize – per the recently enacted law – Joseph Vann's home and property. Bishop wanted the property to pass into the hands of his brother, **Absalom Bishop**, and had no intention of allowing anything to stop him.

Upon reaching the Vann house, Captain Bishop and the Georgia Guard discovered they would first need to dispose of a boarder at the home – a man named **Spencer Riley** – before they could effect the Vann dispossession. Riley was a learned man, and was determined to gain possession of the Vann home for himself. He requested to see the legal papers for the dispossession of the Vann family.

Bishop shortly became outraged with Riley's legal maneuvering and quite literally ordered his men to kill Riley, who then dashed up to his second floor room where he retrieved a brace of pistols. A full-fledged gunfight quickly ensued, with Bishop and his Georgia Guards locked in mortal combat with Riley.

According to Riley's later testimony, he was wounded in the hand, arms and face and one of his weapons was smashed by a bullet from one of Bishop's men's firearms. Bleeding profusely, Riley proved to be a determined opponent, continuing to resist the Guardsmen.

According to the April, 1835 *Georgia Journal* article, all during the exchange, Bishop repeatedly shouted *"Kill the damned rascal!* (referring to Riley). *We've got no use for nullifiers in this country!"*

Badly wounded, Riley eventually retreated back to his room, leaving one of his pistols partially hidden on the stairs and pointed toward his attackers to keep them at bay. He reportedly laid down upon his bed to await his fate.

Meanwhile, Bishop, impatient with the delay, threw a smoldering log onto the stair landing in an attempt to smoke Riley out. After the log set fire to the landing, however, Bishop decided he might have acted a little hastily, and began trying to decide how to extinguish the flames without getting shot by Riley. He ultimately sent Joseph Vann to put out the fire.

It was shortly after this point that a sheriff arrived on the scene, ironically with arrest papers for Spencer Riley. By this time, Mr. Riley apparently was glad to surrender with his life intact, and was taken away to jail.

In the midst of all the gunfire, Joseph Vann and his family had huddled in the cellar of their home. They quite shortly were forced to abandon their plantation and all their wealth, retiring to a cabin with a dirt floor a number of miles away in Tennessee.

Captain Bishop ultimately transferred ownership of the impressive Vann mansion to his brother, Absalom, and seized the Moravian Mission building at the plantation for himself.

Much of the controversial and illegal actions were based purely upon greed. It was greed for money, power and personal property such as the Vann house.

Despite his losses and the unpardonable offenses committed against him, Joseph Vann, just as had his entrepreneurial father, proved to be a resourceful and determined individual. After a period of time, he established a thoroughbred farm where he raised the famous racehorse, **"Lucy Walker."** Between betting upon his horse, and capitalizing on a successful shipping business, he was able to amass yet another substantial fortune.

Meanwhile, back in Georgia, following the removal of the Cherokees in 1838, the Vann house experienced a tumultuous existence, with a total of 18 owners over the 117 years prior to the time the structure was turned over to the Georgia Historical Commission in 1954. One of the owners even turned out to be the indomitable Spencer Riley, who owned the home from 1838 to 1840, somehow wresting ownership from the Bishop brothers.

During many of the following years, the structure was inhabited by tenants who had little or no regard for general maintenance. The outbuildings all fell into disrepair and gradually disappeared; the fences rotted away and general neglect set in.

In 1920, the historic old home was purchased by a Dr. J.E. Bradford. He proved to be the longest owner of the property, retaining it until his dream of its preservation by the Georgia Historical Commission became a reality in 1952.

Prior to its purchase by the Commission, the home had suffered substantially. Impetus for preservation was provided in 1948, when **Will Rogers, Jr.** wrote to the president of the **Whitfield-Murray Co. Historical Society** explaining his family was descended from the Vanns of Spring Place, and expressing an interest in the old home. Rogers' father – the famous humorist – was part Cherokee. The humorist's great-grandfather was Clement Vann Rogers.

Local citizens, with the help of Rogers, eventually raised the $5,000 necessary to purchase the by-then all but ruined mansion and three acres of land still left in the tract. The property was then deeded to the state of Georgia.

Due to its strategic situation on the old Federal Road, the home was visited by many prominent individuals of early American history, including U.S. **President James Monroe**.

The Georgia Historical Commission (predecessor to today's Georgia Department of Natural Resources) spent some $80,000 renovating the site which is open for public tours today.

(The Chief Vann House near present-day Chatsworth, Georgia, is administered by the Georgia Department of Natural Resources, Parks and Historic Sites Division. The site is open Tuesday through Saturday, 9:00 a.m. to 5:00 p.m. and Sundays from 2:00 to 5:30 p.m. A small admission fee is charged. For more information, call 706-695-2598.)

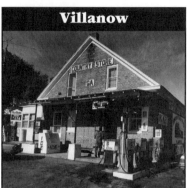

The immense, old structure known historically as **Villanow General Store** still dominates the intersection of two ancient byways (today's Highways 136 and 201) in northwest Georgia's Walker County, just as it has since the days of the pioneers. It has endured the ravages of "Mother Nature" for well over a century, and is one of the oldest free-standing country stores in Georgia.

Old Villanow General Store

From a historic perspective, the three-story brick building is literally bursting at the seams with memories of an era when life was simpler and less hurried. The shelves and bins here contain almost anything a shopper (or collector) could want in the way of necessities for a rural lifestyle. Stuffed deer heads hover above PVC pipe and hardware in round metal bins. From the ceiling hang overalls, hunting gear and hip boots. Newspapers from Walker County and Dalton are stacked neatly near rows of Vienna sausage, gas cans and cartons of worms.

Old glass collectors' bottles, donated by area residents, line the top shelf on one wall of the store. A wheat cradle hangs near a depression mop made of corn shucks.

Martin and Sharon Vess, owners of the historic structure and proprietors of the business located there today, protect the fruits of their labor in the heavy safe brought in by a former owner more than 100 years ago.

An original wall phone still hangs above the old soft drink cooler filled with frosty glass-bottled Cokes. The original roll-up fireplace mantle now serves as a shelf for aspirin and other over-the-counter remedies. A full-size cooler dating to 1928 keeps tobacco fresh. A double-tree yoke with a collar hangs in the couple's third-story bedroom - an area from which coffins were sold in days of yesteryear.

No one knows for certain how early the old store was constructed. **Rodney Edwards** - who owned the building prior to **Martin** and **Sharon Vess** - once suspected the construction date was 1847, but during some research (the store has been listed on the **National Register of Historic Places**), he discovered that a postmaster and blacksmith named **Roland Kinsey** ran a postal route from the site from 1840-1843. The

structure officially became a post office in 1844, so the building apparently was standing a number of years prior to 1847. Since the Cherokee Indians still resided in the woodlands of northwest Georgia as late as 1838, the age of this building quickly becomes obvious.

Parts of the store's shelves, as evidenced by square nails, a wooden money drawer and mail cubbyholes, date back to this time. One of the many interesting items passed down to Martin and Sharon Vess when they purchased the store was its original key, confirmed by an archaeologist to be the type used by post offices in the mid-1800s.

The bricks of the building were hand-made by slaves using clay from East Armuchee Creek (behind the store). The lumber came from trees razed from the original owner's property.

Nails and iron spikes were imbedded into the shutters as an early protective device (whether against Indians or Civil War-era marauders is unknown). In the basement, a hand-dug well provided a safe source of fresh water during times of attack, making the site a well-fortified outpost.

Records indicate that during the **Civil War**, a man named **Micajah Pope** owned a general store at Villanow. It is unknown, however, whether or not his store and Villanow General Store are one and the same. According to records, Pope also owned a cotton gin, and it is a matter of record that a gin once existed to the rear of Villanow General Store.

Little is known of the early years of the store before **Joseph Cavender** purchased it in 1868 or early 1869. Cavender, a very prosperous entrepreneur who owned several businesses in nearby Chattanooga and Whitfield County, kept the store till his death in 1919.

(Villanow General Store is open from 6 a.m. to 7 p.m. Monday - Saturday. To reach the store, take Interstate 75 north toward Chattanooga. Take the Lafayette Exit (Highway 136). Follow 136 westward for seven miles until it dead-ends. Turn right (still GA 136). Continue for 7 miles until you reach the store. For more information, call 706-397-2298.)

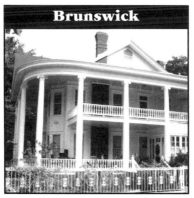

Old Town Brunswick

The city of Brunswick on the Georgia coast is in a state of being re-discovered today, not only by its residents, but by other Georgians and travelers at large. The seaport town includes a popular historic district, as well as residential streets lined with one Victorian home after another. As a result, much of the community is a real estate mecca today, and a flourishing market for real estate sales.

Anchoring this captivating community is Brunswick's historic district, known today as "**Old Town**," which was placed on the **National Register of Historic Places** more than 20 years ago. It exists roughly in a long rectangular shape along Bay Street to H Street behind the courthouse, over to Martin Luther King Boulevard and then down to Fourth Avenue and back to the waterfront. It includes the shops and businesses in downtown Brunswick as well as street after street of historic homes.

"Brunswick has long been recognized as [the community with] the second-highest number of documented historical structures in the state," says Bryan Thompson, director of the Downtown Development Authority. "Only Savannah can rival Brunswick in its number of historic buildings."

Today, one can't help but notice that the city seems to be awakening from a long sleep. A beautifully-restored home might sit next to one that has seen better days, or next to one with ladders and paint buckets leaning against the wall signaling its current renovation.

Old Town is undergoing a quiet revitalization as well, spurred on by the combined efforts of both the city government and the residents. Their goal is to preserve and save this historic district for future generations.

Brunswick's roots reach back to 1771, to the earliest settlers of Georgia. The city still retains structures and streets from the town's original plan. The town was laid out in a style similar to that of Savannah, with a grid pattern and public squares.

To be certain, Brunswick has had its ups and downs over the years. For unknown reasons, it has been slow to develop over the years despite the fact that it became the county seat in 1797 (wresting the designation from nearby St. Simons Island) and has long been a popular port city.

This slow development, however, has had a hidden silver lining. Many of the historic store buildings and homes that might have been demolished have persevered over the years. It is for this reason that Brunswick has many historic structures today where progressive cities such as Atlanta have very few in comparison.

During both the Revolutionary War and the War Between The States, Brunswick was abandoned, and a number of its historic buildings were destroyed by pillagers and neglect. The area also suffered through two yellow fever epidemics and several hurricanes. It somehow even managed to survive the devastating tidal flood of 1898 which swept the Georgia coast.

Despite these setbacks, Brunswick went on to become a major sea port, and by 1888, it boasted a population in excess of 10,000 residents. It was during this time that many of the elegant homes in the town were constructed.

The unique streets and open squares of the historic district reflect the city's English heritage. Many of the street names honor the popular military and political heroes of yesteryear, as well as the royal family. Today, one can still drive down Prince, Gloucester, London, Mansfield, Norwich and Dartmouth streets, and view squares bearing such names as Hanover, Wright, and Halifax. Even the town itself was named after King George II's ancestral home, "Braunsweig."

The homes of Old Town Brunswick were built around the squares by successful railroad employees, presidents of companies, sea captains, and even wealthier individuals. Today, there are at least 722 historical structures to explore within the confines of Old Town.

In order that visitors might appreciate the historic district even more, a booklet called *Driving Tour Of Old Town Brunswick*, Georgia, has been created by the **Old Town Brunswick Preservation Association**, and is sold in many of the downtown shops. It provides directions to, as well as the history of, some 42 structures in the district.

Bob Ciucevich of Quatrefoil Consultants, a historic preservation consulting firm in Savannah, is currently conducting a survey of the structures in Old Town. His research has revealed that houses of all styles are represented in the locale, even styles that were not popular in the South during the late 19th and early 20th centuries. He explains this diversity occurred because Brunswick was a port city, and as such, attracted seafarers and travelers from the North who constructed the type of homes with which they were familiar.

"The stick style of architecture was mainly used in the Northeast," Ciucevich says. "Brunswick is unique in the fact the city has so many houses built in this style."

The **Debellis House**, built in 1867 and located on First Avenue, is a good example of this type of home. "Stick houses" usually have gabled roofs with decorative trusses and overhanging eaves.

Although his home no longer stands today, famed Revolutionary War figure **Benjamin Hart** once owned a home on First Avenue. His wife, **Nancy**, who probably is more famous even than he, lived in this home. Though she was cross-eyed, the red-headed heroine is known to have single-handedly captured a group of Tories during the war.

One of the prettiest avenues in Old Town is Union Street. Here, one can visit the **Lissner House** which is owned by the Old Town Brunswick Preservation Association.

The offices of the Downtown Development Authority are currently located in this historic home, but plans call for the structure to be completely renovated in the near future and opened to the public as a museum.

The Lissner House is built in the Prairie style of architecture and roofed with the famed Ludowici tiles. This red clay tile was manufactured in the nearby town of Ludowici, Georgia, during the early portion of the 20th century and quickly became popular among architects all over the United States.

A few blocks away from the Lissner House is a Greek Revival structure built in 1902. The **Hafner House** may look familiar if one frequents the movies. It was used in the 1973 motion picture *Conrack*, based upon the popular novel of the same name by author **Pat Conroy**. The movie starred **Jon Voight**. Located inside the Lissner House is a carved walnut bed used by **Winnie Davis**, daughter of **Confederate President Jefferson Davis**.

Two streets over on Egmont is another house which was also used in the movie *Conrack*. L.T. McKinnon, a lumber magnate, constructed this elaborate Queen Anne-style home using native cypress wood. The interior woodwork is of ash and magnolia. Today, it is one of several bed-and-breakfast inns in the district.

One of the oldest homes still standing in Brunswick was constructed on Union Street by **Henry Riffault duBignon**, whose family once owned **Jekyll**. DuBignon built the house for his bride in 1869, but unfortunately died within a few years of completing it.

The duBignon house has a mansard roof and decorative brackets at the cornice which was a very popular architectural style during the 1800s. Mansard roofs were first constructed in France where taxes were levied upon each floor contained in a home. The roofline allowed one to use the attic as a room and not be taxed for a third level.

Another member of the duBignon family – **John duBignon** – built a Queen Anne nearby that is dominated by a wraparound porch. This house has an interesting array of shapes and turrets. Its most unusual aspect is the fact that it has a full basement. Since Brunswick is situated just a few feet above sea level, basements are not usually built in the area's homes due to the potential for flooding.

No visit to Brunswick would be complete without a visit to "**Lovers' Oak**" at the intersection of Prince and Albany streets. This large live oak tree is said to be over 900 years old and is famous for being the meeting place of lovers since the days of the Indians in the area. A plaque beside the tree reads, "The National Arborist Association and the International Society of Arborculture jointly recognize this significant tree in the Bicentennial year (1787-1987) as having lived here at the time of the signing of our Constitution."

If you think you might want to knock on the doors of some of these historic private homes just to get a peek inside, you might consider visiting Brunswick the first weekend in May when a tour of homes is conducted by the Old Town Brunswick Historic Association. The houses and gardens will be open to the public.

The majority of the shops in Old Town date to the late 1800s and early 1900s. Only a few shops remain, however, that were built prior to the War Between The States. These original tabby structures were covered over with brick in the early portion of the 20th century, but with careful observation, one can still see the tabby foundations.

Most of Brunswick's shops were originally "Mom and Pop" stores selling everything from groceries to clothing. Today, however, one can find quilt shops, antiques stores, restaurants and more mixed in with the traditional hardware stores and jewelry shops. Restoration projects are plentiful and some owners live above their shops in loft apartments.

The **Ritz Theater** on Newcastle Street was once known as the **Grand Opera House** and was used for multiple purposes. Not only was it the location for entertainment, but, according to Tyler E. Bagwell in the May 14, 2002 issue of *Harbor Sound*, "the first floor rented space for stores and on the second and third floors were the offices of the Brunswick and Birmingham Railroad."

At the opposite end of Newcastle is the very ornate "**Old City Hall**" built in 1888. The corners of the building are decorated with beautiful gargoyles and angels as well as other details. It was constructed in the Richardsonian Romanesque style of architecture with Queen Anne affinities.

The historic **Glynn County Courthouse** is located on Magnolia Square and was completed in 1907. It was designed by Charles Alling Gifford who also served as architect for many of the luxurious homes of the tycoons who once lived on Jekyll at the Jekyll Island Club.

Across the street from the courthouse on Reynolds stands a home almost beyond comparison. The **Mahoney-McGarvey house** was built in 1891 by an official with the railroad. The plans were drawn by J.A. Wood and the home is decorated with very intricate details. Mr. Wood also designed and built the **Tampa Bay Hotel** in Tampa Bay, and the now demolished **Oglethorpe Hotel** which once stood in Brunswick. The Mahoney-McGarvey house is considered by most to be the best example of Carpenter Gothic Style in the state of Georgia.

(Group tours of Brunswick Old Town are occasionally offered by the Old Town Brunswick Historic Preservation Association and by the Brunswick Downtown Development Authority, as well as Coastal Georgia Community College. For more information, log onto www.brunswickgeorgia.net or contact the Development Authority at 912-265-4032.)

5 SOUTHEAST GEORGIA

There is no place quite like Cumberland Island on the Georgia coast. It's history pre-dates that recorded by mankind, and this magnificent pearl just off the Georgia coast has attracted the wealthy and privileged for hundreds of years. Today, it is a protected property and a sanctuary for a popular public inn, a number of historic homes and an array of unusual wildlife.

Cumberland's wildness is poetic; its waves echo against the island's shoreline with the quiet rhythm of a seagull's wings; its palmettos sway and sing in cadence with salty sea breezes.

Accessible only by private boat, private ferry from the stone's-throw-away **Fernandina Beach**, Florida, or public ferry from **St. Marys**, Georgia – a historic waterfront town near the island – Cumberland is natural beauty at its rarified best. Just a smidgen less than eighteen miles long and a scant three miles wide, the tiny island's history and splendor are as deeply rooted as its melange of forests.

The largest and southernmost of Georgia's barrier islands, Cumberland's lure fringes on the mystical; even its sunlight is as silvery and silky as a dream. The profuse, unbroken canopy of treetops stretches across the island like intricately tatted lace, hiding a cache of nature's secrets: a painted bunting, vibrant and jewel-like, flitting about the live oaks; a raccoon skittering after a fiddler crab; an armadillo sunning himself on a sandy knoll; a whitetail deer nibbling on a bed of pungent mushrooms; a bobcat – its species only recently reintroduced to the island – shadowing its next meal of an unsuspecting field mouse.

Here, quietness reigns supreme, with the silence punctuated only occasionally by the throaty bellow of an alligator searching for a mate, or perhaps the drone of a passenger jet as it streams its way across the sky high above the clouds. And as a saffron-dappled butterfly brushes its way across my path, I even imagine that I could hear the fluttering whispers of its

Historic Cumberland Island

delicate wings.

Today, there are two types of exotic species on the island – feral horses and hogs. The animals are descendants of stock once owned by plantation owners on the island. At some point in time, the animals either escaped their pens or were simply abandoned by their owners. Over the years, they have bred outside of domestication, and upwards of 250 horses have roamed Cumberland in more modern times.

The feral horses are but a small portion of the magnetism of the island, a wilderness not altogether untouched by industry. A century or more ago, the massive live oaks were sawn for ship timbers, and the island's fallow fields, now mostly overgrown with wildflowers and weeds, were once cleared to cultivate crops such as sea island cotton, indigo, and yellow pine.

The island's topography – ideal for the cultivation of such crops – is diverse and divided into three distinct land types: the salt marsh on the western end, the maritime forest – characterized by live oak and palmetto – that dominates the island's center, and the eastern beach, a series of dunes and shoreline carved by the Atlantic Ocean.

The salt marsh, at first glance a bland prairie of tall grasses striated with tidal rivers, comes alive with the surreptitious movement of river otters, fat-beaked pelicans, slithery snakes, and fiddler crabs. At daybreak, its richness glows with all of the glorious colors of a tequila sunrise: pomegranate pink, grenadine red, and subtle orange. Sunsets are magical on the marsh; it seems afire as it simmers and burns in golden shards of light.

The marsh and forest soon meld gently into steep windswept dunes and wide expanses of beach. Just offshore, Atlantic bottlenose dolphins dance in the water as an occasional northern right whale lumbers through their playground. Rare loggerhead turtles – imposing in size – trudge ashore along the seventeen miles of unbroken, unspoiled beach to lay their eggs in the soft-as-confectioner's-sugar sand. Terns and seagulls soar and chatter overhead in the pure ocean air as the feral horses, seemingly everywhere, gallop along the beach.

The first humans to enjoy Cumberland's captivating beauty were probably the **Timucuan Indians**, who hunted and fished this place they first called **Missoe** (which translates to "beautiful") and **Wissoe** (which translates to "sassafras"). The Timucuans were followed by the **Spanish** in the mid-1500s who named the island **San Pedro** and built several missions over the next hundred years or so, including **San Pedro de Mocama**, **Puturiba**, and **San Phelipe**.

The British were the next to come to the island. Under the leadership of **General James Edward Oglethorpe, a**n early explorer of Georgia's coast, two forts – **Prince William** and **St. Andrew** – were built in the 1700s to protect the English settlements from the unruly Spanish in Florida. Oglethorpe also ordered the construction of a hunting lodge on Cumberland. He christened it "**Dungeness.**"

It was only after the **American Revolution**, however, that development of the island began in earnest. **General Nathaniel Greene**, a Revolutionary War hero, purchased land on Cumberland in 1783 and made plans to build a huge mansion near the site of Oglethorpe's hunting lodge.

"Greene's idea was to log oak off the island for ships of the line, which was our military fleet at the time," explains Andy Ferguson, a management analyst with the National Park Service. "He had lost a lot of money during the war, and he wanted to make some of it back. Unfortunately, he died before he was able to regain his fortune. His wife, Catherine, remarried to a man named **Phineas Miller**, and together, they built the next Dungeness."

Following Greene's original designs, the Millers built the impressive four-story mansion on top of a shell mound. Constructed of tabby – Georgia's "coastal concrete" that is a mixture of equal parts of lime, sand, oyster shells, and water – the home had six-foot thick walls at its base and contained sixteen fireplaces.

"The four-story Dungeness was so grand," states Ferguson, "that people used to come over to the island prior to the Civil War just to see the house."

Adding even more to the Southern appeal of Dungeness, **General "Lighthorse" Harry**

Lee, a friend of Greene's from the Revolutionary War and father of famed **Confederate General Robert E. Lee**, came to Cumberland in 1818. Already quite ill by the time he reached the island, he died within a month's time and was buried there. Robert E Lee had a tombstone erected upon his father's grave, but in 1913, the body was removed to Lexington, Virginia, to be placed beside that of his famous son. The tombstone back on Cumberland, however, was left untouched.

Cumberland then became home to several working plantations, including the 8,000-acre **Stafford Plantation**, which today remains in private ownership. After the War Between The States, freed slaves remained on the island and developed their own communities, including **The Settlement**, an area on **Halfmoon Bluff** perched on the far northern end of the island.

Today, among the other structures at The Settlement may be found the **First African Baptist Church**. This simplistic one-room, eleven-pew wooden structure attracted worldwide attention in September of 1996, when the late **John F. Kennedy, Jr.** and **Carolyn Bessette** wed there in stunning secrecy.

The plantation era on Cumberland came to an end after the war because there were no slaves to work the fields and keep up the homes. Dungeness slowly deteriorated and the Miller family eventually moved away. In 1866, the once-stately mansion burned to cinders.

Two versions of the origin of the great fire at the mansion have been handed down through the years. One maintains that it was started by freed slaves, while the other holds it was set by departing Union troops as they left the island.

In the years following the war, the island remained largely neglected and essentially abandoned until the 1880s, which was smack in the middle of the thriving **Winter Resort Era**. Well-moneyed and industrious Yankees – the **Rockefellers**, **Vanderbilts**, and **Pulitzers** among them – began buying coastal Georgia islands as private hunting retreats where they could escape the harsh winters of the northeast.

Thomas Carnegie, a Pittsburgh millionaire who was the brother and partner of steel magnate **Andrew Carnegie**, acquired the Dungeness property for his own personal use. He and his wife, Lucy, rebuilt the mansion on the same Oglethorpe-Greene-Miller building site, even using some of the same materials, and landscaped the surrounding twelve acres in a series of trellised formal gardens and immaculate, lush lawns. This became the third Dungeness, a 44-room, 40-building monolith that resembled a Scottish castle. When it was completed in 1887, the home had electrical power – a remarkable feat, considering the time and the island's remoteness.

Although Thomas Carnegie died around the time Dungeness was completed, Lucy nevertheless remained on Cumberland. She offered to build a home on the island for each of her nine children, four of whom accepted her generosity. From there, Cumberland's modern history grew.

The Carnegies ultimately built five additional homes on the island, three of which still exist today: **Stafford Plantation**, which is privately owned; **Plum Orchard**, owned by the National Park Service and which is currently under renovation; and **Greyfield**, owned by the descendants of Lucy Carnegie and which has been transformed into one of the most exclusive inns in America.

Lucy built Plum Orchard for her son, George, and his wife, Margaret Thaw. The 1898 Georgian Revival mansion commands the center portion of a magnolia-flecked hill overlooking an alligator- and egret-filled pond. Its former grandeur is evident with its massive Greek Revival columns gracing the entranceway and twelve-foot indoor diving pool.

"[The] Plum Orchard [property] was actually the first [publicly accessible] part of Cumberland Island," Ferguson adds. "This structure and the twelve acres around it were [designated as] Cumberland Island National Seashore."

Donated to the National Park Foundation in 1971 by the Carnegie family, Plum Orchard, once in danger of collapse, has now been renovated and preserved. The Park Service spent millions – much of it from private donors – in the preservation.

At one time, there were great hopes that Plum Orchard could be turned into something similar to an artists' colony, an authors' retreat, or even a bed and breakfast inn, but for the present time, the mansion remains empty, with the exception of volunteers who are making many needed improvements.

Part of the problem – in addition to the financial aspect – is the site's inaccessibility. Portions of **Cumberland Island National Seashore** are designated as wilderness, which means that mechanized vehicles – including even bicycles – are not allowed in the area. Only island residents and guests of **Greyfield Inn** are permitted to drive there, so any other visitors are forced to walk the nearly 15-mile roundtrip journey around the island from either of the public boat docks. For now, the future of Plum Orchard and its usage is still uncertain.

Greyfield, however, is another story entirely. "This home came about as a wedding present that Lucy Carnegie presented to her daughter, Margaret, when she married a gentleman by the name of Oliver Ricketson," explains Greyfield's Aubrey Ralph. "The home was completed in 1901, but upon completion, the Ricketsons were here very little. . . and it became a sort of weekend place for them. The home came into main use about 1930 or so when [the Ricketsons] gave it to their daughter, who was also named Lucy."

Opened as an inn in 1962 by Lucy Ricketson Ferguson, Margaret's daughter, Greyfield remains in Carnegie family hands and looks much the same as it did when it was built around the turn of the century. While there is electricity, there are no electronic gizmos of any kind, including telephones, televisions, or radios. Many of the same books originally enjoyed by the Carnegies are still in place in the library. Family portraits grace the walls of the parlor, and Greyfield's furnishings include the wonderfully eclectic Carnegie heirlooms.

Greyfield is an uncomplicated, undemanding place that immediately soothes a weary mind. This is your grandmother's home: its wooden floors creak, the smells of fresh-from-the-oven homemade bread filter through its walls, and its wide verandahs and cushioned rocking chairs beckon you to stay for a while.

Cumberland Island rose to prominence once again as a result of the Kennedy-Bessette wedding, and the warm and inviting Greyfield, the only place outside of a campsite or private home with accommodations, enjoyed a surge of publicity. While the just-wed Kennedys didn't honeymoon at the inn – they stayed at a private residence – most of the wedding party did obtain accommodations at Greyfield.

Over the years, Greyfield has also provided accommodations for a number of other celebrities. It has hosted former **Atlanta Falcons football team owner Rankin Smith**, curmudgeonly singer **Jimmy Buffet**, and **William and Rose Styron**, to name a few.

Greyfield has an advantage in that it has its own private ferry service – the *Lucy Ferguson* or the *Robert W. Ferguson* – from Fernandina Beach. From the dock, getting to the inn is much easier than getting to Plum Orchard. Guests are met at the Carnegie family-owned dock and are provided van transportation to the inn over family-owned roads. If desired, guests may also walk the five-minute walk to the inn.

As for Dungeness, it once again suffered the fate of a death by fire, burning in 1959. According to reports, a Dungeness caretaker shot a deer poacher who had come over from the mainland. Despite his wound, the poacher reportedly escaped, but ended up in a hospital nonetheless. A few days after the poacher was released from the hospital, the Dungeness yacht "mysteriously" sank and the mansion was set ablaze.

Over time, the salt air and the sun have seared to whiteness the aged bones of the old mansion. Varmints like rattlesnakes and bobcats now lurk in the old tabby ruins, making it seem almost ludicrous that Dungeness was once one of the largest and most splendid homes in any era of American history. Lucy Carnegie was well-known for her high society soirees at the mansion, now long departed.

Also scattered about Cumberland are a series of chimneys that serve as reminders of another time long since gone. "The chimneys are all that remain of the slave quarters," adds Ferguson. "There are no wooden or tabby structures at all, and the chimneys are in various stages of disrepair. The National Park Service is developing a plan for the chimneys so that we can stabilize them so they don't deteriorate any further. They are, however, on private land and not accessible by the general public."

In the mid-1950s, the National Park Service described Cumberland Island as "one of the two most outstanding undeveloped seashore areas along the Atlantic and gulf coasts." The other place was scenic Cape Cod in Massachusetts. While Cumberland's significance as a natural area increased with that designation, virtually nothing was done to protect it from development.

Then the unthinkable happened. In the late 1960s, **Charles Fraser**, who was the original – and quite controversial – developer of **Hilton Head Island**, bought a fifth of Cumberland's acreage from two Carnegie cousins. He envisioned a resort much like Hilton Head. The plan sounded the alarm that Cumberland's bucolic paradise was very much in danger of disappearing, and the rest of the Carnegie clan came out kicking and screaming about the environmental toll such a development would take.

The Carnegies began to sell or donate their property to the National Park Service, and the Georgia Conservancy helped push through a bill introduced by then-Congressmen **Bill Stuckey** and **Bo Ginn** that established Cumberland Island as a national seashore. Also, the **Mellon Foundation**, in a gesture of conservation-minded good will, donated $7.5 million to buy the remaining property, including Fraser's parcel, which was all then deeded to the federal government.

While the Carnegie family once owned most of Cumberland Island, only about 1,300 acres remain in the family today, and most of that is around Greyfield Inn. The remaining acreage is now in the hands of the National Park Service and 30 or 40 island residents. Camping and hiking are allowed on the island, but only for no more than 300 visitors a day. New structures are not built on Cumberland; instead, says Ferguson, "We take existing structures and renovate them."

The park's boundaries also include Little Cumberland Island, part of the archipelago of barrier islands that is separated from Cumberland by Christmas Creek. "[It] is under private ownership," states Ferguson. "While it is within the park's boundaries, there are covenants that have been signed with the landowners and the Secretary of Interior back when the park was developed and inaugurated. The two islands get along quite well and are very good neighbors."

From its spellbinding beauty to its distinctive history, the hypnotic allure of Cumberland Island and its peaceful respite can calm even the most troubled soul.

(For more information or camping and ferry reservations – which are required – contact Cumberland Island National Seashore, P.O. Box 806, St. Mary's, Georgia, 31558. Website: www.nps.gov/cuis Telephone toll-free 888-817-3421. Greyfield Inn's main office is located in Fernandina Beach, Florida, and may be reached at 904-261-6408. Website: www.greyfield-inn.com. Email: seashore@greyfieldinn.com)

Jekyll Island

The Jekyll Island Club Hotel

In colonial days, much of Jekyll Island was a large plantation. In 1886, it became a huge playground for America's royalty – the families of wealthy industrialists – and for more than 50 years, their Victorian mansions and an impressive hotel dominated the island landscape. In 1942, however, with German U-Boats prowling the Georgia coast, everything changed forever.

Long before the legendary **Jekyll Island Club** was an exclusive hotel, the property was already remarkable for several reasons, the foremost probably being its prime location on one of the Golden Isles, part of the gently strung cluster of barrier islands on Georgia's coast. The impressive Victorian-style hotel on Jekyll was founded in 1886, and it served as a playground for an exclusive group of our nation's societal elite for half a century. Though much of the club's grandeur was lost over the years to weathering, neglect, and thieves, some of the opulent homes and other accommodations once inhabited by historic families from yesteryear may still be viewed at this site today.

Such notables as the **Vanderbilts**, **Morgans**, **Pulitzers**, and **Rockefellers** once journeyed to this pristine island of sand, surf, and natural beauty to relax, hunt, and, of course, to escape the harsh winters of the North. For many years (1886-1942), they spent the winter months of each year and left their mark at the Jekyll Island Club.

The drive to this aged inn from yesteryear is a delightful experience in itself today. The billowy marsh breezes provide just the right amount of salty scent, adding to the allure of the hotel's unique blend of isolation and privacy. Dazzling sunrises and sunsets await visitors to this uncommon place, which always seems cloaked in shards of sunlight steeped in every imaginable shade of gold.

The salt-tinged fragrance of the sea offers a splendid backdrop for quiet evenings spent on one of the many verandahs which enfold the hotel. The gentle coastal climate allows grass to flourish, nurturing it to a deep emerald hue, even during winter months. Spanish moss draped from scores of massive live oaks, the lively scent of sweet magnolias, and gently swaying palms complete this picture of serenity.

"The Jekyll Island Club sprang out of an idea of **Newton Finney**, a New York merchant," says John Hunter, who serves as chief curator and assistant director of operations and the museum of the Jekyll Island Authority. "Finney was the brother-in-law of **John Eugene duBignon**, a descendant of one of the early colonial landowners on the island."

Finney had links through his business associations to the Union Club in New York, one of the most exclusive clubs in the world at that time – a tradition continued today. In the 1880s, the membership roster of the club read like a "Who's Who" of business and industry in New York. It included the likes of **William Rockefeller**, **William K. Vanderbilt**, **J.P. Morgan**, **Joseph Pulitzer**, **Marshall Field**, **Frank Henry Goodyea**r, and many others.

In the 1880s, the railroad through Georgia terminated in Thomasville, so Florida was still relatively undiscovered and wild. Because of that, South Georgia had become the resort retreat of choice by wealthy Northerners bent on escaping the harsh winters. Jekyll Island became a natural progression of this seasonal migration.

"The idea was becoming very popular for the Union Club's members and their families to have hunting or winter retreats to which they would periodically travel," Hunter states. "This was not long after the **Carnegies** purchased **Cumberland Island**. **Sapelo Island** nearby was being purchased, and **St. Simon's Island** was starting to be a little bit of a resort area. After borrowing money to purchase Jekyll and develop it into a hunting club site, Finney and duBignon incorporated the Jekyll Island Club, and then sold shares for $600 apiece to members of the Union Club. The two men, in essence, sold the island to the club for $125,000, which in 1886 in South Georgia was a tremendous amount of money. In today's dollars, that's about $2.5 to $3 million."

Initially, there were a hundred members in the Jekyll Island Club, a number that remained fairly consistent throughout its history. Some of the first members of the club constituted not only the likes of Morgan, Vanderbilt, Rockefeller, Goodyear, Field, and Pulitzer, but also men such as **Theodore Vail**, president of AT&T and one of the early leaders of what is known today as the telecommunications industry.

Following their purchase of the acreage, the club members then invested more money to build a substantial clubhouse. Additionally, lots for exclusive private homes were laid out around the clubhouse property to be sold along with the memberships. The clubhouse, with its Queen Anne architecture, indoor plumbing, dozens of fireplaces, wraparound porches, and dramatic turret, was completed in time for the beginning of the winter season in January of 1888.

"The typical club season would begin – depending upon whether or not one had a cottage or stayed at the clubhouse – as early as Thanksgiving and last through mid-March," Hunter explains. "Those who had cottages would come down around Thanksgiving to mid-December. Most of the time, the other club members would come down just after New Year's and stay until February."

Between 1886 and 1928, other services were added to the club, including a dining room complete with Ionic columns, telephone service, and even an elevator. During this time, members also built lavish "cottages" that were reflective of their lifestyles during that period.

During the last years of the 19th century and the first few years of the 20th century, the club flourished in its stateliness and even contributed small slivers of modern history to the world. For instance, the framework for the **Aldrich Act**, which became the **Federal Reserve Act**, was drafted there in 1910, and the **first transcontinental telephone call** was made by Theodore Vail from the clubhouse in 1915.

"Vail was at the club because he had injured his leg," says Hunter. "He was supposed to be in Washington, D.C., with **Woodrow Wilson** for the first call, but he was in a wheelchair and couldn't make the trip. He had his engineers string and connect the lines, which they brought across the marsh and hooked up in the basement of the clubhouse. For the call, Vail was here, Woodrow Wilson was in Washington, **Alexander Graham Bell** was in New York, and **Dr. Watson** was in San Francisco."

By the 1920s, however, important and defining changes had gripped the country. The jazz age was coming into vogue, and West Palm Beach and Miami were being opened up to tourism because of the railroad. South Florida had become a much more "happening" place with its Mediterranean styles and hot nightlife. Everything was all Hemingway, F. Scott Fitzgerald, and pink flamingoes. The Jekyll Island Club, with its old money blue-blood family ties and aging members, tried to keep pace with the times, but just couldn't.

To add to its woe, the club's isolation and its circumstances as a retreat from the hustle and bustle of the city became both a blessing and a curse. As the original club members who had joined in the 1880s grew older and began to die out, the club, says Hunter, wasn't seen as a family legacy, and [in many instances over time], the houses weren't handed down to family descendants. They were simply turned back in to the club, which then attempted to sell the property to new club members.

By the late 1930s, major conflicts in Europe were causing a ripple-effect in America, bringing with them a concern and anxiety about travel. In the spring of 1942, **German U-Boats** began prowling the east coast of the United States and sinking commercial vessels. A number of the craft were torpedoed and sunk within sight of the Georgia coast – some only a few miles from Jekyll. As a result, those remaining on the island were evacuated, and throughout the war years, the site remained essentially abandoned. The club became insolvent and was closed down and forgotten.

After World War II ended in 1945, efforts to revive the club were initiated by **Frank Gould**. He was the son of **Edwin Gould**, who was a club member, and the grandson of **Jay Gould**, a financier and railroad magnate. Frank's older brother, Edwin Jr., died on Jekyll Island in a hunting accident, and because of family connections to the island, he didn't want to give up on the old traditions.

Gould partnered with Bill Jones of the **Sea Island Company** to reinvigorate the club. The pair intended to model the club after **The Cloister**, an even more luxurious resort located on Sea Island a few miles to the north. Unfortunately, Gould – who was only in his mid-forties at the time – dropped dead after a massive heart attack one morning at his breakfast table. Jones and others in the investment group never recovered from the loss of their leader, and ultimately abandoned any further attempts to reopen the club.

Sue Andersson, who works in public relations and guest programs today at the Jekyll Island Club Hotel, says that when the old club members abandoned the club in the 1940s, the buildings and grounds were left with no maintenance for the ensuing years.

"By 1947, when virtually none of the members had returned, the mortgages, dues, and fees came due and were not paid," Andersson explains. "There was no money with which to continue maintenance or upkeep of the place."

That was when the State of Georgia stepped in. Under its direction, Jekyll Island was to be turned into a state park to make it accessible to all citizens. The state bought all outstanding shares of stock for $675,000.

For a while, it looked as if the state had a white elephant on its hands. "There was considerable concern about what would be done with Jekyll Island for the people of the state," Andersson continues. "They didn't have a loyalty to it. They didn't have fond memories of a childhood here because it had always been owned exclusively by club members from 1886 until 1942. No Georgia citizens [had been allowed to come] here because it was privately owned by the club members."

Eventually, the **Jekyll Island Authority**, an entity that continues to manage the island on the state's behalf today, was formed in 1950. The clubhouse was then opened as a sort of bed-and-breakfast, Andersson says, with some "minor politicians" being sent down to manage the property. But in the 1950s the only people who traveled to Jekyll Island were those who owned boats or had friends who owned boats, because the causeway had not yet been built that connected the island to the mainland. Certainly, then, tourists and their dollars were really very few and far between, and Jekyll Island continued to be difficult to both reach and maintain.

By the early 1970s, the clubhouse had been virtually shut down, because parts of it – including its once majestic verandahs – had deteriorated to the point of becoming unsafe. It was also during this period that many of the priceless furnishings, decorative items, and trappings – such as the solid silver window latches of the luxurious homes – were stolen by thieves and pilferers who carried the treasures by boat back to the mainland.

Sadly, the hotel continued to deteriorate until the 1980s, when a man named **Barry**

Evans came to Jekyll to play golf. Evans, an architect, happened to drive past the old clubhouse and was intrigued by the site. He researched the property and found that it had been the exclusive hunting retreat for the likes of the Morgans, Astors, Vanderbilts, and the hundreds of others who once had enjoyed its unparalleled character.

"[Mr. Evans] thought how wonderful it would be to breathe life back into it," Ms. Andersson smiles. "He had made a career of seeking out properties that could be retrofitted to serve a contemporary, useful function. He and his partners transformed the Jekyll Island Club into a hotel and resort."

And that's where the Jekyll Island Club Hotel is today. From its richly appointed rooms to the intricate scrollwork to its manicured gardens, the hotel is once again a palatial resort. Its Victorian style – including that spectacular turret and the dozens of bay windows – reminds visitors of the good taste and grace of the "Gay 90s."

One legend surrounding the aged hotel maintains that the original members were required to dine in the clubhouse's dining room where they were often served sumptuous 10-course meals. Today's guests will find that the Grand Dining Room – its historic Ionic columns still in place – continues to offer a variety of specialty dishes like crusted grouper rolled in Georgia pecans; Grilled Pork Vidalia, which is a tangy pork loin topped with a Vidalia onion marmalade; or Plantation Shrimp, carefully prepared with Georgia white shrimp, all of which will tempt the palate of even the most distinguished guests.

Imprinting it in history, the hotel was recognized as a *National Historic Landmark* in 1978, and just recently was designated a **Historic Hotel of American** by the **National Trust for Historic Preservation**. Today, the Jekyll Island Authority owns all of the historic structures on the island, which includes anything built prior to 1947. The historic district, which is spread over 240 acres and comprised of 33 buildings including the hotel, cottages, and other structures such as stables and tennis courts, looks basically the same as it did during the island's heydays.

(The Jekyll Island Club is located at 371 Riverview Drive, Jekyll Island. The telephone number is (912) 635-2600 or toll-free (800) 535-9547. You may also visit the website at www.jekyllclub.com.)

Southeast Georgia

Georgia's Historic Coastal Forts

Along the length of the coast of Georgia, a string of aged military fortifications from yesteryear offer an interesting destination for travelers, and a page out of the history of the formative years of our nation.

They stand silent today, but in years past, their voices boomed in loud defiance along Georgia's coast. They are the sentinels of wars past; our coastal forts from yesteryear.

Some of these relics have been lost or built over and are gone forever. The ones that remain are in widely varying conditions. Some are still almost complete. Others are little more than mounds of earth – perhaps with a few remnants of buildings.

The forts that one may find on the map today are: **Jackson**, **Pulaski**, **Screvin**, **McAllister**, **Morris**, **King George**, and **Frederica**. They are located at sites along the coast from Savannah to St. Simons Island.

As one might expect, four of these fortifications were built to protect the important early port city of Savannah. This historic town enjoys a natural defensive barrier of coastal marshes, and the forts were designed to garrison the rivers.

Fort Jackson

Begun in 1808, this fort sits on the south side of the Savannah River, three miles east of the old city. This site was chosen because it is here that all the river channels converge, with a deep anchoring spot aptly named "Five Fathom Hole."

Any boat traveling to Savannah had to pass Fort Jackson, and the same circumstances still apply today. Jackson was constructed as a primary defensive element in the United States' "Second System" of coastal fortifications initiated by **President Thomas Jefferson**. These were all masonry installations with case-mated gun emplacements built to replace the inadequate open batteries and earth parapets which existed at that time around major U.S. harbors.

Fort Jackson is Georgia's oldest standing brick fortification, and is in remarkably good condition considering its history. The entire main wall – or "scarp" – is intact, surrounded by a wet-moat. The entrance or "sallyport" is complete with a drawbridge.

Inside, the central "parade yard" is surrounded by barracks areas, powder magazines, work areas, and even old privies.

Jackson originally had nine cannons in all. These included five 32-pound smoothbores, one 32-pound rifled bore, two 8-inch Columbiads, and one mountain howitzer. A few of the 32-pounders can be visited by climbing a flight of steps up to the "terreplein."

Visitors to Fort Jackson may view Civil War artifacts, visit a blacksmith shop, enjoy a 15-minute push-the-button video presentation, and purchase mementos at the site's gift shop. For schedules and other details about this fort, call 912-232-3945, or log onto www.chsgeorgia.org.

Martello Tower & Fort Wayne

Two other Second System forts were built in the Savannah vicinity in the early 1800s. **Martello Tower** on Tybee Island was constructed in 1815. Built of tabby (a mixture of sand, seashells, and lime), it was four stories high and had 360 degrees of firing circumference. **Fort Wayne** – adjacent to the eastern edge of Savannah – was built just prior to Martello Tower.

It was during this time that a visual "early warning system" was initiated to aid in the area's defenses. This was accomplished with a signal from the lighthouse on **Tybee Island** to an observation post on **Cockspur Island**, then relayed to Fort Jackson and on to Fort Wayne. All remnants of both Martello and Wayne disappeared years ago.

Although the Second System forts enjoyed some successes during the war of 1812, it quickly became apparent that a new "modern" system of coastal fortifications was needed to provide an adequate defense.

Fort Pulaski

As a "Third System" bulwark, Fort Pulaski began to rise out of the mud on Cockspur Island in 1829. Fort Jackson then became a back-up, and Fort Wayne became obsolete.

At the beginning of the U.S. Civil War, both the North and the South considered Pulaski and the other Third System forts along the east coast to be a critical factor in achieving victory. They were massive, and had tremendous firepower as well as flanking defenses. Despite these factors, as it turned out, the forts faced even more-modern adversaries than had been anticipated. One of the new weapons – the recently conceived ironclad shallow-draft steamships – could withstand a terrible barrage from the previously-deadly cannon fire from the forts, and the spinning rounds from the rifled cannons on the ships could drive right through the heavy masonry walls.

Fort Pulaski – like Fort Jackson – is a must-see site for historic fort enthusiasts traveling in the Savannah area. The 25-foot-high walls (scarp) are a minimum of seven and one-half feet thick, contain 25 million bricks, and form a pentagon with an interior parade area of two and one-half acres. A large triangular earthwork called the "demilune" protects the front scarp and the sallyport. A wet-moat encircles the fort and the demilune.

Both side walls and the two angled rear walls each have twelve vaulted casemates. Each casement had a single cannon and "embrasure" or firing port.

Some of the early engineering of Fort Pulaski was done by a young lieutenant named **Robert E. Lee**, who, along with **Joseph Totten**, chief of the U.S. Army Engineers in 1862, were certain that the fort walls would never be breached by cannon fire. Then came the rifled cannons and suddenly the walls weren't impervious anymore.

The Federals built several batteries one to two miles distant from Pulaski. In two days, they hurled almost 5,300 projectiles at the fort. After spinning rounds had breached one of the walls, and exploding shells were threatening a powder magazine, **Colonel Charles Olmstead** ultimately was forced to surrender the fort.

Fort Pulaski is a National Monument today. For more information call 912-786-5787.

Fort Screvin

The construction of Fort Screven – a group of gun batteries – was begun in 1897 on the north end of Tybee Island. Screvin eventually had 23 guns and mortars.

Over the years, this fort has been used for government office space and even as a diving school. In 1945, it was sold to the town of Savannah Beach. Today, it is a mix of private and city property. Visitors can see part of the old run-down fort as they also visit Tybee Island Lighthouse.

Fort McAllister

The Savannah area is sandwiched between two rivers – the Savannah, and, further south, the Ogeechee. Fort McAllister, built prior to the U.S. Civil War, is located twelve miles south of Savannah on the southern bank of the Ogeechee. In modern highway terms, McAllister is located ten miles east of Interstate 95 on Georgia 144 Spur.

Constructionwise, McAllister has no high brick scarps, but it does include the best-preserved earthworks fortification of the Confederacy. McAllister was built with wooden palisades around its periphery. Today, as one approaches the fort's sand and mud wall, the deep ditch – or moat – is first encountered, with palisades embedded in the moat itself. These large "fence posts" – with sharpened tops – offered little protection against cannon-fire, but did provide a somewhat impenetrable barrier against foot soldiers.

Around the interior of the earthen wall, there are some 20 gun emplacements, along with several powder magazines and a hot shot furnace. Rising out of the Parade area is the "Central Bombproof," which was used as a hospital as well as a refuge during naval bombardments.

Interestingly, the earthen walls of Fort McAllister proved much more durable than the brick walls in absorbing the impact of the new, heavier projectiles, and the new rifled cannons. For almost two years, Fort McAllister withstood a total of seven major naval attacks by Federal forces.

In early March of 1863, McAllister withstood a seven-hour bombardment by several Union warships, and amazingly suffered only minor damage. The only reported fatality was that of a tomcat, the garrison's mascot. Mention of the cat's death was even included in the next official report to General Beauregard.

Designed to fight river battles, McAllister's "Achilles' heel" proved to be its "back door." On December 13, 1864, the troops of **General William T. Sherman** did what the gunboats had been unable to accomplish: they overran the fort.

For more information on Fort McAllister, telephone 912-727-2339, or log onto www.gastateparks.org.

Fort Morris

As the crow flies, Fort Morris lies only ten miles south of Fort McAllister. Modern-day visitors, however, must take Georgia Highway 38 east from Interstate 95, then the Fort Morris Road (watch for it), then travel a short distance on Old Sunbury Road. Here, the visitor will find the remains of the only earthworks in Georgia that date back to the Revolutionary War.

Built in 1776 adjacent to the Medway River, Fort Morris was designed to guard the town of **Sunbury** from a British invasion. At that time, Sunbury was a busy port town, second only to Savannah in importance on the Georgia coast.

Fort Morris nevertheless fell to the British, and, after the war had ended, both Sunbury and the fort were left in ruins. The ruined compound was later revived under the name of **Fort Defiance** for the War of 1812, and was again garrisoned during the early part of the Civil War by Confederates.

Today, Fort Morris is a beautiful "park" beside the river, with colorful azaleas (in springtime) amidst huge live oaks. From the earthworks, visitors can look downstream to St. Catherine's Sound seven miles away.

The Visitors' Center at Fort Morris can be contacted at 912-884-5999, and more information can be found at www.gastateparks.org.

Fort King George

Built by the British in 1720, Fort King George is located approximately one mile east of **Darien**, a charming (and very historic) little town on the Altamaha River, probably best known as the site of an annual "**Blessing of the Fleet Festival**" held each April. **Colonel John Barnwell** – a South Carolina planter and Indian fighter – convinced the London Board of Trade that a fort was needed on the mouth of the Altamaha to protect against the French to the north and west, and the Spanish on the south, so King George was built.

Following the fort's construction, the British garrison therein suffered tremendous hardships from disease, malnutrition, exposure and a constant hoard of biting insects, not to mention constant threats from Spanish and the native Indians. In 1727, the entire garrison – with the exception of two very brave lookouts – withdrew to South Carolina.

General Oglethorpe later recruited a group of hardy Highland Scots and stationed them at the fort in 1736, but soon moved them to a higher bluff where he built "Fort Darien."

Unfortunately, later saw-milling activities in the Darien area destroyed all remains of the original Fort King George, but the present-day compound on the site is an authentic reproduction of the original. Inside the parapet are cannon installations, loading and firing steps, guardhouses, and a large blockhouse with overhanging upper stories. The enlisted barracks and numerous small buildings complete the picture.

Various educational programs are offered throughout the year at King George. Site Manager Ken Akins – in a colorful bright Redcoat uniform – regularly welcomes school groups. In addition to the Georgia state parks website, information on Fort King George may be obtained from Ken at 912-437-4770.

Fort Frederica

Today, this former British colonial fort is a beautiful place to visit. Located on St. Simons Island, it is twelve miles from Brunswick.

Named for King George II's only son – Frederick – Fort Frederica was not just a fort, but also a well-planned and thriving seaport. Today, very little remains of this town or the fort, but the foundations of several of the town's houses and shops have been excavated and preserved for public viewing.

A section of the Fort's historic magazine still stands as well, as does a portion of the soldiers' barracks. Most of the town's former streets have been rediscovered and identified, and Broad Street includes a number of information plaques which explain many details of the former town and fort, including the history, architecture, and even information about some of the individuals who once lived in the homes there. Interestingly, much information on the town and its residents was documented by the British, aiding in the relocation and identification of various aspects of the fort today.

The garrison troops at Fort Frederica defended the area several times against the Spanish, defeating them most notably at the now-famous **Battle of Bloody Marsh** a short distance from Frederica. After the departure of the Spanish from what today is Florida, and the subsequent removal of British troops from Frederica, the fort became obsolete and eventually was completely abandoned.

For more information on this interesting historic site, call 912-638-3639, or log onto www.nps.gov/fofr.

Colquitt

Enjoy folk life dramatic productions? The residents of the small Georgia town of Colquitt have cooked up a real doozie. If you appreciate that sort of thing, you might enjoy a little taste of this "**theater in the square**."

You won't find "**swamp gravy**" in most dictionaries, but the term is part of the vocabulary of most southwest Georgia residents, particularly in the area around the community of Colquitt. If Webster had included it, the definition would read something like this: swamp gravy 1. A popular south Georgia stew made from whatever is available and cooked in the drippings after fish is fried. 2. Georgia's Folk Life Play, presented in the fall and in the spring, in Colquitt, Georgia.

The play takes its name from the regional dish because it too combines many disparate ingredients into a new creation while preserving the original flavors and textures. In fact, one of the songs in the production is entitled "**Cooking Up Swamp Gravy**" and talks about "taking what you have and making something unique." It's also about celebrating what you've got instead of lamenting what you don't have.

A decade ago, the small town of Colquitt had little going for it, and its already small population was declining. Women involved in the local arts council – looking for a way to help their community grow – listened attentively to theater director and teacher Richard Owen Geer. He convinced them that a drama derived from folk tales of the region could "put Colquitt on the map" and stimulate economic growth.

Soon a number of local citizens were being trained to interview native old-timers and collect oral history. This included colorful expressions and "old saws," which were woven into the narratives of the folk tales. Performance workshops trained Colquitt townspeople to transform stories into dramatic scenes.

The first production, entitled "**Swamp**

A Taste of "Swamp Gravy"

Gravy Sketches," was performed in 1992 and was put together with virtually no budget. The simple sets were made of crates, bales, and sacks. Old-time costumes were improvised or borrowed from those who had sewn them for annual "Old Timer" festivals sponsored by some of the country churches in the area.

Excited about the project, those involved began working on a more extensive version of the play to be presented in 1994. An old brick cotton warehouse was renovated to become the permanent performance hall for "Swamp Gravy." An estimated two thousand hours of volunteer labor went into its transformation. Attendance at the eleven performances held that year averaged filling 95% of the theater's 300-seat capacity.

As word spread, success followed success. The editor of the *Macon Telegraph* described the play as "the most compelling experience I have ever had in the theater. Those people were acting and singing their lives and their community's history."

The **Georgia State Legislature** proclaimed *"Swamp Gravy"* the "**official folklife play of Georgia**." The production has been performed at the **1996 Summer Olympic Games** in Atlanta, the **Kennedy Center** in Washington, D.C., and in many cities throughout the southeastern United States.

"Swamp Gravy" is presented twice a year for four weekends in October and four weekends in March/April. The stories presented in the fall are reprised in the spring but are different from one year to the next.

The cast of the production is made up of over a hundred local people from all walks of life, white and black, old-timers and newcomers, ranging in age from four to 80. They are all volunteers who contribute their time because they love what they do.

One of the funniest vignettes in the latest

production shows a small girl painting her father's toenails with bright red polish while he is taking a nap. The man later awakens, notices his unusually decorated toes, but has just enough time to quickly pull on his boots as his two buddies arrive to pick him up to go hunting.

Later that night in camp, the fellow suddenly remembers the color of his toenails and gets into his sleeping bag with his boots on. When his buddies insist that he remove the dirty boots, they see his painted toenails and begin razzing him unmercifully.

The humor of the situation increases as the men begin trying – unsuccessfully – to remove the polish with gasoline. One of the men suddenly complains mirthfully, "It's too dark to see a thing. Hand me a match." The hapless fellow finally gets the offending polish removed at the local beauty shop.

In contrast to the humor above, one of the most poignant stories involves a father whose son is "Missing In Action" as World War II draws to a close. The father visits many veterans' hospitals around the country and travels as far away as France in his desperate search for his missing son.

Before each trip, the man tells his wife, "If I don't find him, I'll telephone to let you know I'll be home for dinner on Sunday." The uncertainty of not knowing whether their son is dead or alive is finally laid to rest when the son's remains are returned in a flag-draped coffin.

The doors of Cotton Hall open a couple of hours before performance time to allow visitors an opportunity to view various exhibits and visit the museum also located in the building. The performance area is theater-in-the-round, or rather "in-the-square." The audience sits in tiered wooden seats on three sides.

A stage of sorts occupies the fourth side, but much of the action takes place on three smaller raised platforms located in the pit in the center, one of which is a flatbed truck. The dramatized scenes are alternated with music, including traditional hymns and spirituals as well as songs composed for "Swamp Gravy." One of the soloists is a black woman whose rich voice fills the auditorium.

To make a long story short, Swamp Gravy is a regional dramatic production which is well worth the trip to tiny Colquitt, Georgia. It's a story about a community coming together and working for a common cause. It's a story about people and the collective goodness that should be – but often isn't – the foundation of every community in the world today.

("Swamp Gravy" is produced by the Colquitt/Miller Arts Council. Tickets are $22.00 for reserved seats, $12.00 general admission, and $6.00 general admission for children. Group rates are available. For more information and to order tickets, call 229-758-5450, or visit the website www.swampgravy.com.)

Colquitt

Recreation Opportunities in Miller County

Colquitt (population 2,000) is located in the southwest corner of Georgia, an equal distance (50 miles) from Albany, Georgia, Tallahassee, Florida, and Dothan, Alabama. It was originally called "**Springtown**" when Miller County (current population 6,700) was created in 1856 from the lower section of Early County.

Interestingly, there reportedly was "much discussion, debate, and fist fights over where to locate the county seat" until Judge Isaac Bush offered a five-acre tract as the site of the county courthouse.

Sadly, the historic **Miller County Courthouse** would be almost 150 years old today, but it burned in the 1970s, and has been replaced by a contemporary building. The imposing pillared older structure will not be forgotten, however, since its likeness has been memorialized in one of the colorful murals painted by four artists on several of Colquitt's present-day buildings. Like the scenes in the town's renowned dramatic production "**Swamp Gravy**" which is presented each season in Colquitt, each of the murals relates a story about the area's history.

In addition to the "Swamp Gravy" production, Colquitt also has a **Swamp Gravy Storytelling Festival** which takes place in August, and a **Mayhaw Festival** in April. For those who don't know, "mayhaws" are the tart fruit from hawthorn shrubs that grow in swampy areas, and are often harvested with boats and nets. The juice of the fruit makes a delicious rosy jelly.

In addition to Colquitt's festivals, dramatic productions, and outdoor murals, the area offers numerous other attractions to visitors, such as **antique shops**, a **"Market on The Square"** a boardwalk through ecologically-fragile wetlands at **Spring Creek Park**, and golfing at **Clydesdale Meadows Golf Club**.

Spring Creek Park and the **Mayhaw Wildlife Management Area** offer year-round opportunities for bird-watching in an area rich in avian diversity. Other recreational opportunities in the area include hunting, fishing, boating, and tennis.

(For more information on Miller County, contact the Miller County Chamber of Commerce at 229-758-2400.)

The Tarrar Bed & Breakfast Inn

Going to see the dramatic production "**Swamp Gravy**" in Colquitt? Excellent accommodations are available right across the town square in the historic **Tarrar Inn**.

The Tarrar, now almost a century old, has stood on the Colquitt town square since 1905, and has become a popular stop in recent years for individuals interested in historic overnight accommodations.

Beautifully restored in 1994, the aged inn has served a number of notables over the years, and still offers excellent accommodations today. Among the inn's distinguished guests in years past have been **President Jimmy Carter** and others.

The Tarrar is listed on the **National Register of Historic Places**, and is a winner of the prestigious **Georgia Trust Award for Historic Preservation**. It has been featured in *Southern Living* magazine and is AAA approved.

All of the inn's twelve guest rooms feature attractive Victorian décor, including period antiques, hand-painted fireplace mantels, and embroidered bed linens. Television sets and coffee makers are concealed in armoires so they do not intrude upon the inn's historic atmosphere.

The Tarrar is also famous for its Southern cuisine. An old-fashioned breakfast featuring melt-in-your-mouth biscuits, locally-made mayhaw jelly, bacon, eggs, grits, country sausage, and fresh fruit is included in the price of an overnight stay.

The inn's three dining rooms are usually full for Sunday dinner, so don't tarry if you plan on dining at the Tarrar. It offers a grand smorgasbord of dishes, including fried green tomatoes, swamp gravy, and blackberry cobbler with ice cream.

[For inquiries and reservations, call the Tarrar Inn at 229-758-2888 or 888-282-7737, or visit the inn's website (everyone seems to have one these days) at www.tarrarinn.com.]

Grantville

Historic Bonnie Castle

Traffic flows steadily – sometimes quite heavily – on Interstate 85 between Atlanta and the Alabama state line as tourists and commuters travel to and fro pursuing the busy lives of the 21st century. However, for those who chance to stop off at Exit 7 in **Grantville**, a simple mile and a half drive leads them to a landmark from a bygone era.

A castle – Bonnie Castle – at the center of a tiny Southern town may sound incredible. Perhaps it's not a castle, but this stately 1896 Romanesque Revival Victorian mansion might just as well be. It is grand – huge – in the truest sense, as well as elegant, and very reminiscent of a castle from yesteryear. Even today, its grounds cover practically a quarter of Grantville's downtown district.

Listed on the **National Register of Historic Places**, the two-story brick house reflects the wealth and prominence of the family who built it, **J.W.** and **Itura Colley**, prominent figures on the political and social scene of Coweta County at the turn-of-the-century.

The Colley family – of Scottish descent – gave the mansion its charming name. Because of the uniqueness of both the Colley family and their home, a number of famous guests have visited the mansion over the years. These have included **President Franklin D. Roosevelt**, **President Jimmy Carter** and **Madam Chiang Kai-shek** to name a few.

An ancient wrought-iron gate encircles Bonnie Castle, and a century-old hitching post greets guests in the front yard. The sprawling veranda whispers Southern hospitality with rocking chairs aplenty where guests can "sit a spell" to enjoy the herb and ornamental gardens and a small Victorian goldfish pond.

J.W. built the house in the late 19th century after it was designed by his wife Itura. The mansion was constructed of locally-made bricks, granite from Georgia's **Stone Mountain**, and pure heart pine from the many trees in the area.

Upon entering this unusual edifice, visitors are immediately confronted with a grand staircase that leads past three elaborate stained glass windows on the way to the second floor. Across from the windows is a built-in prayer bench. Half of a wooden heart, carved into delicate fretwork, greets the eye at the staircase entrance, and a miniature heart rests at the apex. The hearts are a tribute to the first lady of the house, whom friends of her era nicknamed "Miss Love."

Oak paneling and oak motifs are prominent throughout the mansion. Other features include massive pocket doors, hardwood floors, an exquisite gilded ceiling in the drawing room, and an original fresco adorning the octagonal ceiling of the adjoining dining room.

The huge home has seven fireplaces which once provided its only source of heat. Original built-in bookcases and walls adorned with art seethe romance and refinement. The fixtures and draperies are original, including oversize dark green drapes reminiscent of those in Scarlett O'Hara's fictional home – Tara – which she used to fashion a gown in the immortal motion picture, *Gone With The Wind*. The intrigue of the Victorian era adds warmth to the mansion's 20 rooms.

Bed & Breakfast

Darwin and **Patti Palmer** purchased the massive 5,200-square-foot home in 1992, and operate it today as a unique bed and breakfast inn with four tastefully-decorated guest rooms on the second floor. The Palmers reside in the "servant's quarters" on the first floor.

Darwin, a retired medical entomologist from the U.S. Army Medical Service Corps, and Patti, a high-risk OB nurse, left Peachtree City a decade ago in search of a slower-paced life. When they discovered the impressive estate at 2 Post Street in Grantville, they knew they had found their new home.

All things considered, the Palmers discovered their "castle" was in excellent condition, not only physically, but aesthetically as well. "We were simply lucky the people who lived here before didn't have enough money to remodel or change things," says Patti.

While the charm of the castle remained intact, there was still plenty of work to be done. The Palmers' first months in the mansion were spent upgrading electricity and plumbing, adding central heat and air and repairing leaks in the roof to bring the dwelling up to standard.

Designed to enchant visitors, the Henrietta Suite and Stewart Suite sparkle with Southern romance and cozy charm. The Civil War Suite features two twin hospital beds from Ft. McAllister and an assortment of stuffed animals and toys, making it a favorite of children. The

SOUTHWEST GEORGIA 6

Prophet's Chamber, so-dubbed because it served as a stopover for traveling preachers in the Castle's earlier days, has double and twin beds with a separate sitting area.

Each of the bedchambers is decorated with antique furnishings, and displayed throughout the house is artwork the Palmers have collected from all over the world during their 32-year marriage.

True to the Victorian era, the Castle's distinctive features include a claw-foot tub, feather beds and even ironed pillowcases.

A sumptuous breakfast prepared by Patti is served with silver, china and crystal each morning.

An Interesting History

J.W. and Itura Colley married in 1885. They designed and built Bonnie Castle, moving in after construction was completed in 1896, following a prosperous year of cotton production. J.W. founded the **Grantville Hosiery Mill** and opened **The Bank of Grantville** at the turn-of-the-century. Among the couple's other holdings were warehouses, land, and a lodge building – investments that established them as one of the area's most prominent families.

Deeply in love, the couple had four sons, including one who reportedly died when only three days old. Sadly, just six years after moving into Bonnie Castle, J.W. died of tuberculosis, still a deadly disease in those days. Several years later, his widow, Miss Love, married Edmond Leigh, an act which created a new and unique name for the home's mistress. **Love Leigh** is a suitable name, says Patti, for a woman whose charm and good nature caused her to be considered a bright spot in the lives of community residents.

Sara O'Kelley, a third grade teacher who still lives down the street, remembers "Miss Love" as a practical joker who could mimic animal sounds or voices of other people. "She'd mimic an animal then act [as if nothing was amiss] when others looked around to see where the sound was coming from," she explained.

Sometimes Miss Love's practical jokes were more elaborate – even bordering on eccentric. According to Mrs. O'Kelley, Itura had a fondness for teasing visiting pastors. Pretending to hear an unusual noise, she would send a preacher up to the second floor to check it out, and when he opened the second door on the left, a manikin she had carefully positioned against the door would tumble out, almost always causing the horrified preacher – who thought he had discovered a dead body – to run red-faced and screaming downstairs. There, a beaming Miss Love would howl with laughter while chastising the panicked preacher.

"You're a minister of the cloth," Miss Love reportedly would squeal between guffaws. "You shouldn't be afraid of death!"

"She was a hoot," says Patti. "What a great sense of humor!"

Believing there should be only one mistress in a house, Itura, in her last years, gave Bonnie Castle to her daughter-in-law, Mary, and, interestingly, paid rent the rest of her life while living out her years in the home. She died at Bonnie Castle in 1955.

Mary, who married the Colley's son, Charles, brought a new realm of visitors to the mansion. As chairperson of the **Committee to Reelect President Franklin Roosevelt**, she entertained a variety of political figures, including F.D.R. himself who stopped by sometimes on his way to Warm Springs.

Mary made history another way as well. Her daughter, **Henrietta Yoder**, was the first female born in the Colley family in 158 years – a distinction that made the **Guinness Book of World Records** for the longest span between female births in one family, according to Patti. The Palmers have heard that Henrietta's wedding was featured in *LIFE* magazine and continue to search for a copy of the article.

Bonnie Castle remained in the Colley family until 1981 when, upon Mary's death, Henrietta sold the estate. The mansion changed hands several times during the following decade before being purchased by the Palmers in 1992.

Grandma Made Dolls

While exploring the attic one afternoon, Patti came across tiny apron patterns on fragments of aged paper, seemingly meant for a doll of some sort. During a visit at Bonnie Castle by Henrietta in 1994, Patti inquired about the fragments of paper.

"Oh those," Henrietta reportedly responded. "Grandma made dolls."

To her abject amazement, Patti later learned that a century ago, Itura had created what became folk art treasures once sold throughout the United States and several foreign countries. Her creations were such a mini-success that she employed a number of assistants to join her in the house where an "assembly line" was formed to turn out the unique creations which she patented in 1930 as "**Loveleigh Novelties**."

The doll heads were made from painted walnuts and the bodies of the dolls were constructed from wire armature. Miss Love used scraps of cloth, beads, string and buttons to fashion clothing for the whimsical toys. Featuring dark faces, the dolls reportedly depicted various members of the local black community around Grantville, according to Patti.

Fascinated with the quaint creations which Itura gave names such as "Old black Joe," "Aunt Lucy," and "Mammy's Little Angel Child," Patti made it her mission to locate some of the dolls crafted decades ago in her home. Enlisting the help of Henrietta, she secured photographs of the dolls and made "wanted posters" that were distributed to antique dealers far and wide.

A year later, the Palmers, to their delight, were presented their first doll – ironically donated by someone living right there in Grantville. As the collection grew, the folk art dolls were placed in the mansion's turret room, which has been remodeled as the **Colley Family Museum**. To date, the Palmers have about 50 of the original dolls displayed in the museum.

A few years ago, the Palmers also obtained the original supply cabinet Itura used to store the materials from which the dolls were constructed. Unseemly on the outside, the cabinet was a treasure trove on the inside, according to Patti, who was overjoyed to find it still contained its original contents, including beads, doll-making tools, wire, clothing, patterns for doll hats and other assorted odds and ends.

With her connection to Itura growing stronger as each year passed (She had earlier discovered that she and Darwin amazingly were married on the same unusual day as were Itura and J.W. – August 12, on a Wednesday at 1:00 p.m.), Patti found it a natural progression to take up doll-making herself, right where Itura had left off so many years ago. With the same patterns used by the first mistress of Bonnie Castle, Patti started crafting her own delightful dolls. She calls her reproductions **Loveleigh Novelties 1997**, and her first doll is a recreation of Mammy's Little Angel Child. These special edition pieces are limited to 500 units, with each doll being hand-made, signed, dated and numbered. After 500 are completed, Patti moves on to recreate another of Miss Love's characters.

"Reborn in the same house from which they originated, [right down to the use of the same construction materials from] the little supply cabinet, these dolls are accurately reproduced to represent the original dolls using the same materials, construction techniques and character identities," Patti smiles. "We even use acorns to make doll hats from the same oak trees in the backyard that Miss Love used."

Friendly Spirits

The Palmers maintain that aside from its other unique qualities, Bonnie Castle has – how shall we describe it – "spirits." They had heard the usual talk about how spirits dwelled in the mansion, and though Patti was not one to believe in ghosts, she was not one to dismiss them out of hand either.

"The day before we moved in, I had what I call a 'church chat' with whoever might be lingering upstairs," she says. "I told them what we wanted to do and that if there was anybody here, we wouldn't bother them."

About a week after they moved in, Darwin and Patti heard a noise in the middle of the night. It sounded like something had shattered.

"Darwin figured it would still be broken in the morning, so we went back to bed," Patti laughs. The next morning, she says the two of them searched the house from top to bottom and found nothing out of place. "We figured the ghost had either cleaned it up or put [whatever was broken] back together, one or the other."

Later one evening, the Palmers detected what Patti described as "a musty smell" in the house. They wondered about it but dismissed it when the odor was absent the following morning. The next night, however, the smell returned, only it was worse, "as if something had died, and it was only in our bedroom," says Patti. The couple searched the room but found nothing, and the next morning, the smell once again was gone.

On the third night, the odor was back again, but this time, it was so strong the couple had to sleep in a guest room upstairs. "It smelled like the mummies in a natural history museum," Patti relates.

To their surprise, the couple discovered that they could make the odor go away by stating out loud, "May I help you?"

Patti hesitates after explaining this to me. "I still feel uncomfortable telling this story in the house," she admits. "I figured it was time we had another 'church chat.'"

Recalling what Itura had told Mary about how there could only be one head of the house, Patti lit a candle in her bedroom and had a heart-to-heart with the spirit. "I told her there could be only one mistress in this house and that now, I was it," she recalls. "I felt cold chills all of a sudden, oh-my-gosh, and sensed that she really had heard me!" From that day forward, Patti said the smell was gone from the house.

Patti adds that she and Darwin believe the spirit that continues to reside at Bonnie Castle is probably Itura, although it could be Mary or even both of them. "She's not malevolent or sinister," Patti continues. "She just loved her home and hates to leave it."

The presence manifests itself in the usual ghostly methods – switching lights on and off and turning on radios. While their church chats keep "the girls" at bay, Patti says she occasionally gives the spirit(s) permission to cut up.

"We've had a good time here," Patti chuckles in conclusion. "Can you tell?"

(Bonnie Castle is located at 2 Post Street, Grantville, Georgia, 30220, a mile and a half west of Interstate 85 south at Exit 7. Call 770-583-3090 or 800-261-3090 for reservations. Check out their website too at www.bonnie-castle.com.)

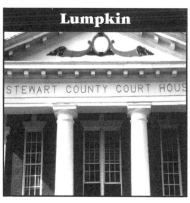

1850 is the magic number in Stewart County. The living-history community of **Westville** advertises that *"It's always 1850 in Westville,"* and only eight miles away is spectacular **Providence Canyon State Park**, whose gullies began to gain canyon status about 1850.

The starting point for a day-trip to both Westville and Providence Canyon is **Lumpkin**, Georgia, the seat of government for Stewart County. It too is worth a visit while you're in the area.

The town center is the courthouse square, and the attractive courthouse at this site has a white columned portico, along with very pretty gold leaf work above the cornice.

The south side of the square has a number of small shops which offer good browsing opportunities. One of these businesses – **The Singer Company** – is known as Georgia's oldest hardware store.

Stewart County is a Chattahoochee River county, located on the southern side of the Columbus, Georgia area. Lumpkin is located at the intersection of U.S. Highway 27 and State Highway 27, approximately 30 miles south of Columbus, 50 miles northwest of Albany, and 35 miles west of Americus.

On the east side of the Lumpkin town square, take Mulberry Street and travel approximately one mile south, and you'll find yourself at Westville. The stated mission of Westville is *"to conserve and demonstrate handicrafts, artifacts, landscape, and the overall environment of a pre-industrial west Georgia village."* In other words, it's a re-creation of a pioneer Georgia town.

This working community – complete with authentic buildings, gardens, period furnishings and dirt streets – does a very good job of completing this mission too. The village is laid out in the county seat grid pattern typical of many present-day south Georgia towns which originated in much this same pattern.

Since opening its "Gates To The Past" permanently in 1970, Westville has grown to over 30 buildings with over 5,000 authentic artifacts from the past. The pre-Civil War buildings range from log cabins to large, two-story structures.

Scenic Stewart County

Most of the logs in the historic structures in Westville were cut from old-growth heart pine, and still show the hewing marks from the broadax used to fell them. Boards of the frame buildings were planed by hand, and were secured with the old-type square (and very hard) nails. A common misconception maintains that all homes and shops of this era were painted white. In point of fact – they weren't - and the buildings of Westville have been repainted to match their original colors.

In addition to a general store, doctor's office and many other edifices, visitors to Westville will see a working blacksmith, a potter, boot maker, and a cabinet maker among many other artisans from yesteryear. These folks make their products using the same tools and techniques as did their predecessors back in 1850. Other crafts showcased here include basket weaving, candle making, quilting, spinning and weaving, and cooking (Don't miss the biscuits baked on the fireplace's hearth.).

At Westville, the "residents" raise crops just as they were raised in the old days. Everything is done the pioneer way. You'll see the last-remaining mule-powered cotton gin in the world, as well as a mule-powered sugar cane mill.

Since 1981, Westville's educational programs have grown to serve 25,000 students in well over 600 schools in several states. Cultural history classes have been provided to teachers in nine area counties.

The authenticity of the community has been confirmed many times. It has been documented in numerous books and articles, even attracting several Hollywood filmmakers such as Disney and ABC Television who used the town as the filming site for several major motion pictures in years past.

Scheduled special events at Westville include a spring festival, summertime vintage baseball games, a food-and-game-filled Fourth of July celebration, and a harvest-time fair.

Westville is open every day except Monday. Hours are from 10:00 a.m. to 5:00 p.m. Tuesday through Saturday, and 1:00 p.m. to 5:00 p.m. on Sunday afternoons. For more information on Westville, telephone 912-838-

6310. The web site address is www.westville.org.

Returning to our starting point on the town square at Lumpkin, turn left and follow Georgia Highway 27 out to U.S. Highway 27 (approximately ?-mile away). Turn right, change lanes, then take the first left onto Georgia Highway 39-C. Seven miles later, you'll be at beautiful **Providence Canyon State Conservation Park**.

The 1,109 acres of Providence are a collection of at least 16 canyons (the park is continually changing), the deepest being approximately 150 feet. Nine of these canyons are alongside a day-use driving area; the others can be seen by hiking or backpacking into the canyon.

The beauty of Providence confronts the senses even at the first parking area. The rugged, irregular canyon walls are a breathtaking palate of pastel hues: reds, orange, pinks and purples. Couple this array with a brilliant blue Georgia sky, and the greenery of trees and bushes growing in the canyons, and you have a photographer's paradise. It's no wonder that Providence has been labeled "**Georgia's Little Grand Canyon**."

Providence has been beautifully sculpted by water, but in the beginning, nature had a lot of help from man. When pioneer settlers in the area began cultivating crops they used a number of ill-advised farming methods. They stripped away the vegetation and plowed up and down the hills instead of contouring around the hills. When the rains came, the topsoil was quickly washed away and the land was gradually abandoned by the farmers because crops would no longer grow on it. With subsequent rainfalls, more and more of the loose, unstable sand-clay sediments were also washed downstream. By 1850, the furrows had become gullies, and the gullies soon graduated into the beginnings of the canyons seen today in this vicinity.

Two distinct geologic formations are layered in the canyons: the Clayton and the namesake Providence. Clayton is the top layer, and is basically clay with some sand. The beautiful tints of red in the upper levels of the many spires in the canyons are caused by deposits of iron ore.

The Providence layer is basically sand, with some clay interspersed. It is the thickest layer, being 120 feet deep in places. The Providence varies in color from tan to salmon to pink – and even to lavender where traces of manganese exist. This layer also contains veins of kaolin – the gray-to-white clay that is mined extensively from Macon to Augusta (and on into South Carolina).

After the run-off water had cut through the Clayton and hit the looser Providence, soil erosion became almost unstoppable. As the surface water cut vertically, the groundwater cut laterally. The impermeable "lenses" of kaolin have a very significant accelerating effect on the lateral erosion.

Today, the downward or vertical erosion appears to have halted in most areas due to the lower portion of the Providence layer known as the Perote. Composed mostly of clay, the Perote is comparatively impermeable and acts as a sealer, stunting the effects of surface erosion. Today, trees, bushes and other vegetation now growing on the floors of the canyons have combined to further stabilize this area.

Lateral erosion, however, continues basically unchecked, and consumes several feet of soil per year, gradually widening the canyons. This widening appears to be accelerating too, probably due to the clearing of land in the vicinity.

An added attraction inside this scenic park is the **Providence United Methodist Church**, with its nearby graveyard. The church was chased from its original location by lateral erosion of the canyon. The present structure was built in 1859. The names and epitaphs on the tombstones in the cemetery offer a glimpse into the past.

Providence Canyon State Park is open year-round. From April 15 to September 14, the park is open from 7:00 a.m. to 9:00 p.m. For the other months of the year, it is open from 7:00 a.m. to 6:00 p.m.

The office and interpretive center of the park are open from 8:00 a.m. to 5:00 p.m. year-round. Facilities include picnic tables and shelters, a group shelter, a pioneer campground, and primitive camping for backpackers.

The largest in-the-wild collection of the rare plumleaf azalea blooms in the canyon floor in late June, early July. There is a three-mile loop trail for hiking, and seven miles of back packing trails.

Other than the pioneer and primitive camping areas, there are no overnight facilities in the park, but nearby **Florence Marina State Park** is "just down the road," eight miles west on Highway 30-C. Florence has RV sites, camping, cottages, and efficiency units.

(For more information on Providence Canyon State Park, call 229-838-6202. Florence Marina may be contacted by telephoning 229-838-6870. For information via the internet, go to www.gastateparks.org.)

Southwest Georgia

Riding the Rails on the Historic SAM Shortline

A historic rail line, built in the 1880s during the days when **Doc Holliday** and **Wyatt Earp** were in their prime, has been put back into use. Today, an excursion train travels this route once again, taking sightseers to a collection of unique destinations in the southwestern corner of the state.

Southwest Georgia is an area rich in history and nostalgia. It is full of small towns where life moves slowly, and historic sites that have helped to shape our state's history. A new attraction – the **SAM Shortline Railroad** – is taking advantage of the tourism opportunities offered by these towns.

SAM, short for the Savannah, Americus and Montgomery Railroad Company which once operated on the same tracks in the 1880s, is a state-sponsored excursion train which began operations in southwest Georgia this past October. Referred to by some as "**Georgia's Rolling State Park,**" the SAM Shortline passes through two counties and five towns.

The train ride takes passengers through some of the most beautiful scenery in southwestern Georgia: fields white with cotton and orchards thick with pecan trees loaded with nuts; past aged country homes with green roofs and wrap-around porches, and across a trestle over picturesque **Lake Blackshear**.

The shortline train – which is quickly becoming a popular weekend getaway opportunity – consists of three vintage passenger cars, a commissary car which includes a gift shop and a snack bar, and the Samuel H. Hawkins dining car, which is named for the founder of the Savannah, Americus and Montgomery Railway.

Just a scant 40 miles or so down the road in Valdosta is the boyhood home of **John Henry "Doc" Holliday**, one of the heroes of the Old West gunfight at **O.K. Corral** in 1881. There are many other historic sites and scenic attractions in the vicinity of Cordele (where the SAM Shortline begins) too, so if a vacationer wanted to make this a week-long getaway, there are plenty of things to see and do.

The SAM Shortline is operated by the Georgia Department of Natural Resources (DNR) under the guidance of the Southwest Georgia Railway Excursion Authority. The engine which pulls the SAM train is owned and operated by the Heart of Georgia Railroad Company, which runs freight on the same lines Monday through Thursday.

SAM Shortline also has a prominent native son who is providing support and promotion for the endeavor. Former **U.S. President Jimmy Carter** – Sumter County's own – has been heavily involved in the development of the shortline since its conception.

Local officials hope that the SAM Shortline will bring economic development and stimulate tourism in the area. Besides the regular tourists who are interested in seeing beautiful and historic southwest Georgia, it is hoped the SAM Shortline will appeal to motor coach tours and school field trips as well. Participants can be dropped off by bus at any one of the train stops along the route and then picked up miles down the road at another stop.

On its regular excursions, SAM departs from Cordele and travels west with stops at the **Georgia State Veteran's State Park** and the towns of Leslie, Americus, Plains and Archery. Each stop offers a number of historic attractions and shopping opportunities. Passengers may board the train at any of the stops and return the same day. Depending on the train's schedule, passengers may also spend the night in a town and catch the train back to their point of origin the next day.

The SAM Railroad Company brought growth to southwest Georgia in the 1880s, allowing local farmers an opportunity to ship their products all over the country. Many of the towns that are still along the line today originated from this burst of commerce over 100 years ago.

Another big market the modern-day version of the railroad expects to "farm" is the under 40ish crowd – those raised after the days when passenger trains were the main mode of transportation. For those people, the SAM

6 SOUTHWEST GEORGIA

Shortline will be a great way to enjoy the experience of a passenger train ride and the excitement it offers.

"All Aboard In Cordele"

The official starting point of the SAM Shortline is Cordele, Georgia, conveniently located right off of Interstate 75. Home to the **Georgia State Farmers Market** and billed as the "**Watermelon Capital Of The World**," Cordele has twelve hotels where out-of-towners can spend the night before catching the train. Nearby, Lake Blackshear offers fishing, boating and camping.

State Representative Johnny Floyd (D-Cordele), has been involved in the formation of the shortline from the beginning. He explained that the idea for SAM was a collaborative effort on the part of people from Cordele, Plains, Americus and Leslie, to enhance tourism along the **Jimmy Carter Historic Trail**.

"We think it's a great idea," Floyd said. "Interstate 75 runs right through Cordele and if we can draw people off the interstate, the sales tax dollars will mean a lot to us. So the shortline is important to us on two levels: economically and as a means of preserving the history of the area."

Georgia Veterans Memorial State Park

The first stop on the shortline – the **Georgia Veteran's Memorial State Park** – is barely 15 miles from the starting point in Cordele, but it could be the last stop for many passengers. Situated on Lake Blackshear, the 1,322-acre park offers an 18-hole golf course, a swimming pool and beach, nature trails and fishing.

Cottages, tents, and recreational vehicle sites are available. For those with more comfort in mind, **The Retreat At Lake Blackshear** opened this past autumn. With 88 rooms, a restaurant, a marina, conference facilities and more, The Retreat offers accommodations for groups up to 450.

Established first and foremost as a memorial to U.S. veterans, the Georgia Veteran's Memorial Park features a museum inside the welcome center which highlights America's involvement from the Revolutionary War through the Gulf War. Uniforms, guns, and other items are displayed.

An additional room to celebrate the contributions of Cordele native **Mac Hyman**, author of the best-selling novel *No Time For Sergeants*, is under construction. Based upon Hyman's own experiences in the military, *No Time For Sergeants* was turned into an award-winning Broadway play. The movie version, filmed in 1958, is considered the vehicle that launched the career of television star **Andy Griffith**.

Outside the museum are many other exhibits which include tanks, bombers and helicopters from World War I through the Vietnam War. A Boeing B-29 – the only one still in existence – is also located at this site.

Lovely Leslie

Leslie, a charming community of about 455 citizens, defines small-town perfection. This little slice of Southern Americana is located half-way between Americus and Albany. "For Sale" signs on the homes in this town usually don't last very long at all. Young couples usually snap up the homes here that are close to their jobs, yet "out in the country" enough to allow a "Mayberry" sort of existence.

It might well be that any economic boom the shortline brings to southwest Georgia will be heard the loudest in Leslie. Already, shops within walking distance of the train depot are being refurbished. A new antiques shop has opened; a welcome center and a park are planned, as is a new restaurant.

Bobby Hines – who has lived in Leslie since he was six years old – is the owner of Callie's Collectibles, an antiques store that has been in downtown Leslie for over 11 years. Hines says he plans to meet each and every train that stops in his town. His store occupies space that once was the Leslie Drug Company.

Hines is just one of many people who have expressed pleasure at the thought of a train stopping in town again. He says he remembers when a passenger train stopped there regularly, although that was many years ago.

Leslie is also home to the **Georgia Rural Telephone Museum**, housed in a renovated 1920s cotton warehouse. Contained in the museum is one of the largest collections of antique telephones and telephone memorabilia in the world. Some of the pieces date back to 1876.

Admiring Americus

In Americus, the train will stop directly across from the **Habitat for Humanity's Global Village and Discovery Center**, a six-acre complex. When completed, the Global Village will display model Habitat homes from 40 countries and house an international marketplace.

While Americus has always had an on-going effort to maintain the appearance and viability of its downtown area, additional revitalization has occurred as a result of the SAM railroad. Several new businesses have moved into town, and the city has restored several previously-unoccupied buildings.

Downtown Americus is within walking distance of the Shortline's depot, and is a shopper's dream come true. A wide variety of consumer products are available – from upscale children's clothing at the Tot Shop to fresh produce at the Farmer's Market.

Americus may be the perfect place to turn the train ride into a weekend getaway too. The **Windsor Hotel**, which opened in 1892, is the most recognizable building downtown. Right down the street from the Windsor, you can catch a show at the **Rylander Theater**, built in the 1920s, which offers regular tours as well as live performances and plays.

Americus is also the boyhood home of former **Atlanta Falcons Head Coach Dan Reeves** and **Georgia Tech Head Coach Chan Gailey**. A number of other notables grew up in this story-book town.

A President In Plains

After visiting the town of **Plains**, it's easy to understand why a former President of the United States and his First Lady would choose to live here after having lived in the White House in Washington, D.C. With its distinctive small-town flavor, Plains is lovely to say the least. Visitors may or may not run into the Carters while in Plains, but the next best thing is meeting people that actually know them.

The SAM Shortline stops in Plains right across the street from **The Plains Inn & Antiques** which opened in February of 2003. The inn is owned by the city and is operated under the "Better Hometown" program. It features seven suites, each decorated with items from a distinct decade from the 1920s to the 1980s, representing the decades of President Carter's life from his birth through his presidency.

The Carters were closely involved in the design of the inn. Mrs. Carter worked with a decorator designing each room in its particular furnishings – right down to the clawfoot bathtubs and the rotary dial phones.

There is also a common room where breakfast is available each morning; a television room, and the inn's most wonderful feature – a front porch on the second floor which affords a view of the entire town. The first floor of the inn is filled with antiques from over 20 dealers across the South. Sandra Walters and her husband, C.L., manage the inn for the city.

School classes were still held at the Plains High School up until 1979. Today, the building houses the museum and visitor center of the **Jimmy Carter National Historical Site.** Visitors can see films and exhibits which depict the history of Plains and the town's famous son.

Other sites of interest are the **Plains Depot**, which served as the **campaign headquarters for Jimmy Carter during his U.S. Presidential bid**. A short distance away is the **United Methodist Church** where **Jimmy and Rosalyn were married**. Even **Billy Carter's Service Station** and the business district which dates back to the 1890s have been preserved.

On Sundays, when he's in town, Jimmy Carter teaches Sunday school at the Maranatha Baptist Church. This attractive church has a membership of approximately 150, but it receives over 10,000 visitors a year.

Aiming At Archery

The final stop on the SAM Shortline is the first stop in the story of America's 39th President. **Jimmy Carter's boyhood home** in the little town of **Archery** is still a working farm where black-eyed peas, collards, squash and of course – peanuts – are grown each season between the house, barns, and other buildings. Carter lived on the farm until 1941 when he departed for college.

As one walks around the farm today, he or she will hear – via recorded narratives – President Carter describe the childhood he spent there. Viewing the humble surroundings which include an outhouse and a hand-pump for water, visitors leave with the distinct impression that a good education and hard work can take anybody to the White House.

While riders are visiting the President's boyhood home, the SAM Shortline turns around to ready itself for the return trip back to Cordele. The train covers 69 miles of historical stops, and the entire train ride – from departure to return to Cordele – takes approximately eight hours.

Interestingly, most of the historic sites and attractions in the towns at which the train stops are free, or have only a small admission charge. The trip can be appealing to all age groups and interests. The day-long venture is also very "child friendly" with many things that reportedly will intrigue young children and teenagers.

Representatives with the SAM Shortline say there are many special events planned with the train in the months ahead, including a ride on the train with Santa and a series of special shopping excursion trips.

(Times, schedules and ticket prices vary, but the SAM Shortline has an excellent web site at www.samshortline.com. Interested persons may also call for more information about the Shortline at (800) 864-7275. The web site offers links to each town and attraction on the route.)

6 SOUTHWEST GEORGIA

Thomasville

Thomasville Rose Festival

The attractive little town originated from the commercial needs of a collection of plantations in the fertile valleys of Thomas County in extreme southwestern Georgia. It later prospered as a winter retreat for wealthy Northern industrialists prior to the development of Florida. With a strong sense of civic pride, an impressive event was organized that continues to this day. Now, "everything comes up roses" in Thomasville.

"A rose is more than a rose in Thomasville, Georgia." So said the *Atlanta Journal* magazine in its June 13, 1948 issue. The lead paragraph went on to say that the rose was "a city-wide passion." The article was describing the city's annual **Rose Festival**, saying that it was "more like Mardi Gras than a flower show," referring to the parade that took 30 minutes to complete.

In that 1948 parade, there were seven floats bedecked with hundreds of roses from the "**City of Roses**," as well as nearby towns in south Georgia and northern Florida. In addition, three high school bands from Thomasville, Moultrie, and Monticello, Florida, marched to their own music as they serenaded thousands of onlookers. Reining supreme over this version of the Festival was Thomasville's first "**Rose Queen**," **Miss Doris Gothard**, elected by the students of Thomasville High School. And this was in 1948!

Reviving The Show

Although this was the city's first **Rose Parade**, it, in fact was Thomasville's 27th annual Rose Festival. The parade was part of a concerted effort in 1948 to revive the faded glory of the "Rose Show," a "Roaring Twenties" event which had almost been killed off completely by World War II.

The Thomasville Garden Club had managed to pull the show through the war years, sometimes charging a 25-cent admission fee, with profits going to buy Defense Bonds. The addition of a parade, however, in 1948, was deemed the best way to renew the old Rose Show enthusiasm. Little did they know what they were creating.

The following year, the parade had 30 floats and eight marching bands! This parade passion has continued right up to the present day, too.

Although it had been a Friday morning tradition for years, the parade is now held on Friday evening.

The event now has a younger sibling too called "**The Rosebud Parade.**" As you might guess, it is reserved strictly for the kids. Almost anything goes too, and the kids – with a lot of help from parents, teachers and friends – enjoy as much fun as is reasonably possible.

The main event however – the Rose Show – is now held in a large barn-like building at the **Exchange Club Fairgrounds** on Pavo Road, within sight of U.S. Highway 19. This coveted event hosts thousands of competition-level roses each year. Single entries, beautiful artistic arrangements, and huge sprays of roses vie for prizes. Large elaborate displays by local and out-of-town nurseries showcase hundreds more versions of the beautiful flowers. Other flower species compete as well, but it is the captivating rose which dominates this event.

The Rose Show opens at 1:30 p.m. on Friday, with the crowning of the year's Rose Queen. The Show is open until 6:00 p.m., and then again on Saturday from 9:30 a.m. until 4:00 p.m.

Just like any other rose show, of which there are many all around the country, right? Well, not quite. Aside from the sheer beauty of the flowers at this event, and the fun-filled activities, one needs to know a bit about the history of the Thomasville Rose Show to really understand its magnitude.

Origin Of The Town

The roots of this gala event go back far

beyond the first show. Over a century ago, Thomasville was considered one of the most fashionable places in the United States to visit, especially if you were a Northerner with lots of money. Then, as now, Thomasville enjoys a location surrounded by some of the most fertile farmland in the country. As a result, many antebellum plantations were built in the vicinity. Many of them still survive today – approximately 70 at last count – covering more than 300,000 acres.

When Thomasville was incorporated in 1827, the town was already well-established due to the many plantations. Though it has no river, and did not even have a railroad until 1861, the area nonetheless prospered due to the richness of the soil. This was, and is, the land of graceful Live Oaks, Dogwood, Azalia, and Wisteria plantations.

Another factor – perhaps even the main one – which aided the town's early growth, was its close proximity to Florida, which, in the latter half of the 19th century, teemed with malaria. The dryer Thomasville area had none, and as a result, many wealthy Northern families – particularly in the Victorian Era – adopted Thomasville as their grand winter resort (instead of the warmer but malaria-plagued Florida).

By 1885, the city had several very large and elaborate hotels that catered to the rich industrialists from up North. There were also 15 to 20 boarding houses, and a wealth of luxury apartments. Most of these early "snowbirds" traveled to Thomasville by way of the railroad, which was convenient and dependable.

As a result of this influence, Thomasville enjoyed an early cultural growth. Big name entertainers performed in the town in the late 1880s and 1890s, including **John Phillip Sousa** and his band and many others.

Many of the wealthy visitors liked Thomasville so well that they built their own "winter cottages" in the city. More than 50 of these grand old Victorian homes still grace the streets of this beautiful city.

This combination of factors – large plantations with great soil, an early rise to national prominence as a winter resort, and then the gift of scores of beautiful Victorian homes – has produced the Thomasville known today,

including the **Thomas County Museum of History**, world-class musical performances and plays at the **Thomasville Cultural Center**, the city's Rose Garden with over 500 varieties of roses, the revered 300-year-old Live Oak (the largest east of the Mississippi) in the center of town, the **National Historic Landmark Lapham-Patterson House**, the elegant **Pebble Hill Plantation** with 40 rooms and 3,000 acres, and the list goes on and on.

<u>Rose Show Early Years</u>

The Rose Show itself had a rather humble beginning in 1920. At that time, it didn't include roses at all, but rather a showing of vegetables! Competition at the first "vegetable show" earned the winner a $25 first prize. The money was donated to the Thomasville Garden Club and became the seed money for a flower show, "preferably a rose show." Little did they know. . .

The Garden Club met with local nurserymen, and a Mr. **George Neel** who owned a department store on Broad Street in downtown Thomasville. Mr. Neel offered his millinery department, in the front corner of his store, as a display space for a flower show.

The first show was held on Tuesday, April 25, 1922. People brought so many roses – along with other types of flowers – that all the millinery counters were filled, and the show overflowed into the upstairs balcony.

As a result of this excitement, the Thomasville Rose Show was off and running, but it was already obvious that the space at Neel's was not large enough to accommodate all the people who wanted to display their flowers. After using the local Buick showroom in 1924, the show moved to the basketball shell of East Side School. The basketball seats were probably responsible for the stair-step arrangement of flowers that was used so often in later years.

By this time, the Chamber of Commerce was also involved in the show, and secured a downtown tobacco warehouse for the event. Six Rose Shows were held there, beginning in 1926. The warehouse offered plenty of room, and the shows were arranged with exhibits (some being very elaborate) around the sides of the large facility, with single flowers (for judging) and other decorated tables in the middle. This format has been the "standard" for many flower shows ever since.

Birth Of A Festival

By 1928, "side events" had been added to the Rose Show. These included golf matches, motor tours to the nearby estates and plantations, a baseball game, a band concert, and a dance at the local American Legion. The Rose Show was now a festival!

Tom Hill with the Thomas County Museum of History maintains the years that began in the tobacco warehouse were the "heydays" of the Rose Show. During this time, local nurseries produced very elaborate displays. One memorable version had over 11,000 roses. During these years, owners of the large plantations would send their gardening crews to construct the amazing exhibits.

Mill Pond Plantation reportedly sent its entire staff of 25 gardeners to build for ten days – all for a one-day show. They set up the entire 100-foot width of the warehouse with real grass, ponds, water wheels, and, of course, thousands of flowers.

Not to be outdone by the gardeners, the Thomasville Ice Company developed a technique to produce beautiful rose displays – frozen in huge blocks of ice!

In 1931, the Depression finally left its mark on the tobacco business in town, and the warehouse folded. The Rose Show then moved to an airplane hangar at nearby **Vose Field**. The hangar had a dirt floor which the rose folks covered with sawdust. This became the home of the Show through 1941.

These "hangar years" are very special memories for Mary Grubbs, a former 5th grade teacher, school principal, basketball player and coach. Mary spent many hours – in various capacities – working in the Rose Festivals.

During these heydays, Mary fondly recalls that the folks of Thomasville did the Rose Show for themselves. Practically everybody in town had one or two roses in the show. . . . not as a result of passionate competition, but simply because they were part of the community. Just about everyone grew at least a few roses, and they wanted to learn from the show's judging.

In those days, all roses still had that wonderful fragrant smell too, and Mary says she can still smell the show at the airport hangar. The sawdust on the floor and the walls covered with pine boughs added "just a hint of pine" to the overwhelming bouquet of thousands of roses!

The Rose Festival is a large reflection of the individual and civic pride that is Thomasville. That pride lives on today. Mary Grubbs says that Thomasville is "still such a special, wonderful place, where civic pride runs high, and the people like to show off their city. Thomasville IS the City of Roses. . . . and the Festival is a way of getting people here to see just how special it is."

From the 1920s right up to today, everything comes up roses in Thomasville, Georgia.

(For more information on the Thomasville Rose Festival, contact the Thomasville Welcome Center at 229-228-7977 or 800-704-2350. Visit their website at www.thomasvillega.com.)

SOUTHWEST GEORGIA 6

Thomasville

Historic Thomasville

From 1870 to 1900 – before there was a Miami, Florida – Thomasville, Georgia, was the destination of choice of Northerners who wished to escape harsh winter weather. And prior to these "snowbirds," there were so many Southern plantations in this area that it later became known as "**Plantation Alley.**" Today, as a result of all this history, the "City of Roses" and its environs offer a plethora of breathtaking architecture.

Life moves at a gentle slow pace in Thomasville, Georgia. Deep in the farthest reaches of the southwestern part of the state, just a few miles from the Florida line, this sleepy Southern town is the quintessential place at which time seems to have stood still. The quiet lull of delicate breezes through the tall pines, punctuated occasionally by the whistle of a bobwhite quail, sets the stage for an unforgettable journey into the past.

Thomasville is exactly what one would expect of rural south Georgia: rolling green hills; red clay furrowed in hues of carmine, mahogany, and cinnamon; graceful plantations that bespeak of a time long since departed in other areas; kudzu-covered roadsides; immense magnolia and oak trees drizzling with Spanish moss; amazing homes from yesteryear; and, of course, plenty of warm Southern hospitality.

Once a hunting site for the Lower Creek and Apalachee Indians, pioneer settlers began moving into the area following the **Treaty of Fort Jackson** in 1814 and land grants from the Creeks in 1818. It is Thomasville's natural beauty, however, that began luring visitors in 1825, when Thomas County was formed from parts of Irwin and Decatur Counties.

Thomas Jefferson Johnson, who owned and built **Pebble Hill Plantation**, introduced legislation that brought Thomas County into being. Both the city and county are believed to have been named for Major General Jett Thomas, who served in the state militia in the War of 1812.

Over the next few decades – up until the War Between the States – Thomasville evolved slowly from Indian hunting grounds to a cotton and plantation society that is classically Old South. Known locally as the "Antebellum Plantation Era," it was a time when "King Cotton" ruled, although it certainly wasn't the only crop grown in Thomas County. Some of the plantations also produced high quality tobacco, corn, pecans, and pears.

"There is not another area in the United States that has a history of plantations like we do," says local historian Thomas Hill. "And one of the things that is so unusual about the plantations is that they are *still* here."

Of the seventy-one plantations strewn over 300,000 acres on **Plantation Parkway** between Thomasville and Tallahassee, only two are open to the public. The others are private homes and quail-hunting retreats that have hosted former presidents **William McKinley**, **Dwight D. Eisenhower**, and **Jimmy Carter**, as well as dignitaries such as **Jacqueline Kennedy Onassis**, actress **Dixie Carter**, and the United Kingdom's **Duke of Windsor**.

The first of the two plantations open to the public is Pebble Hill, a house museum rich in art and history that was once a "shooting" or "quail" plantation. Whitney White oversees the plantation's special projects today.

"Pebble Hill's history dates back to the 1820s, and we were *'the'* place for people to spend winters during the Resort Era from 1870 to the turn of the century," White explains.

Taking more than eighteen months to build from the time the plantation was commissioned by Thomas Jefferson Johnson to its completion in 1827, Pebble Hill is a white-columned masterpiece of architecture. Originally a cotton plantation that remained in the Johnson family until 1896, the property eventually was purchased by **Howard Melville Hanna**, a Cleveland, Ohio, industrialist and executive of Standard Oil Company who wintered in the Thomasville each year.

Hanna, an avid sportsman who enjoyed quail hunting, presented the plantation in 1901 to his daughter, Kate. She married Robert Ireland, and the two turned Pebble Hill into one of the finest homes in the South. Along with her second husband, Perry Williams Harvey, Kate continued to make improvements, adding rooms and gardens as they saw fit.

Tragically, in 1934, the home was all but destroyed by fire. The east wing of the historic structure was all that could be saved. The present house was re-built under the direction of **Abram**

6
SOUTHWEST GEORGIA

Garfield, the son of **Chester A. Garfield**, the nation's 20th president. Floor-to-ceiling windows, complemented with lengthy hallways stretching from here to yonder, allow generous sunlight that provides natural warmth and beauty.

Elisabeth Ireland Poe, the free-spirited but very private daughter of Kate and Robert Ireland, was the last of the Hanna heirs to own Pebble Hill. A gracious host, collector and patron of the arts, and avid sportswoman, "Miss Pansy," as she was affectionately known, willed her home to be opened to the public upon her death so that others could view her extensive collection of Indian artifacts, crystal, antiques, porcelain, carvings, sculptures of her beloved dogs and horses, and other artwork, including more than thirty Audubon originals and an untold number of paintings and prints depicting sporting scenes and wildlife.

Now comprising 3,000 acres of timberland, pastures, and gardens, as well as forty rooms filled with Miss Pansy's collections, Pebble Hill is known as the "South's premier plantation," and was featured on **A&E's Television's** *America's Castles* in 1997.

Melhana, touted as the "Grand Plantation," is the second of the two plantations open to the public, and it is the only one in the Thomasville area that is open for overnight guests. Now owned by Charlie and Fran Lewis, Melhana Plantation is the epitome of Southern elegance and beauty, which is only enhanced by its quite lengthy and significant history.

At its height, the plantation contained more than 7,500 acres. In 1825, Pulaski County attorney Paul Coalson bought the first 750 acres of Melhana's timberlands and fields, paying a grand total of $730 for the entire spread, which was less than one dollar for each acre. He is also credited with building the first original home on the property that is known today as "**The Inn at Melhana**."

After Coalson's death in 1830, his widow, Mary Elizabeth, then married her first cousin, Henry Wyche, who purchased an additional 750 acres of surrounding land. The plantation remained in the Wyche family until 1862 when it was sold to William Gignilliat, a rice planter from the Georgia's coast. In 1869, Gignilliat sold the property to another coastal resident, Dr. Samuel John Jones. Upon Jones's death, his widow, Lizzie, sold the plantation to Charles M. Chapin of New Jersey.

Chapin was the son of Salome M. Hanna and George W. Chapin. He became the first member of the Hanna family to own the plantation. He bought the home from Jones in 1889, but in 1896, sold it to Howard Melville Hanna, who had also acquired Pebble Hill. After purchasing the property, Hanna named it **Melrose Plantation**, and it was he who increased the acreage to 7,500 by buying part of adjoining **Sinkola Plantation**. Melrose remained intact in the Hanna family until 1986.

In the hundred years or so of Hanna family ownership, dozens of historic buildings were added to the property, including stables, garages, offices, a milking barn, a dairy building, a carriage house, an indoor pool house where Hanna family friend and **actress Joan Crawford** once swam, and the **Showboat**, a private theater built to resemble a riverboat and where *Gone with the Wind* was originally screened in 1939. At that time, Howard Melville Hanna Jr., owned Melrose. His friend and neighbor, **John Hay Whitney**, was a major investor in the film. Prior to the premier of *GWTW* in Atlanta, Whitney and Hanna Jr., invited about forty of their closest friends to Melrose to preview the movie at the Showboat.

In 1986, roughly 31 acres that included the main house and stable complex were sold by the Hanna heirs to Dr. William F. and Mary Hogan of Thomasville. In 1994, the Lewises, the current owners, bought approximately 40 acres from the Hogans and the Hannas. In honor of the Hanna family, the Lewises renamed the property Melhana – The Grand Plantation.

Today, Charlie and Fran Lewis have graciously restored the plantation with traditional authenticity and period furnishings. The grounds are just as astoundingly pretty as the house: peacocks and squirrels amble and play while hummingbirds, quail, and cardinals flit about in the trees and shrubbery. The wide verandahs, abundant wicker, and kaleidoscopic azaleas, camellias, angel wing begonias, and hibiscus complement formal English gardens and luxurious accommodations. Melhana's uniqueness as a plantation – *and* an inn – attracts guests from all over the world.

As the plantation and cotton society flourished and homes such as Melhana and Pebble Hill were being constructed, the first railroad came to Thomasville in 1861 – out of sheer necessity – if not for mere convenience.

As more and more Northerners made their way southward to Thomasville, word spread that the area was lush with wildlife. Wealthy hunters began to flock to the town, and many of them stayed on permanently or built second homes there. These "winter cottages" as they were known, would become an integral part of Thomasville's history.

"The entire Resort Era was a pivotal point because of the influx of money," explains Ann Harrison, director of the Thomas County Historic Society. "At that time, the rural South, even with Reconstruction, was reeling financially, but Thomasville continued to prosper. This particular time was very important for the town, because so much of our architecture goes back to that era."

The Resort Era ended around the turn of the century when rail lines snaked their way into Florida. Thomasville then found itself unable to compete with the more favorable weather and sandy beaches of the Atlantic Ocean and Gulf of Mexico. Thomasville's architecture, however, reaped the benefits of the combination of the Antebellum Plantation Era and Resort Era. Most of the cottages and homes are still in existence, and while most of them remain private, others have been transformed into bed-and-breakfast inns or historic attractions.

Each home that has been restored as a bed-and-breakfast is uniquely different. For example, the 1884 **Paxton House**, located in a quiet residential historic district, is a Victorian-style inn that boasts twelve fireplaces and double heart pine floors. The 1854 **Wright House** is an antebellum Greek Revival cottage that is set amidst a stand of spectacular oaks. The **Mitchell-Young-Anderson House**, built in the late 1800s, is an African-American home filled with century-old furniture; and, for added intrigue, this home has the distinction of once having been a brothel.

Several of the historic bed-and-breakfast inns are adorned with white columns, including the **Magnolia Leaf Bed and Business** – its renovations were designed with the business traveler in mind, hence the distinct name – and the **Neel House Lodging**, a Neo-Classical home built in 1907 for **Elijah Leonidas Neel**, a successful South Georgia businessman and landowner. Its paired Ionic columns, wrap porch, and an ocular window help make this property one of the most charming inns in Thomasville.

The **Lapham-Patterson House**, another of Thomasville's one-of-a-kind homes, has the peculiarity of having been built with no right angles. The home, now a state historic site, was constructed between 1884 and 1885 as a winter home for C.W. Lapham of Chicago, a wealthy shoe merchant. In a city filled with incomparable architecture, the Lapham-Patterson House is a standout even among standouts. Named a **National Historic Landmark** in 1975, the home includes a double-flue chimney, a walk-through staircase, fish-scale shingles, a cantilevered balcony, and longleaf pine inlaid floors.

Another historically significant home open to the public is the **Hardy Bryan House**, considered the oldest two-story house in Thomasville. Hardy Bryan's brother, Loverd, and Elizabeth Wyche were among the first couples to be married in the newly formed Thomas County; their wedding date was June 30, 1826. The home, once a small farm, was built in two stages in 1833 and 1837. It is now the headquarters for Thomasville

Landmarks, Inc., a group that recognizes the significance of historic preservation.

Tucked in among the Victorian homes and inns of Thomasville is the 318-year-old "**Big Oak**." Dating to 1685 and located at the corner of Crawford and East Monroe Streets, this is the largest oak tree east of the Mississippi River. Fully covering two-thirds of an acre, its long, gnarly limbs make it wider than Niagara Falls is deep. According to local lore, **President Dwight D. Eisenhower** visited the tree while he was a guest of George Humphreys. He was so impressed with its massiveness that he took several photographs of it himself.

For a comprehensive look at Thomasville from the earliest settlers to the Resort Era after Reconstruction to the present day, the Thomas County Museum of History – spread over a city block shrouded with magnolias and crepe myrtles – provides a captivating look at the area's uncommon history. Dedicated to preserving and sharing the story of Thomas County, visitors are allowed glimpses into the past through exhibits showcasing memorabilia and costumes from the 1820s to the 1940s, military relics from the Civil War through World War II, a cumulative plantation history – including the unique lifestyle of African-American families who lived and worked on the plantations – antique cars, and historic buildings, including the Rufus Smith House.

Nicknamed the "City of Roses," Thomasville lives up to its name. The **Thomasville Rose Garden**, one of more than a hundred gardens in town, is a dazzling display of colors and scents. Located along the waters of Cherokee Lake, the rose garden is complete with a Victorian gazebo. The **Thomasville Rose Show** and **Festival** are held each April, drawing in thousands from all over the world to see more than seven thousand roses planted throughout the city.

While Thomasville's history is one of the most colorful of all of the cities in Georgia, its matchless Victorian architecture and tree-laden brick streets and sidewalks were a boost to its being honored as a Georgia **Main Street City**. Thomasville is still a small town by most standards, and but even so, its "never ordinary, always extraordinary" downtown provides an endless selection of shopping opportunities, festivals, and fairs that draw visitors from all over the Southeast.

Once simply the end of the railroad line in Georgia, Thomasville has always been a well-kept secret because of its remote location. Today, visitors are rediscovering the town and its environs as a place to sojourn into the past.

(For more information on Thomasville, contact Destination Thomasville Tourism Authority at (800) 704-2350 or (229) 227-7099, or visit the website at www.thomasvillega.com.)

Warm Springs

The Little White House

The historic site is quiet today. Gone are the **Secret Service**, the Presidential staff, and the intrigue which once surrounded this peaceful retreat. At one time, however, in the 1930s and '40s, it was considered the ultimate getaway by the 32nd **President of the United States**.

Millions of people were listening that April afternoon in 1945 as a radio drama about Daniel Boone entitled *Wilderness Road* emanated from Studio 28 of the **Columbia Broadcasting System (CBS)** in New York City. Suddenly, three bells rang on a teletype machine and pandemonium broke out in the newsroom.

Newsman **John Daly** (who later gained fame as the emcee of a quiz show called *What's My Line*), preparing for the evening news broadcast, read the words on the yellow paper in disbelief and then quickly signaled technicians to break into the Daniel Boone program.

At 5:49 p.m., Eastern Standard Time, on April 12, 1945, Daly reported quickly but succinctly, "We interrupt this program to bring you a special news bulletin. **President Franklin Delano Roosevelt** is dead."

Warm Springs, Georgia, where Roosevelt died, held FDR's attention longer than any place on earth, except, possibly, his **Hyde Park, New York** ancestral home. The President's frequent visits (41 in all) to Warm Springs began in 1924 and continued until his death. His desire to make the warm mineral springs in the area available to others suffering from polio (infantile paralysis) made the small Georgia town instantly familiar by name to most Americans.

Memories of Roosevelt are carefully preserved at Warm Springs, where both a museum and FDR's retreat – kept exactly as it was the day he died – are open to the public today. A million people come annually to visit what was known during the **Great Depression** and **World War II** as "**the Little White House.**"

FDR – The Early Days

In 1921, Franklin Roosevelt, age 39, while relaxing at his family's vacation home on **Campobello**, an island off the southwestern coast of New Brunswick, Canada, was suddenly stricken with the terrible disease, polio. He had just emerged from a swim in the icy waters of the Bay of Fundy.

From the beginning, Roosevelt downplayed his devastating illness. "I have renewed my youth in a rather unpleasant manner," he wrote in late 1921, "by contracting what is, fortunately, a rather mild case of infantile paralysis." Actually, the prognosis was far worse.

Though he and his doctors all believed he suffered from polio, he might actually have suffered from a different affliction. A recent analysis suggests that Roosevelt, whose work on behalf of polio patients gave rise to the amazing research program **The March of Dimes**, instead may have had *Guillain-Barre syndrome*, a disease barely known by physicians of that day.

Three years later, the future President chanced to hear of a young man also suffering from polio who had spent summers bathing in the waters found at **Warm Springs, Georgia**. The man had, at first, been assisted into the warm water in a nearly helpless condition. However, extensive exercise seemed to increase the man's muscular strength to the point that, by the end of the third summer, he was able to discard his leg braces and walk, using a cane. This got FDR's attention, and he decided he would try Warm Springs too.

When he arrived in the little southwestern Georgia town, Roosevelt's life was decidedly downcast. In the previous four years, he had seen a promising political career come crashing down. In 1920, he was the Democratic Party's nominee for Vice President, but **Warren Harding** defeated the Democrats. A year later, polio struck.

After arriving at the Warm Springs train station, a valet lifted FDR into a car and drove him to the **Meriwether Hotel**. Every day, FDR was lifted into and out of the Warm Springs water. At the end of three weeks, he wrote jubilantly to friends that he was feeling "life in my toes."

News spread quickly. Roosevelt's presence in the small Georgia town drew other polio victims. Soon, "Dr. Roosevelt," as he was known, was the cheerful, laughing leader in games of water polo and other activities.

FDR eventually decided to promote an organization that would place the recuperative work under expert guidance. On July 28, 1927, the **Georgia Warm Springs Foundation** was incorporated under New York State law as a charitable, therapeutic institution.

FDR was quickly smitten with the site. Desperate to regain the use of his paralyzed legs, he exercised frequently in the warm waters.

One day, Roosevelt decided improvements were needed at Warm Springs. The invalids who were constantly arriving at the site shaped his big idea.

The invalids – all sizes from toddlers to people older than the afflicted President – were deposited with their wheelchairs by the Warm Springs train station. All had to be physically accommodated, so FDR had walls knocked down and ramps installed in the ramshackle Meriwether Hotel. He then had several nearby cottages renovated for nurses and physical therapists.

From one man's interest, the greatest research-and-treatment program ever mounted in history against a single disease – the **National Foundation for Infantile Paralysis** – was developed. Under its aegis, polio victims received the best treatment known at the time, and it was provided at no expense to the invalids.

FDR personally selected the site on which his house was to be built. When it was completed in 1932, the President invited all the area residents to come by to "the Little White House" for a house-warming. Telephone operators were busy for days getting the word out to area farmers that FDR expected them to drop by for coffee and cake.

Visiting The Site Today

As visitors enter the Little White House grounds today, they proceed to a fountain, then follow the Walk of the Stones and Flags of the States to a museum. Inside, photos, memorabilia and other personal items trace Roosevelt's early life, his battle with polio and his meteoric political career. Also enshrined here are FDR's heavy leg braces and a collection of walking canes, as is his famous cigarette holder, his telephone and the breakfast tray from which he dined on his last morning alive in April of 1945.

A 12-minute film, *FDR in Georgia*, depicting scenes of his activities in and around Warm Springs, is shown continuously in the museum's auditorium. The film shows him receiving therapy, frolicking in the pool with child patients, picnicking, riding horses, playing with his dog **Fala**, and carving Thanksgiving turkey for other polio patients. **Merriman Smith**, the dean of White House correspondents who was in Warm Springs when FDR died, narrates the film.

Returning to the fountain area, visitors follow a driveway to the Little White House. Approaching the cottage, one notes that the ground slopes toward a ravine. On the left is a guest house; on the right, the garage.

Between these two buildings, set back on the ravine's edge, is the white cottage. The six-room house, which is open to visitors for regular tours, cost Roosevelt a grand total of $8,738.00 to build. It was the nation's second most famous address for 13 years.

Despite its columned entryway, the house is remarkably simple. It has three small bedrooms, two baths and a kitchen, as well as a foyer and a combined living-dining room.

The living-dining room is spacious without seeming large. A dining table is at one side; a stone fireplace at the other. Near the fireplace is the leather chair in which Roosevelt was sitting when he declared, "I have a terrific headache," and then slumped down unconscious.

Opposite the entrance to the living-dining room, wide windows and a door open to a high rear porch, which curves out like the fantail of a ship. On the left is the bedroom Roosevelt always used and where he died at 3:35 p.m. on an April afternoon.

Visitors to the Little White House can also read the scribble on a kitchen wall where, that afternoon, a grief-stricken hand wrote with a pencil, "Daisy Bonner cooked the first meal and the last one in this cottage for president Roosevelt."

The interior of the Little White House, now a national memorial, reflects Roosevelt's desire for simplicity, and his need for a slow-paced getaway where he might escape the pressures of the political world. The fireplace, as well, still holds remnants – charred logs – left from the day he died.

In the garage, FDR's cars can be seen as well. The blue 1938 Ford convertible, fitted with special hand controls, was his favorite. On its front bumper, it bears the last of the Georgia license tags made especially for the President:

"FDR 1 1945." Many car fanciers visit the Little White House expressly to see this automobile.

Despite his handicap, Roosevelt drove extensively around the Warm Springs area. He especially liked to take off alone and delighted in outwitting his Secret Service protectors.

Visitors may drive their own cars up a road that Roosevelt designed which leads to one of his favorite picnic spots – **Dowdell's Knob** – above scenic **Pine Mountain Valley**. The landscape looks almost exactly as it did the day FDR left it 58 years ago – an expansive countryside of piney hills etched with clear streams and green valleys.

Warm Springs Today

The community of Warm Springs is located 75 miles south of Atlanta. Despite this somewhat close proximity to the present-day Atlanta metropolis, Warm Springs was considered to be a very remote location in the 1930s and '40s.

Meriwether County blends its historic past with the present by maintaining its heritage and providing for its future. Aside from its historic sites, the town of Warm Springs has over 60 interesting shops and nine restaurants, all situated within one square mile of the historic village.

Nearby, other sites of enjoyment include **F.D. Roosevelt State Park** for campers, the U.S.D.I. Fish Hatchery and Aquarium, a historic covered bridge, an 1800s-era church, and much more. Nearby festivals such as "**Railroad Days**," "**The Cotton Pickin' Fair**," and "**The Candlelight Tour**" draw visitors from around the nation.

The old Meriwether Hotel which provided accommodations during Roosevelt's early visits was torn down in the 1920s for the construction of the polio facility in the same vicinity. One other very aged hotel, however – the **Hotel Warm Springs** which was in existence in Roosevelt's day – can still be seen today in downtown Warm Springs.

The rails for the railroad were taken up long ago, and the aged **Warm Springs Depot** was torn down in 1947. However, a replica of the depot has been reconstructed on the site of the original beside the original railroad-bed on which Roosevelt's body traveled on the long sad trip back to Washington, D.C. The Warm Springs station had witnessed the comings and goings of FDR for many years. The very famous photograph – which was published internationally – of the black musician weeping at the departure of Roosevelt's body, is believed to have been taken at this depot.

Historic Footnotes

"Warm Springs" refers to a mountain, a valley, a village and a pool of warm water. The thermal springs in the area gush forth at the rate of 1,800 gallons per minute from an Appalachian foothill. The springs had long been a place of healing for Native Americans who preceded the white man in the area. Around 1821, whites began frequenting the area. In the 1920s, it became known to Roosevelt.

FDR viewed the Little White House as a somewhat secret place, where one could find refuge and rejuvenation. A visitor can still find these qualities of life there even today.

Interestingly, when he died, FDR was financially insolvent (broke). In early 1945, he had informed his wife, **Eleanor**, that they would have to sell their Hyde Park mansion after he left the White House, because they could not afford to pay for its upkeep and taxes. Much of his savings and ready cash, interestingly, had gone into his favorite project – Warm Springs.

One last sidebar to the Warm Springs story which is nowhere near as secret today as it once was, is the fact that when he died, his mistress – **Lucy Rutherford** – was present. Eleanor Roosevelt was not.

In a later biography, one of Roosevelt's sons commented on the fact that Mrs. Roosevelt, after the birth of their last child, informed the President that she had all the children she wanted, and that was it (meaning no more sex). Thereafter, Lucy Rutherford filled in those duties.

The common assumption is that Lucy was staying in a cottage on the grounds of the Little White House. She may even have been staying in an adjoining bedroom at the time of the President's death. It is known by this writer that upon hearing of FDR's death, Eleanor ordered Lucy ushered out of town immediately.

(To reach Warm Springs, take Interstate 85 south to Exit 8, then Alternate Route 27 south to the town. The Little White House is open daily from 9:00 a.m. to 4:45 p.m., year-round except Thanksgiving, Christmas and New Year's Day. Admission is $2 to $5. Group rates are available. For more information, telephone 706-655-5870.)

From museums and national parks to planetariums and studio tours, Georgia's free attractions and events offer good opportunities for things that are fun and – best of all – free!

Interestingly, some of the best things in a Georgia resident's life are free, like the amethyst and crimson sunset touching the Blue Ridge Mountains, a welcoming covered dish supper at the neighborhood church fellowship hall, crafts festivals showcasing

47 Free Fun Things to Do in Georgia

Appalachian talents and culture, cane-pole fishing in chilly, freshwater streams, and just plain good old Southern hospitality among neighbors.

The old cliché about the best things in life being free also applies to many of Georgia's summertime attractions and events, so put away your wallet because these fun things listed below won't cost you a cent. Just be sure you call ahead before traveling to any of these opportunities, so you can make certain the freebie is still scheduled.

North Georgia

1. Stargaze through a telescope and discover the constellations at a planetarium show at **Rollins Planetarium**, open each Friday evening at **Young Harris** College in the scenic north Georgia mountains. (Tel.: 706-379-4312)

2. Observe a **Civil War** demonstration at **Chickamauga**, the first and largest national military park in the United States, and learn the significance the area played in the U.S. Civil War and the battles that led to the strategic control of Chattanooga, Tennessee. (Tel.: 706-866-9241)

3. Enjoy the free carnival rides at the **Georgia Mountain Fair** in **Hiawassee** (Tel.: 706-896-4191)

4. Armed with brochures from the Lumpkin County Welcome Center, take a walking tour of **Dahlonega's historic district**

and observe the many historic structures remaining in this charming mining town born by the 1828 gold rush. (Tel.: 706-864-3711)

5. Examine antique anesthesia machinery and an antebellum apothecary shop while paying tribute to the man who discovered surgical anesthesia at the **Crawford W. Long Museum** in Jefferson, Georgia. (Tel.: 706-367-5307)

6. Climb the spiral staircase to the top of the 100-foot brick water tower and 1871-built **Clock Tower Museum** for a panoramic view of historic downtown **Rome**. (Tel.: 706-236-4416)

7. Feed fish from the boardwalk or hike along three miles of lake loop trails at **James H. "Sloppy" Floyd State Park** in **Summerville**. (Tel.: 800-864-7275)

8. Walk the historic **Silver Comet Trail** along a newly-refurbished segment of the historic Seaboard Railroad line from Paulding to Polk counties, viewing wildlife, many scenic attractions, historic sites and much more. (Tel.: 770-684-8774)

Atlanta

9. Take in the tunes of the chart-topping talent against Atlanta's spectacular skyline every Friday night at **Centennial Olympic Park's "On The Bricks"** outdoor music concerts. (Tel.: 404-222-7275)

10. Recline in your lawn chair and watch classic flicks on a huge movie screen under the summer stars at **Screen-on-the-Green** at **Piedmont Park**. (Tel.: 1-877-262-5866)

110. Be a part of the largest fireworks show in the Southeast as **Lenox Square** lights up the beautiful Buckhead district with a huge pyrotechnic extravaganza on **July 4.** (Tel.: 404-233-7575)

12. Celebrate the life and accomplishments of America's most revered Civil Rights leader at the **Martin Luther King, Jr. National Historic**

7
STATEWIDE GEORGIA

Site and the Center for Nonviolent Social Change. (Tel.: 404-331-5190)

13. View the final resting place of author **Margaret Mitchell**, golfing great **Bobby Jones**, and many other celebrities from yesteryear at **Oakland Cemetery**, an outdoor museum with elaborate monuments, mausoleums and statues commemorating the deceased stars entombed therein. (Tel.: 404-688-2107)

14. Play archeologist and "discover" the mummies, coffins and Egyptian art on display at the **Michael C. Carlos Museum** at Emory University. (Tel.: 404-727-4282)

15. Try on a blue suit, similar to the ones worn by researchers in the Level 4 Biosafety Laboratory, and view a hazardous waste site display at the **Centers for Disease Control's** "**Global Health Odyssey.**" (Tel.: 404-639-0830)

16. Roam the marble floors, grand staircases and the Georgia history collections at the gold dome-topped **Georgia State Capitol**, where Georgia Senators and Representatives enact the state's laws. (Tel.: 404-656-2844)

17. See an average of $11 million in soiled or ripped bills pulled from circulation and sent to a shredder at the **Federal Reserve Bank Museum**. (Tel.: 404-498-8764)

18. Tour the 30-room Greek Revival **Governor's Mansion**, the official residence of Georgia's governor. (Tel.: 404-261-1776)

19. Learn how **WSB-Television** (Channel 2) meteorologists use a blue wall, a Chromakey system, camera angles and noncommittal hand gestures to report the weather on a **WSB Studios Tour**. (Tel.: 404-897-7369)

20. Observe achievements in art and design and shop for hand blown glass, graceful sculpture and intriguing ethnographic art each Wednesday at the **Atlanta International Museum**. (Tel.: 404-688-2467)

21. Hear how **Alexander Graham Bell** and his assistant, **Thomas A. Watson**, invented the telephone in 1876 at the **Bell South Museum**. (Tel.: 404-529-0971)

22. Gaze into a 36-inch reflecting telescope to view celestial objects and photometry of double stars at the **Fernbank Science Center's** observatory. (Tel.: 678-874-7102)

23. Stroll the 30-acre oasis of meandering paths and vast swaths of grass and delight in the conservatory's tropical, desert and endangered plants from around the world each Thursday from 3-7 p.m. at the **Atlanta Botanical Garden**. (Tel.: 404-876-5859)

24. Encourage your teens to attend a weekly open studio to receive professional instruction in the visual arts medium of their choice at the **Youth Art Connection**. (Tel.: 404-614-6233)

25. Attend **Centennial Olympic Park's Independence Day Celebration** for a variety of music, children's activities, games and fireworks displayed against the downtown skyline on **July 4**. (Tel.: 404-222-7275)

26. Go underground and saunter the six city blocks of restaurants, specialty shops, entertainment emporiums and street-cart merchants in the subterranean hideaway known as **Underground Atlanta**. (Tel.: 404-523-2311)

27. Hike or picnic among more than 11 miles of earthen breastworks remaining from the **Civil War** at beautiful and scenic **Kennesaw Mountain National Battlefield Park**. (Tel.: 770-427-4686)

28. Sway to soul-stirring gospel performances by choirs, soloists, quartets and instrumentalists at historic **Ebenezer Baptist Church** during Martin Luther King, Jr. National Historic Site's free First Saturdays concert series. (Tel.: 404-331-5190)

Middle Georgia

29. See replicas of a pre-Columbian Native American dwelling, a turn-of-the-century schoolroom, a 1930s shotgun house, and much much more at the **Columbus Museum**, the second largest museum in the state. (Tel.: 706-649-0713)

30. Tour Braselton's **Mayfield Dairy**, where 150,000 gallons of milk are produced and poured into the famous yellow jugs every day, and browse the gift shop for Mayfield Jersey cows and "Got Milk?" paraphernalia. (Tel.: 706-654-9180)

31. Relive the greatest moments in **Georgia Bulldogs** sports history and recall your favorite UGA athletes at **Butts-Mehre Heritage Hall** in Athens. (Tel.: 706-542-1621)

32. Behold a premier collection of 90 aircraft and missiles dating from an early 1896 glider to modern-era aircraft at the **Museum of**

Aviation in Warner Robins. (Tel.: 478-926-6870)

33. Imagine yourself rounding the 12 turns of the 2.54-mile **Grand Prix Course** at 110 miles per hour while on a tour of **Road Atlanta** in Braselton. (Tel.: 770-967-6143)

34. Wander the landscaped grounds, behold the **Abbey Church**, shop the greenhouse or meditate in the 50-room retreat house of **Conyers Monastery**. (Tel.: 770-483-8705)

35. Hike the white trail, which parallels the Middle Oconee River for several hundred yards and extends into the upland plateau areas of hardwood forests at the **State Botanical Garden** in Athens. (Tel.: 706-542-1244)

36. Discover unusual mounds built by Native Americans more than 500 years before Columbus sailed to the New World at **Ocmulgee National Monument** near Macon. (Tel.: 478-752-8257)

37. Paint with video graphics, communicate through whisper tubes, dig for fossils and touch a hissing cockroach from Madagascar each Monday at the **Museum of Arts & Sciences** in Macon. (Tel.: 478-477-3232)

38. Visit the only **double-barreled cannon** ever built (and designed for use in the Civil War) and **"The Tree That Owns Itself,"** in Athens. (Tel.: 706-357-4430)

39. Explore the **Church-Waddel-Brumby House**, which is believed to be the oldest home in Athens. (Tel.: 706-353-1820)

40. Take a tour of the **Ware-Lyndon House**, one of the few antebellum homes with Italianate elements remaining in the Athens area, which also serves as the centerpiece of the **Lyndon House Arts Center**. (Tel.: 706-613-3623)

41. Learn about the history of Augusta,

meander through the Japanese garden, toy on the children's playground and survey a replica paddlewheel from the *Kathryn S* along the **Augusta Riverwalk**, a five-block promenade of pathways and gardens stretching along the Savannah River between Fifth and Tenth Streets in Augusta. (Tel.: 800-726-0243)

42. Explore the butterfly conservatory where more than 1,000 butterflies and hummingbirds fly freely among tropical foliage at **Callaway Gardens**, where admission is free each Monday for up to five guests accompanying a child five and under. (Tel.: 800-225-5292)

South Georgia

43. Wander through the simple four-story townhouse where the famous Georgia author was born at the **Flannery O'Connor Childhood Home** in Savannah. (Tel.: 912-233-6014)

44. Observe the site of the plant introduction experiments and the largest grove of bamboo in the United States at the **Bamboo Farm & Coastal Gardens** near Richmond Hill. (Tel.: 912-921-5460)

45. Spy alligators, turtles and owls at the **Savannah National Wildlife Refuge**. (Tel.: 912-652-4415)

46. Explore the historic halls of Savannah's **Christ Episcopal Church**, the first congregation organized in the colony of Georgia, and the site where **John Wesley** held the first Sunday school class in North America. (Tel.: 912-232-4131)

47. Backpack through the breathtaking colors of Georgia's **Little Grand Canyon** at **Lumpkin's Providence Canyon State Park**, where admission is free every Wednesday. (Tel.: 229-838-6202)

7
STATEWIDE
GEORGIA

To order additional copies of this 2005 edition of Georgia Backroads Traveler...

- -

Please send me _____ copies of
Georgia Backoads Traveler

(PLEASE PRINT)

Name _____

Address _____

City _____

State _____ Zip _____

Phone (_____) _____

PAYMENT TYPE:
❏ Check ❏ Money Order ❏ Visa ❏ MasterCard

If paying by credit card, please provide the following:

Card No.: _____ Expiration Date:_____

Signature: _____

Enclose $18.50 per copy plus $3.00 postage and tax per copy.

TOTAL ENCLOSED: $_____

MAIL ORDERS TO: Legacy Communications, Inc., P.O. Box 127, Roswell, GA 30077
Or call toll-free to order: 1-800-547-1625   Please allow 2 weeks for delivery.

- -

Please send me _____ copies of
Georgia Backroads Traveler

(PLEASE PRINT)

Name _____

Address _____

City _____

State _____ Zip _____

Phone (_____) _____

PAYMENT TYPE:
❏ Check ❏ Money Order ❏ Visa ❏ MasterCard

If paying by credit card, please provide the following:

Card No.: _____ Expiration Date:_____

Signature: _____

Enclose $18.50 per copy plus $3.00 postage and tax per copy.

TOTAL ENCLOSED: $_____

MAIL ORDERS TO: Legacy Communications, Inc., P.O. Box 127, Roswell, GA 30077
Or call toll-free to order: 1-800-547-1625   Please allow 2 weeks for delivery.